D0147480

Rethinking Organizational & Managerial Communication From Feminist Perspectives

Rethinking
Organizational
& Managerial
Communication
From Feminist
Perspectives

Patrice M. Buzzanell
Editor

DISCARDED
UNIVERSITY OF TULSA LIBRARY

Sage Publications, Inc.
International Educational and Professional Publisher
Thousand Oaks ▪ London ▪ New Delhi

Copyright © 2000 by Sage Publications, Inc.

All rights reserved. No part of this book may be reproduced or utilized in any form or by any means, electronic or mechanical, including photocopying, recording, or by any information storage and retrieval system, without permission in writing from the publisher.

For information:

Sage Publications, Inc.
2455 Teller Road
Thousand Oaks, California 91320
E-mail: order@sagepub.com

Sage Publications Ltd.
6 Bonhill Street
London EC2A 4PU
United Kingdom

Sage Publications India Pvt. Ltd.
M-32 Market
Greater Kailash I
New Delhi 110 048 India

Printed in the United States of America

Library of Congress Cataloging-in-Publication Data

Main entry under title:

   Rethinking organizational and managerial communication from feminist
perspectives / [edited by] Patrice M. Buzzanell.
        p. cm.
   Includes bibliographical references and indexes.
   Rev. papers presented at the 1996 National Communication Association
conference, held in San Diego, Calif.
   ISBN 0-7619-1278-9 (cloth: alk. paper) — ISBN 0-7619-1279-7 (pbk.: alk. paper)
   1. Communication in organization—Congresses. 2. Communication in
management—Congresses. 3. Feminist theory—Congresses. 4. Women in
communication—Congresses. 5. Women—Communication—Congresses. 6.
Communication—Sex differences—Congresses. I. Buzzanell, Patrice M.
   HD30.3 .R475 2000
   658.4´5´082—dc21   00-008077

00   01   02   03   04   05   06   7   6   5   4   3   2   1

Acquiring Editor: Margaret H. Seawell
Editorial Assistant: Sandra Krumholz
Production Editor: Astrid Virding
Editorial Assistant: Victoria Cheng
Typesetter: Tina Hill
Indexer: Cristina Haley
Cover Designer: Candice Harman

D30

R475

.OOO

*To my parents, Francis G. and Marie J. Buzzanell,
and my siblings, Charles A. Buzzanell, M.D.,
and Doreen Buzzanell Koehler.*

Contents

PART I: CONFRONTING OUR PAST

PART II: RETHINKING PRESENT PROCESSES

PART III: AUTHORING OUR FUTURE

CONCLUDING CHAPTER

Preface

Patrice M. Buzzanell

This edited book began with an invitation to submit a book prospectus on organizational communication for a possible feminist series with Sage. Sonja Foss requested works that could contribute to a more holistic understanding of specific areas within communication through feminist analyses. Her invitation prompted me to begin a discussion with several feminist organizational communication scholars about how different theories, research, and practices could be reconsidered from multiple feminisms. These scholars enthusiastically responded to my request that they participate in a 1996 National Communication Association (NCA; then called the Speech Communication Association) conference panel held in San Diego, California. They each identified an area in organizational and managerial communication studies that they believed could be enhanced through feminist analyses. Our NCA panel was a well-attended (beyond our expectations) and very encouraging beginning to this edited volume.

After the conference, the authors revised their conference presentations into draft chapters that were then reviewed by feminist researchers, non-feminist organizational and managerial communication experts, and myself. What emerged is an edited volume that offers a counterpoint to the ordinary ways in which organizational and managerial communication researchers have approached topics such as socialization, ethics, and negotiation. As such, our chapters in *Rethinking Organizational and Managerial Communication From Feminist Perspectives* intend to critique and supplement existing approaches with alternative insights, practices, and research agendas.

Our chapters are not as much about "women's issues" as about the ways that conventional approaches often exclude the concerns, values, and life experiences voiced by members of traditionally underrepresented groups. Our hope is that, within this volume, the reanalysis of some aspects of organizational and managerial communication will stimulate greater thinking about how organizing itself can be gendered and exclusionary and about how we (as researchers and organization members) can prompt continued change toward greater equality, dignity, and justice for women and for men (Buzzanell, 1995, 1999). As M. G. Fine (1993) argues,

> A feminist perspective tells us why we study organizational communication—to create organizations that allow all people to express fully their human potential, and that allow them a genuine and free voice rather than a voice constrained by false ideology. A feminist perspective rejects research that is intended to further the economic goals of the organization without regard to the well-being of the people who constitute the organization. (p. 132)

In short, feminist approaches to organizational and managerial communication are grounded in the belief that we can create an equitable and ethical vision for organizational lives and processes.

Rethinking Organizational and Managerial Communication From Feminist Perspectives continues the ongoing feminist critique of traditional organizational and organizational communication theory and research (e.g., Bullis, 1993; Buzzanell, 1994, 1999; Calás & Smircich, 1996; Fine, 1993; Marshall, 1993; Mumby, 1996, 1998). As our field has progressed from a variable analytic sex/gender difference approach to a more complex and situated understanding of gendered processes, we have seen feminist reanalyses of phenomena such as diversity (e.g., Allen, 1995a), bounded rationality/emotionality (e.g., Mumby & Putnam, 1992), ethics (Mattson & Buzzanell, 1999), and pay for (house)work (e.g., Clair & Thompson, 1996).

Just as these trends have emerged in gendered organizing, we can see related themes reflected in this volume. The first commonality among the chapter authors is their desire to suffuse, rather than insert, in their writings what has been excluded from traditional organizational and managerial communication: namely, the complexities of sex and gender, race and ethnicity, class, and sexual-social orientation. In this way, they delve into taken-for-granted assumptions that expose invisible gendered relations. Second, the authors ground their feminist analyses in processes rather than in singular aspects of organizing, sense making, and communicating. Not only do they focus on sites where multiple feminisms offer distinctive contributions to knowledge and practice, but they also note where and how change can be enacted. Third, the authors retain the centrality of communication as the fundamental organizing process that produces and reproduces both inequity and justice in daily life. In all cases, the authors eschew the metaphor of organization as container by blending concerns of work and family, organization and environment, public and private, and inclusion and exclusion (see Putnam, Phillips, & Chapman, 1996, for an overview of metaphors). Finally, the authors envision their chapters as works in progress. They may vary in style, but each chapter explores and stimulates dialogue on some concerns rather than providing a comprehensive or best analysis of issues.

These themes of feminist organizational communication scholarship and of *Rethinking Organizational and Managerial Communication From Feminist Perspectives* have helped us create a book that can serve both research and pedagogical purposes. *Rethinking Organizational and Managerial Communication From Feminist Perspectives* provides critical and heuristic analyses of organization by outstanding researchers. As a research tool, this book can assist graduate students and professors in organizational and managerial communication, women's studies, organizational behavior, organization theory, and organizational sociology. These materials can be used for reference or be incorporated into classrooms (e.g., as the main text, a special topics course reading, or a supplementary text that extends—and often counters—the teachings of traditional organizational and managerial communication textbooks), particularly in graduate seminars or upper-division undergraduate courses. At present, there is no other edited or authored feminist book that can be used as a companion to advanced undergraduate and graduate texts and handbooks of organizational communication.

Because of our research and teaching goals, most chapters begin with either references to or critiques of literature in specific areas of organizational and managerial communication, such as chaos theory, leadership, or careers. Sometimes this overview is relatively brief, but readers will find that the initial combination of mainstream and alternative thinking about particular communication phenomena enables authors and readers to revisit issues, examine changes in scholarship and practice, and offer feminist analyses and change initiatives. Readers also will note that there has been no attempt to cover all possible topics or to use every feminist perspective. There have been recent overviews of organizational communication: Jablin and Putnam's (in press) *The New Handbook of Organizational Communication* and Putnam et al.'s (1996) chapter in *The Handbook of Organizational Studies*. There have also been refereed articles and yearbook chapters that have provided broad feminist overviews of organizational communication and organization theory (e.g., Bullis, 1993; Buzzanell, 1994, 1999; Calás & Smircich, 1996; Fine, 1993; Marshall, 1993; Mumby, 1996). Rather than publish another broad overview or include all feminisms, we intended to provide an in-depth feminist treatment of some major issues.

There are many individuals who deserve acknowledgment in this preface. Each chapter lists reviewers who commented on earlier drafts. I have not repeated their names here but they deserve (and have) my undying gratitude. Their enthusiasm for this project and detailed comments for individual chapters are greatly appreciated. In addition, I would like to thank Sonja Foss, Julia Wood, and Linda Putnam, and the members of the Organization for the Study of Communication, Language, and Gender (OSCLG) for their support and insights over the years. In addition, Erin Smith and Judi Dallinger helped with text-reference checks—Judi and I sat on the airport floor before our flight from an OSCLG conference in Maine checking off references.

I also thank the fabulous editors and production staff at Sage, particularly Margaret Seawell and Marquita Flemming whose humor and warmth have made this process and journal editing so very enjoyable.

Finally, I would like to thank my partner (Steve Wilson) and my six children (Brendan C. Sheahan, Sheridan A. Sheahan, Ashlee M. Sheahan, Lisette M. Sheahan, Annie Grace Sheahan, and Robyn F. Wilson) for their love and ability to always draw me back to what matters most in life.

This book is dedicated to my parents, Francis G. and Marie J. Buzzanell, and my siblings, Charles A. Buzzanell, MD and Doreen Buzzanell Koehler.

Introduction: In *Medias Res*

Patrice M. Buzzanell

Our first chapter begins "in the middle of things." The chapters in this book continue the current trend of rethinking organizational and managerial communication from critical, particularly feminist, approaches. In 1993, Sheryl Perlmutter Bowen and Nancy Wyatt published an edited book, *Transforming Visions: Feminist Critiques in Communication Studies,* that focused on how feminisms could prompt scholars to pose research questions and use methods different from those conventionally employed in the primary areas of the communication discipline (e.g., performance studies, interpersonal communication, and organizational communication). Until *Rethinking Organizational and Managerial Communication From Feminist Perspectives,* there has not been a single organizational communication volume similar to Bowen and Wyatt's (1993) project. *Rethinking Organizational and Managerial Communication From Feminist Perspectives* is designed to fill this gap and is expected to roughly coincide with the publication of *The New Handbook of Organizational Communication* (Jablin & Putnam, in press).

Rethinking Organizational and Managerial Communication From Feminist Perspectives focuses attention on feminist approaches to some organizational communication issues. As such, it begins in *medias res* and contributes to the ongoing dialogue about reframing communication to better incorporate diverse perspectives and members. This edited book is not intended to be a comprehensive treatment of current organizational communication issues. Rather, our chapters delve into specific topics and provide frameworks and analyses that could be useful for additional feminist organizational communication critiques. I see these chapters as illuminating traditional organizational and managerial communication work. Like Western medieval religious documents in which the pictures told stories both separate from and coinciding with the words, our chapters add to the conventional text by highlighting emotions, embodied experience, and standpoints of traditionally underrepresented groups. Our work does not intend to dismantle the past but to augment the rich scholarly tradition of our discipline.

There are three main sections in *Rethinking Organizational and Managerial Communication From Feminist Perspectives:* Part I, "Confronting Our Past"; Part II, "Rethinking Present Processes"; and Part III, "Authoring Our Future." The sections progress from theoretical analyses that reconceptualize and extend boundaries in our thinking about work and organizing processes; through the use of marginalized voices to question ordinary acts, identities, and critiques of organizational constructs; to the incorporation of difference in such a way that questions and proposes concrete remedies for those micropractices and structures that (re)construct injustice. Each chapter within these three parts is a self-contained feminist analysis of some aspect of organizational life.

PART I

The four chapters in Part I, "Confronting Our Past," discuss themes of binary oppositions, exclusion, contradictions, and power in organizational and managerial communication literature. Each proposes an alternative view of public-private discourse, stakeholder ethics, socialization processes, or negotiation by contrasting traditional approaches with feminist values.

In Chapter 1, "Communication, Organization, and the Public Sphere: A Feminist Perspective," Mumby returns to some of the foundations of the field to describe the ways in which traditional conceptualizations of the public sphere in democratic institutions are linked to individuals' rhetorical effectiveness and identities. Mumby proposes that the public-private issues from a critical feminist approach are how the *relationship* between the public and private spheres is articulated discursively and how this *articulation process* (re)produces power imbalances and/or creates opportunities for resistance and transformation. Opportunities for individuals to make their arguments public depend on availability, resources, and ideological associations. These opportunities assume a reified social structure in which members of marginalized groups are restricted because they voice competing interests and needs.

Mumby defines the public sphere as "a discursively constructed space for argument in which different interest groups compete to articulate conflicting worldviews," and he argues for a multiplicity of overlapping public spheres. By using feminist analysis to critique binary thinking and to propose action that can eliminate the oppression of women (and others), Mumby illuminates the complexities within and between spheres. If public spheres are contested sites, then organizational and managerial communication researchers can reframe the public sphere to open possibilities for participatory exchanges. This means that forms of discourse and knowledge traditionally associated with different spheres (e.g., the private sphere and personal opinion, and the public sphere and social knowledge) can no longer be considered legitimate, can no longer serve dominant interests, and can no longer limit possibilities for dissent and alternative views. A feminist articulation of participatory democracy requires: admission of social inequities; further development of discursive spaces in which women renegotiate identities (i.e., spaces to formulate "oppositional interpretations of their identities, interests, and needs"; Fraser, 1990-1991, p. 67); and problematizing what "counts" as public and private matters. Through a critical feminist analysis of public-private relationships, Mumby exposes the "contradictions between the rhetoric of democracy and enfranchisement, on the one hand, and the reality of social, political, and economic inequality, on the other."

Haas and Deetz also examine conditions necessary for participatory exchange. In Chapter 2, "Between the Generalized and the Concrete Other: Approaching Organizational Ethics From Feminist Perspectives," they claim that multiple-stakeholder models can address the complexities of varied political interests and values that need representation in internal corporate decision making.

They address two ethical concerns: the implementation of procedures to identify stakeholders' interests and values, and the implementation of procedures to ensure that stakeholders' interests and values are represented in corporate decision-making processes. They use Benhabib's (1985, 1986, 1987, 1990, 1992) feminist perspective on ethics to extend Habermas's (1973, 1984, 1987, 1990, 1993) theory of communicative action, discourse ethics, and his description of the ideal speech situation. Specifically, Benhabib contends that generalized and concrete other standpoints operate as moral orientations that reflect binary thinking (e.g., autonomy/nurturance, public/private, independence/interdependence, commonality/individuality, impartiality/connection, universalistic norms/contextually sensitive criteria, and "ethic of justice and rights"/"ethic of care and responsibility"). Benhabib (1992) requires the use of both standpoints simultaneously in moral conversation to transcend dualities. The objective of moral conversation is the willingness to engage in discussion that can affect understanding and, perhaps, consensus.

Although Benhabib (1992) argues that moral conversation does not require copresence because individuals can have an "imaginary dialogue" with others, Haas and Deetz believe that an "actual dialogue" among participants—even if participants are not in the same spatiotemporal location—is necessary for an ethical stakeholder model of internal corporate decision making. Their reasoning is that management often is so isolated from corporate stakeholders that it lacks the imaginary resources to adequately represent divergent interests. They suggest some preliminary applications of their theorizing to corporate decision-making processes but caution that their ethical ideal may be difficult to pursue in practice.

Chapter 3 also addresses ways to include marginalized voices in our theorizing. Rather than reframing public-private to incorporate discourse previously belonging exclusively to one sphere (Mumby) or establishing conditions necessary for the inclusion of disparate stakeholder interests through the use of concrete and generalized others (Haas & Deetz), Bullis and Stout argue that greater attention to class and race ("Both go unmentioned and are thereby erased"), among other contextualizing processes and outcomes, can help researchers better understand oppression, resistance, and change. In "Organizational Socialization: A Feminist Standpoint Approach," they critique the usual socialization assumptions to demonstrate how feminist organizational and managerial communication researchers can enlarge traditional emphases. In general, researchers have most often studied socialization strategies and tactics, newcomers' sense-making and information-seeking strategies, and communication processes. Bullis and Stout position standpoint feminisms as a means of advocating "oppositional, politically conscious understandings with the hope that such understandings provide resources for a critique of domination as well as change."

Bullis and Stout suggest several possible lines of inquiry. First, communication researchers can explore the meanings of organizational boundaries and the ways in which containment metaphors maintain dominant/subordinate relationships. Second, by focusing on the variability of experiences that are inadequately represented by phase models and trajectories, feminist scholars may better depict the experiences of those who otherwise might be considered "outliers." Finally, researchers can question the assumption that individuals and organizations mutually influence each other. They conclude with a review of published work that can serve as exemplars for how organizational and managerial communication theory and methods can be changed.

The final chapter in Part I displays how negotiation and bargaining can be changed. In Chapter 4, "Rethinking Negotiation: Feminist Views of Communication and Exchange," Putnam and Kolb argue that distributive, integrative, and principled negotiation and bargaining are gendered because they privilege masculine characteristics of exchange over feminine qualities of connectedness and co-construction. To develop an alternative approach, they highlight normative aspects of the normative negotiation model and contrast these with parallel but feminist processes. In this way, they explore the assumptions and communicative implications of conventional negotiation dimensions (i.e., exchange, instrumental goals and optimal settlements, and independent parties). Through contrastive analyses, they advocate: co-construction (mutual inquiry that encourages expansive thinking and con-textualization of issues within a communal approach); goals of self- and mutual understanding and jointly developed courses of action; and relational interdependence that emerges during bargaining processes and reflects trust, empathy, and shared emotional expressions.

Like the other authors in Part I, Putnam and Kolb expand our conceptual-izations of organizational and managerial approaches. They explore what these feminist dimensions would mean for bargaining processes. Rather than exchanging proposals, generating options, and exchanging concessions, negotiators in the alternative approach would reframe the ways multiple par-ties understand the situation. They would use dialogue as a process of co-learning and inquiry, rather than as problem solving for option generation. Instead of converging on debate and persuasion as core processes, negotiators in the alternative perspective would center on invitational rhetoric and circu-lar questioning as fundamental social interaction processes. Invitational rhet-oric "urges participants to move beyond the here-and-now issues and raise questions about peak experiences, times of exceptional performance, and what people value most about their lives, careers, and work." Circular ques-tioning is a series of queries that begins with personal experience and assesses responsibility. This inquiry cycles back to narrative details about the shared personal experience so that the original experiences are destabilized and, thus, open to alternative interpretations. By critiquing, then extending current negotiation models, Putnam and Kolb develop an alternative model guided by feminist thinking.

PART II

Whereas the authors in Part I lay some conceptual groundwork about exclusionary discourse, interests, and experiences, the authors of the three chapters in Part II, "Rethinking Present Processes," present (mostly white) women's voices through interview excerpts, poems, diary entries, stories, and personal involvement with these constructs. They explore the ways in which these concrete details of ordinary lives represent missing facets and nuances of our organizational and managerial communication work. These chapters are the least "finished" because all the authors raise issues that defy closure. Each of their overviews and feminist reanalyses acts as a springboard for addi-tional research.

In her work on embodied experience, Trethewey links the development of sophisticated control mechanisms with the ways in which women's bodies are disciplined by themselves and others. In Chapter 5, "Revisioning Control: A Feminist Critique of Disciplined Bodies," Trethewey develops Foucauldian and poststructuralist analyses of female workers' bodies as sites of power and resistance. Women's embodied experiences enable and constrain their self-identities and material results (i.e., competence evaluations and outcomes) to such an extent that the terms *female bodies* and *professional bodies* appear contradictory. Through analyses of her interview data on (primarily white heterosexual) professional women's embodied experiences, she finds that women's discourse repeatedly portrays professional women's bodies as fit, as tools to emit intentional messages, and as excessive. Unable to meet the masculine ideal of a professional body despite self- and other-disciplinary action, women's bodies mark them as "other."

Trethewey admits that her analyses do not account for the ways that many women celebrate and resist disciplinary mechanisms. She argues that greater attention to the social construction of women's embodied identities could illuminate the kinds of resistance that can lead to organizational change and innovative organizational (and managerial) communication research programs.

In Chapter 6, "Walking the High Wire: Leadership Theorizing, Daily Acts, and Tensions," Fine and Buzzanell use a revisionist/revalorist feminist analysis to create a vision of leadership, administration, and management as serving. This vision exposes the deficiencies of both mainstream and alternative views of leadership. Fine and Buzzanell first explore how traditional (adaptive, transformational, and self-leadership and superleadership) and alternative (gendered and servant) leadership and management aspects are exclusionary and/or incomplete. By using feminist epistemological and methodological commitments (i.e., women's ways of knowing, feminist problematics, feminist synalytics, and revolutionary pragmatism; see Fine, 1993), they bring together their own life experiences (in the form of diary entries) and theory in such a way that tensions among differing values and approaches are exposed and sustained.

They find that four main paradoxes emerge when *servant, leadership,* and *feminine* are examined simultaneously. When women lead by serving, they face double binds because (a) the juxtapositions of subordinate/servant and superordinate/served gain power for males but fulfill traditional (unvalued) roles for women; (b) the qualities built into the servant leadership role are evaluated according to their instrumental worth, making most feminine ways of enacting and describing servant leadership devalued; (c) the implications that leaders can change styles easily to suit situations do not rest easily with "serving" as a lifelong ethical process; and (d) women who serve threaten the status quo. To revision *serving* as a feminist form of leadership, Fine and Buzzanell situate serving as a form of resistance. Women who serve resist others' definitions of what they should do and how they should do it. They resist judgments of selfishness and unfemininity that often occur when women prioritize service by and for themselves *as highly as* service for others. And they resist static notions of serving by constantly reevaluating whether their serving is ethical (i.e., whether serving empowers or makes different stakeholders vulnerable and whether serving creates a more equitable world for white women and members of other traditionally underrepresented groups).

Serving embodies the struggle to move toward feminist transformation. Serving is transformative and emancipatory because it provides freedom to confront oneself and to act for the betterment of women and men. Serving challenges community-diminishing norms by its very existence. However, serving also can lead to the development of strategies and practices that initiate "microemancipation" (Alvesson & Wilmott, 1992) within the organization because of the self-reflexivity that serving prompts in others and in organizations.

In the final chapter of Part II, Mattson, Clair, Sanger, and Kunkel use the storytelling of narratives and poems to draw readers into a reframing of what stress means in our everyday lives and why those meanings do not reflect the experiences of women. In Chapter 7, "A Feminist Reframing of Stress: Rose's Story," they observe that traditional research has resulted in prescriptive measures for reducing stress; however,

> none of the prescriptive measures suggest altering the way we do business so that we do not have "high-pressure deadlines" . . . [or altering the] onus for change [that] is placed on the individual rather than on the way we organize our work practices.

Moreover, stress typically is described as negative. Popular writings about time management are presented as ways of managing deadlines, demands, and outcomes of burnout. Models that incorporate communication as a means of alleviating stress propose either that social support operates as a buffer against the harmful effects of stressful life events or that emotional communication can lessen the impact of stress on burnout. Other lines of research connect interpersonal linkages and attributes of workers with different stress levels.

To reframe stress, Mattson et al. recommend that organizational and managerial communication researchers be "open to the sequestered stories, the marginalized stories, or the stories of stress that are labeled as categories other than stress." As one example, they recount Hazell's (1997) narrative of a call to a radio talk show in which Rose, a young mother with five children under the age of 3, pleaded for help after social services had rejected her appeals. Mattson et al. point out that popular and academic reports would not categorize the story as stress, work, or public policy but as "domestic." This framing does not question who assigns meaning to an event or how power imbalances can be made visible so that frames can be challenged, resisted, and opened to change. The more that frames are accepted as taken for granted, the more they become reified. Their communicative potential for creating and persuading self and others about realities becomes less obvious.

Mattson et al. draw from core feminist concerns rather than single feminist approaches. They endeavor

> to highlight stressful situations that may not have received the same legitimation as current "workplace" conceptualizations of stress; to advance a more holistic understanding of stress as a sociopolitical phenomenon; to point out the discursive as well as the material aspects of stress; and to expose the ways in which women's work-related stress is far too often privatized.

Each of these "reframings" is elaborated on but also is connected to Rose's story and the stories of others whose tolerance for life's demands and deadlines is exceeded. They recommend that these four areas provide a counterpoint for traditional research.

PART 3

Part III, "Authoring Our Future," contains three chapters that rewrite organizational and managerial communication constructs. These chapters not only offer alternative reconceptualizations but also suggest specific tactics and long-term strategies derived from feminisms to revise organizational and managerial communication processes and practices. These chapters deal with intersections of sex and gender, race and ethnicity, and class not by adding phrases like "and people of color" but by delving into concerns raised when women and men of color and economically disadvantaged groups are excluded from organizational and managerial communication theory, research, and practice. These chapters lay bare—with no excuses—how limited our views of organizational life have been. Indeed, by failing to think about difference holistically, we have unwittingly perpetuated exclusionary thinking, micropractices, and macrostructures. These chapters question our taken-for-granted assumptions in theorizing and practices and find our prior work lacking. They are most explicit in their recommendations for the transformation of daily practices and organizational policies.

As Allen explains in Chapter 8, "'Learning the Ropes': A Black Feminist Standpoint Analysis," she can offer a personalized and contextualized account of organizational socialization by describing and critiquing her experience as an "outsider within" (i.e., a black woman in the U.S. white male academe; see Allen, 1998a; Collins, 1991). Although the communicative content and work-related communication may differ, Allen's standpoint analysis is applicable to nonacademic organizations and to members of other marginalized groups. Allen weaves theory, research, and routine practices with reflections about her own experiences. She identifies her role and role-set members, her treatment as a newcomer, the ways in which role-set members often communicate based on stereotypes of black women (e.g., mammy and matriarch) and on token status, and how others often make insensitive or patronizing comments and requests. She voices the constant inner struggles that black women feel as they (re)live the power dynamics that mark them as outsiders and that make sense making different from those experiences and emotions portrayed in socialization literature. She uses her "'outsider within' status to help create black feminist thought," resist marginalization (and build a supportive community), and "infuse elements of my black woman cultural experience into my work" through examples of positive black experiences, "call and response" teaching styles, and concern for others. As Allen summarizes her strategies, she remarks, "I engage in a variety of activities that allow me to honor and nurture many facets of my multicultural identity."

Based on her experiences, Allen offers suggestions for those interacting with members of traditionally marginalized groups and for newcomers. She encourages sensitivity to newcomers, self-reflexivity, and self-challenges to transform academe (and society) in ways that could benefit *all* newcomers. She recommends that black female academicians be proactive in their socialization processes and in their solicitation of feedback about their work. If these women know what they want, keep these priorities in mind, and maintain a varied support network, they can resist their own complicity and others' inclinations to disempower them and other newcomers.

Allen primarily describes detailed micropractices to question taken-for-granted assumptions and to revise theory and organizational practice. In Chapter 9, Buzzanell shifts between micro and macro issues but focuses mostly on macrolevel concerns in "The Promise and Practice of the New Career and Social Contract: Illusions Exposed and Suggestions for Reform." In this second chapter in Part III, Buzzanell challenges our acceptance of new career forms (i.e., series of work contracts over the course of a lifetime) and related social contracts (i.e., normative expectations for employee-employer exchange relationships) and psychological contracts (i.e., temporary terms of exchange stipulated in specific employee-employer agreements). Through a poststructuralist feminist analysis, she exposes the illusions that the new career and contracts are more realistic, more just, and less paternalistic than older career and contract forms.

Buzzanell contrasts the career and contract discourse and discursive practices found in writings by managerial, organizational, and career researchers and practitioners with data produced by government documents (e.g., U.S. Department of Labor reports and projections), PBS focus group transcripts, and research on the effects of career insecurity, unemployment, displacement, underemployment, and lack of work on individual, organizational, societal, and global levels. Buzzanell displays how the discourse actually disenfranchises workforce members, benefits managerial ideology, and curtails discussions of underlying premises and alternative solutions. When inequities, particularly unfair treatment and outcomes for individuals and workforce cohorts most vulnerable in our society, are made visible, then the potential to create change is realized.

Buzzanell advocates four avenues of change organized according to the organizational communication problematics outlined by Mumby and Stohl (1996). The *rationality problematic* suggests that management and organizational communication researchers and practitioners devise and educate others about career models, definitions, and language that systematically promote feminine/feminist values of relationship, interconnectedness, collaboration, and long-term focus. The *problematic of voice* demands publication of the ways the new career and social contract disadvantage white women, people of color, the lower class, and less educated members of the workforce who are both female and male. The *problematic of organization* mandates the authoring of new texts that explicitly promote values of fairness, interrelationships, and community support within and beyond sites of employment. The *problematic of organization-society relationships* requires that we find ways to treat all stakeholders as legitimate contributors to dialogue about blurred boundaries and moral responses to corporate environments and community concerns.

Finally, in Chapter 10, "Chaos Theory and the Glass Ceiling," Reuther and Fairhurst display how a system's inherent order suggested by some organizational chaos theorists may perpetuate gender and/or race ideologies that can lead to glass-ceiling processes and effects. Although the glass ceiling is often defined as the disproportionate representation of white women and people of color in top organizational levels, they focus on "ideologies, language patterns, and organizing practices [particularly racist ideologies and practices] that establish and reify this invisible barrier."

Reuther and Fairhurst believe that insights from the new sciences may better account for the complexities in language and social interaction that undergird discriminatory glass-ceiling effects. The experiences of white males are replicated, while different identities are suppressed (strange-attractor branch of chaos theory). Organizational members can devise means for disrupting or resisting ("unlearning") discriminatory practices (order-out-of-chaos branch of chaos theory). Through different feminist transformation processes, organizational members and organizational and managerial communication researchers can educate others in feminist principles, use praxis, and employ deconstruction of oppositions to affect change. On a daily level, members and researchers can challenge thinking that precludes avenues for change, can engage in micropractices that resist patriarchal systems in small (but incremental and unforeseeable) ways, and can initiate more macro efforts toward reform that address the complexities of organizational systems. Through action and reflection, members can resist the replication of discriminatory patterns. For researchers, Reuther and Fairhurst suggest a research agenda that not only devises possible interventions but also creates the potential for radical self-organizing.

CONCLUDING CHAPTER

The final chapter, "Dialoguing . . . ," draws together several themes occurring throughout *Rethinking Organizational and Managerial Communication From Feminist Perspectives* and encourages a continuation of chapter authors' conversations with readers. In this concluding chapter, feminist concerns articulated by the authors are positioned within ongoing feminist (including third-wave feminist) discussion. Rather than concluding this edited book, our final chapter encourages extension and critique of the issues raised throughout *Rethinking Organizational and Managerial Communication From Feminist Perspectives*.

PART I

CONFRONTING OUR PAST

Communication, Organization, and the Public Sphere

A Feminist Perspective

Dennis K. Mumby

With the emergence in recent years of a growing body of feminist theory and research devoted to organization studies, critical scholars have to take seriously the idea that organizations are the site of gendered communication practices (Acker, 1990; Buzzanell, 1994, 1995; Calás & Smircich, 1992; Mumby, 1996). In contrast to much previous research, this critical work conceives of gender not as an addendum to already established structures and practices but, rather, as a constitutive feature of organizing processes. In Acker's (1990) terms,

> To say that an organization . . . is gendered means that advantage and disadvantage, exploitation and coercion, action and emotion, meaning and identity, are patterned through and in terms of a distinction between male and female, masculine and feminine. Gender is not an addition to ongoing processes, conceived as gender neutral. Rather, it is an integral part of those processes, which cannot be properly understood without an analysis of gender. (p. 146)

AUTHOR'S NOTE: I would like to thank Patrice Buzzanell, George Cheney, and Karen Foss for their extremely helpful feedback on an earlier draft of this chapter.

Put another way, organization members "do gender" (West & Zimmerman, 1987) in the course of their mundane, everyday organizational practices. Whether in formal meetings or talking informally by the water cooler, social actors are constantly engaged in the process of enacting systems of meaning that construct identities in a gendered manner. In this sense, gender is not an individual characteristic of discrete organization members but is both a medium and an outcome (Giddens, 1979) of structured organizational practices.

The recognition that organizing is enacted through gendered social practices has arisen simultaneously with a body of work that focuses on organizations as important sites of participatory decision-making processes (Cheney, 1995; Deetz, 1992, 1995b; T. Harrison, 1994). The major thrust of such research lies in developing communication-based models of organizational democracy that premise organizational decision making and structures on the basis of empowerment and emancipation from capitalist systems of control. For example, Deetz (1992) argues that communication *as a field* traditionally has been rooted in effectiveness models that privilege conceptions of the individual as unitary and undifferentiated, a control orientation toward human interaction, and efficiency-based definitions of successful communication. On the other hand, Deetz (1992) develops a participatory model of communication rooted in dialogue, mutual understanding, and a move toward overcoming any fixed sense of subjectivity. Thus, "the moral foundation for democracy is in the daily practices of communication, the presumptions that each of us makes as we talk with each other" (pp. 350-351). Such a model of communicative democracy is articulated in the context of a critique of the corporate colonization of the life world and an appeal for a need to reclaim the workplace as an important political site of participatory decision making and identity formation.

Much of this critical work, particularly Deetz's, is rooted partly in rendering problematic the traditional notions of the public sphere of decision making and argumentation. Rather than viewing organizations as private, corporate individuals, it is argued instead that organizations must be reconceptualized as important public spheres in which identities and worldviews are fundamentally shaped. In other words, organizations play an important role in the discursive formation of core societal values through the generation of shared understanding about what is good, right, and true (Phillips, 1996). Certainly, feminist research has contributed heavily to this view, particularly the research into alternative organizational forms. Although most of this research has occurred outside the field of communication, it reflects a deep-rooted concern that extant institutional forms produce and reproduce communication practices and forms of rationality that are patriarchal. As such, alternative forms of organizing are seen as an important means by which to articulate nonpatriarchal, noncapitalist forms of meaning and identity (Ferguson, 1984; Ferree & Martin, 1995; Martin, 1990).

One issue that has only recently been addressed directly and thematically in the critical feminist organizational communication literature is the *relationship* between the public and private spheres of human interaction (e.g., Murphy, 1998) and, more specifically, the processes through which this relationship is constituted. In this chapter, I argue that feminist studies have provided ways for us to radically rethink extant notions of organizing by reframing the relationship between the "public" and "private" spheres. In particular, a critical feminist framework suggests how corporate organizations—as important sites of meaning formation in contemporary society—operate on a limited and problematic conception of these spheres. By showing how critical feminist theory is able to critique this dominant conception, we can move toward a more democratic, participatory, and communication-based notion of community.

This chapter is constructed in the following manner: First, I provide a brief critical discussion of prevailing conceptions of the public sphere. Second, I suggest how critical feminist thought can provide a more fruitful and compelling understanding of the relationship between the public and private spheres of discourse. Finally, through several examples, I provide an analysis that demonstrates how critical feminism can deconstruct and rearticulate the relationships between organizations and these spheres.

CONCEPTIONS OF THE PUBLIC SPHERE: A CRITICAL APPRAISAL

In the field of communication, we are particularly interested in the role of the public realm in the growth of democratic institutions. Quintillian's (1922) notion of the orator as "a good man, skilled in speaking" situates communication at the center of a rhetorical model in which the ethical and public dimensions of life are equated with each other. As a field, therefore, we have long been interested in promoting a public conception of communication in which access to the democratic process is dictated, at least in part, by the individual's rhetorical skills. In recent years, scholars in the area of rhetorical studies have increasingly recognized the complexity of the issues associated with developing useful conceptions of the public sphere (Bitzer, 1987; Goodnight, 1981, 1987; Hauser, 1997; Phillips, 1996). In this section, I provide a review and critique of some of these conceptions and suggest how critical feminism can extend this work through a more nuanced reading of the connection between the public sphere and democracy. More specifically, I suggest that critical feminism can increase our understanding of this connection by problematizing the relationship between the public and private spheres of society—a relationship that, I argue, has been given short shrift by rhetorical scholars in the field of communication. Fraser (1990-1991) appears to share this position:

> In general, critical theory needs to take a harder, more critical look at the terms "private" and "public." These terms . . . are not simply straightforward designations of societal spheres; they are cultural classifications and rhetorical labels. In political discourse, they are powerful terms that are frequently deployed to delegitimate some interests, views, and topics and to valorize others. (p. 73)

In other words, what "counts" as "public" or "private" is the product of discursive practices that shape our understanding of who we are as both citizens and individuals. Moreover, conceptions of public communication and the public sphere frequently adopt a de facto bifurcation of the public and private realms of discourse, with little reflection given to why certain issues are assigned to one domain or the other. The importance of critical feminist theory lies in its ability to deconstruct the discursive articulation of the public-private relationship and to demonstrate the ways in which different conceptions of this relationship serve different interests.

Although there are certainly gendered dimensions to the public-private dichotomy, it is not my intent to argue that this dichotomy is always inimical to women and disempowered minority groups. Indeed, it could be argued that, on the one hand, the situating of particular issues in the private realm serves the interests of women and minorities and creates possibilities for resistance (e.g., Murphy, 1998; Scott, 1990; Trethewey, 1997c), while, on the other hand, the blurring of the two spheres serves corporate interests and increases institutional limitations of people's rights (e.g., increasing organizational surveillance and monitoring of employee health issues). The central issues from a critical feminist perspective are *How does the relationship between the public and private spheres get discursively articulated, and how does this articulation process function to produce and reproduce extant power relations and/or create possibilities for resistance and transformation?* Two brief examples from critical feminist research help to illustrate this point.

Trethewey's (1997c) feminist analysis of client resistance in a human service organization (whose purpose is to enable low-income, unemployed parents to become self-sufficient) provides an interesting example of how clients can invoke privacy issues as a way to subvert the discursive articulation of their identities as open to bureaucratic scrutiny and definition. Trethewey provides an example of a client who refused to answer her questions when she accompanied the caseworker on a home visit:

> During the course of the home visit, Allyson [the client] made it exceedingly clear that she resented having to confess her life story to strangers, including social workers and researchers like me. . . . Allyson also let her social worker know, in no uncertain terms, how displeased she was that Fern assumed she would be willing to discuss her life with a researcher she did not know. (p. 290)

Trethewey shows how this client resists the perceived invasion of privacy and simultaneously negates "the social worker's attempts to position her as a client who unquestioningly and passively confessed to knowing experts" (p. 290). On the contrary, Allyson discursively situates herself as the "knowing subject" who controls the form and content of confessional practices. In this example, the female client refuses the discursive construction of her identity as open to public scrutiny, assessment, and definition. As such, she invokes the separation of public and private spheres as a means to resist what she perceives as an inappropriate scrutiny of her life.

The second example illustrates how this invocation of a separation of spheres can lead to precisely the opposite result. Clair's (1993b) feminist analysis of women's narratives about workplace sexual harassment reveals how sometimes women engage in discursive practices that sequester their experiences of harassment. For instance, Clair shows how some women discursively address harassment by situating it as part of their private lives, "thus dismissing it as an organizational problem and relegating it to the private domain" (p. 121). In one situation, a woman responded to unwelcome sexual advances by bringing her boyfriend to the workplace to discourage the offender. In other situations, women discursively sequestered sexual harassment experiences by framing them as too embarrassing to talk about; in such instances, the possibility of public, organization-level action is foreclosed. Here, then, we have an example of an organizational communication context in which the separation of spheres serves to reproduce the patriarchal ideology and furthers women's subordination.

My point, then, is that a sufficiently nuanced conception of the relationship between the public and private spheres requires an understanding of the complex relations among discourse, power, gender, and identity. By viewing the public sphere as a contested discursive space that is itself subject constantly to refinement and change, we are less likely to reify it in a way that limits possibilities for participatory forms of democracy. Given this context, the remainder of this section provides a brief overview of some of the principal arguments regarding the role and function of the public sphere.

Jasinski (1987) notes that "the task of public communication scholarship is to identify and analyze the constituent features and recurrent practices of the public sphere" (p. 424). I would modify this statement somewhat and suggest that, in addition, public communication should be concerned with identifying and critiquing the *relationship* between the public and private spheres. Such a shift in focus allows one to examine more closely the legitimacy of categorizing some discourses as public (and therefore worthy of analysis) and some as private (and therefore not as worthy). Below, I examine some of the constituent features of the public sphere and suggest how certain extant notions associated with its framing limit our conceptions of democracy in contemporary society. Let me begin by providing some currently espoused definitions of the public sphere.

Goodnight (1987) understands the public sphere to be "that domain of dis-cursive practices open to those whose opinions count in contesting a decision of consequence to a community" (p. 431). Attached to this definition are four hypotheses: (a) Public discourse is in principle controversial; (b) public dis-course occurs in forums that allow communication processes to be inspected; (c) public discourse both emerges from and shapes time and space; and (d) public discourse addresses an audience whose consent is requested and opti-mally provides knowledge for informed decisions by those people urged to act (pp. 430-431).

In addition, Goodnight (1981, 1987) situates the public sphere by juxtapos-ing it against what he refers to as the personal sphere (characterized by private conversation involving open-ended language use, with consequences mainly for the interlocutors) and the technical sphere (constituted through formal codes and the production of technical knowledge). As Schiappa (1989) has indicated, such a tripartite distinction between spheres of discourse and knowledge is clearly in the classic liberal tradition, which carefully separates the public and private realms. The logic of this liberal "distinct spheres" approach is tied up with the preservation of individual rights, in the sense that it is premised on the right to privacy, through which certain issues are ex-cluded from public debate and contestation. In general, the private sphere is deemed to encompass the domestic/familial realm as well as certain dimen-sions of the economic realm, such as rights of ownership and the right to make a profit. At the same time, the public realm is seen ideally as consisting of in-dividuals who, regardless of their position in the social hierarchy, are able to come together to deliberate over contested issues. In this sense, the bourgeois liberal conception of the public sphere is premised on the basis of a *sovereign* subject.

In Goodnight's distinction among spheres, we can also see an attempt to differentiate various epistemic products (Schiappa, 1989). That is, each of Goodnight's spheres is deemed to produce largely differentiated forms of knowledge. The private sphere produces private opinion, the technical sphere produces technical knowledge, and the public sphere produces social knowl-edge. The result of this careful separation of knowledge into different realms (spheres of argument) is that discourse is deemed legitimate only to the extent that it is articulated within the appropriate sphere. For example, technical knowledge requires specialized discursive practices and is therefore not usu-ally open to public debate. Although this separation of spheres may provide a system of checks and balances in society, such a position sets up dichotomous relationships between forms of knowledge and, by extension, forms of dis-course that potentially make relatively arbitrary judgments about the legiti-macy of issues open to public debate. I would argue that a more important and more fundamental question than "In which sphere of argument does this issue belong?" is the question *By what set of criteria and in whose interests is it to structure the respective spheres so that only specific issues are deemed admissible?*

This latter question implies a much more radical-critical conception of the public-private dichotomy. It suggests that, rather than functioning as a structure in which both individual rights and the public good are ensured, this dichotomy is rooted in specific ideological practices that privilege certain forms of argument and modes of knowledge over others. Phillips (1996) makes a similar case when he argues that the dominant conception of the public sphere is rooted in a communication model of consensus that limits possibilities for dissension and alternative worldviews. For example, he suggests that, although the consensus model operates under a presumption of openness, the reality is that "the public sphere becomes merely another discursive site with its own unique forms of exclusion, coercion, and judgment" (p. 238). Similarly, by maintaining a strict separation of spheres, the consensus model appears to foreclose discussion of the relevance for public debate of discourses associated with marginalized groups such as women and minorities. Though it can be argued that Phillips overstates the oppressive, consensus-driven qualities of the public sphere and its negating of possibilities for dissent (Goodnight, 1997; Hauser, 1997), his essay does point to the need to conceptualize the relationship between the public and private realms as essentially contested and ideological.

One of the most important theorists of the public sphere is Habermas (1974, 1989). Habermas argues that, originally, the bourgeoisie conceived the public sphere as the realm that mediated between society and the state. In other words, it embodies "the principle of information which once had to be fought for against the arcane policies of monarchies and which since that time has made possible the democratic control of state activities" (Habermas, 1974, p. 50). However, Habermas also argues that, although this liberal model is still in principle an instructive one (in terms of its ability to critique state power), it can no longer be applied to the conditions that currently operate in late capitalist, welfare-state mass democracy. The public sphere has by and large lost its importance as an instrument of political discussion, not because the role of the citizen is less important but because of the overlapping of state and society:

> With the interweaving of the public and private realm, not only do the political authorities assume certain functions in the sphere of commodity exchange and social labor, but conversely social powers now assume political functions. This leads to a kind of "refeudalization" of the public sphere. Large organizations strive for political compromises with the state and with each other, excluding the public sphere whenever possible. But at the same time the large organizations must assure themselves of at least plebiscitary support from the mass of the population through an apparent display of openness. (Habermas, 1974, p. 54)

In this sense, any notion of a critical public sphere is chimerical because "the process of making public simply serves the arcane policies of special interests; in the form of 'publicity' it wins public prestige for people or affairs, thus making them worthy of acclamation in a climate of non-public opinion" (1974, p. 55).

Habermas thus enables us to see how any possibility for meaningful debate within the public sphere is effectively undermined because of combined state and corporate interests within the social realm and the economy. By and large, those major decisions of potentially public significance "short circuit" the public sphere and are presented as a "fait accompli" to the citizenry.

Habermas's critique of the liberal model of the public sphere is important because it allows us to see how a still largely accepted dichotomy between public and private has been transformed in late capitalism. To argue for an unproblematic distinction between the public and private spheres is essentially to overlook not only the extent to which the two realms intertwine but also the extent to which the citizen as the sovereign subject of rationality has been undermined and disempowered. The opportunity for the "private" citizen to make his or her case in a discursive public space is largely negated because (a) the institution of the public sphere is not equally available to everyone; (b) those with the resources to make use of the public sphere also have the resources to control the ways in which different and competing interests, needs, and beliefs are interpreted; and (c) the public-private dichotomy structurally and ideologically disempowers certain social groups because it regulates admission of issues into the public sphere, thus determining the extent to which such issues are "open to contestation."

Habermas maintains that something like the public sphere is indispensable to the rational contestation of issues of public welfare, but at the same time he offers an important critique of why the public sphere, as currently constituted, is unable to function in its appropriate critical, mediatory role. However, while he recognizes the aporia in the liberal bourgeois model, he is unable to appropriately problematize the relationship between the private and public realms. It is this problematic that the liberal bourgeois model specifically ignores and that, I would argue, must be more closely examined if we are to articulate a more democratic conception of participation in political processes.

At this point, it would be helpful to provide a working definition of the public sphere as a context for my discussion of critical feminism and its implications for the public-private relationship. I view the public sphere as a discursively constructed space for argument in which different interest groups compete to articulate conflicting worldviews. The boundaries of the public sphere are both conventional (i.e., humanly constructed) and permeable, so the relationship between the public and private spheres is continuously open to contestation. Furthermore, following Fraser (1990-1991), I reject the notion of a single public sphere in favor of a multiplicity of spheres that impinge in different ways on society. These spheres are interrelated, drawing on a complex system of overlapping discursive communities that have varying degrees of cultural, economic, and political capital.

For example, large multinational corporations clearly possess greater political, cultural, and economic resources than, say, women's and gay rights groups, and, as such, they are able to marshal these resources in ways that heavily influence public debate and policy. At the same time, relatively powerless groups can have an impact on public discourse and debate; witness, for instance, Disney's extension of its health care plan to include domestic partners of employees regardless of sexual orientation. Such a policy change, it might be argued, would be unthinkable without the important role of the gay community in shifting the parameters of public debate over homosexual rights. On the other hand, Disney's new policy triggered a response from conservative groups such as Focus on the Family, leading to a boycott—albeit unsuccessful—of Disney products. To complicate matters further, Disney has been a frequent target of leftist critics, particularly feminists, because of its cultural imperialism and its mass marketing of conservative values and gender identities.

What we see in this example is an incredibly complex and frequently contradictory picture of the relations among discourse, publics, and individual and group rights. Some of the issues relevant to this example include competing definitions of "the family," the boundaries between the public and private spheres (Is the legitimacy of certain forms of sexuality open to public debate or not?), and the role of the modern corporation in shaping cultural identities and values. My point is that any attempt to characterize "the public sphere" in monolithic terms and, concomitantly, to posit a straightforward and fixed relationship between the public and private spheres fails to do justice to the complexity of the spheres and their relationship to each other. In the next section, I explore the role of critical feminist theory in attempting to develop a more nuanced conception of the relationship between the public and private realms of discourse. Following this, I suggest how such a conception can provide greater insight into the relations among the public and private spheres, organizations, and democracy.

THE PUBLIC-PRIVATE DICHOTOMY: A FEMINIST CRITIQUE

It is both impossible and undesirable to provide an accurate and inclusive description of "the feminist project" given the many and diverse intellectual currents that have emerged over the last 20 years or so. However, in the context of this chapter and in terms of the type of analysis I wish to conduct, we can think of feminism in its broadest sense as the critique of binary thinking

(Fox-Genovese, 1991; Fraser, 1989; Gergen, 1988; Mumby & Putnam, 1992; Nicholson, 1990; Nielsen, 1990).

This type of critique falls into two analytically distinct but related domains. First, feminist theory has consistently addressed and critiqued the binary assumptions associated with traditional Western, patriarchal epistemology. Thus, apparently natural oppositions such as rational/irrational, culture/nature, and mind/body (in which the first, male, term in each dichotomy is privileged over the second, female, term) are shown by many feminists to be arbitrary constructions that maintain and reproduce men's dominance over women (Flax, 1990; Hekman, 1990). For example, the "rational/irrational" opposition is shown to be an ideological construction that traditionally has justified women's exclusion from the realm of ideas and the public sphere of rational argument (Hekman, 1990, pp. 10-61). Related to this, the tendency of traditional science to dichotomize the relationship between the researcher and the object of study (generically termed the "subject/object split") has been critiqued by many feminists as inappropriately reifying and separating elements that are interdependent in important ways—ontologically, epistemologically, politically, and so on. Feminist researchers such as Oakley (1981), for example, have shown how knowledge claims are coproduced by the researcher and informants and are very much tied up with the political choices made by the former. As such, feminists eschew the notion of objective, political-neutral knowledge, arguing that all knowledge arises out of the standpoint one assumes (Allen, 1996; Collins, 1991; Hekman, 1997).

Second, feminism as a social movement has focused attention on the various ways in which social and political practices systematically subordinate women (Buzzanell, 1995; Clair, 1993b; Ferguson, 1984). By drawing attention to the gendered features of societal inequality, feminism has provided a context for both debate and action. It has demonstrated the extent to which the differences between social groups are not natural and inevitable but, rather, are shaped by the production and reproduction of specific semantic, political, and economic systems. In this sense, feminism has critiqued the construction of a binary system of difference in contemporary society.

In the context of this chapter, the feminist critique of both patriarchal ways of knowing and gendered systems of oppression provides a framework for the analysis of the relationship between the public and private spheres. First, in epistemological terms, feminist theory has shown that "the ruling paradigms or theoretical frameworks in social science are flawed by a masculinist bias which is indicated in an arbitrary privileging of the public aspect of social existence" (Yeatman, 1987, p. 159). The erstwhile privileging in rhetorical studies of "great speakers" is one manifestation of this bias. While women may be viewed as a legitimate object of study for social science, the tendency has been to treat gender as a variable rather than as a central construct for thematizing social issues (see Spitzack & Carter, 1987, for a critique of this

tendency). In Foucault's (1979) terms, it might be said that women traditionally have been "the object of information, never a subject in communication"
(p. 200). In addition, although women may be accommodated in traditional
forms of social science, they generally are assumed to have a "distinctive"
role in the domestic realm—a realm that is defined as the lesser dimension of
the dual ordering (public/private) of social life.

Second, the masculinist bias in social theory and research mirrors (and is
mirrored by) the gendered character of the "citizen" role. The liberal bourgeois concept of the public sphere is gendered in terms of its privileging of
masculinist speech styles, forms of association, and so forth. Indeed, Fraser
(1990-1991, p. 58) even points to the etymological connection between "testimony" and "testicle" as an indicator of how thoroughly patriarchal our conception of the public sphere is. But as several feminists have pointed out, this
structuring of a male-oriented public domain is dependent on the ability to
articulate a domestic (i.e., private) realm that supports it. This gendered split
between the public and private realms thus becomes the foundation for social
order. In her analysis of the mutual development of capitalism and individualism, Fox-Genovese (1991) notes,

> Individualism, rationalism, and universalism were all interpreted in strictly male
> terms. Worse, in some measure, they all rested upon a more or less explicit repudia-
> tion of women as the opposite of the desired male norm and the celebration of them
> as the emotional anchor necessary to the functioning of that norm under conditions
> of intense competition. Having rejected dependency in favor of autonomy, the
> dominant male culture nonetheless itself depended, in the lives of individual men,
> upon a repressed domestic sphere that was represented as custodian of all the qual-
> ities the public sphere could not tolerate. (pp. 16-17)

Feminist theory, then, allows us to problematize and deconstruct the "ideology of separate spheres" (Fox-Genovese, 1991, p. 22) and to demonstrate
the extent to which the cleavage between the public and private realms is constructed via the privileging of a specifically gender-political social system. In
essence, it can be argued that the central construct around which this deconstruction process revolves is that of "power." Here, I do not mean "power" in
a simply coercive sense but, rather, as the process through which a certain
constellation of interests is structured so that the needs of certain groups take
precedence over the needs of other groups. In a Gramscian (1971) sense, we
can say that the currently articulated relationship between the public and private spheres provides the foundation for a hegemonic social structure in
which certain groups (particularly women and minorities) are denied access
to the dominant "means of interpretation and communication (MIC)" (Fraser,
1989, p. 164).

For example, the debate over "welfare" tends to be so dominated by conservative political interests that the term *welfare mother* immediately conjures up, in many people's minds, the image of a single, minority (probably crack-using) mother who gets pregnant for the sole purpose of increasing her welfare payments. In this definitional struggle, "welfare" becomes the signifier for the failure of a specific class of individuals rather than for an economic system that creates huge economic and political disparities between the "haves" and "have nots."

Fraser's (1989, 1990-1991) analysis of the public-private relationship is worth examining at length because it provides an important means of moving beyond the tendency to treat that relationship as largely reified. Specifically, Fraser (1989) provides what she terms a "discursive-political" model of "needs talk." Here, "needs talk" refers to those issues that come to constitute what is generally considered the public sphere and about which there is debate among different interest groups. However, Fraser argues that such needs talk cannot be taken at face value but must instead be contextualized in terms of the struggle over how such needs should be defined and interpreted. One way to clarify this orientation is to contrast the characteristics of her "thick" model of needs talk with the "thin" approach that she attributes to most traditional treatments of publicly declared needs. According to Fraser (1989), traditional approaches are subject to the following difficulties: (a) "They take the interpretation of people's needs as simply given and unproblematic"; (b) it is assumed that who interprets the needs and in light of what interests is unimportant; (c) it is taken for granted that the currently authorized public discourse available for needs interpretation is adequate and fair; and (d) such approaches "fail to problematize the social and institutional logic of processes of need interpretation" (p. 164).

In contrast, Fraser (1989) proposes

> a more politically critical, discourse-oriented alternative. I take the politics of needs to comprise three moments that are analytically distinct but interrelated in practice. The first is the struggle to establish or deny the political status of a given need, the struggle to validate the need as a matter of legitimate political concern or to enclave it as a nonpolitical matter. The second is the struggle over the interpretation of the need, the struggle for the power to define it and, so, to determine what would satisfy it. The third moment is the struggle over the satisfaction of the need, the struggle to secure or withhold provision. (p. 164)

Fraser contextualizes this model of the politics of needs within a model of social discourse (her MIC). Such a model is not simply a means of stressing the importance of the communicative process in the expression and representation of individual and group needs. Rather, it thematizes the extent to which discursive practices are integral to the constitution of identity—both individual and group. Fraser (1989) suggests the following discursive resources that members of a given social group have available in articulating their needs in opposition to other groups:

1. The officially recognized idioms in which one can press claims; for example, needs talk, rights talk, interests talk
2. The vocabularies available for instantiating claims in these recognized idioms . . .; for example, therapeutic vocabularies, administrative vocabularies, . . . feminist vocabularies
3. The paradigms of argumentation accepted as authoritative in adjudicating conflicting claims [e.g., appeals to scientific experts, to majority rule, etc.]
4. The narrative conventions available for constructing the individual and collective stories that are constitutive of people's social identities
5. Modes of subjectification; the ways in which various discourses position the people to whom they are addressed as specific sorts of subjects . . . as "normal" or "deviant," . . . as victims or as potential activists. (pp. 163-165)

On the basis of Fraser's (1989) model of "needs talk," we are able to explicitly problematize the process by which certain systems of communication and modes of interpretation come to constitute the sphere of public discourse. In essence, the problem is one of examining the ways in which discourses are politicized or sequestered as nonpolitical. In other words, to what extent is an issue contested across different social groups that occupy different discursive arenas? Based on the discursive-political model that Fraser develops, the relationship between the public and private realms can be examined by exploring the various discursive practices that ideologically situate specific issues either as open to public contestation or as restricted to specific, "nonpolitical" arenas.

From a critical feminist perspective, the prevailing tendency in patriarchal, liberal bourgeois society is—discursively and ideologically—to establish a tripartite relationship among the political, economic, and domestic/private spheres (Fraser, 1989, p. 168). By definition, then, both the economic and domestic/private realms are characterized by discursive practices that restrict specific issues to those arenas and thus deem them "nonpolitical." Thus, the merits of capitalism as an economic system are—for the most part—not open to debate, and corporations are free to pursue the accumulation of capital as long as they do not break the law (or at least as long as they are not caught breaking the law). In this sense, even though various groups may debate the ethics of certain economic practices (e.g., moving production to Third World countries to decrease labor costs or to escape "draconian" environmental policies), the right of corporations to vigorously pursue a wide profit margin is viewed as a nonpartisan, nonpolitical issue.

Similarly, in the domestic sphere, certain issues are discursively situated as "private" matters and therefore beyond public contestation. As a case in point, the sequestering of spouse abuse within the domestic realm is viewed by feminists as one way that patriarchal society depoliticizes a political issue. The subordination of women is reproduced by the male-dominated establishment's ability to control the forms of discourse that articulate the question of spouse abuse. Thus, if this issue is discursively constituted as a personal, private, domestic matter that takes place between specific individuals within a family situation, then it can be potentially addressed by expert discourses associated with social work, family law, clinical psychology, and so forth. Fraser (1989, p. 174) would argue that such expert discourses are depoliticizing in that they position people as "cases" rather than as belonging to a specific social group or movement. Furthermore, "they are rendered passive, positioned as potential recipients of predefined services rather than as agents involved in interpreting their needs and shaping their life conditions" (Fraser, 1989, p. 174).

Of course, feminists have long struggled against this tendency toward depoliticization by constituting oppositional discourses that declare the "personal as political" and that demonstrate the extent to which domestic violence is rooted in complex social, political, economic, and gendered structures of domination. As such, it is argued that the liberal bourgeois notion of the right to privacy, as manifested in the dichotomous relationship between the public and private spheres, is founded on the suppression and trivializing of the private sphere and the simultaneous valorization of a (monolithic) public sphere as the only realm in which issues are politically contested.

The feminist deconstruction of the public-private dichotomy can be summarized by suggesting several lines of critique that theorists pursue (Fox-Genovese, 1991; Fraser, 1989; Pateman, 1983; Pateman & Gross, 1987). First, *feminists expose as chimerical the notion that the liberal bourgeois public sphere is accessible to a wide variety of interest groups, regardless of social inequalities.* Instead of bracketing such inequalities, feminist theorists argue for their thematization to examine the various ways in which discursive-political structures function to produce and reproduce exclusionary structures of domination. Participatory democracy, it is argued, can never flourish as long as it is assumed that social inequality is not an impediment to access to the public sphere. Such a perspective represents a direct critique of the liberal, pluralist model of power and rights as advocated by theorists such as Dahl (1961) and Hunter (1953), who argue that—far from being monopolized by an elite few—power is widely dispersed in U.S. society. As Lukes (1974) and others have pointed out, however, this pluralist model focuses exclusively on visible, vocal interest groups, thus overlooking the fact that certain voices can be silenced through sequestration—precisely the issue with which critical feminists such as Fraser are concerned.

Second, *the development of feminist counterpublics over the last two decades has provided the context for discursive spaces in which women can renegotiate and reinterpret identities imposed on them by a male-dominated social structure.* As such, feminist theorists have critiqued the basic liberal bourgeois notion of the existence of a single, unified public sphere. Indeed, scholars such as Fraser (1990-1991) have argued that, within a nonegalitarian society such as the United States, a plurality of publics better addresses the needs and concerns of subordinated groups. Such a plurality does not represent the kind of pluralist model advocated by Dahl (1961) but is more consistent with a Foucauldian (1979, 1980) model of power in which various subaltern voices constantly appear on the margins of the established order in attempts to redefine the terrain of legitimate public debate. In this context, Fraser stresses the importance of the development of "subaltern counterpublics"—that is, "parallel discursive arenas where members of subordinated social groups invent and circulate counterdiscourses, which in turn permit them to formulate oppositional interpretations of their identities, interests, and needs" (Fraser, 1990-1991, p. 67). An example of this process in operation is discussed in the case of the women's shelter (Maguire & Mohtar, 1994) presented in the next section. Furthermore, the introduction into the general public consciousness of terms such as *sexual harassment, date rape,* and *sexism* suggests the extent to which the ability to "speak in one's own voice" and articulate an oppositional view of social reality can influence the wider public sphere and, hence, reframe social relations.

Third, and perhaps most important, *feminist theorists have made a strong case for fundamentally problematizing what, under the bourgeois liberal model, is to count as a public versus a private matter.* As mentioned above, critical theory in general and feminist theory in particular have challenged the notion that these terms simply designate a concrete, objectively existing social structure. Instead, they are viewed as discursively constructed spheres that function ideologically to legitimate and delegitimate various interests, beliefs, and worldviews. Thus, the fundamental concern is not with the straightforward classification of an issue as either public or private (although clearly this remains an important question) but with how it is that certain issues come to be situated as one or the other. In a Foucauldian (1976/1990, 1979) sense, we can argue that definitions of the relationship between the public and private realms are structured according to a set of power-knowledge relations that articulate oppositions between different groups. From a feminist perspective, such oppositions discursively and rhetorically situate women as "other," that is, as subordinated, domesticated, privatized, and disempowered in relation to a valorized male norm of publicity and empowerment. By recognizing, for example, that the liberal bourgeois gendered discourse of domestic

privacy seeks to exclude issues such as domestic violence from the public
sphere by personalizing and/or familializing them, we can come to appreciate the extent to which the public-private dichotomy is ideological and
discursive-political rather than objectively founded.

In the final section, I show how these issues can be applied to the analysis
of the relationships among organizations, community, identity, and resistance. Specifically, I examine three instances of resistance among members of
three different organizations. My point is to illustrate the importance of developing a gendered understanding of the public and private spheres and their
relationship to issues of community and democracy.

GENDERING ORGANIZATIONAL HEGEMONY:
IDENTITY AND RESISTANCE IN THE WORKPLACE

Gramsci's (1971) concept of hegemony provides an important means by
which to examine processes of control and resistance in organizations. For
Gramsci, hegemony refers not to control through coercion but to "the 'spontaneous' consent given by the great masses of the population to the general
direction imposed on social life by the dominant fundamental group" (p. 12).
Important to my argument, Gramsci views hegemony as exercised primarily
in the realm of civil society—that is, those institutions that function as elements of the public sphere (e.g., the mass media, the education system, and
religious organizations) and that function ideologically to shape experience,
knowledge, and identity.

Although Gramsci does not directly discuss the corporate form as part of
civil society, it can be argued that the modern corporation has a large impact
on issues of knowledge production and identity formation (Deetz, 1992;
Mumby, 1997). As such, the modern corporation is directly implicated in the
shaping of the relationship between the public and private spheres. Two
important studies that assess the impact of gender on how hegemony "is produced at the point of production" (Burawoy, 1979, p. xii) are Benson's (1992)
analysis of the "clerking sisterhood" and Collinson's (1988, 1992) study of
masculinity and humor in the components division of a truck factory. Both
studies, in very different ways, assess the relations among gender, identity,
community, and resistance in the workplace. Examining the work of saleswomen in U.S. department stores between 1890 and 1960, Benson (1992)
demonstrates that

> At least in this major women's occupation, the effect of changes in management
> practice in the twentieth century was, ironically, to increase the level of workers'
> skill and thus inadvertently to permit the development of a powerful and enduring
> work culture. (p. 168)

Thus, in contrast to Braverman's (1974) generalized "deskilling" thesis, Benson shows that the "clerking sisterhood" developed strong informal work groups that resisted management intervention and assisted in the enrichment of jobs through sharing expertise, helping fellow workers, and so forth. In addition, the development of a strong work culture enabled the female clerks to work against management interests by resisting attempts to increase output by adopting an informal quota among themselves and by collectively resisting management-fostered intradepartmental competition. As a result, Benson (1992) notes,

> Social interaction on the selling floor was friendly and supportive. The tendency of saleswomen to "huddle" or "congregate" on the floor was the aspect of their behavior most frequently remarked by managers and customers alike. . . . Saleswomen in the more solitary departments shared stockwork and paperwork even when it was assigned to individuals, and reinforced day-to-day contact with parties, both on the job and after hours. They integrated the rituals of women's culture into their work culture; showers and parties to commemorate engagements, marriages, and births . . . are reported in employee newspapers by the score. (p. 176)

Benson's study is significant in its articulation of a gendered response to the thesis of deskilling. While it is true that, in an undifferentiated sense, the separation of conception from execution of labor is a pervasive characteristic of the workplace, Benson provides a subtler reading of this struggle for control of the labor process through a gendered analysis of work. Just as significant, however, is her reading of the ways in which worker resistance, identity, and sense of community are derived from a fundamental blurring of the relationship between the private and public spheres of life. The female clerks' resistance to the deskilling process and to management efforts to carefully control the selling process is successful because of a sense of solidarity that arises from a "women's culture" traditionally sequestered in the private, domestic realm. In this sense, the women are able to collectively (and only collectively) refuse the logic of a managerial rationality that dictates a workplace environment rooted in the privileging of technical, instrumental forms of knowledge. This issue becomes particularly important when contrasted with Collinson's (1988, 1992) study of workplace resistance.

Collinson's study is significant for two reasons. First, it provides important insights into the everyday communicative practices of workers, addressing the relationships among communication, identity, power, and resistance. Second, as a gendered analysis, it focuses explicitly on the construction of *masculine* workplace identity. Although not unique (e.g., Willis, 1977), such an analysis is unusual in its problematizing of masculinity as a socially constructed phenomenon. Collinson focuses on the use of humor in the workplace, arguing that humor functions simultaneously as a means of resisting boredom and management control practices, as a way of exerting social pressure to conform to working-class definitions of masculinity, and as a means of controlling those workers perceived to be not "pulling their weight." The most interesting dimension of this study, however, is that, contrary to Willis's (1977) view of working-class resistance and solidarity, Collinson finds solidarity among the workers to be rather weak and superficial, compromised by a masculine identity that focuses on "having a laff" and maximizing wages to provide for dependents. The contradiction between worker solidarity and strong masculine (sexual) identity is captured well in the following:

> One male self-identity, as sexually rampant, was superceded by another, that of the responsible family breadwinner. In both cases, however, shop-floor workers were expected to subscribe to the masculine assumptions of the joking culture. Yet these demands to conform inevitably generated a form of reluctant compliance from some workers which rendered shop-floor unity at best precarious and fragile. The oppositional values of personal freedom, masculine independence and autonomy, enshrined in the breadwinner role, contributed to these divisions, in particular, by compounding the separation between the "public" sphere of work and the "private" world of home. The collective experience of shared masculinity at work often contradicted the individualistic orientation to life outside. (Collinson, 1988, p. 192)

It is interesting to compare Benson's (1992) discussion of the close connections among women clerks' sense of identity, community, and resistance with Collinson's claim that working-class masculine identity, community, and resistance are, in some respects, inimical to each other. The careful male working-class separation of the public and private realms results in a very different sense of community and identity from that of the female clerks in Benson's study. Indeed, one could argue that, for the engineers, identity ("the collective experience of shared masculinity") is strongly rooted in a competitive individualism that constructs the demonstration of one's sexual prowess and breadwinner status as superseding collective resistance to management. In fact, even though the masculine culture of the workplace is clearly strong, it functions—at least in part—as a vehicle for the expression of individual identity. Furthermore, the masculinist reification of the boundaries between the public and private spheres actually helps to maintain and reproduce a managerial system of logic because workers are defined (and define themselves) as elements in the production process who must perform to a particular level to be effective.

Another way of situating this critique is to argue that, within the ideology of liberalism, the engineers in Collinson's study are constructed as subjects through two different, and contradictory, discourses: First, they are situated as free, autonomous, self-constituting citizens, and, second, they are constructed as alienated labor, subject to the autocratic and capricious logic of capitalism and managerial rationality. However, the logic of liberalism hides the contradictory nature of these two forms of subjectivity—independent agency and economic subjugation—by stressing a different "truth" associated with each: a political truth with the former and an economic truth with the latter (Huspek, 1994). The ideology of liberalism holds sway by keeping the political and economic spheres distinct. The engineers reproduce these discourses of truth by engaging in communicative practices (humor) that position them as autonomous, free-willed individuals whose identities are defined economically and sexually. Indeed, one could argue that the workers' self-identification with aggressive sexuality is partly a response to their recognition of themselves as alienated, disenfranchised labor within capitalist economic relations. By discursively constructing themselves as sexually active, they resist—at the individual level—the everyday oppressions of the workplace. However, this form of resistance merely can serve to reproduce the liberal separation of spheres by reducing worker resistance to individuated, noncollective acts.

In sum, the tendency of the male workers to maintain a rigid bifurcation of the public and private spheres serves to disempower them by articulating a sense of community and identity that furthers the interests of capital, rendering resistance to managerial logic ineffectual and largely symbolic in form. On the other hand, the female clerks' reframing of the workplace as an extension of the private realm of home and sisterhood creates possibilities for empowerment and a collective means of resisting managerially imposed limitations on what is considered appropriate organizational behavior. Such findings provide insight into the gendered construction of identity and suggest the importance of avoiding blanket and totalizing claims about relationships among discourse, power, identity, and resistance in organizations.

One final example of the relationship between gender, identity, community, and the public and private spheres helps to point out the constitutive role of discourse in creating "subaltern counterpublics" (Fraser, 1990-1991). Indeed, one could even make the case that, in addition to having different structures and decision-making processes, feminist alternative organizations are best characterized as alternative discourse (or speech) communities. As such, they provide contexts for the expression of needs and interests that are traditionally "organized" outside of public discourse. Thus, as Fraser (1990-1991) argues, "the idea of an egalitarian, multi-cultural society only makes sense if we suppose a plurality of public arenas in which groups with diverse values and rhetorics participate. By definition, such a society must contain a multiplicity of publics" (p. 69).

What issues "count" as public versus private are, as we have discussed, open to discursive contestation. Fraser argues that various feminist counterpublics have played an important role in reconfiguring the ways in which issues are framed as either private/domestic or public/political. Many feminist organizations can be understood as subaltern counterpublics that discursively challenge prevailing understandings of the ways in which gender, identity, power, and politics intersect. One example of a study that directly takes up Fraser's conceptual framework is Maguire and Mohtar's (1994) study of the counterdiscourses of a women's center. Although the center experienced the usual tensions between the need for hierarchical structure and the development of egalitarian relationships, the members also defined themselves in terms of three discursive moves that functioned to situate them in an oppositional relationship to the mainstream culture:

> In the first move they identify the common practice of hierarchically structured state-run social service agencies as incompetent and point to the systematic dysfunction of those agencies. . . . Their praise for the Center as a positive alternative is exemplified in two phrases heard throughout the script/interviews: "The Women's Center is non-racist, non-sexist, and non-homophobic" and "our goal is to help women help themselves.". . . In a second discursive strategy they attempt to re-educate these members of the dominant public [police department, hospital staff, state agencies, etc.] about survivor/victim assistance and the dynamics of domestic violence and sexual assault.
>
> In a third discursive move, members of the community identify the scorn, derision, false assumptions, and stereotypes generated about them by members of the dominant public. The verbal attacks the community has suffered over the years act to position them as outsiders, at the same time the community members retell these stories. In this way, both the attacks and the responses to the attacks reinforce their outsider status. (Maguire & Mohtar, 1994, pp. 241-242)

The importance of this study lies in its conceptualization of an organizational community not in terms of its structures, roles, and responsibilities but in terms of a set of discursive processes that provide community members with a set of interpretive procedures by which to construct their relationship to other mainstream organizations. The defining of this community as a constellation of discursive moments means that the relation between the public and private realms becomes problematized. The members of this community blur the boundaries between the economic, political, and domestic realms, discursively positioning themselves as challenging and resisting liberal conceptions of what "counts" as appropriate issues for public debate.

Thus, the members of this organization bring together a focus on community and collective action and a concern with "the other" and engagement in resistance through discursive strategies. This process is exemplified through a tension between, on the one hand, the recognition that the collective articulation of an alternative way of being and doing is possible and, on the other hand, the awareness that such an alternative is tenuous, precarious, and founded primarily in the group's ability to articulate its marginality in the face of powerful discursive and nondiscursive hegemonic forces that shape the "will to truth" and definitions of what counts as publicly contestable issues.

CONCLUSION

This chapter has attempted to outline some of the issues and problems associated with the widely accepted liberal bourgeois conception of the relationship between the public and private spheres of discourse and its implications for organizational communication studies. In particular, I have tried to show how these two spheres are not objectively given but, rather, are constructed through the discursive articulation of certain social, political, and economic interests. The adoption of a critical feminist framework to conduct such an analysis is particularly compelling because it can be argued that the public-private distinction is largely conventional and is structured around the interests of dominant groups. A critical feminist analysis of this distinction provides insight into how a male-centered conception of the public realm is dependent on a complementary and subordinated domestic/private realm. This ideology of separate spheres provides the foundation for social order and functions to perpetuate social inequities.

This critical feminist analysis of the relationship between the public and private spheres also enables us to rethink issues of organization, identity, and resistance. Through an examination of specific instances of organizational life, we gain insight into how problematizing the liberal conception of these spheres creates possibilities for transforming that which counts as political. By focusing on the ways in which the public-private dichotomy is discursively constructed, we can come to a more nuanced understanding of the processes involved in the legitimation of some views of the world and the marginalization of others. Feminist theory plays a pivotal role in exposing the contradictions between the rhetoric of democracy and enfranchisement, on the one hand, and the reality of social, political, and economic inequality, on the other.

2

Between the Generalized and the Concrete Other

Approaching Organizational Ethics From Feminist Perspectives

Tanni Haas
Stanley Deetz

Our objective is to apply feminist theorizing on ethics to discussions about how the corporation may address its two primary "ethical" concerns in relation to its various stakeholders. These ethical concerns are (a) the implementation of ethical procedures for identifying which stakeholders have legitimate values and political interests in need of representation and for identifying the character of those values and political interests, and (b) the implementation of ethical procedures that ensure that stakeholder values and political interests, once identified, are adequately represented in the corporation's internal decision-making processes.

The plural *perspectives* was intentional in the title. No simple unitary feminist perspective exists, and feminist theorizing on ethics may contribute to organizational ethics in multiple ways. We have chosen one way from those available. The feminist writings of interest here have provided two important

AUTHORS' NOTE: We would like to thank Richard L. Johannesen for his thoughtful comments.

contributions to the study of corporations. First, they have thoroughly critiqued the exclusivity of the consensus-based rational/economic model of corporations, thereby aiding the conceptual development of what we more generally refer to as conflict-based stakeholder models. And, second, they have enriched the development of the concept and practice of ethical decision-making processes in corporations by focusing on the notions of care and responsibility. As a further limit to this essay, we focus primarily on this second contribution through the works of Benhabib (1985, 1986, 1987, 1990, 1992).

The two contributions are not independent, however. We agree with Burton and Dunn (1996) that "stakeholder theory . . . must be grounded by a theory of ethics" and that "traditional ethics of justice and rights cannot completely ground the theory" (p. 133). A feminist theory of ethical decision-making processes is important to stakeholder theory generally. The conception of corporations in relation to stakeholders and the practice of ethical decision-making processes are intertwined. The relations are complex, and the feminist writings of interest here provide an important part, but not the whole, of the relation. We argue that a dynamic tension exists between stakeholder theory morally guided by ethical theories arising from argumentation, competition, and justice/rights and ethical theories arising from conversation, cooperation, and care/responsibility. Rather than resolving this tension with feminist theories, we reflect on the ways certain feminist theorists keep it alive.

The chapter develops the argument as follows. First, we discuss recent developments in stakeholder theory by distinguishing between an "economic model" and a "multiple-stakeholder model" of the relationship between the corporation and its various stakeholders (see Deetz, 1995a, 1995b; Freeman & Gilbert, 1992). We argue that the economic model provides an inherently problematic conception of the relationship between the corporation and its various stakeholders. In contrast, the multiple-stakeholder model provides a normative ideal of how this relationship ought to be conceptualized. Next, we argue that the further conceptual development of stakeholder theory may benefit considerably from attending to recent developments in feminist theorizing on ethics.

Second, we discuss discourse ethics as a guide to the types of ethical decision-making processes necessary for a multiple-stakeholder model to function in practice. Initially, we discuss the way Habermas's (1984, 1987, 1990, 1993) theory of communicative action and discourse ethics, and especially his description of the "ideal speech situation" (Habermas, 1973), have served as a normative heuristic for the development of ethical decision-making processes within corporations. Next, we discuss how certain feminist theorists have built on and transformed Habermas's analysis. In particular, the feminist perspective on ethics developed by Benhabib (1985, 1986, 1987, 1990, 1992) provides a basis on which it may be possible to analyze the relationship between management and the corporation's stakeholders and provide tentative answers about how management and other stakeholders may engage in ethical decision-making processes. This theoretical perspective is particularly relevant not only because of its own intrinsic merits but because it provides useful conceptual distinctions to discuss the relations between an "ethic of justice and rights" and an "ethic of care and responsibility."

Third, we argue that management ought to assume the standpoint of what Benhabib has termed the "generalized other" (à la Habermas) and the "concrete other" (as care/responsibility) simultaneously during the initial identification of which stakeholders ought to be represented in the corporation's internal decision-making processes and during the initial identification of the character of their values and political interests. Related to this, we argue that management ought to engage in what Benhabib has termed the "moral conversation" during the actual representation of stakeholder values and political interests within the corporation's internal decision-making processes.

Finally, we discuss some important practical problems associated with assuming the standpoint of the concrete other during instances of communicative interaction in which management and the corporation's stakeholders are situated in different spatiotemporal contexts. Although the assumption of the standpoint of the concrete other ideally requires that the participants be situated in the context of spatiotemporal copresence, communicating through face-to-face interaction, management often may be forced to apply either "mediated interaction" or "mediated quasi-interaction" instead (see Thompson, 1995). We argue that, although both types of communicative interaction are inherently problematic from the standpoint of concern with the concrete other, the application of mediated interaction provides the most potential for assuming this standpoint because it entails a "dialogical" mode of communicative interaction aimed at "specific others."

In sum, this chapter provides a discussion of how Benhabib's feminist perspective on ethics may inform a conceptual shift from an economic model to a multiple-stakeholder model of the relationship between the corporation and its various stakeholders. Specifically, we discuss how the conceptual distinction Benhabib draws between assuming the standpoint of the generalized and the concrete other in terms of a moral conversation provides a basis for delineating how the corporation may address its two primary ethical concerns in terms of the conceptual logic of the multiple-stakeholder model. These ethical concerns are (a) the implementation of ethical procedures for identifying which stakeholders have legitimate values and political interests in need of representation and for the identification of the character of those values and political interests, and (b) the implementation of ethical procedures that ensure that stakeholder values and political interests, once identified, are adequately represented in the corporation's internal decision-making processes.

THE ECONOMIC AND THE
MULTIPLE-STAKEHOLDER MODELS

The relationship between management and the corporation's internal and external constituencies (or "stakeholders") may be attended to in terms of two conceptually distinct models: the economic model and the multiple-stakeholder model, respectively (Deetz, 1995a, 1995b). Fundamentally, the economic model conceptualizes corporations as "economic" institutions functioning to satisfy the (primarily economic) objectives of their owners and stockholders, and the multiple-stakeholder model conceptualizes corporations as "social" institutions functioning to accomplish multiple social objectives for a variety of societal groups who have a stake in them. Whereas the economic model constitutes an ideal-typical representation of how corporations have traditionally conceptualized their relationships with others, the multiple-stakeholder model constitutes an ideal-typical representation of how corporations are increasingly conceptualizing their relationships with others.

The Economic Model

Traditionally, the corporation has been conceptualized as consisting of management, with all other stakeholders being situated external to the corporation and controlled by managerial strategic actions. By conceptually separating management from all other stakeholders, the interests of other stakeholders are considered to be potential costs to the corporation, and control is justified as "cost containment." Potential political conflicts of interest among societal groups with a stake in corporate decisions are reduced to economic calculations (Power, 1992). The relationship between the corporation and its stakeholders is therefore not considered to be based on representation rights of the stakeholders within the corporation's internal decision-making processes but, rather, is transformed into a cost-containment activity. Economic rationality and management's desire for control merge in this model. This control-oriented economic rationality legitimizes management's attempts to "colonize" other stakeholders (Deetz, 1992; Habermas, 1987). Feminist theorists from Ferguson (1984) onward have thoroughly critiqued the patriarchal worldview present in this model, the narrow concept of masculine rationality, the marginalization of the body, emotions and the feminine, and the ever presence of bureaucratic and unobtrusive control processes.

Furthermore, the conceptual distinction drawn between the corporation, embodied by management, and other stakeholders is based on the classical liberal democratic distinction between the "private sphere" and the "public sphere." Within this conceptual logic, corporate decisions are conceptualized as taking place within the private sphere and as being primarily of economic character. The primary objective of the corporation is to create profit, and the responsibility of management is to be accountable to the corporation's own-ers/stockholders. Representation rights of the corporation's various other stakeholders are suspended because of accepted contractual relations of sub-ordination and the primacy of property rights.

The conceptual distinction drawn between the private sphere and the public sphere is problematic, however, because the corporation is increasingly mak-ing decisions affecting various societal groups that previously have been made through democratic state processes. This conceptual distinction is there-fore politically significant because it defines the space for political debates outside the private sphere by situating the corporation as an extension of pri-vate property conceptually, and often legally, outside the sphere of demo-cratic state processes. The assumption that the corporation represents only an economic institution also neglects to account for the presence of extrarational and extraeconomic managerial values within the corporation's internal deci-sion-making processes. The economic imperative therefore represents a value-laden but presumably impartial and neutral system of conflict resolu-tion that distorts the expression of values and suppresses awareness of poten-tially significant political conflicts of interest within the corporation. The conceptual distinction drawn between the private sphere and the public sphere is therefore not value neutral. It is maintained for the advancement of certain (often managerial) values and political interests, such as the prevention of public intrusion into the corporation's internal decision-making processes. Again, feminist theorists have contributed much to our understanding of how the private-public dichotomy has not only supported the economic domina-tion of stakeholders by corporations but has also marginalized women as a distinct stakeholder group in various ways (e.g., Barrentine, 1993; Eastland, 1991; Iannello, 1993).

The problems associated with drawing a conceptual distinction between the private sphere and the public sphere finally are exacerbated by the fact that the control of the corporation has increasingly shifted from primarily profit-oriented owners/stockholders to primarily career-oriented managers. Whereas for the owners/stockholders, the corporation represents primarily a means to profit, management is primarily concerned with the long-term stabil-ity and growth of the corporation, which a number of organizational theorists have termed "managerialism" (e.g., Edwards, 1979; Ingersoll & Adams, 1986; Pitelis & Sugden, 1986; Scott, 1985). Management therefore often functions as an independent entity within the corporation, attempting to pur-sue particular values and political interests of its own.

The Multiple-Stakeholder Model

In recent years, an important theoretical perspective has emerged within organizational studies under the name of "stakeholder theory" (e.g., Carroll,

1989; Freeman, 1984; Freeman & Gilbert, 1988). Central to this theoretical perspective is the recognition that the corporation is increasingly making decisions affecting various societal groups that previously have been made through democratic state processes (see Deetz, 1992). It has therefore been argued that a multiplicity of stakeholders other than the corporation's management and owners/stockholders have values and political interests in need of representation in the corporation's internal decision-making processes. There is also considerable evidence that corporations that have active and ongoing interactions with multiple stakeholders are more adaptive, efficient, and profitable (e.g., Cotton, 1993; Lawler, 1986; Miller & Monge, 1985; Rubinstein, Bennett, & Kochan, 1993). Ironically, the economic model may be increasingly detrimental to the economic well-being of corporations in a time of general environmental turbulence, including ecological tradeoffs, fickle consumers, and knowledge-intensive product production.

The corporation may be conceptualized more accurately as a complex "political" site in both process and outcome. It represents a space in which values and political interests are embodied and articulated within its internal decision-making processes. The corporation may be conceptualized more accurately as having a multiplicity of stakeholders with different and potentially conflicting, yet legitimate, values and political interests in need of representation. The feminist emphasis on "relational connectedness" rather than "competitive individualism" directs this recognition toward cooperation rather than competition between the corporation and its various stakeholders.

To recognize the existence of a multiplicity of stakeholders is not to make the corporation more political but, rather, to recognize the values and political interests that already are present. This dimension has been denied or obscured in the traditional economic model because of its conceptualization of the corporation's internal decision-making processes as being purely economic rather than inherently value-laden (Gorz, 1987; Schmookler, 1993).

According to the multiple-stakeholder model, the responsibility of management is not primarily to create profit on behalf of the corporation's owners/stockholders but to facilitate the articulation of the potentially conflicting values and political interests of a multiplicity of stakeholders within the corporation's internal decision-making processes. Under many circumstances, this may require management to act as a disinterested facilitator of conflict-resolution processes rather than as an interested party. Management's responsibility is to optimally coordinate the meeting of all stakeholder values and political interests as if these values and political interests were those of the corporation itself.

Management therefore needs to increase stakeholder representation within the corporation's internal decision-making processes by determining which stakeholders have legitimate values and political interests in need of representation and by determining the character of those values and political interests. Ideally, stakeholder representation ought to be part of the corporation's internal decision-making processes so that the transformation of values and political interests takes place inside the corporation rather than management attempting to enforce them from the outside.

Within the conceptual logic of the multiple-stakeholder model, management therefore has two primary "ethical" concerns in relation to the corporation's various stakeholders: (a) the implementation of ethical procedures for identifying which stakeholders have legitimate values and political interests in need of representation and for identifying the character of those values and political interests, and (b) the implementation of ethical procedures that ensure that stakeholder values and political interests, once identified, are adequately represented within the corporation's internal decision-making processes.

What guidance may management and others derive from communication theory to help devise such ethical procedures? Generally, feminist theorizing has contributed much to answering this question. Feminism can develop stakeholder theory more specifically by emphasizing the distinct interests of women as a stakeholder group in corporate decision-making processes, by identifying the overly rational/economic and consensus-based character of most stakeholder models, and by demonstrating the complex and internally conflictual nature of stakeholder groups and group values and political interests. Rather than getting into the full complexity of these issues, we turn in one direction that one might take in these ethical concerns by highlighting communication theoretical reformulations arising from feminist theorizing on ethics.

FROM RESPONSIBILITY TO RESPONSIVENESS: BENHABIB'S CRITIQUE OF THE THEORY OF COMMUNICATIVE ACTION AND DISCOURSE ETHICS

Initially, stakeholder theory situated its own moral justification in the theory and language of legal "rights and responsibilities" and had a rather naive theory of communication and of the workings of power in corporations. Much like the more general theory of liberal democracy and corporate social responsibility, the assumption was that the primary task was one of justifying the "rights" of stakeholders and the "responsibilities" of corporations. The assumption was that, if the rights of representation of the corporation's stakeholders within the corporation's internal decision-making processes were assured, normal communication processes would facilitate the development of ethical decision-making processes. This overlooked both the wide societal rejection of foundational ethics and the understanding of liberal democracy as based on an inadequate theory of language, communication, and power. Habermas's (1984, 1987, 1990, 1993) theory of communicative action and discourse ethics, and especially his description of the "ideal speech situation" (Habermas, 1973), offered a viable alternative development. Because Habermas's work provides an important turn in the conceptual development of stakeholder theory and serves as a point of departure for Benhabib's feminist critique, we discuss a number of key concepts (see Deetz, 1992).

The Theory of Communicative Action and Discourse Ethics

Habermas (1984, 1987) has argued that every "speech act" functions during instances of communicative interaction only by virtue of certain "presuppositions" made by the participants. Even when these presuppositions are not honored by the participants, they serve as the basis of appeal, for failed instances of communicative interaction turn to "rational-critical discourse" concerning the disputed "validity claims." The basic presuppositions and validity claims arise out of four domains of reality: the external world, human relations, the individual's internal world, and language. The claims raised in each validity claim are truth, correctness, sincerity, and intelligibility, respectively. Every instance of communicative interaction therefore presupposes the representation of facts (the external world), establishes legitimate social relations (human relations), discloses the speaker's point of view (the individual's internal world), and is understandable (language). Any validity claim that may be disputed by the participants serves as a basis for what Habermas (1970) has described as "systematically distorted communication." A communication situation in which these validity claims are honored by the participants, however, is termed an "ideal speech situation" (Habermas, 1973), or what Habermas (1990) has subsequently termed the "universal and necessary communicative presuppositions of argumentative speech."

The ideal speech situation therefore signifies a communication situation in which potential conflicts of interest among the participants are rationally resolved through a mode of communicative interaction that is "free of manipulation" and in which only "the force of the better argument" prevails. The participants are guaranteed the "reciprocal" and "symmetric" opportunity to apply all types of speech acts during communicative interaction.

The redemption of these four validity claims may serve as a basis for delineating how management may ensure that its communicative interactions with the corporation's stakeholders are conducted in an ethical manner. First, the pursuit of a rationally motivated consensus presupposes the reciprocal and symmetric distribution of opportunities to choose and apply various types of speech acts. This entails the minimal conditions of skills and opportunities for expression, including access to adequate forums and means of communication. When these opportunities are extended to a consideration of the applied means of communication, the focus ought to be on the provision of equal access, the distribution of training opportunities, and the development of means of communication that may be applied to express a variety of human experiences. Such a principle argues against privileged expression forms or routines and rules that advantage certain experiences or expressions.

Second, the understanding and representation of the external world ought to be freed from privileged preconceptions in the social development of truth. The participants ought to be provided with opportunities to express explanations and interpretations of conflicts of interest that are resolved in reciprocal claims and counterclaims without privileging certain epistemologies or forms of data. The freedom from privileged preconceptions in the social development of truth entails an examination of values and political interests that may privilege certain modes of discourse, disqualify certain participants, and universalize sectional interests. The applied means of communication ought to be examined for how they function ideologically to privilege certain epistemologies or forms of data.

Third, the participants ought to be provided with opportunities to establish legitimate social relations and norms for communicative interaction. The rights and responsibilities of the participants should not be given in advance by nature or by a privileged universal value structure. Rather, these ought to be negotiated through communicative interaction. The reification of organizational structures and their maintenance without questioning and the presence of managerial prerogatives are examples of potentially illegitimate social relations. Acceptance of views because of a participant's privilege or authority or because of the character of the applied means of communication also represents a potentially illegitimate social relation. Authority is legitimate only if it is redeemable by appeal to an open interactional formation of social relations freed from the appeal to other (and higher) authorities. To the extent that the applied means of communication embody values and political interests, hide authority relations, or reify social relations, they therefore participate in the development of systematically distorted communication.

Finally, the participants ought to be provided with opportunities to express their own authentic interests, needs, and feelings. This entails freedom from various coercive and ideological processes by which the participants are unable to form experiences openly, to develop and maintain conflicting interests, and to form expressions that adequately represent their interests. Certain means of communication may produce particular imagistic relations and establish a type of distance that reduces the formation of otherness and interrogation of the self. In this sense, they function unethically. An examination of the applied means of communication in their structuring of the interior is important for recognizing their potential effects on the accomplishment of such ethical ideals.

Benhabib's Feminist Perspective on Ethics

Benhabib's (1992) perspective on ethics represents what she has termed "an anticipatory-utopian critique of universalistic moral theory from a feminist perspective" (p. 152). She argues that, historically, the predominant conception of the moral domain and the ideals of moral impartiality/neutrality, offered by moral philosophers from Hobbes to Rawls, led to the privatization of women's experiences and the exclusion of their consideration from the moral point of view. In this historical tradition, the moral self was conceptualized as disembedded and disembodied, and moral impartiality/neutrality implied that an individual learned how to recognize the claims of the other who was similar to himself or herself. Therefore she shows why it is necessary to develop a universalistic perspective on moral theory that defines the moral point of view in light of the reversibility of perspectives and an "enlarged mentality" (a term originating with Arendt, 1961). Such a universalistic perspective on moral theory, she contends, ought to be "interactive not legislative, cognizant of gender differences not gender blind, contextually sensitive and not situation indifferent" (p. 3).

The Generalized and the Concrete Other

Inspired by the influential debate between Kohlberg (1981, 1984) and Gilligan (1982; Murphy & Gilligan, 1980) concerning cognitive developmental moral psychology, Benhabib (1992) argues that a broadened conception of the moral point of view may be developed by attending to two distinct conceptions of self-other relations that delineate both moral perspectives and communicative structures: the standpoint of the "generalized other" (a term originating with Mead, 1934, and applied by Habermas) and the "concrete other" (see Manning, 1992; Noddings, 1984; Wood, 1994, for a similar emphasis on the other as a concrete other). Benhabib argues that these two moral orientations reflect traditional dichotomies between autonomy and nurturance, independence and bonding, the public and private spheres, and, more broadly, between normative issues of justice and rights and evaluative issues of the good life. For Benhabib (1992), to assume the standpoint of the generalized other

> requires us to view each and every individual as a rational being entitled to the same rights and duties we would want to ascribe to ourselves. In assuming this standpoint, we abstract from the individuality and concrete identity of the other. We assume that the other, like ourselves, is a being who has concrete needs, desires and affects, but that what constitutes his or her moral dignity is not what differentiates us from each other, but rather what we, as speaking and acting rational agents,

have in common. Our relation to the other is governed by the norms of formal equality and reciprocity: each is entitled to expect and to assume from us what we can expect and assume from him or her. The norms of our interactions are primarily public and institutional ones. (pp. 158-159)

To assume the standpoint of the concrete other, on the other hand,

requires us to view each and every rational being as an individual with a concrete history, identity and affective-emotional constitution. In assuming this standpoint, we abstract from what constitutes our commonality, and focus on individuality. We seek to comprehend the needs of the other, his or her motivations, what s/he searches for, and what s/he desires. Our relation to the other is governed by the norms of equity and complementary reciprocity: each is entitled to expect and to assume from the other forms of behavior through which the other feels recognized and confirmed as a concrete, individual being with specific needs, talents and capacities. Our differences in this case complement rather than exclude one another. The norms of our interaction are usually, although not exclusively, private, non-institutional ones. (p. 159)

The problem associated with only assuming the morally impartial and neutral standpoint of the generalized other is that it entails a conception of self-other relations that makes it difficult to individuate among different selves. The other as distinct from the self, or the "otherness of the other," is likely to disappear. Benhabib (1992) argues that neither the concreteness nor the otherness of the other may be recognized in the absence of the "voice" of the other. The characteristics of the concrete other emerge as distinct only as the result of "self-definition" on the part of the other.

It should be considered that Benhabib's (1992) conception of self-other relations has been critiqued by a number of (especially postmodern-inspired) feminist theorists. Young (1990a), for example, has argued that assuming the standpoint of the concrete other represents a problematic "ideal of shared subjectivity, or the transparency of subjects to one another, [that] denies difference in the sense of the basic asymmetry of subjects" (p. 309). This critique, which is based on what Derrida (1976) has termed a "metaphysics of presence" and Adorno (1973) has termed a "logic of identity," is unfounded, however. To assume the standpoint of the concrete other does not presuppose a transparency between self and other. Rather, as we subsequently discuss in further detail, it only entails that one attempt to comprehend and take into consideration individuating characteristics of the other as defined by him- or herself to be better able to interact with the other in an ethical manner.

The conception of the self implied by the concept of the generalized other is, as Benhabib (1992) argues, incompatible with the criteria of reversibility of perspectives and universalizability advocated by universalistic moral philosophers, such as Habermas's (1990, 1993) appropriation of the Meadian

(1934) concept of "ideal role-taking" or Rawls's (1971) concept of the "veil of ignorance" in terms of an "original position." Benhabib argues that "one consequence of limiting procedures of universalizability to the standpoint of the generalized other has been that the other as distinct from the self has disappeared in universalizing moral discourse" (p. 10).

It should be considered, however, that Habermas (1993) has responded directly to Benhabib's (1992) contention that to assume the standpoint of the concrete other becomes difficult. In a recent interview, Habermas (1993) argued that the impression that his discourse ethics renders the assumption of the standpoint of the concrete other difficult is associated with a one-sided preoccupation with questions of justification: "The unique disposition of a particular case that calls for regulation, and the concrete characteristics of the people involved, come into view only after problems of justification have been resolved" (pp. 153-154). Therefore, Habermas (1993) argues, "[Moral-practical] reason is not fully realized in discourses of justification. Whereas in justifying norms [moral-practical] reason finds expression in the principle of universalization, in the application of norms it takes the form of a principle of appropriateness" (p. 154).

The conceptual distinction Habermas (1993) draws between a "universal-istic" justification of norms and a "contextually sensitive" application of norms does not adequately resolve the issue, however. To assume the stand-point of the concrete other requires that one thematize individuating charac-teristics of the other right from the outset rather than introduce their thematization during the subsequent decision on how to interact with the other in an ethical manner. In contrast, Habermas's (1993) approach entails an ini-tial bracketing of individuating characteristics of the other (during the justifi-cation of norms) that makes it difficult to introduce their subsequent thematization (during the application of norms). In this important respect, Habermas's (1993) approach is associated with the problematic contention that one initially ought to assume the (universalistic) standpoint of the gener-alized other, followed by the assumption of the (contextually sensitive) stand-point of the concrete other. In other words, there is a problematic two-step process: "In justificatory discourses it is necessary to abstract from the contin-gent contextual embeddedness of a proposed norm only to ensure that the norm, assuming it withstands the generalization test, is sufficiently open to context-sensitive application" (p. 58).

The Moral Conversation

For Benhabib (1992), a broadened conception of the moral point of view requires that one simultaneously assume the standpoint of the generalized other and the concrete other, which entails a shift from a "substantialistic" to a "discursive" conception of rationality. This may be accomplished by engaging in an open-ended "moral conversation" that requires

> (1) that we recognize the rights of all beings capable of speech and action to be participants in the moral conversation—I will call this the principle of universal moral respect; (2) these conditions further stipulate that within such conversations each has the same symmetrical rights to various speech acts, to initiate new topics, to ask for reflection about the presuppositions of the conversation, etc. Let me call this the principle of egalitarian reciprocity. (Benhabib, 1992, p. 29)

The purpose of engaging in the moral conversation, Benhabib (1992) argues in a critique of Habermas's (1990, 1993) discourse ethics, is not to reach a rationally motivated consensus concerning the respective values and political interests of the participants. Rather, the objective ought to be "the anticipated communication with others with whom [one] must finally come to some agreement" (p. 9). Therefore, to engage in the moral conversation does not guarantee that a rationally motivated consensus may ultimately be reached among the participants. Instead, to engage in the moral conversation "demonstrates the will and readiness to seek understanding with the other and to reach some reasonable agreement" (p. 9). A moral conversation that is genuinely open and reflexive and does not operate on the basis of any epistemic limitations may therefore lead to a mutual understanding of otherness. It actualizes a moral dialogue between different selves who are considered to be both generalized others, in the sense of equal moral agents, and concrete others, in the sense of individuals with irreducible differences.

To engage in the moral conversation does not necessarily require the actual presence of the other:

> To think from the perspective of everyone else is to know how to listen to what the other is saying, or when the voices of others are absent, to imagine to oneself a conversation with the other as [the] dialogue partner. (Benhabib, 1992, p. 137)

Benhabib's (1992) contention that the moral conversation may also take the form of an "imaginary dialogue" between the self and the other represents an implicit critique of Habermas (1990, 1993), who repeatedly argues that the moral conversation may take the form only of an "actual dialogue" between different selves. In this respect, Benhabib (1992) adheres to the Kantian categorical imperative that asserts that the meaning of moral validity may be adequately grasped from the perspective of an individual reflecting on his or her motives of action. However, only a moral conversation conceptualized as an "actual dialogue" between the participants involved represents an ethical solution of how to ensure adequate stakeholder representation within the corporation's internal decision-making processes.

For Benhabib (1992), this way of conceptualizing the moral conversation represents a transcendence of the classical moral philosophical distinction between an "ethic of justice and rights" and an "ethic of care and responsibility":

> If in discourses the agenda of the conversation is radically open, if participants can bring any and all matters under critical scrutiny and questioning, then there is no way to predefine the nature of the issues discussed as being public ones of justice versus private ones of the good life. Distinctions such as between justice and the good life are subsequent and not prior to the process of discursive will formation. (p. 110)

Fraser (1990-1991) has leveled a similar argument in a critique of the conceptual distinction Habermas (1989) draws between what ought to count as issues of private and public interest—and thereby the appropriate mode of communicative interaction in the public sphere. Specifically, Fraser argues that what ought to count as issues of public interest should be decided through communicative interaction between the participants themselves rather than being determined in advance.

Thus conceptualized, Benhabib's (1992) argument that the moral conversation represents a transcendence of the classical moral philosophical distinction between an ethic of justice and rights and an ethic of care and responsibility is a critique of a number of influential feminists as well as nonfeminist ethical theorists who have argued that these are not complementary but represent contrasting moral orientations (e.g., Gilligan, 1982; Habermas, 1990, 1993; Kohlberg, 1981, 1984; Noddings, 1984; Ruddick, 1989).

Feminist Ethics and the Multiple-Stakeholder Model

Benhabib's (1992) feminist perspective on ethics provides a useful basis for discussing the relationship between management and the corporation's stakeholders and for providing tentative answers about how management may conceptualize and interact with the corporation's stakeholders in an ethical manner (in terms of the conceptual logic of the multiple-stakeholder model). For reasons of conceptual clarity, we first discuss how management may implement ethical procedures for identifying which stakeholders have legitimate values and political interests in need of representation and for identifying the character of their values and political interests. Second, we discuss how management may implement ethical procedures that ensure the adequate representation of stakeholder values and political interests within the corporation's internal decision-making processes.

Although the conceptual distinction drawn between the "identification" and "representation" of stakeholder values and political interests is useful for the purposes of the present investigation, it may be difficult to maintain this conceptual distinction in practice. The representation of stakeholder values and political interests within the corporation's internal decision-making processes ought to entail a perpetual reconsideration of entrenched values and political interests in order to recover genuine conflicts of interest.

The Identification of Stakeholder Values and Political Interests

When management identifies which stakeholders have legitimate values and political interests in need of representation within the corporation's internal decision-making processes and the character of their values and political interests, it is important that management not assume only the standpoint of the generalized other. The standpoint of the generalized other is, as previously discussed, associated with a stance of moral impartiality and neutrality. Management may never assume a standpoint of absolute moral impartiality and neutrality in relation to the corporation's stakeholders. As the corporate entity responsible for the overall functioning of the corporation, management is inevitably concerned with whether the introduction of stakeholder values and political interests into the corporation's internal decision-making processes may be beneficial or detrimental to the overall functioning of the corporation.

The pursuit of moral impartiality and neutrality on the part of management is therefore likely to lead to what a number of organizational theorists have termed "managerialism." By not recognizing that it inevitably will attempt to further certain interests of its own, management's ideals of moral impartiality and neutrality are likely to suppress the corporation's stakeholders' awareness of those values and political interests and their genuine discussions thereof. Management ought to acknowledge that it does not represent a morally impartial and neutral entity within the corporation and that the values and political interests pursued inevitably will influence its valorization of those of the corporation's stakeholders. It may be beneficial for management to reflect on what Bernstein (1983), following Gadamer (1975), has termed its "prejudices" (in this case, values and political interests) in order to be able to distinguish those that are "blind" from those that are "enabling." In this particular context, blind prejudices may be conceptualized as those that make it difficult for management to recognize that the corporation's stakeholders are likely to have different and potentially conflicting, yet legitimate, values and political interests in need of representation. Enabling prejudices may be conceptualized as those that make it possible for management to recognize those stakeholder values and political interests that are arguably legitimate and in need of representation within the corporation's internal decision-making processes.

Related to this, it is important that management not assume only the standpoint of the generalized other, because this standpoint would lead to the assumption that what management shares in common with the corporation's stakeholders is more important than what distinguishes them from one another. By focusing on commonalities rather than differences, management may be in danger of assuming a "consensual" rather than "conflictual" orientation toward the corporation's stakeholders. In doing so, management is likely to deprive itself of recognizing genuine conflicts of interest both in its relationships to the corporation's stakeholders and among the different stakeholder groups internally. In the vocabulary of Benhabib (1992), an undue emphasis on "commonalities" rather than "differences" is likely to lead to a conception of self-other relations that makes it difficult to individuate among different selves. The other as distinct from the self, or the "otherness of the other," is likely to disappear because this turn lacks the criteria for individuating among different selves. To only assume the standpoint of the generalized other is not only ethically problematic but may also be detrimental to the overall functioning of the corporation.

If management only assumes the standpoint of the generalized other in relation to the corporation's stakeholders, it is also likely to adhere, intentionally or unintentionally, to the economic model rather than the multiple-stakeholder model. The emphasis on commonalities rather than differences is likely to lead to a situation in which management "colonizes" the corporation's stakeholders in terms of economic imperatives. Needing a seemingly impartial and neutral means of conflict resolution, management is likely to evaluate the values and political interests of the corporation's stakeholders in terms of an economic logic. This may be detrimental to the transcendence of the classical liberal democratic distinction between the "private sphere" and the "public sphere" implied by the multiple-stakeholder model. Management is likely to attend to the economic interests of the corporation's stakeholders (which pertain to the private sphere) rather than to their various noneconomic interests (which pertain to the public sphere). The noneconomic interests of the corporation's stakeholders, which to Benhabib (1992) represent "evaluative issues of the good life," are likely to be perceived by management as being based on irreducible differences. These perceived differences make it difficult to identify commonalities both between management and the corporation's stakeholders and among the different stakeholder groups internally.

Management may find it beneficial to assume the standpoint of the generalized and the concrete other simultaneously by "thematizing" rather than "bracketing" differences among the values and political interests of the corporation's stakeholders. Thematizing entails conceptualizing each stakeholder group as a concrete other with irreducible, yet legitimate, differences and at the same time conceptualizing the individual members of a stakeholder group as generalized others (i.e., as identical representatives of a stakeholder group). Although it may be ethically and ideally worthwhile to assume the standpoint of the concrete other toward the individual members of a stakeholder group, it clearly is difficult to do so in practice. Stakeholder groups often comprise so many members that it becomes practically unfeasible to attend to salient differences between the individual members. By assuming the standpoint of the generalized and the concrete other simultaneously, management may be able to recognize that the values and political interests of the corporation's stakeholders may be radically different from and potentially conflicting with its own, yet legitimate and worthy of representation within the corporation's internal decision-making processes.

The Representation of Stakeholder Values and Political Interests

Management should not only implement ethical procedures for identifying which of the corporation's stakeholders are in need of representation within the corporation's internal decision-making processes and identifying the character of their values and political interests. It should also ensure that, once they are identified, they are represented within the corporation's internal decision-making processes in an ethical manner. In thinking about how the corporation's stakeholders may be represented within the corporation's internal decision-making processes in an ethical manner, the concept of the moral conversation is of much relevance.

Many companies, especially those engaged in environmentally sensitive areas and/or whose activities place the public at risk, provide forums for stakeholder response. Most of these "public" meetings encourage venting more than creative decision making. They often are based on dated "liberal democratic" conceptions of communication that rarely enhance voice and may serve primarily as places for company officials to reaffirm their positions (see Deetz, 1995a, 1995b). A much stronger conception of communication and meetings is necessary to guide these practices in productive and ethical directions (see Pearce & Littlejohn, 1997).

Benhabib (1992) conceptualizes the pursuit of the moral conversation in two distinct ways that initially can provide guidance for the development of better practices. She shows that the moral conversation may (a) take the form of an "actual dialogue" between different selves who are considered to be both generalized others, in the sense of equal moral agents, and concrete others, in the sense of individuals with irreducible differences, or (b) "when the voices of others are absent, [one may] imagine to oneself a conversation with the other as [the] dialogue partner" (p. 137).

The conceptual distinction drawn between the moral conversation as an "actual dialogue" and an "imaginary dialogue" is important for thinking about how the corporation's stakeholders may be represented within the corporation's internal decision-making processes in an ethical manner. Whereas the first way of conceptualizing the moral conversation requires that the corporation's stakeholders are provided with opportunities to actively "participate" within the corporation's internal decision-making processes, the second way requires only that management is in a position to adequately "represent" the values and political interests of the corporation's stakeholders within the corporation's internal decision-making processes. Although the conceptual distinction drawn between the participation and representation of the corporation's stakeholders may be useful for conceptual purposes, we believe that only the active and ongoing participation of the corporation's stakeholders within the corporation's internal decision-making processes is adequate.

Because management is often situated at a considerable distance from the stakeholders with which the corporation interacts or ought to interact, it is unlikely that management will be able to exhibit the "moral imagination" necessary to represent the values and political interests of the corporation's stakeholders as well as those articulated by the stakeholders themselves. Often, managers assume that purchasing patterns are in fact an adequate way for wider public values to be represented. Few recognize the implicit value system and representation distortions inherent in a market economy (see Schmookler, 1993). Most do not recognize that political (citizen) and economic (consumer) choices may differ greatly (e.g., people may watch the violent programs on television that they as citizens would wish to prohibit). Furthermore, many managers have used their wealth to fundamentally separate themselves and their families from the ordinary life conditions of other societal members. Managers are thus only rarely in a position to adequately represent the values and political interests of the corporation's stakeholders in the absence of the stakeholders themselves. As Benhabib (1992) argues, the characteristics of the concrete other emerge as distinct only as the result of "self-definition" on the part of the other. It is the other who makes one aware of his or her concreteness and otherness.

Two excellent examples come from the early days of the Saturn automobile company. In both cases, the unique structural guarantee of its management and its employee participation (a partial stakeholder model) required a discussion of the issues and led to creative representative decisions. In the first case, Saturn managers discovered that the plant could not produce the new car at the desired price and quality if it relied on U.S. parts manufacturers. On behalf (as they saw it) of the company and the economic health of the Saturn workforce, the managers argued for overseas purchases. The employee representatives, using a different value system, insisted on buying "American." The result of representing both interests led to a "quality" training program for American parts manufacturers that enabled high-quality, less-expensive American parts to be available, as well as other social benefits. In the second case, Saturn could not keep up with the demand for its cars. Its managers argued for reducing quality, while its employees argued that poor quality—not price—had hurt American car companies. The result was a reengineering of the car that enabled higher quality at faster production speeds. In each case, the managers thought they were representing employee interests, but they were so guided by their own decision premises and by their desire to overlook what they saw as "political" issues that they made bad decisions for investors and workers. Only the direct employee involvement in decision making produced beneficial solutions.

If our argument is correct, then adequate representation of the values and political interests of the corporation's stakeholders requires that stakeholders be provided with opportunities to participate actively in the corporation's internal decision-making processes as equal participants alongside management and the corporation's owners/stockholders. Benhabib (1992) argues that the moral conversation, conceptualized as an actual dialogue between different selves, requires the adherence to two fundamental principles that she termed the principle of universal moral respect (i.e., the recognition of the rights of all beings capable of speech and action to be participants in the moral conversation) and the principle of egalitarian reciprocity (i.e., the recognition of the rights of all participants to the same symmetrical rights, including rights to various speech acts, to initiate new topics, and to ask for reflection about the presuppositions of the conversation). These principles are derived, of course, from Habermas's (1990, 1993) discourse ethics, but the approach is no longer general and universalistic but concrete and contextually sensitive.

THE CONCRETE OTHER AND THE PROBLEM OF SPATIOTEMPORAL DISTANCIATION

In the preceding sections, we have argued that to assume the standpoint of what Benhabib (1992) has termed the generalized and the concrete other simultaneously ought to be considered the ethical ideal for communicative interaction between management and the corporation's stakeholders. Although this ethical ideal is worthy of consideration, it may be difficult to pursue in practice. To assume the standpoint of the concrete other requires that participants be situated in the context of spatiotemporal copresence, communicating through face-to-face interaction. Without the context of spatiotemporal copresence, it is arguably difficult to achieve a recognition of the other in all of his or her complexity.

The modern corporation is increasingly structured in such a way that management is situated at a distance from the corporation's stakeholders (i.e., the transnational or international corporation), maintaining communicative relationships with them through the application of different technical means of communication. The basis on which the corporation's stakeholders may participate actively within the corporation's internal decision-making processes is therefore increasingly based less on spatiotemporal copresence but, rather, on "spatiotemporal distanciation" (see Thompson, 1995).

Mediated Interaction and Mediated Quasi-Interaction

The important question, then, is whether communicative relationships based on the spatiotemporal distanciation of the participants provide the conditions under which management may assume the standpoint of the concrete other in relation to the corporation's stakeholders. To shed further light on this question, it may be useful to distinguish between two conceptually distinct modes of communicative interaction. Mediated interaction signifies a "dialogical" mode of communicative interaction facilitated by a technical medium that permits messages to be transmitted between communicators who are situated in different spatiotemporal contexts (e.g., letter writing or telephone conversations; Thompson, 1995). This mode of communication is oriented toward "specific others." Mediated quasi-interaction, on the other hand, signifies a "monological" mode of communicative interaction facilitated by media of mass communication (e.g., newspapers, radio, and television; Thompson, 1995). This mode of communication is oriented toward an "indefinite range of potential receivers."

The conceptual distinction between communicative interaction based on mediated interaction and mediated quasi-interaction provides a useful basis for discussing whether it may be possible to assume the standpoint of the concrete other when the participants are situated in different spatiotemporal contexts. Although both modes of communicative interaction are inherently problematic because the participants are not situated in the context of spatiotemporal copresence, mediated interaction provides the most potential for assuming the standpoint of the concrete other. This mode of communicative interaction is both dialogical in character, permitting the participants to engage in actual dialogue, and directed toward specific others, permitting a recognition of individuating differences. Mediated quasi-interaction is inherently problematic. This mode of communicative interaction is both monological in character and oriented toward an indefinite range of potential receivers, so it becomes difficult to assume the standpoint of the concrete other.

Direct and Indirect Social Relationships

The application of mediated interaction, rather than mediated quasi-interaction, may also permit management to establish relationships with the corporation's stakeholders, conceptualized as "social" relationships, that resemble what Calhoun (1995; see also 1986, 1988, 1991, 1992) has termed "direct" rather than "indirect" social relationships. Calhoun argues that a conceptual distinction may be drawn between the experiences gleaned from "nonmediated interpersonal relationships" (direct social relationships) and "mediated mass communicational relationships" (indirect social relationships) that are established when social actions affect others through the mediation of mass media of communication, interpersonal markets, or complex organizations. When social relationships are mediated, understandings of others are based not on a recognition of the character of their relationship to oneself but on categorical differences. Although these categories may imply certain concrete modes of conceptualizing others, the abstract category is likely to take precedence.

These insights point to one of the important problems associated with assuming the standpoint of the concrete other during instances of mediated quasi-interaction. Although it may be possible to conceptualize and interact with others as concrete others through the application of mediated interaction (direct social relationships), it is difficult to conceptualize and interact with others as concrete others through the application of mediated quasi-interaction (indirect social relationships). Indirect social relationships are likely to be based on categorical differences (or stereotypes) in which others are conceptualized as abstract representatives.

CONCLUSION

Further conceptual development of stakeholder theory may benefit considerably from attending to recent developments in feminist theorizing on ethics. Benhabib's critique of Habermas's theory of communicative action and discourse ethics is particularly relevant because it draws an important conceptual distinction between assuming the standpoint of the generalized and the concrete other and because it provides a useful delineation of the principles underlying the moral conversation. The pursuit of the multiple-stakeholder model may be aided if management assumes the standpoint of the generalized and the concrete other simultaneously and if management adheres to the principles of the moral conversation during communicative interaction with the corporation's stakeholders. Our discussion indicates, however, that if management assumes only the standpoint of the generalized other and/or breaches the principles of the moral conversation, management not only behaves unethically toward the corporation's stakeholders but, equally important, is in danger of adhering to the conceptual logic of the economic model rather than the multiple-stakeholder model.

Although assuming the standpoint of the generalized and the concrete other simultaneously and adhering to the principles of the moral conversation ought to be considered the ethical ideal for communicative interaction between management and the corporation's stakeholders, it may be difficult to pursue these ethical ideals in practice. Because management and the corporation's stakeholders often are situated in different spatiotemporal contexts, it is difficult for management to assume the standpoint of the concrete other. Management may be forced to use either mediated interaction or mediated quasi-interaction instead of face-to-face communication. Although both modes of communicative interaction are inherently problematic from the standpoint of concern with the concrete other, mediated interaction offers the most potential for assuming this standpoint because it entails a dialogical mode of communicative interaction aimed at specific others.

Even though it may be difficult for management to assume the standpoint of the generalized and the concrete other simultaneously in an ideal sense, there is much that management can do on a day-to-day basis to approximate this ideal. Management can challenge its own entrenched ways of conceptualizing and interacting with the corporation's various stakeholders. Fundamental to such a reorientation is the implementation of a different way of understanding the purpose of engaging in communicative interaction with the corporation's stakeholders. Rather than considering communication to be primarily a means for successful "self-expression," management may find it useful to consider communication as a means for successful "self-destruction." By communication as self-destruction, management may attempt to overcome fixed ways of conceptualizing its own responsibilities as an organizational entity and may overcome fixed ways of conceptualizing its relationships with the corporation's stakeholders. In practical terms, communication as self-destruction requires that management engage in attempts to "denaturalize" and "deneutralize" the ways it traditionally has conceptualized its own responsibilities as an organizational entity and its relationships with the corporation's stakeholders. Rather than considering these relations to be natural, in the sense of being given by nature, and neutral, in the sense of being free of underlying values and political interests, management should acknowledge that these relationships may more accurately be conceptualized as being the results of numerous (value-laden) microinteractions occurring on a day-to-day basis.

By opening itself up to the corporation's stakeholders and by providing them with opportunities to challenge entrenched ways of conceptualizing their relationships, management can engage in interactions with the stakeholders that may, over time, become "productive" rather than "reproductive" in character. By productive interactions, we mean interactions that enable management and the corporation's stakeholders to perpetually produce new and more mutually satisfying relationships together rather than old and unsatisfying ones.

3

Organizational Socialization

A Feminist Standpoint Approach

Connie Bullis
Karen Rohrbauck Stout

Organizational socialization has been examined by organizational and managerial communication researchers for at least the past two decades. The increased focus on organizational socialization by communication researchers seems to temporally parallel the trend toward viewing organizations as cultures. As organizational communication scholars turned toward conceptualizing organizations as cultures (Pacanowsky & O'Donnell-Trujillo, 1982), it was sensible to turn increased attention to how newcomers learn to participate in unique organizational cultures. Similarly, the socialization of people into particular cultural roles is associated with how cultures maintain and reproduce themselves.[1] More recently, with the emergence of feminist perspectives, organizational cultures have been criticized as male dominated (Marshall, 1993; Sheppard, 1989).

As theorizing continues to produce more varied understandings of organizational communication, we need to both maintain and reconsider past con-

AUTHORS' NOTE: We would like to thank Betsy Wackernagel Bach, Patrice Buzzanell, Kathleen Krone, and Eileen Berlin Ray for their thoughtful comments on and critique of an earlier version of this chapter.

ceptualizations while we consider what future conceptualizations are possible (Bullis, 1993). The feminist theorizing developed in this book provides one such set of perspectives. A variety of such theories are needed (see Calás & Smircich, 1996; Fine, 1994) "to create theory and research which enable us to think about how we recreate gender relations" (Buzzanell, 1994, p. 339) and to "offer a comprehensive view on why and how women's contributions to organizational life are devalued consciously, and unconsciously, by both men and women" (Buzzanell, p. 340). It is important to note that feminist theories begin with these assumptions, whereas traditional organizational socialization work begins from different assumptions. In other words, we need to criticize traditional work in order to define its limits and domain so that we see alternatives. However, in doing so, we acknowledge that we view past work assumptions for their failure to deal adequately with gender relations—a task they were never designed to accomplish. As conversations evolve, we anticipate a continued adaptation, rather than a dismantling, of existing assumptions and approaches.

In this chapter, we focus specifically on feminist standpoint theory. Feminist standpoint theory is appropriate because it assumes that, by starting with the experiences and knowledges of the subordinated, we can better understand how dominations occur. Although she did not explicitly recommend socialization as a topic of inquiry, Buzzanell (1994) described the value of this approach (among others) and commented on the importance of socialization processes in reproducing gendered relations. We address ways in which feminist standpoint theory may be helpful in reconsidering and expanding organizational socialization theorizing and research. We first identify common assumptions that have guided socialization research and then review some specific questions and findings that emanate from those assumptions. Second, we summarize standpoint feminism as a perspective that offers an alternative set of assumptions. Third, we illustrate the potential value of feminist standpoint theory by using it to review and critique extant work. We focus on reframing assumptions, examining existing research by identifying its exclusions and traditional research processes, and examine one exemplar of research in detail to illustrate the kind of critique feminist standpoint theory can generate. Finally, we summarize the suggestions for future work embedded in our discussion.

We locate ourselves as scholars interested in organizational communication as it pertains to organizational socialization. We consider ourselves to be participants in an ongoing scholarly conversation and have participated as "traditional" thinkers and researchers, as feminist critics, and (regardless of theoretical approaches adopted) as white, heterosexual, First World, middle-class women interested in understanding socialization. Here, we adopt feminist standpoint views.[2]

ORGANIZATIONAL SOCIALIZATION

When organizational and managerial communication scholars consider organizational socialization scholarship, we typically turn to Jablin's work (1982, 1984, 1987; Jablin & Krone, 1987) as providing the most comprehensive reviews and guiding frameworks. His reviews incorporate studies and approaches derived from older managerial models. However, they have been at least as valuable for informing our understandings of organizational socialization in cases in which organizations are assumed to be cultures as they have been in cases in which organizations are viewed as containers, machines, or organisms. In general, the basic conceptualization of socialization is that it is a process in which organizational "outsiders" become "insiders." Three main assumptions are considered here. First, socialization scholarship assumes that organizations are bounded entities. Second, individuals enter, are socialized (or enculturated or assimilated) into, adopt roles in, become members of, and leave these entities through general stages. Third, these processes occur through interactions engaged in by individuals as active agents. After summarizing these assumptions, we summarize socialization research, illustrating how it is typically aimed at examining processes that lead to socialization outcomes associated with the transition from outsider to insider.

Assumptions Guiding Socialization Research

Organizations Are Bounded Entities

To adopt an assumption that outsiders become insiders, we assume that organizations have boundaries through which individuals cross. Organizational communication research has imported this assumption from management theory. Perhaps Schein's model (1970, 1971) most clearly clarifies the boundaries. It illustrates the organization as a stable, hierarchically shaped cone. Arrows depict the individuals' movement over time across barriers. The first barrier that individuals cross is the boundary separating the inside from the outside. Later, individuals are depicted as moving toward the center and top of the organization. This assumption shapes socialization research so that it seeks to understand the processes, strategies, and communicative patterns through which these boundary crossings are negotiated. Research has sought to identify which processes are most successful.

Socialization Occurs Through Phases

Individuals are assumed to cross boundaries in phases. Individual-organization relationships develop over time, and several stages mark the

increasing degree to which the individual is positioned as inside the organization (see Buchanan, 1974; Feldman, 1976; Jablin, 1987; Porter, Lawler, &
Hackman, 1975; Schein, 1978; Van Maanen, 1978; Wanous, 1980). These
models often identify three or four stages. Jablin's (1987) model is a broad
descriptive model that is used to integrate past socialization research into an
overall heuristic view of the cyclical phases of anticipatory socialization,
encounter, metamorphosis, and exit through which individuals move as they
anticipate, enter, and eventually exit specific organizations.

The initial entry process, anticipatory socialization, includes vocational
anticipatory socialization, during which individuals intentionally and unintentionally gather information regarding occupations from a variety of
sources. They compare that information to their self-concepts and weigh it
accordingly. Anticipatory socialization also includes organizational anticipatory socialization, during which individuals gather information from organizational sources that affects their expectations about the job and the organization. During this phase, expectations are refined. Expectations about the
organization, the work, one's role, and the communication environment that
may pervade the organization result from this phase (Jablin, 1987).

Jablin describes the encounter phase as similar to Van Maanen's (1975)
description of the "breaking in" period. During this phase, newcomers learn
the requirements of their roles, organizational expectations, and norms.
Expectations are tested and may or may not be met. Newcomers encounter
varied experiences such as surprise (Louis, 1980) and role shock (Hughes,
1958; Minkler & Biller, 1979). Once encounter has occurred, organizational
assimilation, the process of the newcomer's integration into the culture or
"reality" of the organization, occurs (Jablin, 1982). This is a reciprocal process during which the organization attempts to socialize newcomers to the
organization's needs and values while, at the same time, newcomers attempt
to individualize or create and develop their own roles in the organization.
Metamorphosis is an important part of this process; individuals gradually
internalize organizational expectations by modifying their attitudes and
behaviors so that they are more compatible with the organization's expectations. Eventually, individuals internalize the rules that govern everyday interaction and construct meaning within the organization. Finally, exit occurs.
For various reasons and through various processes, individuals leave organizations. This phase is, perhaps, the least studied.

For each phase, Jablin (1987) describes specific information sources, different types of information exchanged, and strategies employed. He provides a thorough review of stage research that we do not reiterate here. In
general, research reports depict organizations as stable while individuals
move through the stages in systematic and sequential patterns (see Jablin,
1987).

Individuals as Well as Organizations Are Active Agents

Early socialization research typically assumed that organizations or organizational agents socialize individuals. Socialization in this view was seen as a one-way relationship, with organizations as active participants and newcomers as passive recipients. Buchanan (1974) perhaps most clearly articulated this assumption when he labeled newcomers "tabula rasa." More recently, researchers have typically agreed that socialization relationships are mutually defined by individuals and organizations or organizational agents (e.g., Falcione & Wilson, 1988; Hess, 1993; Jablin, 1987; Jorgensen-Earp & Staton, 1993; Staton-Spicer & Darling, 1986). For example, supervisors and newcomers engage in exchanges in which newcomers seek information and supervisors adapt to newcomers. Jablin (1987) specifically adopted an unusual meaning for the term *assimilation* to include both the processes through which the organization attempts to socialize the individual newcomer and the processes through which the individual newcomer personalizes the role taken in the organization. Uncertainty reduction is frequently assumed to stimulate newcomer activity. As newcomers seek to reduce uncertainty inherent in boundary crossing, they actively seek information (see Kramer, 1993).

Socialization Research:
The Study of Socialization Processes and Outcomes

Guided by the assumptions mentioned above, the bulk of the socialization research examines linkages between communication processes and socialization outcomes (see Mowday, Porter, & Steers, 1982). As a community of scholars, we have typically assumed that socialization consists of a process in which outsiders become insiders. We have assumed that these outsiders cross boundaries, becoming encultured through several general phases, and mutually negotiate relationships and roles. It is only sensible that communication scholars would focus attention on a variety of communication processes through which this socialization process occurs. Moreover, communication scholars naturally have focused on the socialization outcomes associated with these processes. Given that scholars are interested in identifying processes that are successful, we review some of this research to provide an understanding of the specific kinds of questions and findings that are generated by the assumptions summarized above.

Organizational Socialization Strategies

Socialization strategies and tactics have been studied as one important process. This process has been related to role-taking styles as an important socialization outcome (Allen & Meyer, 1990; Hart, 1991; Jones, 1986; Van Maanen & Schein, 1979). Some more formalized types of organizational strategies have been associated with more passive role-taking styles, while other more informal and individualized types of strategies have been associated with more active, innovative role-taking styles. Crow and Glascock (1995) examined a nontraditional principal training program and found that, in addition to the formal program, the principals' cohorts played a very important role in conjunction with the formal training program in enabling innovative role adoption. DiSanza (1993) described framing, reinforcing, and quota setting as strategies used to train tellers to carry out organizational duties. Pribble (1990) examined the formal socialization process of orientation programs as a rhetorical process that both reveals an organization's objectives and works to shape a newcomer's ethical conduct. The orientation communicates what the organization views as an ideal employee. Through identification rhetoric, organizational veterans attempt to influence newcomers into accepting their ethical stance. Strategies to induce identification were identified by Cheney (1983b) in corporate house organs. These include common ground, unifying symbols, identification by antithesis, and the assumed "we."

Newcomers' Experiences and Strategies

As more emphasis was placed on individuals as active agents, research focused on individuals to balance out the focus on organizational strategies. Louis's (1980) classic work described newcomer experiences and ways in which they make sense of new situations to reduce the uncertainty and surprise they experience.

Information-seeking behaviors were examined in relation to several outcomes. Miller and Jablin (1991) identified types of feedback, methods of eliciting feedback, and sources of feedback that newcomers employ to reduce uncertainty. Kramer, Callister, and Turban (1995) found that unsolicited information receiving was positively associated with intention to quit. Information giving through modeling was negatively associated with intention to quit. Teboul (1997) studied the content learned by newcomers in their proactive efforts to cope with uncertainty. For example, newcomers reported learning that they could ask questions or learn idiosyncratic rules. Moreover, newcomers generally reported using what they had learned in later situations. Bach (1990b) described how pledges to a sorority coped with their entry experiences. Their socialization was enacted in their talk. Their talk not only helped them make sense of their new membership but also helped reveal the cultural meaning of their interactions as well as demonstrate their membership to themselves, other organizational members, and outsiders.

Several studies focused on how newcomers' turning points affected organizational commitment or identification. Bullis and Bach (1989a, 1989b) identified turning points reported by graduate students and identified those more and less associated with identification. They also found that, for newcomers who reported strong identification with their mentors, identification did not necessarily translate to the larger organization. Kirk and Todd-Mancillas (1991) extended the examination of graduate student turning points to gain an understanding of how negative experiences reported by women and minorities might negatively affect these students' identification with the graduate program to such an extent that they would choose not to enter academe as a career. They expressed concern that such choices would reproduce the unequal gender and race/ethnicity nature of higher education.

Teboul (1995) extended the examination of information seeking by combining into a single study the individual, relational, and organizational-level factors that predict newcomer information-seeking behaviors and choice of sources.

Communication Processes

A number of communication processes have been identified in single studies and have been examined for their impact on socialization outcomes. One such study was conducted by Reichers (1987). It may be instructive to note that, although Reichers was not a communication scholar, he nevertheless posited the importance of communication to the socialization process. The study focused on the amount of interaction without specifying particular kinds of interaction or communicative processes. However, amount of interaction was associated with successful socialization.

Communication scholars typically specify communication processes with much greater detail. Stohl (1986) studied memorable messages that newcomers receive. Through these messages, organizational veterans communicated norms, values, and expected behaviors to individual newcomers. She concluded that these messages had a lasting impact on receivers' behavior and work lives. Brown (1985) studied how organizational stories told by veterans function to socialize newcomers. DiSanza (1995) described bank teller socialization processes, including stress as a meaningful result. Kramer (1989) identified patterns of communication in a specific type of barrier crossing. He examined communication in loosening, transitional, and tightening phases of job transfers.

Socialization Relationships

Given the importance of the relationships through which socialization is assumed to occur, it is not surprising that researchers have examined types of socialization relationships to discover what types are most helpful. Because the "organization" is a fairly abstract actor, research typically assumes that identifiable organizational agents such as supervisors and peers provide the relational partners through which socialization occurs. Kramer (1994) found that feedback and closer communication relationships predicted adjustment. Drawing on the leader-member exchange model, Kramer (1995) found that supervisor-subordinate relationships that were neither close partnerships nor strong overseer relationships were associated with the most positive new-comer adjustment. Newcomers, then, thrived when they negotiated relationships with their supervisors that were not overly egalitarian or overly directive. In another study using Kram and Isabella's (1985) peer relationships typology to study both supervisory and peer relationships, Kramer found that relationships with supervisors characterized as collegial or special relationships led to more understanding of relevant knowledge than did more distant informational relationships. Adjustments were most positive when there were higher proportions of closer peer relationships and lower proportions of peer informational relationships. Jablin (1984), too, found that the development of closer relationships was associated with better adjustment. Bullis and Bach (1991) found that multiplex relationships were associated with higher organizational identification.

Summary

This brief review illustrates that the assumptions adopted about socialization have guided socialization research. Much socialization research has focused on identifying a variety of processes associated with positive socialization outcomes. Some research focuses on organizational strategies, whereas other research focuses more on the individual as the active agent engaging in activities that lead to socialization outcomes. Still other research focuses on mutual communicative patterns, and other studies examine the types of relationships that lead to positive outcomes. Finally, studies of organizational transitions describe success in a specific kind of barrier crossing. In general, these studies have emanated from the assumption that individuals enter organizations, are socialized by the organization, actively participate in the process of becoming insiders, and form relationships that are more or less conducive to successful socialization. These assumptions have been particularly useful when organizations were viewed as machines, organisms, or cultures.

As new metaphors of organization and organizational communication emerge (see Putnam, Phillips, & Chapman, 1996), our understandings of socialization evolve as well. One emerging view considers organizations as nodes in larger, deeply gendered, classed, and raced, relatively stable discursive formations. When this view of organizations is adopted, alternative approaches to understanding socialization are useful. We turn now to standpoint feminism to provide a critical alternative perspective from which socialization scholarship may be reconsidered.

STANDPOINT FEMINISM

Standpoint feminism is one of a number of specific views that have emerged as critical and feminist approaches have gained increasing attention in organizational communication (see Buzzanell, 1994). Some of the general themes prevalent in standpoint feminism are shared by contemporary critical theories. However, as reviews (Buzzanell, 1994; Putnam, 1990a) have illustrated, standpoint feminism also provides a unique contribution. Wood (1992a) has specifically advocated the use of standpoint feminism in communication to encourage questions that start from women's standpoints.[3]

Positioning of Locations and Voices

As we have commented elsewhere (Bullis, 1993; Bullis & Bach, 1996), standpoint feminism may be viewed as being positioned in between liberal and postmodern feminist voices. Liberal feminism advocates the inclusion of women into current arrangements so that they may participate equally with men (and/or "dominants" or "insiders"), whereas postmodern feminism practices the deconstruction and interrogation of gendered arrangements (see Calás & Smircich, 1996; Mumby & Putnam, 1992). Put simply, standpoint feminism assumes that, through social processes and institutional arrangements, some voices are positioned as dominant or master voices while others are positioned as marginalized, excluded, or servant voices. When applied to people, this assumption is very similar to Hegel's (1807/1967) master-bondsman relationship. The "other," or bondsman, is that through which the "self" is defined. The "other" is, in large part, what the self is not and what the self defines itself against. In Hegel's example, the master's definition of self as subject is dependent on defining the bondsman as "other," or object. Hegel suggests that both relational participants are locked into oppression. Clearly, however, the oppressions are not equal. The possibilities open to the master and bondsman are neither identical nor equal. However, by examining the relationship and the "other," a more comprehensive understanding of social life and a more complete understanding of the self are possible. Moreover, alternatives become visible. The "self" is a pervasive assumption of Western life, as is its necessary but underexamined counterpart, the "other" (see Hegel, 1807/1967; Sartre, 1943/1956). As a critical theory, standpoint feminism advocates this understanding for the purpose of revealing relationships that need to be transformed.

Standpoints, then, typically refer first to the locations of the marginalized, or the "others." If we consider the servant as the most overt case, we touch on the history of standpoint feminism. Drawing on Marx, "the" woman's standpoint was sought as a critical, transformative, positioned voice. This woman's standpoint was based on the assumption of a common location of women. Specifically, they were located in positions to provide work that was valuable for its "use" rather than its "exchange" value. For example, Smith (1987a) describes women's provision of work in support of the school system in their role of helping children with homework. This work is hidden, unpaid, devalued, and essential to the smooth functioning of the school system. Ultimately, women's role in helping children with homework supports capitalism by providing competent labor. Yet it remains invisible. The prototypical example of this type of work is the work that women have been assigned in caring for men and in reproducing laborers. In other words, women's work was to serve the capitalist system in necessary but invisible ways.

Adams (1990), in her insightful analysis of animal eating, has developed the "absent referent" as a useful analytic tool. For example, eating animals relies on killing and dismembering animal bodies. Yet by invisible institutional and discursive practices, the killing and dismembering is ignored, or absenced. Animal eating is divorced from the animal bodies on which it inherently depends. Instead, we purchase "food" from the store and eat "meat" or "protein." Adams (1997) illustrates how the mistreatment of terminal animals (those raised to be killed), in general, and the practice of feeding animal remains to other animals, in particular, were associated with "mad cow" disease. In this case, the use of animals as absent referents visibly cycled back to hurt the oppressor, as people contracted disease from the animals—a relationship we thought impossible. Similarly, women's reproductive work serves as an absent referent to capitalism. Emotional work in organizational life is necessary but unvalued.

Historically, women, by functioning in such positions, were denied political and economic voices. Women were alienated from the productive systems and were isolated in private locations. When women worked for exchange value, they were typically assigned to invisible, servantlike positions of caring for men, such as the secretary, office peacemaker (Kolb, 1992, as cited in Buzzanell, 1994), or the office wife who cares for others' needs (Huff, 1990, as cited in Buzzanell, 1994). Both in these positions and by functioning as homemakers in men's homes, women learned to adopt understandings associated with the "outsider within" (Collins, 1986) location. By functioning in such servant roles, women learned to understand men, current societal arrangements, and unequal relationships as means of survival. Men, however, had no comparable need to understand women. Women's double understandings, then, much like Marx's proletariat understandings, could serve as a critique of patriarchal institutions (Hartsock, 1987) and as valuable resources for bringing about change.

Standpoint feminism's initial impulse of defining a single woman's standpoint was largely dismantled as feminists of color criticized the project for its racial and classist biases. Refusing accounts of the "woman's" standpoint generated by middle-class, First World white women, women of color pointed out the multiple axes of differences among women (see Longino, 1993). Feminists such as bell hooks (1981, 1984, 1989) and Patricia Hill Collins (1991) have successfully insisted on a feminist respect for differences among women. Instead of developing a unified singular "woman's" voice, standpoint feminism has more recently focused on revealing the conditions, experiences, and voices of a wide variety of women. For example, Diamond (1994) has illustrated how the availability of reproductive technology functions to create reproductive freedom for women located in First World countries, functions to enable additional state intrusion for some women in some Third World countries, and is denied to others. For some Native American women in the United States, forced sterilization (attempted genocide) was practiced (and absenced from public discussion). Shiva (1989, 1991) has detailed the devastations foisted on local lands, communities, and women's lives in a variety of situations in India as a result of that nation's participation in international development.

Standpoint feminism, then, has evolved from a Marxist notion of a unified "woman's" standpoint to a focus on differences and multiple women's standpoints. Because multiple and variously overlapping relationships of domination position women in a variety of marginal locations, it is important to understand such relationships and standpoints without assuming uniformity. However, another concern emerged with the evolution toward focusing on multiple standpoints. The danger in identifying multiple subordinations is that the hope of transformation is difficult to retain. In other words, if taken too far, the trend toward championing difference means that the political potential for change is decreased because groups do not recognize the possibility for coalition formation with those who occupy different standpoints.

LaClau and Mouffe (1985) provide an understanding that serves to fill this need. They clarify how varied oppositional standpoints can form resisting and transforming voices through solidarity rather than unity. The process of creating and maintaining a dominant discourse simultaneously creates and maintains different, but not isolated, positions of marginality. For example, if white, First World, middle-class women see themselves as different from Third World women and Native American women who are positioned differently vis-à-vis reproductive technology, opportunities for change-oriented coalitions are minimized. Change that relies on understandings of oppressions that link women and nature (Adams, 1990; Shiva, 1989) or slaughterhouse workers and the animals they torture (Eisnitz, 1997) is unthinkable. Yet these are the linkages necessary to transform dominant-submissive relations. LaClau and Mouffe (1985) use the image of a chain of linkages that may be formed among varied marginalized standpoints. In other words, although the marginalized are positioned and oppressed differently and do not share identical standpoints, because different oppressions intersect, groups may join together to focus on resistance and transformation while still maintaining differences. A feminist overemphasis on differences and underemphasis on potential linkages politically neutralizes feminist transformative potential.

From our discussion thus far, one might draw two misleading conclusions: (a) that feminist standpoint theory addresses only women, and (b) standpoints are merely located positions. We turn to a more comprehensive discussion of standpoints to point out that this theory pertains to relationships of dominance rather than solely to biological women and that standpoints are more than located positions.

Standpoints as Expressions and Achievements

Standpoints include experiences and the locations, conditions, relationships, and processes that produce those experiences (Hartsock, 1983b; Smith, 1987a, 1993). However, they also include a reflexive awareness that results in a political consciousness. Sells (1997) points out that standpoints are achievements rather than perspectives. They are achieved through struggle. In other words, whereas locations and perspectives are created through processes and conditions, standpoints are achieved through reflexive struggle. They entail an awareness of the politics of domination. Similarly, Collins (1991, pp. 25-28) insists that standpoints must be "self-defined."

The struggle needed to achieve self-identified standpoints is difficult because the processes and conditions that encourage particular perspectives often are not obvious to people. Rather, people are socialized to accept the dominant perspectives. For example, as psychologist Miller (1976), among others, points out, one dynamic of oppression is that those who are oppressed may accept the definitions of themselves as defined by dominators. In other words, they often accept their locations as marginal and subordinate, or "other." Their subordination is accepted as natural. For example, words from a popular song in the 1960s proclaim, "I was born to be stepped on, lied to, cheated on and treated like dirt. . . . I was born a woman, didn't have no say, I was born a woman, I'm glad it happened that way."

Some writers advocate the process of recovering denied experiences as a way to begin to develop standpoints. Collins (1991) notes that resistance depends on the oppresseds' ability to share their experiences with each other. When these experiences are articulated, personal experiences are transformed into collective voices that are more prone to stimulate acts of resistance or change. Because the recovery and articulation of such experiences form the basis for understanding standpoints, standpoint scholars need to consider ways to participate in the recovery process.

Standpoint feminism, then, assumes that dominant patterns function to create relationships of dominance and subordination and to mask these relationships so that the subordinated accept the relationships, invisibly providing the necessary resources to maintain and naturalize the dominant arrangements. Standpoint feminism advocates the achievement of standpoints as oppositional, politically conscious understandings with the hope that such understandings provide resources for a critique of domination as well as change.

Basic enlightenment institutions such as science, law, academics, and the professions add to the difficulty of achieving standpoints (see Code, 1991; Harding, 1986, 1991) by adopting the assumption of the neutral, rational observer. As Hartsock (1997) points out, women have never been the subjects of enlightenment theories. They also have not been the subjects of enlightenment institutions. The observer, from a distanced position, observes the object to explain, predict, and control what the object is unable to manage from its own embedded position. Authority over personal decision making, then, is retained in the "expert" and removed from the individual. This is a particularly relevant concern for those of us interested in producing knowledge about socialization because it invites us to consider our own roles and assumptions as scholars.

A STANDPOINT FEMINIST REVIEW
OF SOCIALIZATION

A standpoint feminist perspective encourages careful consideration of the assumptions that are taken for granted in socialization scholarship. Here, we first focus on why socialization is a useful place to draw on feminist standpoint analyses.

Socialization is a site, or a culturally defined set of processes that occur in identifiable locations, where the conditions, relationships, identities, and processes of interest to standpoint feminism are produced and reproduced. Specifically, socialization is a set of communicative processes that produce and reproduce relationships through which domination, subordination, and marginalization occur. Since gendered relationships are pervasive in organizational life (Ferguson, 1984; Marshall, 1993) and in general social and institutional relations, the organizational and more fundamental general socialization practices through which these gendered relations are reinscribed must be understood (Buzzanell, 1994). From a feminist standpoint view in which the awareness of experiences is important and difficult, socialization provides a site where the increased awareness involved in approaching, joining, and leaving organizations should be helpful. Not only are people more alert to their own experiences during socialization, but they are involved in a sense-making process (Louis, 1980) in which they connect their experiences to the contexts around them as they attempt to understand their situation. Similarly, veterans encountering newcomers and exiting members should exhibit an enhanced awareness as they attempt to socialize newcomers, to understand how they themselves are positioned vis-à-vis newcomers, and, as we shall see, to exclude newcomers.

Therefore, feminist standpoint theory is appropriately applied to organizational socialization. To engage this analysis, we reconsider the assumptions of socialization scholarship that we identified earlier. We simultaneously rely on and question these assumptions. We then turn to a reconsideration of the socialization research that has emanated from these assumptions, focusing on exclusions (ignored or absenced groups and processes) and feminist concerns with typical research processes. Finally, we illustrate a more detailed analysis by focusing on a specific study.

Socialization Assumptions

From Boundaries to Containers

Although they do not claim to use a feminist analysis, Smith and Turner (1995) first articulated the formulaic assumptions undergirding socialization research when they identified containment as a root metaphor guiding our understandings of socialization. They point out that the formula, initially articulated by Jablin (1987) and evident in socialization research, assumes that socialization (actions of the organization on the individual) plus individualization (actions of the individual on the role) serve to transform outsiders into insiders. Smith and Turner's work clarifies the dualism inherent in the assumption that there is an outside and an inside marked by an organizational boundary. Whereas traditional socialization research has used this assumption to guide its focus on boundary crossing, and standpoint feminism similarly relies on boundaries that mark marginal, insider, and outsider within locations, Smith and Turner enable a reconsideration by proposing the notion of containment. Socialization scholars, then, can consider the oppression of the "master" or "insider" as well as the subordinated. Several additional questions emerge from a feminist standpoint view.

Most obviously and directly, in contrast to the socialization work reviewed earlier in this chapter, feminist standpoint perspectives turn attention to the outside as the absent referent to examine. Just as socialization focuses on how people enter and successfully become members of an organization, the boundary assumption also inherently relies on an outside. The notion of an organizational member inherently relies on a nonmember. By considering only those who transition to "insiders," socialization scholarship ignores the people, discourses, and institutional arrangements that produce and sustain "outsiders." "Outsiders," then, serve as the invisible but necessary resource that sustains the notion of "insiders."

Second, the commonly accepted pyramid shape (Schein, 1970, 1971) inherently means that everyone "inside" the boundary cannot move to the center and top. There is more space around the perimeter and at the bottom. No one can inhabit the top center of the pyramid unless others inhabit the bottom periphery. In other words, the top inherently depends on the bottom. This assumption may well be associated with the "outsider within" (Collins, 1986). Although people successfully enter the organization, most cannot also successfully cross the many internal barriers. Yet, as Buzzanell and Goldzwig (1991) illustrate, career literature encourages an expectation of progressing up the ladder through one's career. They point out that we do not have language to adequately express the alternative career paths that most people follow. In a study of a professional bureaucracy, one of us (Bullis, 1984) identified a "cadre of the malcontent" in feedback provided to the organization. These employees—often positioned in marginalized, feminized professions—saw no alternative to their employment and no future advancement in the bureaucracy. When presented with the feedback, organizational leaders commented on the number of "graveyard" positions with no potential for internal movement. The leaders generated ways to reward these employees because the organization needed their full participation. In other words, the leaders were implicitly uncomfortable with the outsider within and the power of the "passive resistance" that they had encountered from such locations. Yet they were aware of the constraints producing the malcontent position. In Hegel's terms, both leaders and the malcontent were locked into oppression. This finding was not included in the academic research report because the finding was "outside" the bounds of the theory of interest. A feminist standpoint analysis would examine these subject (or object) positions as socialization outcomes and draw on the experiences to provide a stronger analysis of the organizational structure and the related discourses that produce and sustain the position. Reports of resistance strategies (e.g., stockpiling older versions of forms so that the older version could be used longer in the face of a less desirable newer version) and their implications would be the focus of such analyses. We could ask, How is it that some socialization experiences result in these outsiders within? How are their resistances transformative?

Third, analyses of the processes that sustain the container and the boundaries should be examined. For example, Stout's (1995) study serendipitously identified exclusionary practices that served to maintain both internal-external boundaries and boundaries between the periphery and center of an organization. Buzzanell (1994) also suggests that organizational discourse and structure exclude women through socialization practices and organizational opportunities, respectively. Buzzanell and Goldzwig (1991) identified strategies such as mythical alternative career tracks through which internal barriers are maintained. Considerable literatures on employment interviewing (Jablin, 1987) and career development (Buzzanell & Goldzwig, 1991) exist, yet very little research examines interviewing and career development as boundary maintenance.[4]

Finally, by identifying this implicit assumption, alternatives can be considered in the future. Socialization scholars may pursue a deconstruction of the containment assumption. Forward and Scheerhorn (1996) suggest that considering organizations as "things" encourages the absencing of changes in the organization and environment as well as ignoring the identity negotiation processes inherent in socialization. Standpoint feminism encourages a lens that focuses on the patterned discourse (or discursive formations), institutions, and institutional arrangements (relationships between home and work) through which power relations maintain dominant-subordinate relationships. By focusing solely on organizational boundaries, these larger discursive formations and institutional arrangements that maintain dominant-subordinate relationships and subject locations are not as obvious as they are when containers are not visible. We can understand how analytically relying on bounded entities submerges larger dynamics. For example, whiteness (e.g., Friedman, 1995; Nakayama & Krizek, 1995), the market (e.g., Mander & Goldsmith, 1996), and discourses about work (Clair, 1996) transcend organizational boundaries and function to maintain dominant-subordinate relationships. Although these dynamics operate within particular organizations, neither their existence nor their important impacts on contemporary contexts are evident when socialization research focuses primarily on organizational boundaries.

By focusing on these larger dynamics, it is possible to differentiate between "outsiders" who do not make it into one particular organization and those who never successfully work or participate in the market. We are able to identify those who are more permanently socialized to inhabit object positions and their oppositional resistances. For example, migrant workers are essential to the current market arrangements, but when oppositional consciousness is generated, struggle ensues. Segura (1994) tracked the socialization of Chicana and Mexican immigrant women as they were channeled through training programs into the lowest-level jobs in terms of both pay and status. The global practices of expunging indigenous people, animal species, and the natural world in the name of development and the market are not within the purview of joining particular organizations. Yet an understanding of how socialization processes produce subjects who are willing participants in such practices is within the "boundaries" of socialization research.

From Phase Models to Linear, Universal Trajectories

Researchers from a feminist standpoint identify three primary concerns with phase models. First and foremost, the "universalizing" assumption that specific, linear, male patterns pertain generally to the population is problematic. Phases that describe trajectories through which some people pass are assumed to be such good descriptions of most people's experiences that alternative trajectories are not considered. Second, phases are overly abstract and do not derive directly from lived experiences. Third, they are assumed to be neutral, objective, and apolitical phenomena.

Jablin (1987) contends that,

> Although variability certainly exists, it is probably reasonable to estimate that most people spend between thirty and forty years of their lives working in occupations within some form of organizational setting. . . . The experience of entering, becoming assimilated into, and exiting work organizations is a quite common phenomenon in our society. (p. 679)

In other words, there is an assumption that because "most" people in "our" society are involved in this phenomenon, it is worthy of our attention. Those who differ are simply irrelevant to this model. By superficially considering who might be irrelevant here, we see that the excluded "variability" is often made up of subordinated groups and processes. Traditional women's work (i.e., performed for use rather than exchange) is excluded. Home workers in cottage industries are excluded. Presumably, volunteer organizations, community efforts such as mutual day care groups, and people and "other" societies are rendered invisible by being subsumed in the phrase "certainly, variability exists." Clearly, no one model can "see" every society, process, group, or type of organization, but we point out that feminist views focus on phenomena that are invisible from traditional views. When the absent referent is employed, these phenomena are particularly important to reveal.

Feminists have primarily addressed the model from the perspectives of white middle-class working women who are members of "our society." Bateson (1989) depicts middle-class women's lives as frequently upended and out of their control when they experience disruptions because of their husband's career changes. These women, then, would not expect to follow developmental patterns because they are positioned differently than men are. The linearity inherent in this model has been identified as one that excludes the feminine and positions women in double binds (Buzzanell, 1994).

Englebrecht (1994) succinctly summarizes phase assumptions from a feminist standpoint perspective when she claims that "the model used to depict the woman's experience is a male-based model" (p. 6). Women's experiences, she illustrates, are not represented in socialization phase models. Englebrecht shows that, even for women who do enter organizations as workers, the socialization process may better be described as a game of "blindman's bluff" (p. 7) in which women are wearing blindfolds and ear plugs. In this game, the clearly defined steps of stage models are not visible, and clues are not derived from other players.

Englebrecht (1994) claims that many women simply do not move through socialization stages. Instead, they move through a continuous process of being marked as other and excluded. Englebrecht traces this exclusionary process through anticipatory socialization, organizational assimilation, metamorphosis, and exit. Women learn to expect to engage in women's work throughout their childhood and adolescence. As they enter organizations, they are positioned as organizational wives (Huff, 1990, as cited in Buzzanell, 1994) and faced with sexual harassment (e.g., Wood, 1992b), glass ceilings (e.g., Buzzanell, 1995), and multiple, less overt exclusions.

Women are often never fully assimilated. Instead, they learn to cope and sometimes develop standpoints. Women's submerged discussions of the undiscussable function to help women learn to operate as "outsiders within." For example, professional women are often discouraged from discussing their children. In this way, women's reproductive roles and important life experiences are dismissed and remain invisible and devalued. Englebrecht (1994) advocates the opening of this conversation to create change. The history of sexual harassment similarly includes the sharing of experiences, the development of oppositional consciousness, and the collective pressure to create legal and policy changes (Cornelius, 1998).

Marshall (1993) and Milwid (1992), like Englebrecht, describe how their experiences from marginalized positions as professional white women within institutions contradict and challenge the universal stage assumptions. Marshall (1993) interrogated an established notion of Eastern and Western cultures as, respectively, dense and thin from her standpoint as a woman in a Western academic culture. She illustrated that, from her standpoint, this supposedly thin culture was very dense. Similarly, Milwid (1992) described her own as well as other professional women's stories about working with men. By listening to stories from 125 professional women, she identified and described subtle processes that served to keep women as perpetual outsiders. Stories included early gender socialization, lack of training, informal networks, sexual harassment, and power dynamics. By revealing these patterns, she was able to offer advice to women who seek to overcome these marginalized positions (Stout, 1997). Allen (1995a, 1996, 1998a, this volume) describes her experiences as a black woman, showing that race intersects with gender to produce unique experiences. These authors contradict and challenge the universal stage assumptions. From these voices, previously unexamined marginalized "others" emerge as relevant to socialization research.

Englebrecht (1994) claims that, "It seems almost absurd to discuss organizational exit from women's perspectives, because women may never completely get assimilated to an organization" (p. 14). Instead, women often become disillusioned with accepted organizational practices and leave or "move on" to create alternative work situations (Marshall, 1995). However, very little research has focused on the leaving process. It is as though we, as a community of scholars, prefer to adopt a "happily ever after" myth, suggesting that people enter organizations and stay with them for "full" careers (i.e., careers that include retirement). We should point out that the model encourages the study of the exit process by including exit as an explicit process. Yet the body of research using the model has typically ignored this stage.[5]

The high level of abstraction is a further, related observation. The phases are abstract enough that their descriptions necessarily obscure specific situated lived experiences. Experiences of the lower classes, people of color, and women may be particularly poorly represented (see Allen, 1996). Waring (1988), in her analysis of women's invisibility in the global economic system, describes the work lives of women (and girls) in particular subsistence economies in which work does not entail a relationship with an employing organization. She begins her book with a descriptive contrast of men's and women's work. She describes a man whose (paid) "work" is to sit in a missile silo for 8 hours each day and a young teenage woman who is defined as "not" working as she spends 16 hours each day walking to retrieve wood, water, and food that she uses to cook and clean to sustain her family.

However, it is important to acknowledge that exclusions vary by context. Exclusions are often directed at the feminine rather than at biological females. For example, biologists in the forester-dominated U.S. Forest Service have long been marginalized. Because of their emphasis on "biotic communities" and "webs of life," their voices represented unwelcome criticisms of the more traditional (patriarchal) practices of "tree harvesting." When "tree farms" are grown for harvesting, forestry is a rational practice in which planning and technology produce predetermined results. When the complex ecological systems that sustain trees, animals, clean air, healthy soils, and watersheds are made visible, the harmful underside of patriarchal forestry practice is exposed and the irrationality of the historical practices becomes evident.

The presumed universality and the abstract level of description are related to phase assumptions of neutrality. The phases are presented as though they are simply neutral, objective descriptions derived from a neutral observation. However, as Buzzanell (1994) points out, no theorizing is neutral. Instead, the presumed neutrality serves to mask the preservation of masculine, patriarchal assumptions. For example, as we summarized above, phase models exclude women's developmental trajectories and are thereby of political consequence. Phase model assumptions, then, preserve patriarchal arrangements and ignore subordinated lives. Thus, from a feminist standpoint view, much of what needs to be examined is ignored.

From Newcomers' Experiences and Strategies to Newcomers' Complicity

Feminist standpoint theory questions the facile assumption that individuals and organizations mutually influence one another. As this assumption evolved, scholars began to examine individual experiences in greater detail. We described this trend earlier in this chapter. Although this examination was viewed as an equalizing move in seeking to understand the individual as well as the organization, the focus on individual agency drew attention away from the unequal relationships inherent between organizations and individuals (Forward & Scheerhorn, 1996; Tompkins & Cheney, 1985) and between dominants and nondominants. Seeking to identify the ways in which such relationships are reproduced and/or challenged through socialization, standpoint feminism encourages linking experiences and strategies to the power relationships in which they are embedded. This is particularly important for the increasing proportion of temporary workers (see O'Connell & Louis, 1997) who may be marginalized persistently. However, some temporary workers, making lemonade out of lemons, focus on managing their own careers rather than remaining complicit in their marginalization. The examination of individual agency may be shaped to encourage the development of transformational standpoints rather than to simply reinscribe unexamined assumptions of individual agency.

Socialization Research

As mentioned above, the bulk of the socialization research is grounded in the assumptions we have discussed and is designed to identify linkages between socialization processes and outcomes. From a traditional view, this research has served to increase our understanding of what kinds of processes are associated with a variety of better socialization outcomes, or what we might most generally call person-organization fit (Hess, 1993). Our earlier sampling of this body of research illustrated this approach and the knowledge generated from its application to expand our understanding of the transformation from outsider to insider. Here we turn to a standpoint feminist perspective to provide some contrast.

From a standpoint perspective, this body of work is criticized in two primary ways. First, it is interpreted for its exclusions. Second, it is examined for its assumptions about knowledge and knowledge production. After summarizing these standpoint critiques, we examine a particular research case by way of illustration.

Exclusions

To identify a wider range of standpoints, more fully understand the socialization contexts that produce subjectivities, and examine the political nature of socialization, we need to identify absences. Here, we focus only on the most obvious absences. We turn first to absenced groups of people, considering race, class, and gender. Next, we turn to the processes of exclusion and resistance. Finally, we briefly return to the kinds of groups and "work" that are ignored. At its most basic level, this is a strategy of "mere" adding (i.e., considering groups and processes that have not yet been considered but considering them through the same concepts that have traditionally been studied). However, just as the addition of "others" can change organizations (Bach, 1990a), such additions can reformulate our understandings of socialization given that their locations, experiences, and standpoints may differ from those in past studies.

For the most part, class and race are not reported, considered, or theorized in socialization research (see Anderson & Thomas, 1996; Falcione & Wilson, 1988; Feldman, 1989; Forward & Scheerhorn, 1996; Jablin, 1987). Both go unmentioned and are thereby erased. Class is typically ignored except in rare treatments of specific occupations. Some occupations and types of organizations may implicitly index class.

However, a sampling of the literature illustrates that occupations and organizations are often reported but not further interpreted or considered (Barker & Tompkins, 1994; DiSanza, 1995; Ferraris, Carveth, & Parrish-Sprowl, 1993; Pribble, 1990; Stohl, 1986). Instead, the occupation is treated as an obligatory and unexamined demographic variable. Interpretations are not occupationally specific. Rather, occupation is implicitly assumed to have no effect on more universal organizational socialization patterns (see Allen & Meyer, 1990; Hackett, Bycio, & Hausdorf, 1994; Jablin, 1984; Jones, 1986; Ostroff & Kozlowski, 1992, 1993; Sass & Canary, 1991). This is particularly troubling when the type of occupation is unique at face value, such as graduate students as an organization (Bullis & Bach, 1989b).[6]

Occasionally, race is reported but not theorized because race is not specifically examined for the purposes of the study (see Barker & Tompkins, 1994; DiSanza, 1993, 1995). Allen and Sandine (1996) are an exception to this. They treat race as a key question, focusing on the sense making and experiences that students of color had during their college careers. They posit that understanding these members' socialization processes may assist academy members in helping these students complete their college careers. Such knowledge could help us create orientation programs as well as add to our research. Teboul (1995) calls for careful examinations of the intersections of gender, race, and socialization. Jackson, Stone, and Alvarez (1992) recognize that organizational literature offers little guidance for "managing diversity" when concerns about women's and minorities' experiences in the workplace are increasing. The authors provide a framework for studying socialization in diverse populations. The "demographic" variables affect the behavioral, affective, and cognitive processes that are a part of socialization. Lovelace and Rosen (1996) further probe race by examining differences among diverse managers.

Similarly, sex and gender are often not reported. More often than class and race, biological sex is reported as a characteristic of participants (e.g., Chao, O'Leary-Kelly, Wolf, Klein, & Gardner, 1994; Clark & Corcoran, 1986; Crow & Glascock, 1995; Hackett et al., 1994; Jablin, 1984; Jorgensen-Earp & Staton, 1993; Ostroff & Kozlowski, 1993; Sass & Canary, 1991; Stohl, 1986). However, gender is not considered, theorized, or interpreted as an integral aspect of socialization in most socialization studies. In this way, gender is seemingly acknowledged but only as it is stereotypically identified with sex, and, even then, it is not considered as more than a demographic variable. Ironically, sex and gender are erased when sex is reported.

A few studies specifically examine gender as a variable. While this is commonly eschewed by postmodern perspectives (Mumby, 1996), it is one way in which traditional perspectives are adapted to "see" (if not "hear") women. Mason and Mudrack (1996) discovered gender differences in ethical orientation among employed people, with women appearing "more ethical." Contrary to expectations, there were no gender differences among those not employed. Reynolds (1992) focused on how gender affected the experiences of junior faculty. Reynolds argues that "genderization" encourages males and females to have different worldviews of social interdependence and that this difference affects their socialization experiences. Through a series of five case studies, Reynolds found that worldview type more closely governed socialization experiences than gender did. However, she does argue that gender may shape newcomer experiences, with women reflecting more on acculturation experiences than men do. In essence, this finding suggests that white men expect to be fully integrated as they join organizations, whereas white women and people of color expect to be marginalized—therefore they more carefully make sense of their socialization experiences.

Some processes are also ignored in favor of others. Although processes that are theoretically associated with successful socialization are examined, organizations also engage in exclusionary processes to ensure that successful socialization does not take place (Stout, 1995, 1997; Takahashi, 1997). Other less intentional processes may serve to similarly exclude. Moreover, the unintentional and intentional strategies and processes through which people resist socialization are ignored in socialization research.

More subtly, the processes examined may be those from which women are excluded. For example, Milwid (1992), Marshall (1993), and Buono and Kamm (1983) illustrate that women are often excluded from informal networks even though such networks provide access to important socialization through informal peer interaction. Exclusion from these networks may preclude participation in many other socialization processes such as information seeking, informal socialization strategies, and relationship development. Ibarra (1992, 1995) found that the development and structure of managerial networks are influenced by gender and race. Network configurations in turn affect career benefits. Gender and racial differences in network configurations result in the differential allocation of individual and positional resources that work to create and reinforce gender and racial inequalities in the organizational distribution of power.

Perhaps most fundamental, in an effort to identify those processes and practices associated with successful socialization, the concepts and methods employed inherently rely on absent referents. The emphasis on successful processes and outcomes necessarily implies unsuccessful processes and outcomes. For example, when studies show that a particular set of socialization strategies is associated with successful outcomes, the studies have measured outcomes that are both successful and unsuccessful. Yet the lack of success and the concomitant less-socialized newcomers are not interpreted and discussed. Instead, like those who remain on the "outside," they are necessary to the conceptualization, measurement, and conclusions about what is successful but go unacknowledged. Increased attention to outcomes such as alienation and anomie (Hess, 1993) and stress (DiSanza, 1995; Tetrick & LaRocco, 1987) is warranted. Moreover, the study of critical standpoints should serve to better understand oppressive relationships as well as resistance and change.

In sum, by ignoring race, class, gender, occupation, type of organization, context, exclusionary processes, and many outcomes, the particulars and associated politics of human and organizational life are erased in favor of a universal, abstracted understanding of "the" newcomer being socialized into "the" organization. Contextual factors that differentiate experiences and standpoints are absenced. For example, pay, level of boredom, control, safety, health, meaning, and general working conditions are ignored. From a feminist standpoint perspective, the frequent exclusion of contextualized human experiences in favor of the measurement of relationships between variables means that it is typically difficult to understand the experiences, contexts, and discourses that produce the experiences and the standpoints associated with experiences.[7] In other words, politics are seemingly absenced. We turn now to a feminist standpoint perspective on the production of knowledge to address this second major point.

A Feminist Standpoint Critique of
Research Processes

In general, research processes are consistent with researchers' assumptions about the kinds of knowledge sought. A feminist critique of social science research in general is relevant to the socialization theory and research we have discussed in this chapter. However, standpoint feminism insists that the kind of traditional social science research we have reviewed here is problematic in several ways. First, the search for general, universal patterns is considered not only futile but a way of ignoring important unique patterns and contexts. For example, which general socialization strategies lead to which role orientations is an important question in socialization research. However, from a standpoint feminist perspective, this kind of question begins with assumptions that not only are overly abstracted but also perpetuate interests of management and science. Related to this, the use of broad abstract concepts that are necessary to consider these general, universal patterns (e.g., the general phase models discussed earlier) is also problematic.

Second, feminists eschew the assumption of objective knowledge produced from the position of a neutral researcher or observer. In other words, for standpoint feminists, researchers are located within particular contexts and they approach research with particular interests. Socialization research is as politically embedded as is socialization itself. By assuming that knowledge is objective and neutrally produced, socialization research is clearly located within this problematic tradition.

Third, standpoint feminist research uses accounts of personal experience as data (Smith, 1987a). Accounts are analyzed and organized using relevant theories to account for the experiences reported (Foss & Foss, 1994). For feminist standpoint scholars, research needs to seek the accounts of personal experiences given by people in marginal positions, such as the outsider within, providing the essential but invisible resources that sustain the system.

Fourth, feminists insist on reflexivity in scholarship (Foss & Foss, 1994). Scholars, then, need to consider their own perspectives, interests, and position vis-à-vis the particular studies, but continued reflexive considerations of the evolving bodies of research and theory are also essential. Traditionally, this reflexive questioning is not common.

Finally, research is conducted to improve women's lives by enabling them to make active choices about how they encounter their worlds (Foss & Foss, 1994; Smith, 1987b). Foss and Foss point out that the research process itself is enabling in that women have the opportunity to speak about and reflect on their experiences. Through interaction with feminist scholars, this self-reflexivity in itself operates to develop critical consciousness.

According to these feminist standards, extant socialization research clearly is not feminist in nature. Although some methods of study and presentation do carefully consider individuals' lives (e.g., Bach, 1990b; DiSanza, 1993, 1995), the descriptive/interpretive theories applied typically do not account for the subjectivities or standpoints described or detail resistance. In sum, although exclusions are an important concern, another concern is the production of knowledge. We turn now to a more specific critique.

A Standpoint Critique of Turning-Point Research

In this section, we analyze one exemplar of this research, our own turning-point work, from a standpoint perspective. We select this particular work for two reasons: (a) Its methodology enabled an interpretation consistent with standpoint theory, though such an interpretation was not developed originally, and (b) we prefer to critique our own work to personalize the reflexivity espoused by feminism.[8]

In the first turning-point study (Bullis & Bach, 1989b), we interviewed communication graduate students, asking them to identify turning points in their relationships with their graduate departments that led them to feel more or less identified with their departments. We defined identification as feelings of similarity, membership, and belonging (Cheney, 1983a). We listened to full accounts of newcomers' relationships, focused on their detailed expressions about each turning point, and heard their narratives linking the individual turning points together into complete stories. We then identified a typology of turning points and found that some were more associated with immediate change in identification and others with long-term change in identification. We then replicated the study to see whether members identified different turning points in varied organizational contexts (Clark & Bullis, 1992; Stout & Bullis, 1997). After comparing turning points described by insurance employees, government agents, and medical students, we identified a more general typology and examined the relationships between turning-point types and identification across organizations.

The first study adopted all three traditional assumptions. We purported to study the boundary crossings from outsider to insider, examined the participant accounts at three different stages, and assumed that individual agency and voice were central. Like most studies we discussed, we ignored gender, race, class, and type of organization. Although experiences of exclusion were reported, they were not interpreted as such. We purposively universalized, arguing that graduate departments (and graduate students) are similar to other organizations (and all newcomers). Although we were clearly and directly embedded and located within the research contexts (though in varying positions in the different studies), we ignored our researcher position, implying a neutral, objective location in all three studies.

Moreover, our methodology, although based on listening to participant voices, included the imposition of concepts such as newcomer, turning points, and identification. In this research, we ignored voices of participants who left, counting them as "subject mortality." We abstracted from the accounts by categorizing turning points according to our imposed research questions. The initial accounts and locations from which they were offered, then, were left behind in favor of abstracted categories and relationships among these abstracted categories. Rather than honoring lived experiences and drawing on theories to account for the experiences, we sought relationships among variables to better link individual experiences with an organizationally important outcome. However, the political interests went unacknowledged, despite our grounding in Tompkins and Cheney's (1985) theory of control.

Our work does not examine how experiences are linked with broader institutional relations and discursive formations. Rather, organizations are treated as isolated, autonomous contained entities. For example, lengthy descriptions about how people chose to attend graduate schools and attend particular institutions were treated as opportunities to build rapport but were ignored in the analyses. Turning-point descriptions that emphasized "outside" institutions such as community, family, religious institutions, or the "field" were categorized as "other" and omitted from analysis. Turning-point reports that could have been interpreted as identifying critical, oppositional standpoints were neutralized by the categorizing, abstracting process. Neither people nor their experiences nor the institutions involved were positioned within the broader society.

Although potentially empowering for participants (Foss & Foss, 1994), simply listening to people's stories does not constitute feminist work. The careful listening in our past research was coupled with traditional, non-feminist interpretations to create a prototypical study that ignored feminist concerns. For example, the method and data enabled traditional feminist themes such as emotionality and nonlinearity (Buzzanell, 1994). Interpretations absenced these themes. In other words, through our unacknowledged commitment to traditional assumptions, our past work reproduced patriarchal arrangements through its assumptions and analysis.

TOWARD FEMINIST STANDPOINT RESEARCH

We have pointed to many feminist standpoint possibilities throughout this chapter and here summarize the kinds of foci implied by feminist standpoint concerns. We first mention those that are related most directly to extant work and follow with those that are more distant. Three specific areas of inquiry promoted by standpoint feminism are offered: (a) Socialization scholarship should be expanded so that the absent referents, outsiders within, and marginalized people, processes, outcomes, and contexts are considered; (b) scholarship should incorporate the located contextualized positions of scholars and those studied through approaches, methods, and analyses that develop and reveal standpoints; and (c) research should both examine institutions and processes beyond contained organizations and continue critical analyses of our collective scholarly work.

The kinds of questions associated with an expansion of current inquiries focus on identifying patterns that sustain dominant-subordinate relationships in organizational socialization. How does socialization function to marginalize as well as socialize? Exclude as well as include? Create and maintain "others" such as outsiders and "outsiders within" as well as insiders? Encourage particular identities for particular groups? How do resistance and change occur? What are the roles of the marginalized in these processes? What communicative processes are involved? What processes, roles, and groups are made invisible, and how? Through such work, experiences and the processes by which exclusion occurs become available for further consideration. How are gendered relationships reproduced and/or transformed through socialization processes?

To answer these kinds of questions, feminist methodologies are needed. We find Smith's (1987a) institutional ethnography to be particularly useful. This method starts with identifying accounts of individuals positioned in absent referent roles or those who are in locations identifying communicative processes that are invisible. Working with these initial accounts, institutional ethnography traces connections indicated in the accounts and seeks accounts from people who are mentioned in the initial accounts. The process operates inductively to identify multiple connected accounts. In this way, researchers can track the institutional and discursive relationships that create the kinds of accounts offered. Invisible relationships are revealed, and critical consciousness is developed. The research setting becomes a point of transformation. Through this approach, scholarship intersects more closely with those studied.

Another implication of this approach is the need for continued reflexive monitoring of dominant-subordinate relationships that transcend particular organizations, including our own socialization scholarship. We need to focus on awareness of what is revealed and concealed through socialization theories, questions, and methods as well as what knowledge is produced.

The best example of this kind of organizational communication work of which we are aware has been produced by Brenda Allen. Her most recent published report focuses on the "outsider within," feminist standpoint methods and analyses, and scholarly reflexivity (Allen, 1998a). She provides a description of her experiences as a black woman in academia. Rather than stopping with this description, she describes resistance strategies, champions her standpoint as she claims that she is both "blessed and a blessing," and uses her standpoint as a resource for transformation as she proffers helpful advice to the dominant from her standpoint.

Murphy's (1998) study of flight attendants, though not drawing explicitly on standpoint theory, also illustrates the development of critical transformational standpoints. As flight attendants shared their common experiences of meeting an airline's appearance requirements through hidden transcripts (Scott, 1990), they determined to collectively challenge airline policies and, in one case, negotiated a policy change.

An important extension illustrating the further potential of standpoint theory is provided by Danielson's (1997) work. Rather than locating her work within a particular organization, she visited marginal workers who were attempting to leave welfare situations and enter the labor force. Her located, lengthy interviews provide insights into these "others'" experiences as they attempt to become "workers"; she links their experiences to the knowledges used to make choices as they negotiate marginal positions. Through her study, we gain a broader view of how institutional relations ("work" and "welfare") operate to maintain subordinated and resistant "others."

Shiva (1989), after detailing the many ways in which women's local, survival knowledges are being destroyed in India, suggests that the implications of standpoint theory are relevant beyond our ability to value the subordinated. The dominant and subordinate suffer together when the natural ecosystems on which human societies depend are destroyed. Shiva shows that, by revaluing women's knowledges (e.g., how to interact with the land to enhance long-term local sustenance rather than depleting the land to produce short-term exports), the potential for human survival may yet be recovered.

With these exemplars, we look forward to the continued evolution of feminist approaches, including feminist standpoint theory, for they can produce alternative, transformative knowledges. As P. Collins (1997) comments, "Oppression is not a game, nor is it solely about language—for many of us, it still remains profoundly real" (p. 381).

NOTES

1. We use the general term *socialization* in this chapter and do not examine differences among the three terms. For a consideration of differences between socialization and assimilation as defined by Jablin, see Jablin (1987).

2. We acknowledge that there are multiple feminist standpoint theories but adopt the singular term because we are focused on illustrating the potential of feminist standpoint theories as unique compared with the wider variety of feminist and critical theories.

3. As Wood (1992a) assumes, and we imply above by our equating of men with dominants or insiders, feminism is not related solely to biological women. Instead, stand-

point feminism, as we employ it here, focuses on voices and processes that are marginalized or absenced. As Marshall (1993) indicated, in organizational communication research, qualities traditionally associated with the feminine, such as emotion and relationships, have been ignored and excluded. Many "other" voices (typically listed as those related to race, class, and sexual preference) also have been relegated to the margins and ignored or hidden. Kanter (1977) illustrates how processes of marginalization function in organizations. Her description would pertain as easily to any underrepresented group as to white women and women of color. Moreover, she describes how powerlessness, rather than sex, best theorizes women's organizational marginalization.

4. For exceptions, see Baron (1989) and Ralston and Kirkwood (1995).

5. Although we say that socialization research typically has ignored leaving processes, there are exceptions to this claim (e.g., Cox, 1997; Egdorf, 1994; Jablin, Grady, & Parker, 1994; Mattson & Buzzanell, 1999; Phillips & Bach, 1992). Cox and Kramer (1995) point out that leaving can be more complex than simply voluntary or involuntary exit. Instead, organizations may induce or encourage leaving. Yet the ways in which exclusionary processes occur communicatively are rarely considered.

6. Jablin (1984) offers one exception to the statement that unique occupational types are not considered. He examines teachers attending classes at a university and considers this to be vocational organizational socialization. Similarly, Van Maanen (1975) focuses specifically on the police occupation in his interpretations. Hartmann (1997) addresses socialization relating to volunteers for nonprofit organizations.

7. Allen (1995a, 1996, 1998a) provides the clearest, strongest exception by describing her personal experiences from her own standpoint.

8. It is important to note that we are not including the turning-point study by Kirk and Todd-Mancillas (1991) in this critique. Their work is not implicated in all of the concerns we raise here.

4

Rethinking Negotiation

Feminist Views of Communication and Exchange

Linda L. Putnam
Deborah M. Kolb

One type of social interaction that has become an essential skill for all walks of life is negotiation. At one time, negotiation was viewed as a sordid affair associated with haggling, bartering, and back-room deal making (Kolb & Putnam, 1997). It is now a ubiquitous activity used in solving problems, sharing resources, and making decisions in multiple settings, including family and work environments. In the work setting, negotiation is often the primary form of interaction for hiring, making work assignments, deliberating on budgets, and enacting group decisions. It is not only central to labor-management relationships but is also the mechanism for developing organizational contracts and trade agreements. In an era characterized by corporate mergers and new organizational forms (McPhee & Poole, in press), negotiation is clearly an essential and complex communication skill.

Negotiation is also a special type of social interaction, one that differs from group decision making (Putnam & Roloff, 1992). These differences stem from the characteristics of perceived incompatibility, interdependence be-

AUTHORS' NOTE: We would like to thank Steve Wilson for his comments on this chapter.

tween parties, and simultaneous cooperative and competitive relationships. Social interactions in traditional negotiations, then, rely on exchanges of proposals and counterproposals, making arguments for preferred outcomes, and developing strategies and tactics to obtain desired ends.

These assumptions and characteristics contribute to the conception of bargaining as a "scripted activity" (O'Connor & Adams, 1996). That is, individuals enter a negotiation with a prototype of standard actions. These scripted activities include making offers, defending and refuting positions, discussing issues, exchanging compromises, and reaching an agreement. In general, then, people share a conceptual representation that negotiation is competitive and individualistic, is defined by trades or exchanges, and often results in an impasse. Even young children learn this script and are skilled at taking positions and engaging in tradeoffs to reach a settlement (Sheldon, 1992; Sheldon & Johnson, 1994).

This chapter undertakes a revision of negotiation as a scripted social interaction. In particular, we adopt a feminist perspective to review and critique traditional models of negotiation by focusing on "exchange" as the central element of bargaining. Through an examination of the way that exchange underlies the essence of negotiation, the goals and outcomes, the nature of relationships, and the processes, we set forth an alternative model—one rooted in feminist assumptions of connectedness and co-construction of the process. We contend that, in traditional approaches to negotiation, relationship and connection disappear as the fundamental ways in which people see and define their situations. By focusing on trades, negotiation is concerned with getting to settlements rather than understanding situations. Communication within the traditional model typically serves as information exchange and the execution of bargaining tactics to foster the pursuit of a settlement.

We begin this chapter with an overview of the traditional models of negotiation and the role of exchange in these approaches. Then we present feminist critiques of exchange and position our analysis within this literature. The latter part of the chapter sets up the rudimentary elements of an alternative model by comparing the essence, goals and outcomes, relationships, and processes of this perspective with a prototype of the traditional models. We use a negotiation case to exemplify these comparisons. This chapter concludes with a summary and discussion of the situations in which this alternative might be used as a viable option to traditional approaches to negotiation.

TRADITIONAL MODELS OF NEGOTIATION

Traditional studies in negotiation fall into the arena known as negotiation analysis. This work is based on the belief that descriptions of negotiation grounded in empirical research can assist bargainers in anticipating the other side's behaviors. Negotiation analysts provide prescriptive or normative advice based on projections of how the other party is likely to behave (Sebenius, 1992).

This traditional research emanates from three general types of models: game theory, distributive and integrative bargaining, and principled negotiation. Game theory draws from economic principles and centers on maximizing gains, minimizing losses, assessing utilities of options, and reaching optimal outcomes. By applying economic rationality to decision making, this approach focuses on ascertaining alternative courses of action and shaping rational choice (Luce & Raiffa, 1957; Raiffa, 1982).

Distributive and integrative models of negotiation draw from and react to notions of economic rationality. Distributive negotiation, also called zero-sum bargaining, concentrates on maximizing individual payoffs in situations in which one person's gain is the other person's loss. Negotiators typically set target points for what each person wants and resistance points for each individual's bottom line. For instance, in the sale of a house, both the buyer and seller set target and resistance points. The target points refer to both bargainers' preferred prices, and the resistance points refer to the end amounts to which parties will no longer concede. In the distributive model, bargaining becomes the process of reaching a settlement between the target and resistance points. Each party aims to capture as much of the bargaining range as possible (Lewicki & Litterer, 1985). Negotiation as a distributive process, then, is primarily a form of conflict management aimed at compromise. Successful negotiators start high, concede slowly, exaggerate the value of concessions, minimize the other party's concessions, conceal information, argue forcefully, and capture more of the bargaining zone (Lax & Sebenius, 1986).

In contrast, an integrative approach to negotiation presumes that the goals of the parties are not mutually exclusive; hence, it is possible for participants to achieve joint gains. Thus, through negotiation, individuals find ways to combine their diverse goals into a collective effort (Lewicki & Litterer, 1985). Parties start from preset positions, but through sharing information and creative problem solving, they make trades based on complementary interests that increase the size of joint gains for both individuals (Pruitt, 1981, 1983).

The relationship between integrative and distributive bargaining remains unclear. In some ways, the two approaches are interdependent processes of the same model, and in other ways, they are distinct perspectives on negotiation (Putnam, 1990b). Although Walton and McKersie (1965) depict these processes as descriptive models, they have surfaced in the field as normative approaches aimed at developing principles to guide effective negotiation (Lewicki, Weiss, & Lewin, 1992).

Principled negotiation draws from integrative bargaining and sets forth guidelines for reaching joint gain or win-win settlements. Critical of positional bargaining that typifies the distributive process, principled negotiation urges bargainers to focus on interests, not positions; to separate people from the problem; to invent options for mutual gain; and to use objective criteria to reach settlements (Fisher, Ury, & Patton, 1991). Popular in practice, this perspective has revamped the training of negotiators and spawned major programs on mutual gains bargaining (Cutcher-Gershenfeld, 1994; Cutcher-Gershenfeld, McKersie, & Walton, 1995). However, there are barriers to reaching integrative agreements, including overconfidence about obtaining desired outcomes, framing positive and negative outcomes differently, and reliance on processes rooted in splitting the pie (Neale & Bazerman, 1991). On the prescriptive level, researchers continue to offer advice based on the management of exchanges (e.g., types of opening offers and responses, strategies and tactics to use or avoid, ways of ascertaining interests and needs, and ways to overcome barriers in reaching mutual gains agreements; Friedman, 1992; Heckscher & Hall, 1994).

Each of these perspectives embraces exchange as the essence of negotiation. Gulliver (1979) even defines bargaining as "the presentation and exchange of specific proposals for terms of agreement on issues" (p. 71). In the distributive approach, the exchange of proposals is typically viewed as the vehicle or recommended strategy for settling within the bargaining zone. Exchange begins with both parties stating their asking prices or initial offers. Opening offers set the tone for trading concessions, in which the bargainers move closer to each other by exchanging incremental moves.

Exchange is also the essence of integrative and principled negotiation. In this approach, bargainers exchange information about their needs, ways of reaching a settlement, and criteria for assessing options. Exchange becomes the primary way that parties create value and discover arenas for joint gain (Lax & Sebenius, 1986). In integrative negotiation, exchange is the means through which bargainers learn and alter their perceptions about options available for joint gain (Lewicki & Litterer, 1985).

In each of these three models, exchange is the modus operandi and the very heart of negotiation (Lewicki & Litterer, 1985). It is the means by which bargainers gain a competitive edge, the way the process is enacted, the basis for reaching outcomes, and the way in which bargainers learn about the options available to them (Thompson, 1998).

EXCHANGE AND
NEGOTIATION AS GENDERED ACTIVITIES

Exchange, as it functions in these three perspectives, is a gendered activity. What does it mean to say that a particular practice like exchange is gendered? A practice is seen as gendered if its attributes are more commonly associated with one gender than the other, thus making dimensions linked to the other gender less valued. Parenting, for example, entails nurturance and the giving of care, practices linked to mothering. Acts of fathering, then, often remain hidden and devalued in the process. In this chapter, we contend that both exchange and negotiation are gendered activities because of the ways that trades grow out of individualistic needs, become reduced to commodities, and emerge as instrumental activities that define the nature of outcomes.

Other feminist scholars have presented critiques of social exchange (Howard & Hollander, 1997), exchange theory (Hartsock, 1985), and utility comparisons (Ferber & Nelson, 1993; Strober, 1994). Our chapter draws from these critiques but differs from them in several important ways. First, we view exchange as the essence of the negotiation process; hence, exchange occurs within and aids in defining a particular activity, bargaining. Second, our critique of exchange in negotiations is nested in social relations rather than in the marketplace as an institution (Hartsock, 1985). Moreover, unlike Hartsock, who adopts a feminist standpoint view, our critique and reframing of exchange does not grow out of an essentialist view of women's activity or the positioning of exchange as a materialistic phenomenon. By analyzing the taken-for-granted oppositions embedded in the traditional model of bargaining, we deconstruct negotiation as a gendered activity and set forth an alternative model, one rooted in co-construction rather than in exchange. Thus, we adopt a feminist poststructural stance to critique negotiation and offer an alternative model.

Negotiation, as we have previously argued, is also a gendered activity (Kolb & Putnam, 1997). It is gendered in that the qualities of effective bargainers (e.g., individuality and independence, competition, objectivity, analytic rationality, instrumentality, reasoning from universal principles, and strategic thinking) are linked to masculinity. Those attributes typically labeled as feminine (e.g., community, subjectivity, intuition, emotionality, expressiveness, reasoning from particulars, and ad hoc thinking) are less valued. Negotiation is also gendered because of its emphasis on the framing of issues, the exercise of power in the legal system (Gray, 1994), and the way women lack voice and a sense of place at the bargaining table (Kolb & Coolidge, 1991). From a feminist standpoint, the experiences of women are typically excluded from negotiation theories and research. Furthermore, studies on gender and negotiation typically graft women onto the existing structure of bargaining (Gray, 1994).

This chapter extends this critique by focusing on the centrality of exchange in negotiation and by setting forth an alternative model—one rooted in feminist values and assumptions about social interaction. Just as economics forms the foundation for traditional perspectives, feminist thinking guides the theoretical development of an alternative model. This alternative is not simply a minor repair to existing perspectives or a change in style inserted into the dominant framework. Rather, it represents a shift in the fundamental thinking that underlies the nature and process of negotiation.

At first blush, the alternative approach may seem naive, simple, or unnatural when compared with the traditional model. However, any option that stands in comparison to the dominant discourse will likely appear deficient, devalued, and inadequate since the standards of traditional perspectives have shaped our very knowledge of a particular phenomenon. From a political stance, the traditional model surfaces as hegemonic. The temptation, when exposed to "differance," is to critique the alternative model using the assumptions and criteria of the traditional approach. Thus, a reader might criticize this alternative by arguing that "negotiators won't play by the rules or will use goals and strategies of the alternative model to exploit their opponent." This criticism, however, draws from and functions within the status quo. In many ways, it serves to reinstate the dominant stance of the traditional model rather than to critique its alternative. The alternative approach presented in this chapter must and should be critiqued, but it needs to be examined from a new set of criteria and questions, ones that develop from within and are consistent with the perspective advocated in this chapter.

This chapter, then, aims to recapture many of the features deemed absent or marginalized in traditional approaches to negotiation: namely, relationship, connection, understanding, and dialogue. We present this model as an option, not as a replacement or panacea for problems with existing approaches.

COMMODITY AS THE METAPHOR FOR EXCHANGE

Exchange, as noted previously, is the heart of negotiation. As the essence of bargaining, it not only influences the use of concessions, strategies, and tactics, but also underlies the fundamental image of the process. The dominant metaphor in understanding exchange is commodity (Howard & Hollander, 1997). Even though bargaining centers on symbolic costs and rewards, the commodity metaphor remains dominant in traditional views of negotiation. Social processes in bargaining are converted to economic language and assigned weights and measures; thus, the value of a particular offer is given a numerical weight that complies with patriarchal assumptions of objectivity (Howard & Hollander, 1997). Treating bargaining as the distribution of resources also reinforces the commodity metaphor by presuming clear divisions between costs and benefits (Hartsock, 1985). By conceiving of an exchange as a commodity, negotiators measure their achievements from the criteria of whether they made "a good deal." They simultaneously transfer aspects of their relationship such as emotional support, loyalty, and understanding to processes that can be exchanged; for example, "if you give me a good deal, I will be loyal to you" (Strober, 1994). The commodity metaphor, then, sets forth a language system of rewards, costs, resources, utilities, and trades that pervades the negotiation literature and is rooted in patriarchal values. This metaphor grounds interactions in material resources that shove identity and relationships into the shadow of negotiation (Kolb & Williams, 1999).

A feminist lens highlights elements of negotiation that are typically marginalized in or missing from exchange-based models, such as connectedness, collaboration, expressiveness, and equality. Table 4.1 contrasts the traditional and the alternative models based on four dimensions: the essence of the activity, the goals and outcomes of bargaining, the relationship of the negotiators, and the negotiation process.

A COMPARISON OF THE TRADITIONAL AND THE ALTERNATIVE PERSPECTIVES

In the traditional models, exchange and trades form the essence of the process. Both are limited by reducing the practice of bargaining to individual needs, the use of a commodity metaphor, and reliance on a language system of rewards and costs. Both of them privilege patriarchal values—namely, objectivity and materialism—as ways of depicting social processes. There is nothing inherent in the particulars of a negotiation that would suggest that one model of negotiation would dominate in a given situation. However, the processes that individuals experience in the bargaining entail vastly different approaches. The following example of a negotiation demonstrates how goals, relationships, and outcomes differ when we compare and contrast the traditional and the alternative models.

This negotiation deals with a fee arrangement between Strategic Information Technology Institute (SITI), a consulting firm, and Browne Associates. Karen Davenport, the director of programming at SITI, is in charge of the educational programs that the company offers to information technology professionals and general managers. SITI's basic 3-day educational seminar, Strategic Models in Distributive Systems, has been highly successful. On the basis of this success, Davenport has developed an advanced seminar for professionals who have completed the basic course. Since SITI does not have the resources to run these programs, the company subcontracts the marketing operations of the course to Browne Associates, a marketing and management firm.

Several years ago, Davenport's predecessor negotiated a successful contract for marketing the basic models course. Basically, Browne Associates incurs all the costs to advertise and manage the program, retains the revenues generated, and pays a guaranteed fixed fee to SITI for delivery of each course. The advanced course promises to be a good deal for both SITI and Browne Associates. SITI can use it to develop long-term relationships with companies

TABLE 4.1 A Comparison of Negotiation Models

Traditional Model	*Alternative Model*
Exchange	*Co-Construction*
Trades	Mutual inquiry
Reciprocity	Integration
Balance	Blended
Equity	Equality
Transaction	Collaboration
Goals	
Enlightened self-interest	Self-knowledge
Mutual gain	Mutual understanding
Outcomes	
Settlement	Transformation
Agreements	Jointly developed actions
Win-lose, win-win, lose-lose	Changing conflict
Relationships	
Other as distant	Other as approachable
Interdependence through desired ends	Interdependence through connectedness
Extrinsic	Intrinsic
Instrumental	Expressive
Cooperative/competitive motivation	Motivated through mutual recognition
Trust/distrust	Empathy
Rational	Emotional
Process as Activity	
Proposals/counterproposals	Offering perspectives
Making concessions	Re-sourcement/reframing
Problem solving	Dialogue
Process as Social Interaction	
Debate	Deliberation and invitational rhetoric
Information exchange	Sharing experiences
Strategies and tactics	Expressions and circular questions

and to enhance future consulting jobs. Having another course to market means additional revenue for Browne Associates.

Karen Davenport, SITI's programming director, and Sam Browne, the founder and president of Browne Associates, meet to negotiate the revenue-sharing arrangement for the advanced course. Although offering the advanced seminars appeals to both parties, the negotiations do not begin on an auspicious note. As Karen describes,

> We meet at our usual place for breakfast. Sam hands me his proposal. I am shocked. It is clear that the fee structure that Sam proposes is considerably less than the one that SITI receives for the basic course. SITI cannot afford to deliver the program with this loss of revenue.

The task of developing a mutually acceptable fee arrangement is the goal of the negotiation. Yet the kind of process that follows and the type of agreement reached are not predetermined. This negotiation could go in several different directions. It could follow the traditional distributive or integrative path, or it could be worked out through an alternative model of co-construction. We develop these alternatives by describing how the traditional approaches differ from the alternative model in enacting the essence of the process—exchange versus co-construction.

Exchange Versus Co-Construction

As Table 4.1 illustrates, the traditional views of negotiation are rooted in practices of exchange, with trading, reciprocity, balance, equity, and transaction as the key characteristics. The alternative model, in contrast, is situated in co-construction, with mutual inquiry, promoting integration, blending proposals, facilitating equality, and producing collaboration as the central activities of bargaining. In traditional negotiation, progress toward a settlement is typically measured through frequent exchanges and the use of reciprocal concessions. The term *reciprocal concessions* refers to each party's response to his or her opponent's compromise with a counterproposal that concedes on issues. In bargaining, giving trades or exchanges entails altering original proposals and moving closer to the other side. As part of the unstated script of bargaining, reciprocity aims to equalize bargaining control. However, it often surfaces in actual negotiations as a strategy to promote one side's instrumental gain. Reciprocity of moves demonstrates good faith bargaining and keeps the negotiation moving toward a settlement. Refusal to reciprocate can lead to a stalemate that slows down or even stops the negotiation process (Raiffa, 1982).

As an alternative to exchange, co-construction occurs through connecting and creating mutual understanding. In co-construction, negotiators develop joint actions from mutual inquiry rather than trades. Mutual inquiry differs from trades by centering on the recursive nature in which negotiating generates meanings or interpretations of events. Inquiry pushes parties to question commonly held definitions, to dispute the naming or labeling of issues, and to challenge the status quo by expanding and envisioning alternatives. Rather than using trades to generate joint gain, mutual inquiry encourages expansive thinking and envisions what might be in the future. Rather than moving from counterproposals and reciprocal concessions, mutual inquiry uncovers seeds of change through joint learning. Hence, co-construction and mutual inquiry, activities that are shoved into the background in traditional models, move to the forefront in the proposed alternative view of negotiation. Concomitantly, attributes of connection and community linked to feminist thinking become central rather than marginal in the alternative model.

In the alternative model, progress or forward movement emanates from integrating negotiated issues into the larger system in which they occur. That is, negotiation interaction moves from deliberations about particulars (e.g., issues, positions, and facts) to discussions about the relational and organizational systems (e.g., definitions, background, lines of authority, and coherence within the system). Integration, then, becomes a way of moving negotiation "forward," not through stages or steps but through situating positions and issues within the larger context of the participants. Through integration, parties can describe particular moments in which a system functions effectively and can entertain new options by appreciating the complexity and scope of the situation.

Other contrasting features of the traditional and alternative approaches are equity versus equality and balanced versus blended. The traditional models cast the act of trading as a balanced or equitable process (Rubin & Brown, 1975). Repeated exchanges of rewards and costs provide negotiators with ways "to level the playing field." Reciprocal concessions and matching patterns such as tit for tat aim to balance resources and minimize power differences (Rubin, Pruitt, & Kim, 1994). This notion of equity, however, roots power in the individual control of resources. Negotiators who espouse this belief often fail to recognize how equivalency is different when it surfaces as equal numbers, equal ratio, equitable division, or distribution based on contributions to the group (Howard & Hollander, 1997). Thus, the exchange process that is so fundamental to negotiation embodies a notion of justice rooted in the agentic goals of equity rather than in the communal goals of equality.

The alternative model, in contrast, relies on communal goals rooted in feminist thinking. Based on intimacy, mutuality, and camaraderie, equality arises from the caliber of communication rather than from balancing power differences. It emanates from interaction that is responsive to multiple and emergent voices, that allows participants a chance to speak and be heard, and that legitimates discussion of new vistas and directions (Foss & Griffin, 1995). Proposals in this model are blended through open deliberations rather than balanced through the use of reciprocal trades.

Another contrasting feature between the two approaches is transaction versus collaboration. Traditional bargaining is often called transactional negotiation, referring to a buyer-seller transaction. The concept of transaction, however, implies transfers, calculated exchanges, and mutually rewarding trades. In negotiation, these transfers represent calculations based on utility functions and decisions derived from anticipating the opponent's behavior (Gray, 1994). The concept of transaction, then, reaffirms the view that negotiation is a series of strategic exchanges that can be arranged and rearranged to achieve the most beneficial combination. Communication in the traditional model also appears as a transaction, one in which information and tactical behaviors are transferred back and forth through a give-and-take process.

Unlike the traditional model, the alternative approach draws on a communal perspective to cast negotiation as a collaboration rather than as a transaction. Consistent with feminist thinking, collaboration relies on joint experiences and treats communication as a forum for ongoing and active deliberations that lead to a dialogue about diverse perspectives. Collaboration is a type of communicative competence in which participants build on each other's positions to find opportunities for joint actions and shared experiences (Barrett, 1995).

Thus, a feminist critique and revision of the traditional model of negotiation highlights different and often marginalized elements of the process. The essence of negotiation in this alternative model is co-construction rather than exchange. Co-construction emanates from mutual inquiry, integration of ideas, equality of voice, and collaboration rather than from the traditional elements of trades, reciprocity, equity, and transaction.

Let's return to the example of Karen Davenport to consider how the three different routes might function differently for the same bargaining situation.

Traditional Model 1: Distributive Exchange

In the distributive model, negotiation occurs through the exchange of a series of proposals and counterproposals. Sam claims that his costs for marketing and managing the advanced course are high and that he would be taking all the risks; therefore, he deserves a greater share of the revenues. Karen, who clearly wants this course, realizes that SITI needs Browne Associates more than it does the new course. She looks at Sam's numbers and makes a counterproposal by giving in on her initial revenue demand for SITI. Sam reinforces his position by arguing how much risk is involved and how he must cover the costs for these risks.

Karen reasons that, in the early years, no one imagined that the basic course would be so successful. The costs and the risks were equally high for both parties. Sam was getting a good deal from the basic course seminars. The new course would probably have the same life cycle, and Sam should continue to compromise on the proposed fee that he will have to pay SITI for the course delivery.

As the negotiation progresses, Karen argues that this program is going to be a real moneymaker for Browne Associates, just as the basic models course has been. She then proposes her bottom line—the same revenue arrangement that they currently have for the basic course. She implies that if SITI cannot get this arrangement, then the whole idea of an advanced course will be off the table. The negotiation proceeds with Karen and Sam going back and forth— Sam moaning about the costs and risks to Browne Associates and Karen claiming that Sam's company has minimal risks and has fared well from the original deal. In the end, both parties reach a compromise settlement. Sam pays a lower fee to SITI for the advanced course than he does for the basic seminar, but it is more than he originally proposed. Both parties feel dissatisfied with the process, and both agree to reopen the negotiation next year.

Traditional Model 2: Integrative Exchange

In the integrative model, rather than working from positions, both parties try to decipher each other's interests and make proposals to dovetail these different interests. The integrative bargaining might proceed in this fashion. After Karen recovers from her shock regarding the low fee that Sam proposes to pay, she realizes that she needs to know more about Browne's interests in this arrangement and what is driving Sam's proposal. So Karen asks Sam why the revenue-sharing scheme for the new program is so skewed in his favor. His explanation is simple. The basic models course is a prerequisite for the advanced seminar; hence, Sam must recruit participants from the pool of applicants who have already taken the basic course, which is only about 10,000 people. His risks are high because he fears that the yield will be low, and his company will not sign on the numbers needed to make this venture profitable.

What catches Karen's attention is the risk profile that Sam presents. The new advanced program is more risky than the basic offering. If Sam's entire pool of possible attendees for the advanced course is limited, Browne Associates has no flexibility in marketing. The company could not recruit more attendees simply by sending out another direct-mail campaign. Instead, Browne Associates must target their marketing strategies to a select group.

Karen realizes that she needs an entirely different proposal and that she should not simply engage in a series of tradeoffs on the amount of revenue. She suggests that they meet later, after she has had time to develop alternatives. The next day she gives Sam an alternative proposal. Since Sam is concerned about the risk factor of the new program, Karen proposes that SITI's fee start low but ratchet up as the number of seminar participants increases. When enrollments reach the number that parallels those in the basic course, SITI will receive a higher fee per attendee than it currently does for the basic course. This prorated fee compensates for SITI's revenue loss during the introductory period of the course when it is paid a low fee.

Although Sam responds positively to the idea, he believes that the incremental increase in fees is too steep. He prefers a slow phase-in of the higher fee. However, after tinkering with the revenues associated with the numbers, Karen and Sam reach an agreement. The settlement is a gain for both sides. By linking revenues to the number of attendees, the new course will move forward. Although the deal does not return as much revenue as Karen had hoped, particularly in the early stages, it will generate considerable cash flow in the future—for SITI and for Browne Associates.

An Alternative Model:
Mutual Inquiry and Co-Construction

When Sam hands Karen his proposal, she is shocked. SITI is a major client for Browne, and their relationship has yielded other work for his company. It does not make sense that Sam would try to take advantage of SITI, even though the proposal looks like it. Karen says to herself, "I'm missing something here. We haven't talked enough. I don't understand what's going on. Sam is really upset and not just about the revenue. Maybe I do not fully understand his business."

Karen asks Sam to talk about his business in more detail. Sam tells Karen his situation. To recover his costs, including SITI's fixed fee, Browne needs to recruit 105 attendees for each advanced course. At the start of a mailing cycle, Sam can never predict the yield. If the numbers look low, he sends out more direct mail. Using a formula of 1 attendee per 1,000 mail announcements, Sam knows that he can fill the seminar if Browne sends out enough mail. Karen then realizes that she has never understood Sam's operations. His problems aren't just about the fee structure. In this new arrangement, he can't use a direct-mail campaign to fill the advanced course because he can approach only previous participants. If not enough people sign up for the course, then he is out of pocket. This moment serves as a turning point to pursue the relationship as a basis for negotiation.

Karen mentions to Sam that she is only beginning to see how risky the advanced program is for him. That comment opens the door for Sam to become more expressive and to approach Karen in a new light. He begins to talk about the risks of his business and that he feels he has always borne all the risks in their joint ventures. "When we started," he remarks, "nobody knew the programs would be so successful. I underwrote them. Now that the programs are successful, the institute is not only unappreciative, but you want more."

Sam's unguarded remarks raise a critical element that is driving the negotiation. Both parties consider the other company greedy, and each interprets the actions of the other through this screen. Karen shifts the negotiation away from competition to mutual recognition by affirming Sam. Karen talks about how much SITI values the work of Browne and his team, and Sam points out how much Browne Associates appreciates SITI's contributions to making the seminars successful and effective. This affirmation makes both parties more approachable and builds connectedness in goals.

As Karen inquires more deeply into Sam's business—not just about the nuts and bolts but why he has to make the decisions he does—both parties surface past resentments, renew trust, and gain a new understanding of each other. This new understanding alters the definition and direction of the conflict. It transforms their perceptions of past behaviors and enables them to see their relationship in a new light. Through this mode of negotiation, Karen and Sam discover their real incentives for working together. Their discussion leads them to set aside the fee arrangements and build their interdependence and connectedness by thinking of ways to fill the advanced classes and to expand the pool of recruits. Karen pursues ideas related to the sequence of the courses, and Sam questions why the courses need to be offered sequentially. Then they both develop the idea to offer the two courses simultaneously, thereby giving people the prerequisites while recruiting them into the advanced course. Thus, instead of promoting the new course as a stand-alone offering, they could couple it with the basic course; participants could remain for the 2-day advanced program after they complete the basic course. This way, Sam can approach the 10,000 existing alumni and, at the same time, prospect for new attendees for the basic course.

What is important to Karen and Sam, however, is not the outcome or solution to the problem; rather, it is the connectedness that forms in jointly developing their course of action and in building a new sense of understanding of their situation. In effect, they transform the nature of their relationship by promoting expressiveness, appreciative inquiry, mutual recognition, and collaborative actions. Their relationship has changed because they have built a new foundation for future interactions, one that reduces suspicion and distrust, builds on common ground, and engages in a process of collaboration.

These three scenarios illustrate how the elements of negotiation function differently in each model. In the first two scenarios, exchange surfaces as the fundamental activity of negotiating. In both the distributive and integrative models, Karen and Sam concentrate on their own rewards and costs and on balancing risks and revenues. Balance and reciprocity drive the way that each person weighs the other party's concessions, and they influence the basis of the integrative agreement as Sam and Karen haggle over the revenue figures linked to the number of attendees.

In the alternative scenario, Karen engages in mutual inquiry rather than trading by asking Sam to explain his business. This inquiry, rooted in expansive thinking, allows the parties to raise issues about their relationship and to integrate the particulars of the moment into the larger organizational system that connects the parties. The negotiators collaborate not only in developing a creative solution but also in surfacing their suspicions and fears about each other and in developing a sense of recognition and a new understanding of each other. As they increase their appreciation for each other and their interdependence, they voice their concerns, develop communal goals, and jointly construct an outcome. Negotiation, then, becomes a co-construction rather than an exchange. These scenarios serve as exemplars to compare the goals and outcomes, relationships, and processes of the traditional and the alternative approaches.

Goals and Outcomes

Goals and outcomes in the traditional models are infused with the residue of exchange. Distributive bargainers rely on exchanges to maximize individual payoffs and to achieve settlements close to their opponents' resistance point. Mutual gains negotiators cast these goals as joint profits and strive to optimize gains for both parties. Consistent with the mutual gains model, bargainers aim to achieve the best optimal settlement while realizing that the other party is striving to enhance his or her position. Even though the goals of integrative bargaining include both self and other, the primary concern of enlightened self-interest remains for the individual whose payoffs are increased because joint gain is optimal. To return to our example, when Karen and Sam negotiate under the traditional models, their objectives are clear—to get the best deal that each person can. What differs between the distributive and integrative versions is the operation of enlightened self-interest. In the integrative version of the traditional model, Karen fashions an agreement that takes Sam's interest—in this case, risk—into account. The patriarchal value of individualism, then, remains primary in these approaches to negotiation.

The alternative view of bargaining strives for self-knowledge and mutual understanding rather than enlightened self-interest and mutual gain (see Table 4.1). Self-knowledge differs from self-interest in the way that negotiators are positioned in the process. Enlightened self-interest presumes that both parties are pursuing paths to increase their relative advantage in the situation. Self-knowledge, however, focuses on the way that co-constructing the process enlightens or informs both parties of their true needs, capabilities, and motivations. When Karen and Sam open up the negotiations and begin to hear about the experiences of the other, each learns something new about the other as well as about their own case. Through their collaboration, they come to see their individual interests in a different light and come to define and understand their mutual interests in how each person experiences the relationship. The co-constructed model presumes that parties can learn from negotiation and become aware of their own interests as a result of engaging in the bargaining. The major goal of the alternative model is not mutual gain but, rather, mutual understanding through generating new insights, creating alternative meanings, and expanding horizons. These goals, then, embrace the feminist quality of learning through connectedness.

In the traditional model, the outcome of negotiation is closely tied to the goals of the process. The ultimate resolution of bargaining is a mutually satisfactory settlement, particularly an optimal one in which "neither party can do better in an alternative agreement unless the other party does worse" (Pruitt & Carnevale, 1993, p. 83). A major limitation to treating agreement as the ultimate outcome of bargaining is the way this end drives other features of the process. Negotiation, then, as a complex process of social interaction, becomes an instrument for attaining agreement. Interdependence occurs around the task, not the relationship. In an interesting irony, when interdependence is rooted in the task, the very kinds of creative options that might emerge as solutions are not realized because the parties concentrate on outcomes and the instrumental nature of their talk. Thus, in Traditional Model 2, when Karen proposes a deal that takes Sam's risk into account, Sam remains suspicious and concerned that the terms of this agreement will favor SITI. The emphasis on reaching an agreement and on different types of outcomes, such as win-lose, lose-lose, or win-win, supports the instrumental nature of the process.

Rather than striving for optimal settlements, a model of negotiation based on feminist thinking aims for outcomes rooted in jointly developed courses of action that have the potential to transform the situation. Transformation implies a disjunction or break in preconceived ways of thinking about issues, positions, and relationships (Putnam, 1994). A negotiation that works through the changes that occur in understandings and meanings about issues, relationships, and future actions has the potential to become different from its original conception. Outcomes in the alternative model are not simply prefigured inputs that have been exchanged, rearranged, and repackaged. Rather, they arise from changes in the fundamental understandings of the situation and the participants.

In the alternative scenario, when Karen and Sam jointly develop a definition of and solution to the problem, it represents a new co-construction of their individual views of the situation. Even though the initial purpose of their meeting is to negotiate SITI's fee for the advanced courses, they co-construct a new understanding and rework the problem. This process, in turn, leads to significantly different feelings about the agreement. It is not the nature of the outcome itself that is radically different in the alternative model. (Clearly, the solution of offering both courses simultaneously could have emerged from integrative or principled negotiation.) Rather, it is the joint or collaborative discovery of developing the solution that arises from changes in the relationship and in the ways that parties work through their conflict.

Transformative outcomes are inextricably tied to how a dispute is defined and enacted. Specifically, transformation is often associated with the way a conflict is labeled or named, the process of blame and accusation tied to the dispute, and the ownership of the conflict (Mather & Yngvesson, 1980/1981). Through negotiation, parties in a dispute may come to frame or label the conflict differently. What was initially defined as a conflict about employer contributions to health insurance might emerge from the interaction as a problem with the health care provider or the nature of the health care package. A conflict about the implementation of training and diversity programs in an organization might transform into concerns about fundamental values in the company culture.

Other levels of transformation address the blaming and claiming of a conflict. Parties often approach a dispute by blaming other people for the problem. Sometimes the conflict interaction focuses on who caused this problem or who has contributed to the development of these difficulties. Moving from blaming others to owning the causes and effects of a situation illustrates a transformative moment in the dispute. When Sam and Karen negotiate about the fees, they still hold mutual assumptions about the greed and exploitation of the other. In the background, these feelings affect the kind of deal that can be made. When they work through these feelings and recognize the contribution that each person makes to the situation, their insights into the problem change, and their collective ability to create options changes as well. Through deliberation and reflection, the parties claim or own the problem in new ways; the outcomes, then, evolve from explanations and understandings of the situation that are different from those that the parties originally held.

Transformation also occurs when parties realize how the problems are rooted in the social systems in which both disputants are embedded. In the alternative approach, the solution that Karen and Sam collectively generate comes from moving away from proposals and thinking about the larger social system that they are developing. Thus, rather than aiming for win-win or win-lose outcomes, negotiators in the alternative model seek an enriched understanding of the very situation they are constructing. Jointly developed actions, then, emanate from changes in expectations, explanations, and understandings of the conflict. They grow out of the interaction during the negotiation rather than initiating the process through goals brought into the dispute. Change and transformation are outgrowths of the process of discovery and mutual understanding rather than the culmination of exchanges. Thus, the evolutionary nature of the conflict may lead to transformation, but transformation cannot be imposed on the conflict. The synergy of the process produces a transformation, not the superiority of arguments, the effectiveness of trades, or the optimal nature of the settlement.

Relationships

One primary difference between the traditional and the alternative models of negotiation is the role of relationships. In the traditional model, exchange and outcomes function as the foci, while in the alternative model, relationships and process move to center stage. In the traditional model, relationships serve instrumental ends by helping bargainers reach an optimal solution. Sam Browne is a businessman, and Karen Davenport represents an important client. They have a mutual interest in continuing that lucrative relationship. Consistent with patriarchal assumptions, negotiators are distant, independent, and autonomous. The "other" person in this model constitutes a bundle of interests, needs, and goals that are discrete and distant from one's own needs. In both traditional models, Karen takes the lead in trying to figure out what Sam needs, and she proposes solutions based on her assumptions about these needs.

The alternative model, in contrast, adopts the feminist goal of connecting as the basis of relationships (Fletcher, 1998). The other person is not simply a bundle of interests, goals, and needs; this person is someone to join with, learn from, and create a unique experience with. Hence, bargainers connect with the other person to form a relationship through the process of negotiating. In the alternative scenario, Karen opens up the possibility of examining the relationship when she inquires about Sam's past experiences and frustrations in implementing the courses. Through the negotiation, they start to shape a different relationship—it is still rooted in business, but it becomes defined as a collaborative partnership rather than an instrumental connection. By attending to the relationship, bargainers become attuned to ways of nurturing each other.

Clearly, self-disclosure and expressiveness have the potential to result in conflict escalation. Although a fine line exists between expressiveness and defensiveness, attending to the relationship places negotiators in a position to promote inquiry and probe their joint situation. For example, if Karen had responded to Sam's comment with defensiveness rather than sensing Sam's needs and frustrations, the conflict might have escalated when Sam said, "The institute is not only unappreciative but wants more." By attending to the relationship, Karen seeks to move the conflict in a different direction, one that may not work in all situations. Karen, however, is not taking a major risk to pursue a relational approach first.

In the traditional model, individuals act independently in making decisions, but they depend on the other party to achieve their respective goals. Interdependence, then, is predetermined and instrumental, derived extrinsically from mutual efforts toward interrelated goals (Blau, 1964). In the traditional scenarios, even though Sam and Karen talk about their mutual dependence, it is a dependence based on the exigencies of the situation. Indeed, under these models, negotiation strategists might advise Karen to develop alternative ways to deliver SITI's programs so that SITI would not be totally dependent on Browne Associates.

Contrary to the traditional models, interdependence forms the bond for building relationships in the alternative view. Rather than being predetermined and defined instrumentally, interdependence is co-constructed and emergent through the process of bargaining (see Table 4.1). Sam and Karen get to see how their mutual actions implicate the other company and create the conditions of distance and mistrust in their business relationship. These disclosures lead to a reframing of the relationship; the two parties begin to see each other differently. By probing underlying reasons for actions, Karen and Sam meet each other on new ground with deeper levels of inquiry about their situation (Bakhtin, 1981). Consistent with a feminist orientation, in the alternative model, relationships are defined intrinsically as parties acquire new understandings of each other and their respective situations. Rather than being driven by instrumental goals, both parties are expressive and open to the possibilities of learning something that they do not already know.

In a like manner, issues of trust differ between the traditional and alternative models of negotiation. In the traditional models, trust and distrust function through a cooperative/competitive lens. Motivations to cooperate stem from sharing a common fate; motivations to compete emanate from the desire for maximum gain (Rubin & Brown, 1975). In this situation, trust develops through opening moves that set the tone for cooperation: making concessions during the process, demonstrating similarities to the other party, and accepting the other parties' ideas and suggestions (Michelini, 1971; Swinth, 1967).

By rooting trust in cooperative/competitive orientations, negotiators adhere to a view of social relations defined by commodity exchange (Hartsock, 1985). The bargainers are isolated individuals who meet in an initial atmosphere of suspicion for the purpose of enhancing self-gain. They move toward cooperation to achieve the best bargain and to maintain their mutual association. Although the individuals oscillate between cooperation and competition, the connections between the parties are instrumental and are defined by domination rather than by a sense of community (Hartsock, 1985).

Although integrative bargaining is designed to build trust, negotiators share information and engage in joint problem solving to serve instrumental ends. Trust, if it can really be said to exist, becomes a tool to grease the skid of exchange (Gray, 1994). Negotiators may take risks to engage in joint problem solving, but this activity places trust in the task and the incremental moves of bargaining rather than in the relationship (Fisher et al., 1991; Lax & Sebenius, 1986). In traditional models, mutual distrust characterizes Sam and Karen's interactions. Each negotiator thinks the other person works only for his or her own company and is out to make a deal at the other party's expense. They cooperate to make a deal, but the nature of their interdependence remains fundamentally unchanged.

Feminist theory would suggest an alternative model of social relations, one rooted in connection and empathy. In this model, trust emanates from confidence in the process, one that grows from a shared commitment to the interaction. Trust building occurs from coming together, discovering new understanding, rejecting stereotypes and prejudices, and forming common ground through co-constructed meanings (LeBaron & Carstarphen, 1997; Notter, 1995). The seeds of empathy are planted in the process of connecting and in being open to the mutual understanding that both could create. In the alternative model, Karen legitimates Sam's feelings about his contributions to the success of their joint enterprise. Nurturing his feelings of being misunderstood, her inquiry and desire to hear about his experiences encourage him to be forthcoming. The negotiators internalize the other party's interpretations of issues and events and generate different ideas from the way each person comes to understand the issues (Becker, Chasin, Chasin, Heraiz, & Roth, 1995). As empathy develops, negotiators operate from a mode of inquiry rooted in appreciation rather than suspicion (Barrett & Cooperrider, 1990). Thus, the parties move from distrust to trust by building a connected relationship and a shared reality rather than by oscillating between competition and cooperation.

The traditional models also cast relationships as rational. Emotional or expressive goals are either devalued within bargaining relationships or serve instrumental ends. Bargainers are advised to remain detached from their opponent, to get beyond feelings, and to separate people from the problem (Fisher et al., 1991; Nierenberg, 1973). Emotional expressions in traditional bargaining block clear thinking and make it difficult for a negotiator to process information effectively (Daly, 1991; Fisher et al., 1991). When emotions enter into the traditional models, they often serve instrumental ends. Positive affect becomes valued in negotiation not because it grows out of relationships but because it influences creative problem solving, lowers contentious tactics, and increases cooperative behaviors (Carnevale & Isen, 1986; Isen, Daubman, & Nowicki, 1987; Thompson, 1998).

In contrast, in the alternative model, sharing feelings and experiences is an important factor that contributes to effective negotiation. A feminist lens would suggest that understanding and mutual inquiry emanate from experiential and affective dimensions of conflict (Kolb & Coolidge, 1991). Rather than being the opposite of reason, emotions are ways in which individuals know the world, reflect on and evaluate it, and change their perceptions about it (Buzzanell, 1994; Ferguson, 1984). Emotional moments in negotiation may represent turning points or shifts in the nature of a conflict. For Sam and Karen in the alternative scenario, sharing feelings opened up the process. For the first time, they could appreciate the perspectives that each person brought to the table. These moments of recognition form the groundwork for periods of ambivalence in which parties can pursue new understandings and joint courses of action (Putnam, 1994).

In summary, relationships in the traditional models take a backseat to instrumental goals and outcomes. Negotiators remain distant from one another and act as autonomous decision makers. They approach each other with suspicion and vacillate between competition and cooperation in their search for mutual gain. Bargaining relationships, then, are rational and defined extrinsically by the need to reach a mutually dependent end. In contrast, the alternative model, rooted in feminist thinking, places relationships at the center of the process. Bargainers enact their interdependence by connecting with each other, building trust from co-constructed meanings, and discovering new insights as a result of empathy and appreciation. Feelings and shared experiences are ways that negotiators learn about each other and their situations rather than being used instrumentally as a path to desired ends.

Negotiation Process

The process of negotiation has a direct influence on the relationships, goals, and outcomes of this activity. In the negotiation literature, process surfaces in two ways: as bargaining activity and as the social interaction that enacts negotiation. This section compares traditional and alternative models in each of these two areas.

As Bargaining Activity

Three types of activities characterize process in traditional bargaining models: exchanging proposals and counterproposals, giving concessions, and engaging in problem solving. The exchange processes that dominate traditional models of negotiation influence how proposals are developed, initiated, accepted, and rejected. Proposals refer to the positions that parties hold on issues or their recommendations for action. Basically, proposals are placed on the table as offers that delimit the scope and nature of counteroffers. In the distributive scenario, Karen and Sam confine their negotiation to trading offers and counteroffers of the fee that SITI will receive from the advanced course. Sam presents Karen with an offer, to which she responds with a counteroffer. Their negotiation centers on the justifications of each party's positions. Sam contends that this program is different, more risky than the basic course; therefore, he needs to cover his potential losses by retaining a large share of the revenues. In turn, Karen rejects this idea and sets forth a proposal of her own. The activity of bargaining in the traditional models is confined to a narrow band of ideas and concepts; essentially, it centers on the commodity under discussion.

Disputants in the alternative model offer perspectives or alternative understandings rather than proposals and counterproposals (see Table 4.1). Rooted in feminist thinking, the giving of perspectives treats ideas as the expression of viewpoints (Foss & Griffin, 1995). Unlike proposals, perspectives are tentative notions that represent works in progress. A perspective is one of many legitimate viewpoints expressed; it is the offering of an idea, which is different from advocating or seeking support for it. The offering of a personal experience or story, then, is not used as evidence to support a position—it is simply the giving of a perspective. The sharing of stories in the alternative scenario reveals different information than that exchanged in the monetary proposals and justifications for them. Sam's story about his relationship with SITI reveals to Karen how and why he is approaching the negotiation in this manner and the issues that form the roots of his concerns. Likewise, Sam is able to understand Karen's perspective and why SITI needs to explore proposals that look beyond the short run. Both parties come to understand that any deal has to recognize the life cycle of the seminars, the way that both companies do business, and their mutual goals of filling the classes.

Similarly, rather than exchanging concessions, negotiators in the alternative model respond through a process of re-sourcement, or drawing energy from a different frame or source than the one in which the initial proposals were made (Gearhart, 1982). Parties in the alternative model switch "frameworks, assumptions, and principles" from those suggested by their previous messages (Foss & Griffin, 1995, p. 9). For conflict scholars, this process resembles reframing or the act of altering fields of vision, interpretive schemes, and ways that parties come to understand their situation (Bartunek, 1988; Putnam & Holmer, 1992). It entails acquiring new insights, learning new premises, and altering cues in the social context (Bateson, 1972). By responding with re-sourcement rather than concessions, parties expand the options available to them and envision possibilities never realized in enacting traditional models of negotiation. Another advantage of engaging in re-sourcement is freeing the parties from face concerns linked to concession making in traditional negotiation. In the alternative model, Karen and Sam shift their conversation from proposals to the problems of risk and marketing strategy. As they draw on this new source or frame, their understanding of the problem changes. They are not simply splitting revenues or expanding the pie; rather, they reframe their task, redefine their mutual problem, and shift the focus of their negotiation.

Another difference between the traditional and alternative models is the notion of problem solving (see Table 4.1). As the fundamental activity of integrative bargaining, problem solving fosters brainstorming and bridging solutions, addresses the needs of both sides, and facilitates creative solutions (Lewicki & Litterer, 1985). Although problem solving is not typically regarded as a gendered activity, many aspects of this process parallel patriarchal values of rationality: namely, the isolation of problems into discrete parts, the use of sequential or linear steps, and the defense of particular solutions (Barrett, 1995). The discrete parts of problem solving typically include defining the problem, searching for causes, brainstorming solutions, generating criteria, and selecting the best solution. Critics contend that, by isolating components into parts, problem solving ignores the systemic and interactive nature of issues, consequently distancing problems from their context in time and space (Baruch Bush & Folger, 1994). This segmentation of steps also promotes a linear rather than holistic approach to analyzing situations.

Moreover, dwelling on problems often closes off exploration by reducing the discussion to concerns that have been labeled as problems. These deficiencies suggest that problem solving as a mode of inquiry is limited in producing the knowledge that is necessary for fundamental change (Barrett, 1995). In the integrative scenario, Karen and Sam engage in problem solving. They interact regarding Sam's problem of risk and propose a solution that links the fee compensation to the number of participants. This integrative solution represents a cost-compensation approach that appears to be a good package for both bargainers. However, the negotiation then switches from the activity to the social interaction that will make the deal acceptable to both parties. Because Sam and Karen remain in a tug of war about the sharing of revenues, Karen initiates and owns the deal, leaving Sam suspicious of whether his interests are truly served in the process. Although the deal meets mutual interests, the bargaining process revolves around revenue sharing.

The alternative model of negotiation relies on dialogue rather than problem solving for generating options. Dialogue aims to join with the other person in connective thinking and envisioning alternative courses of action (Bohm, 1996). It is a joint enterprise or a genuine meeting in which people codevelop explanations and options by probing underlying assumptions and reasons why these assumptions operate as they do. Dialogue aims to transform the conversation by focusing on presumptions that people bring to situations and by creating something additive that never existed before (Isaacs, 1993; Johannesen, 1971). As a process of interaction, dialogue focuses on the system as a whole through a type of synergy created from the collective construction of the parties (Evered & Tannenbaum, 1992). In the alternative scenario, Karen and Sam engage in a connected dialogue that broadens the nature of their conversation. They begin with the situation, move to the relationship, and then advance to a redefinition of the problem. As each tries to understand the problem from the other party's perspective, they acquire a more detailed understanding of their situation and shift their foci on the problem. Their new problem, as they now mutually define and own it, is not how to split the revenues from the advanced course but how to increase the marketing base so that their shared risk can be reduced.

A dialogic model of negotiation may seem like an oxymoron in that dialogue, in one sense, involves mutual openness, high levels of trust and disclosure, and empathetic listening (Buber, 1923/1958), elements that rarely enter into highly conflictual situations. However, another approach to dialogue, not necessarily aimed at openness, grows out of conflicting viewpoints and even adversarial relationships. This approach treats dialogue as a process of cooling down, suspending views, mutual learning, and appreciating (Ellinor & Gerard, 1998; Isaacs, 1993; Johannesen, 1996; LeBaron & Carstarphen, 1997). Logically, in a traditional negotiation, Sam and Karen would not discuss issues that threaten their credibility in the other party's eyes. In the alternative model, dialogue, then, unites with the feminist processes of connecting and offering perspectives to alter the very nature and direction of negotiation. Collective actions and joint proposals typically emerge from dialogue, but these endeavors are not the ends that drive the process. Engaging in dialogue becomes both the means and the ends of the activity.

As Social Interaction

Similarly, the two models of negotiation differ in the form of social interaction that characterizes each approach. Debate, the type of discourse that typifies the traditional model, consists of pro and con arguments and rebuttals aimed at reinforcing one's own position and refuting the opponent's claims (Keough, 1992; Putnam & Geist, 1985; Putnam, Wilson, & Turner, 1990). With the avowed purpose of winning, debate tends to close off interaction by encouraging parties to defend their positions and suppress doubts about the validity of their views. As a mode of discourse in traditional negotiation, debate may increase competition when parties match attack and defense patterns (Putnam & Jones, 1982). Hence, as the dominant discourse in negotiation, debate may be problematic as a venue for fundamental change. The interaction of Karen and Sam in the first two examples relies heavily on argumentation and debate. Each negotiator tries to convince the other of the veracity of his or her position. In the distributive model, both parties argue that their view on the fee allocation is right, fair, and appropriate. In the integrative model, Karen attacks Sam's position and strives to win him over to her perspective.

The alternative model posits a different process as a mode of social interaction for negotiation: deliberation (see Table 4.1). Deliberation is a precursor to dialogue in that as parties begin to discuss their needs, they "weigh out" their views by sorting out the ones with which they can agree and disagree. This "weighing out," however, differs from the discourse of "attack-defend" that characterizes debate (Isaacs, 1993). Deliberation opens up thoughts for reflection. It also promotes invitational rhetoric, a process grounded in feminist principles that focuses on sharing knowledge, thinking critically about ideas, and creating understanding (Foss & Griffin, 1995). Parties are invited to enter each other's worlds and to bring a new sense of awareness to the situation. By appreciating multiple perspectives, parties validate the communication process, even if they disagree on issues. Invitational rhetoric also expands thinking through appreciative inquiry. This approach urges participants to move beyond the here-and-now issues and raise questions about peak experiences, times of exceptional performance, and what people value most about their lives, careers, and work (Barrett, 1995; Barrett & Cooperrider, 1990).

In the alternative model, Sam voices his concern about taking all the risks and being in competition with SITI for revenues, and Karen expresses her feelings that Browne Associates gets more than the lion's share of the profits.

The process of appreciative inquiry is critical in changing these perceptions. By asking questions about Sam's business, Karen can begin to understand how and why Sam might feel that SITI has taken advantage of him. Karen can share her appreciation for Sam's contributions while she discloses her suspicions about Sam and her concern for covering the costs of delivering the course. As they talk, Sam and Karen develop a new awareness of their situation. Karen gains a new appreciation for Sam and the role of Browne Associates in the basic course seminars, and Sam begins to understand why Karen might think he is taking advantage of SITI.

The alternative perspective challenges two additional features of negotiation: information exchange and the use of strategies and tactics (see Table 4.1). Information exchange in traditional bargaining focuses on the amount of information shared, the truthfulness or completeness of the information, and the ways for gleaning information from one's opponent (Putnam & Jones, 1982). Information is shared in both tacit and explicit ways, and parties distinguish between the giving and the seeking of information in negotiations. The feminist critique of exchange applies to information management in bargaining. In the traditional models, information functions as a commodity or a material good that bargainers acquire and own. The negotiator's ability to accumulate more facts and manipulate the information environment is often an index of bargaining success (Donohue & Diez, 1985). Even though honest disclosure of information is vital to the effectiveness of integrative bargaining, information is treated primarily as a transaction; data are transmitted to enhance enlightened self-interest or mutual gains.

In the traditional models, bargaining strategies and tactics are also traded, reciprocated, and matched (Brett, Shapiro, & Lytle, 1998; Donohue, Diez, & Hamilton, 1984). A strategy refers to a broad plan or an overall approach that a negotiator pursues. Strategy is linked to exchange in that it directs the patterns of offers and counteroffers, it influences the use of persuasive appeals, and it affects concession making. For example, a strategy of toughness in negotiation entails the exchange of extreme opening offers, small concessions, high expectations, and an unyielding posture (Bartos, 1970). Bargainers also exchange tactics that influence an opponent's perceptions of target and resistance points (e.g., the use of threats, commitment statements, and demands). These exchanges foster the goals of competition and control by promoting the relative advantage of one negotiator over the other. Sam and Karen play this game in both traditional versions of their negotiation. Neither trusts the other, and both are out to get a larger share of the pie.

The patriarchal nature of strategies and tactics is also evident in their linguistic ties to military metaphors (Gray, 1994). In military vernacular, strategies and tactics are maneuvers or game plans that negotiators develop to improve their positions for attack or defense. They are designed to leverage the opponent and bring negotiation strength to bear at the right time (Rubin &

Brown, 1975). The language of conquest permeates traditional bargaining literature with phrases such as "weaken the opponent's stand," "stockpile resources," "tacit warnings," "aggressive and nonaggressive tactics," and "coercive maneuvers" (Wall, 1985). This integration of military images into the exchange process continues to root negotiation in a masculine environment in which the attack/defend model of social interaction is the dominant discourse.

An alternative social process highlights what is often marginalized in traditional models of negotiation: sharing experiences (see Table 4.1). Sharing experiences entails the use of personal narratives, descriptions of incidents and events, and discussions about personal feelings (Foss & Griffin, 1995). Sharing life stories connects people by revealing common values, beliefs, and emotions. In this approach, experiences are not shared simply to fortify positions or provide evidence for a claim. Each perspective in storytelling is unique; thus, sharing experiences is not subjected to argument or agreement/ disagreement (LeBaron & Carstarphen, 1997). The goal of sharing experiences, then, is not to convert someone to another position but to come to a new understanding by extending each other's ideas.

Rather than exchanging strategies and tactics, the alternative model sets forth a process known as circular questioning (Cobb, 1993; Fleuridas, Nelson, & Rosenthal, 1986). Drawn from therapeutic discourse, circular questioning involves a series of queries that collectively create interdependence. This discourse moves from personal narratives and experiences to an analysis of situations in a way that removes blame from the process. Questions include the following: How did a problem begin? What happened before? and When did you notice this difficulty? Thus, the interaction moves in a circular fashion to inquire about events, actors, themes, and time factors in the sharing of experiences. Stories begin to break their original structure and coherence when participants collectively ask questions that alter time frames, characters, and plots of situations (Cobb, 1993).

Karen uses a strategy of circular questioning when she negotiates in the alternative model. First, she asks questions about Sam's business, and then she reinforces what she learns about his work. As he shares his experiences, she acknowledges his risk and the way that it functions with SITI. He tells a story that places Browne Associates as the victim in their joint ventures. Sam's story gives Karen an opportunity to tell SITI's version of their relationship, and together they come to appreciate not only their mutual interests but also their commitment to solve the problem and improve the trust in their relationship. Questions such as what people value, what they want to learn from the situation, and how this situation relates to the larger system in which they function combine circular questioning with promoting appreciative inquiry. Circular questions aid in keeping each person's story open to alternative interpretations (Cobb, 1994).

Negotiation as a ritualistic process is so familiar that theorists often refer to it as a "conflict rite," a "dance," or a "game of chess" (Hocker & Wilmot, 1995). The process is so automatic that few people question the legitimacy of debate as the form of social interaction that dominates the process. Similarly, nearly every textbook on negotiation includes sections on strategies and tactics and the role of information exchange in reaching integrative agreements. These processes, however, are wedded to a set of assumptions that are limited by a view of negotiation as an exchange. The enactment of an alternative model must rely on a radically different form of social interaction. That form of interaction is rooted in dialogue and focuses on deliberation, invitational rhetoric, sharing experiences, storytelling, and circular questioning as the fundamental patterns of communication.

The solution that Karen and Sam generate cannot be separated from the process of negotiating. They reach an agreement through mutual understanding and jointly developing a solution, not through incremental concessions or finding a mutual gains deal. As Sam shares his experiences and his feelings about the relationship, Karen opens up about SITI's resentment over the existing fee arrangement. As they begin sharing, they set aside their suspicions, listen to each other, and learn from each other. The traditional models of negotiation give lip service to the notion of partnership. In the alternative model, Sam and Karen actually experience their relationship as partners who are jointly defining and developing their mutual project.

CONCLUSION AND DISCUSSION

Negotiation is not simply the process of making trades. It is an activity in which conflicting ideas form the basis for questioning, integrating issues into the larger system, representing multiple voices, and producing joint action. This alternative for thinking about negotiation stands in contrast to traditional approaches. Exchange forms the foundation that underlies traditional bargaining—the goals and outcomes, relationships, activity, and social interaction.

We contend that exchange and negotiation are gendered activities in that both processes privilege attributes typically identified with patriarchal values. Specifically, exchange casts commodity, cost-benefit ratios, and utilities as rational, materialistic, and objective approaches to decision making. The principles that underlie exchange such as reciprocity, balance, equity, and transaction also reflect a gender bias by relying on agentic goals and reasoning from universal principles. The goals and outcomes of bargaining highlight the instrumentality of a continual drive to reach a mutually satisfactory settlement.

Relationships in the traditional models reaffirm this gender bias through an emphasis on distance, instrumentality, and rationality. Bargainers are treated as autonomous decision makers who develop interdependence extrinsically by vacillating between competition and cooperation. Emotions and feelings are either overpowered by rational processes or coopted to serve instrumental ends. Exchanging proposals and concessions functions from the principles of reciprocity and balance. Problem solving in integrative negotiation privileges rationality and the separation of interrelated issues into isolated segments.

The alternative model of negotiation, influenced by feminist thinking, accentuates those features that are marginalized in traditional models. Treating negotiation as co-construction elevates relationships to the center stage. Employing dialogue as primary grounds negotiation interaction in community, mutual understanding, and connectedness. The alternative model operates from the principle of equality to strive for integration, collaboration, and mutual inquiry among diverse voices. Negotiation becomes the process of building a relationship, one that strives for mutual recognition and empathy. The types of interactions that characterize the alternative model are sharing experiences, offering perspectives, deliberating about ideas, telling personal narratives, engaging in circular questioning, and envisioning through resourcement and reframing. These forms of social interaction support the feminist practices of intuition, expressiveness, and shared feelings that are typically absent in traditional approaches.

This comparison of traditional and alternative models stems from prototypes, that is, from coherent and isomorphic views of each category. Deviations from these prototypes are more likely the rule rather than the exception. The dichotomous representation of each exaggerates the differences between them. This analysis, however, uncovers marginalized and unappreciated aspects of negotiation, ones that are often ignored in the traditional literature. Thus, the traditional and alternative models are presented as extremes to differentiate between the two approaches, even though the traditional models vary in form and function across types of bargaining.

For some scholars, the alternative model of negotiation may appear to be an entirely different form of social interaction (e.g., therapeutic discourse, social support interaction, or personal conversation). The proposed alternative, however, does not abandon the fundamental features of negotiation— perceived incompatible goals, interdependence, expressed struggle, mixed motive nature, and potential interference in achieving one's goal (Hocker & Wilmot, 1995). These features enter into the alternative model but function in different ways than they do in the traditional models.

Co-construction as an alternative view of negotiation is not an approach that replaces traditional models; it also cannot be used in every bargaining encounter. Some situations that seem particularly appropriate for using this model include informal work negotiations, bargaining in long-term relation-ships, role negotiations, and even intractable disputes. In any negotiation, par-ties can begin from a point of mutuality. In some and perhaps many cases, the other person will connect by pursuing goals, strategies, and processes that dif-fer from traditional models. However, if the other person refuses to engage, to pursue mutual inquiry, and to share mutual recognition, a negotiator can resort to traditional options. Mutual inquiry means that both parties must take risks to engage in a relational orientation to negotiation.

Even though the alternative model may seem unconventional and far-reaching, other theorists have presented similar perspectives on mediation (Baruch Bush & Folger, 1994), legal negotiations (Menkel-Meadow, 1994; Williams, 1996), and workplace dispute resolution (Gwartney-Gibbs & Lach, 1994). These perspectives explore the limitations of problem-solving media-tion; the links between negotiation and the healing process; and the need to examine institutional structures that contribute to dispute management prac-tices. This critique of traditional models of negotiation adds to a growing body of literature aimed at developing options and possibilities that are not easily coopted into the dominant orientation. The development of a truly alter-native model of negotiation, one that is rooted in nonpatriarchal values, is essential to enhancing the discipline's ability to explain communication in conflict management. This chapter takes another step forward in advancing this goal by presenting an alternative to the dominant theories of negotiation, one rooted in feminist thinking and principles.

PART II

RETHINKING PRESENT PROCESSES

5

Revisioning Control

A Feminist Critique
of Disciplined Bodies

Angela Trethewey

In this chapter, I extend extant conceptions of organizational control by laying a foundation for feminist analyses of the body as a site of power/resistance dialectics in contemporary organizational life. I appropriate the work of Foucault (1976/1990, 1979, 1980) and a variety of poststructuralist feminists (Balsamo, 1996; Bartky, 1988; Bordo, 1989, 1993; Butler, 1990; Deveaux, 1994; McNay, 1992; Sawicki, 1991) to revision traditional notions of control. I argue that communication is an agency of disciplinary force and demonstrate how particular communicative practices enable and constrain gendered, embodied subject positions. More specifically, I argue that organizational discourses and their attendant disciplinary practices are, in a very real and material sense, inscribed on female employees' bodies in ways that may narrow the possibilities for women's embodied agency in organizational life.

AUTHOR'S NOTE: I would like to thank Patty Sotirin and Patrice Buzzanell for their insightful and helpful suggestions.

TRADITIONAL TO CONTEMPORARY CONCEPTIONS
OF CONTROL AND DISCIPLINE

Historically, organizational theorists have been plagued with the problem of control. The question that organizational theorists, from Max Weber (1947) to Frederick Taylor (1903) to Chester Barnard (1938/1968) to Herb Simon (1945) to Tom Peters and Bob Waterman (1982), have tried to answer is, How can organizations and/or managers induce organizational members to direct their efforts toward organizational goals and ends? Although no single answer has prevailed, we do have a wealth of theoretical tools to draw on that help us explain why workers work as hard as they do (Burawoy, 1979). In the following paragraphs, I first sketch, in broad strokes, the historical development of control models, beginning with simple control to the more contemporary notions of unobtrusive or concertive control. Second, I address a recent model of disciplinary control as it is manifest in contemporary panoptical organizations (Foucault, 1979). Finally, I suggest that what is missing in the organizational communication literature is an explicit understanding and analysis of organizational control as embodied and of disciplinary practices that have material and ideational implications for gendered identities.

Overt Control: From Simple to Bureaucratic Forms

The development of the modern organization has created the need for increasingly complex forms of control. Simple control, in which capitalists or their appointees can directly oversee and intervene in employees' work processes, is becoming less pronounced in organizations increasingly characterized by spatial and temporal distanciation (Edwards, 1979). Simple forms of control are ill equipped for large, complex organizations, although those more personal and direct forms of control still persist today in organizations such as small businesses. Indeed, simple control, particularly when it is used in the context of expanding, geographically disparate organizational forms, has been subject to employee resistance. Workers resisted their tyrannical bosses' and supervisors' speed-ups and arbitrary rules more successfully as organizations grew because workers became more concentrated, and thus more powerful, through the very growth of enterprise (Edwards, 1979).

As simple control waned, technical control emerged as a more appropriate form for larger, hierarchical organizations (Edwards, 1979). Technical control is epitomized by the assembly line, but since its advent, a wide variety of tasks have been designed so that control mechanisms are built in to the actual work processes. Braverman (1974) convincingly argues that technical control, or "Taylorism," has become a bedrock principle for the design of work. The seemingly more humane human relations approaches to work processes are simply strategies to "adjust the worker to the ongoing production process as that process is designed by the industrial engineer" (Braverman, 1974, p. 87). Technical control is not infallible, however, and is also subject to worker resistance. Early on, workers quickly learned that a small group could effectively cripple an entire operation, as evidenced by the 1936 sit-down strike at the General Motors plant in Flint, Michigan (Edwards, 1979). While technical control continued, particularly in the design of tasks, it became clear that a new system was needed to control unruly laborers.

Bureaucratic control finds its locus in the social structure of the organization rather than in the processes of production. Edwards (1979) argues that "bureaucratic control establishes the impersonal force of 'company rules' or 'company policy' as the basis for control . . . [and] is built into job categories, work rules, discipline, wage scales, definitions of responsibility and the like" (p. 131). Bureaucratic control relies heavily on compliance with impersonal rules, positive incentives, and the creation of an image of the "'good' worker" to which members can aspire and less on the employees' actual work outputs (Edwards, 1979, p. 147). In this scenario, "workers owe not only a hard day's work to the corporation, but also their demeanor and affections" (Edwards, 1979, p. 148). Yet this form, like its earlier counterparts, also failed to resolve the control problem. Edwards argues that bureaucratic control's emphasis on "the rule of corporate law" shifted the locus of resistance from unions and internal grievance mechanisms to more public, legislative conflicts over the rights of workers and the nature of work. Thus, the Equal Employment Opportunity Commission, the Civil Rights Commission, the Occupational Safety and Health Administration, and others have stepped in to shape, dictate, and amend the rules of bureaucratic control (Edwards, 1979). Increasingly, however, governmental bodies' power to intervene on behalf of employees seems to be on the wane, as does the general public's faith in governmental regulatory efforts (Deetz, 1995b).

Although the preceding discussion separated these three forms of control for analytic purposes, these forms have not developed in a simple, linear fashion over time. Remnants of all three forms of control remain in the modern workplace. But, increasingly, more subtle forms of control are beginning to emerge, and I turn to these in the following section.

Identification and Concertive Control

According to Deetz (1995b), organizations have moved away from a "rhetoric of persuasion," which characterized earlier forms of control, to a "rhetoric of identification (of attachment and identity investment in the corporation)" (p. 118). Tompkins and Cheney's (1985) articulation of "concertive control" clearly lays out this newer form of organizational control. In organizations characterized by concertive control, members make "good" decisions because they identify with the organization and accept—indeed, pursue—organizational decision premises. More specifically, members draw conclusions "from the premises (beliefs, values, expectations) inculcated in the decision maker(s) by controlling members of the organization . . . [and] organizations offer inducements to the individual in exchange for accepting its decision premises as controlling his/her decisions" (Tompkins & Cheney, 1985, pp. 188-189). Flexibility, teamwork, innovation, and value consensus are central themes in these organizations. Organizations in which concertive control appears to be particularly effective, and potentially dangerous (Barker, 1993; Kunda, 1992), might be described as having strong cultures (Deal & Kennedy, 1982).

Kunda's (1992) analysis of one such strong culture points to the power of concertive control at work(places) and its encroachment on individuals' processes of identity construction. According to Kunda, under normative (i.e., concertive) control, members act in the best interest of the company because they are driven by a strong identification with company goals, commitment, and an intrinsic satisfaction from work. In this context, "a member role is fashioned and imposed that includes not only behavioral rules but articulated guidelines for experience. In short, under normative control it is the employee's self . . . that is claimed in the name of corporate interest" (Kunda, 1992, p. 11).

These newer forms of "internal" control have been heralded as "more effective" than the more direct or explicit strategies of the past (Tompkins & Cheney, 1985, p. 194). With them, the pressing need for resistance to workplace (explicit and external) controls seems to be diminished (Deetz, 1992). Yet, when we begin to fashion our own decision-making practices and identities in the shadow of the organization, the space for alternative identity construction narrows and becomes more constricting (Kunda, 1992). It is when corporate control practices come to take on the mantle of the normal and are reinforced by the very members they are designed to control that resistance becomes, perhaps, most crucial.

The notion of concertive control has provided a useful framework for many compelling empirical studies that help us to understand the communicative practices that harness employees' attitudes and decision-making processes in favor of the organization (e.g., Adler & Tompkins, 1997; Bullis, 1991; Papa, Auwal, & Singhal, 1997). However, these studies limit our understanding of control by framing it as operating on our cognitive processes exclusively, with little attention given to the ways in which members' material bodies are similarly harnessed for instrumental purposes. As a result, the possibility for resistance to concertive control seems to be located in the "autonomous rational" agent, who is largely a socially constructed fiction (Deetz, 1995b), rather than in embodied (micro)practices.

Discipline, the Panopticon, and Self-Surveillance

Control, in its most insidious form—discipline—operates simultaneously on employee minds and bodies. Organizational communication or discourse (in a Foucauldian sense) articulates meanings, values, and modes of being; discourse steers the normative body of ideas and the corporeal bodies of employees. While, certainly, early models of control were interested in regulating the body, particularly in relation to work tasks,[1] contemporary models of control (discipline) colonize members' bodies in ways that go beyond scientific management strategies. Whereas concertive control works on members' attitudes, beliefs, and identification processes, discipline operates, quite literally, on the body.[2] Foucault (1980) contends that "power seeps into the very grain of individuals, reaches right into their bodies, permeates their gestures, their posture, what they say, how they learn to live and work with other people" (as cited in Martin, 1988, p. 6). Organizational communication scholars have yet to systematically address how control functions as embodied practice. Following Foucault, I argue that what is particularly important about organizational communication is its effects on individuals' embodied identities. Unfortunately, there is a paucity of research in the communication field that explicitly addresses the relationship between specific everyday or mundane discursive practices and members', particularly women's, embodied identities (for an exception, see Corey, 1996).

Foucault's (1979) discussion of the Panopticon provides a framework for examining the ideational and material/bodily consequences of organizational discourse on members' identities. The Panopticon is an architectural structure that creates a situation of perpetual visibility for its inhabitants. Foucault (1979) captures the essence of contemporary disciplinary societies when he suggests that modern organizational forms operate in much the same way that penal institutions do when they create embodied identities by differentiating between their delinquent and law-abiding subjects. The effect of the Panopticon is

> to induce in the inmate a state of conscious and permanent visibility that assures the automatic functioning of power. So to arrange things that the surveillance is permanent in its effects, even if it is discontinuous in its action . . . [establishes a situation in which] the inmates should be caught up in a power situation of which they themselves are the bearers. (Foucault, 1979, p. 201)

Today, organizational members are routinely subjected to panoptic surveillance by themselves and others. Indeed, Botan (1996) argues that a "surveillance culture has emerged in the American workplace" (p. 295). Team-based work groups, for example, exhibit growing levels of surveillance in which members monitor one another's behavior more closely than their superiors might, thus reducing the need for direct supervision and further tightening the "iron cage" of control (Barker, 1993; Barker & Cheney, 1994). Electronic surveillance technology, such as electronic cash registers that monitor grocery clerks and retail salespersons, keyboard monitoring systems, and electronic sensor badges that can track members' movements, was predicted to monitor up to 40 million workers by the year 2000 (Adler & Tompkins, 1997; Botan, 1996). This technology has panoptic effects because it renders the surveiller invisible and the surveilled visible. Unfortunately, the impact of electronic surveillance affects women, who are concentrated in service positions, disproportionately. In 1990, 85% of monitored workers were women (Botan, 1996). Botan (1996) suggests that surveilled workers suffer four effects: a reduced sense of privacy, increased uncertainty, reduced communication, and, possibly, lowered self-esteem. Panoptic surveillance, when it is practiced by those in control, induces discipline and has real effects on members' identities.

What is perhaps most disconcerting about surveillance and discipline is that they are often self-imposed. Most employees today conduct their own self-assessments by bringing their own hopes, dreams, aspirations, indeed, their very identities under their own "private public eye" (Deetz, 1992, p. 257). Deetz's (1995a) study of a large multinational telecommunications corporation suggests that discipline and self-surveillance are tightly connected to members' identities (p. 4). He argues that organizational discourses are literally integrated into the self: "In this logic, work is not supposed to be for body sustenance and support of external relations. Rather the reverse: the body and social relations are positive only in so far as they support work" (Deetz, 1995a, p. 18). More precisely, Deetz (1995a) writes,

> The body is medicated (with caffeine, cold and stomach medications) to mask the symptoms of stress and fatigue, and the heart and home are replaced with the consumption and hope of what we will have. All other institutions and their demands are conceptualized as constraints on employees' work success. . . . The employee colonizes the [body], home, community, educational institutions, state and church. The managers in the name of the corporation need not do so. (pp. 18-19)

Deetz's study highlights the extraordinary power of discipline and the almost frightening degree to which employees willingly control and monitor themselves and their bodies in the name of the organization. "The self," says Deetz (1995a), "is seen as a confused, imperfect rendition of the [organizational] model. Effort is put not into maintaining a front, but into self-surveillance and social technologies of control in order to get the self to behave" (p. 22). As will be discussed further in later sections, this is particularly true for women who struggle to perform and embody professional identities that are nearly impossible to achieve—yet still demand and inspire constant vigilance. Female professionals invest a great deal of time, energy, and material resources in efforts to get their seemingly undisciplined and leaky bodies under control and in line with normative ideals (Nadesan & Trethewey, 1998; Trethewey, 1997a, 1999).

The ability of the subject to form his or her identity through alternative discourses is constrained when organizational discourse constitutes the subject in the corporation's image. Disciplinary control may undermine the foundations of collective action when members respond to family, community, and the body politic in the way that corporate discourse demands. Without alternative discourses in which members can choose various subject positions, disciplinary power may ultimately "narrow the human character" (Deetz, 1992, p. 43).[3]

UN/COVERING THE BODY:
A POSTSTRUCTURALIST FEMINIST RETHINKING
OF CONTROL AS EMBODIED PRACTICE

Although Foucault provided us with an important conceptual framework for examining the effects of control in contemporary life, he failed to fully articulate the gendered character of so many contemporary disciplinary techniques. Fortunately, poststructuralist feminists, in particular, are beginning to provide accounts of how women's bodies are disciplined and, often, made docile in culturally and historically specific ways (Balsamo, 1996; Bordo, 1993; McNay, 1992; Sawicki, 1991; Trethewey, 1997a, 1999). It is important to note here that the body is a social, historical, and cultural production. It is "a reality constantly produced, an effect of techniques promoting specific gestures and postures, sensations and feelings" (Balsamo, 1996, p. 3). Furthermore, the body is both a product and a process. Balsamo (1996) argues,

> As a *product,* it is the material embodiment of ethnic, racial, and gender identities, as well as a staged performance of personal identity, of beauty, of health (among other things). As a *process,* it is a way of knowing and marking the world, as well as a way of knowing and marking a "self." (p. 3)

As both product and process, the body is a locus of social control. This locus becomes exceedingly evident when the disciplinary techniques of gender are examined critically.

Disciplinary Techniques of Femininity and Gendered Identity

Gendered ways of performing identities—walking, working, sitting, comportment, and dressing—

are regimes of the body which seek to subjectify in terms of a certain truth of gender, inscribing a particular relation to oneself in a corporeal regime: prescribed, rationalized, and taught in manuals of advice, etiquette and manners and enjoined by sanctions as well as seductions. (Rose, 1996, p. 137)

Perhaps nowhere is this more true than in the context of organizational life.

Women learn to discipline their bodies well before they begin their professional lives. Young (1990b) argues that women learn to control their bodies in distinctly "feminine" ways as young children.[4] Not only do women learn to "throw like a girl," they also learn to sit, stand, walk, tilt their heads, gesture, carry objects, and comport themselves like a girl. Girls' bodies are socialized into moving in a feminine and thus more constrained manner than their male counterparts. Young (1990b) explains that the "more a girl assumes her status as feminine, the more she takes herself to be fragile and immobile and the more she actively enacts her own body inhibition" (p. 154). Moreover, young women learn to experience their bodies as an object, a thing: "The objectified bodily existence accounts for the self-consciousness of the feminine in relation to her body and the resulting distance she takes from her body" (Young, 1990b, p. 155). In addition to the objectification women experience in sexist societies, women also live with the threat of invasion of their bodies, the most extreme form of which is rape. Thus, to open her body in a free, active, open (read masculine) fashion is to invite objectification and invasion.

Bartky (1988) extends Young's (1990b) phenomenological analysis by explaining how (white, middle-class) women's bodies are controlled and ordered within contemporary disciplinary regimes of femininity. She describes three disciplinary practices that contribute to current social/historical constructions of femininity. First, diet and exercise regimes are designed to attain the ideal female body size and configuration (Bordo, 1993; Trethewey, 1997a, 1999; Wood, 1999). For example, women are increasingly recasting the natural weight of healthy, normal women as "the existential female dilemma" (Wolf, 1991, p. 67). Second, women pay close attention to comportment, gestures, movements, and other nonverbal behaviors. Finally, women employ techniques, such as the application of makeup, that display the female body as an ornamental surface, especially in professional contexts (Murphy, 1998; Wolf, 1991). Our notions of professionalism are thus intimately and inextricably connected to a particular type of embodied and disciplined femininity.

Bartky (1988) claims that these disciplinary practices are not simply individual, aesthetic choices for women; rather, they are part of the process by which the "ideal" body of femininity is constructed against a pervasive sense of bodily deficiency. This ideal body is the organizing fulcrum among the various disciplinary regimes that constitute the discursive power of (a socially constructed) femininity. Women engage in self-surveillance and disciplinary practices under the onus of a sense of deficiency and abnormality. Chernik (1995) articulates the self-talk that many women employ in the service of self-surveillance:

> When our bodies take up more space than a size eight (as most of our bodies do), we say *too big*. When our appetites demand more than a Lean Cuisine, we say *too much*. When we want a piece of a friend's birthday cake, we say *too bad*. Don't eat too much, don't talk too loudly, don't take up too much space . . . don't seem hungry. (p. 83)

Certainly, these self-disciplining practices have consequences beyond women's self-image and self-esteem; they distract women from sociopolitical concerns. Bordo (1989) maintains that, through the disciplinary techniques of diet, makeup, and dress, women's bodies have become docile, meaning that women "are rendered less socially oriented" and more focused on "self-modification" (p. 14). Women's concerns with diet, weight, exercise, makeup, and bodily comportment are *political* concerns, *not* medical ones. Tavris (1987) points out that "it is political because it keeps women attending to their looks instead of the circumstances of their lives, it pits woman against woman against woman, it destroys physical fitness and energy" and drains resources, including time and money (p. 114). In brief, my argument is not that women are "docile bodies" but that the politics of disciplinary techniques ultimately narrows the possibilities for women's embodied agency. This (primarily) poststructuralist account makes clear that the "body is political" and demands active(ist) feminist inquiry.

Women's Bodies and Professional Bodies: A Contradiction in Terms?

The political struggles around women's bodies are furthered in organizational contexts in which the feminized body is both marginalized and disciplined (Hearn, Sheppard, Tancred-Sheriff, & Burrell, 1989; Marshall, 1993; Mumby & Putnam, 1992; Sheppard, 1989). Organizational communication scholars argue that the prevailing organizational context in which women and men communicate is dominated by masculine values and forms. Organizational discourses valorize traits and characteristics that are stereotypically masculine, including an emphasis on rationality, assertiveness, and the drive for individual success. In contrast, the traits typically attributed to women, such as an emphasis on feeling or emotion, an orientation toward affiliative relationships, and connectedness, are often denied legitimacy in organizational life (Fine, 1993; Hearn et al., 1989; Mumby & Putnam, 1992). Thus, enacting and embodying a feminine gender becomes particularly problematic for women in masculine organizations. Indeed, Sheppard (1989) argues that women "share a perception of gender as a *managed status:* being a woman in male-dominated environments demands handling one's gender in particular ways and this process is done with reference to one's interpretation of prevailing power structures in the organization" (p. 145). For organizational women, managing gender involves containing or displaying an appropriate sexuality and presenting an appropriate professional image through verbal and non-verbal communication.

The task of managing "femaleness" is difficult given a masculine context, and professional women are often caught in double binds (Jamieson, 1995). The female body is associated with characteristics such as nurturance, dependence, passivity, and incompetence, whereas the male body connotes strength, ability, and intelligence. Therefore, women who want to be perceived as competent must look less feminine and more "male-ish" (Tavris, 1992, p. 31). At the same time, however, there are negative consequences for women if they look or dress in ways that are too masculine (Garber, 1992). Bordo (1989) suggests,

> "Upwardly mobile" women today continue to be taught traditionally "feminine" virtues, to the degree that the professional arena has opened up to them, they must also learn to *embody* [italics added] the "masculine" language and values of that arena—self-control, determination, cool emotional discipline, mastery, and so on. Female bodies now speak symbolically of this necessity in their slender spare shapes. . . . [Women] are also becoming more and more practiced at the "male" values of control and self-mastery. (p. 19)

Learning to navigate one's body through these complex, ambiguous, and precarious "in-betweens" (e.g., masculinity and femininity, revealing and hiding one's body, conservative and fashionable dress, social conformity and individual creativity, and sexuality and asexuality) becomes a tantamount concern, as well as a political struggle, for women in their professional lives.

Although dress, appearance, and image may appear to be rather innocuous and even frivolous concerns for women in the workplace given more seemingly pressing issues such as current wage disparities between men and women (Laabs, 1996), increased incidents of sexual harassment, and the persistence of the glass ceiling and walls (Wood, 1999), the way in which women display and present their professional bodies has very real, material consequences for women. For example, dress influences judgments about a woman's chances for success and promotion in business environments (Kimle & Damhorst, 1997). Women's competence continues to be evaluated based in part on dress and appearance, and wearing "appropriate" dress makes women more role-confident (Bartlett, 1994).

In addition, in organizational life, "those who fail to do their gender right are regularly punished" (Butler, 1988, p. 522). There are negative repercussions in terms of job opportunities and personal relationships for women who fail to discipline their own bodies. For instance, nonverbal communication research suggests that physically "attractive" individuals are more likely to be hired than those with lower levels of attractiveness (Manusov & Billingsley, 1997). At the same time, however, the desire to control one's body, to do "gender right," can lead to severe problems for professional women. Women who value achievement and professional careers are especially likely to be obsessed with thinness and to suffer from eating disorders (Bordo, 1993; Tavris, 1992). Organizational discourses, then, have very real consequences for the women who try and feel compelled to embody them.

Struggling With Their Bodies: Professional Women Speak

An empirical example may highlight how women's embodied selves are controlled in and through organizational and gendered discourses at work. My research with professional women suggests that they do struggle with embodying an "appropriate" professional identity in the workplace, and they firmly believe that their bodily presentation of self has very real consequences for their own and others' success or failure (Nadesan & Trethewey, 1998; Trethewey, 1999).[5] Moreover, the professional women I interviewed invested time and energy in disciplining their own and other women's, sometimes uncontrollable, bodies. These women articulate three themes that characterize how women experience, present, and display a professional embodied identity: (a) A professional body is a fit body; (b) a professional body (purposefully) emits signs and messages through bodily comportment, nonverbal behaviors, and performances (thus, the body is conceived as a text to be read); and (c) a professional woman's body is excessive. The task of controlling the female body is made more difficult because the female body has a tendency to leak. The undisciplined body also points to the female body's otherness in a masculine context. These three themes indicate how professional women's bodies are normalized and made docile in organizational contexts. Finally, these women imply that both men and women are disciplinarians.

Professional Body as "Fit" Body

When asked "What does a professional body look like?" many women described it as "fit." Beth, a management communication consultant, said without hesitation,

> I think the new standard is fit. With our young people, it is. . . . And I've seen more and more pressure to be fit in the workplace than I've ever seen before. Yeah, yeah, that's how I would define [a professional body].

Later in the conversation, Beth emphasized that being fit "means control. That would very, very much be so." Sunshine, a 50-something owner of a consulting firm, noted that the increased pressure for employees' bodies to conform to particular standards is a relatively recent historical phenomenon:

> We've always had standards, but I don't think we've ever put them on body types. And I think we're doing that more now. We're looking for people that exemplify those healthier lifestyles . . . as pictures of what we'd want our company to look like. That's why so many young people are brought into quasi-management positions, because they exude that look of youth and vitality that they want the corporate culture to look like.

Finally, Kim stated, "In order for you to be successful, you have to be fit, physically and emotionally, and that gives you the ability to be more productive and more efficient and more in control, more machine-like."

For many of the interviewees, the connection between professionalism and a (particular sociohistorical) notion of fitness was almost taken for granted. The participants seemed to provide at least two reasons for why fitness is an appropriate indicator of professionalism. First, a fit (as opposed to fat) body quite literally indicates that a woman is disciplined and in control. The "firm, developed body has become a symbol of the correct *attitude;* it means that one 'cares' about oneself and how one appears to others, suggesting willpower, energy, control over infantile impulses, the ability to 'shape your life'" (Bordo, 1993, p. 195). For example, Success argued, "If you can control yourself [and your weight], I know that you are going to take care of me. If you can't do that for yourself, how am I to trust in whatever you're gonna do for me?" Second, a fit body is better able to perform the duties required of a professional woman. Nan claims that

> having a body that is an appropriate size gives you lots of energy, and it takes a lot of energy to be a professional, especially a professional woman. Because you have to do all that makeup and stuff. Takes time!

Women need to be fit, in part, because the disciplinary regimes of femininity are time and labor intensive. In addition to needing endurance to work, women need endurance to work at being women.

Similarly, Many Hats complained that one of her biggest struggles is "pushing her body to work as many hours as I need to without burning it out, that's the big one right now." To accomplish that goal, Many Hats installed a refrigerator and a small cabinet to store food in her office at a law firm. Her colleagues and receptionist have to remind her to eat. In an era of increasing time pressures (Hochschild, 1997; Schor, 1991), many women recognize the utility of a fit body. What these women fail to recognize, or at least articulate, is that not only are home and hearth colonized by corporate demands, but their very bodies are being harnessed in normalizing ways.

Professional Bodily Displays

In addition to "fitness," the participants used comportment, nonverbal behaviors, and performances as strategies for creating and maintaining professional identities. More specifically, the interviewees discussed their, sometimes deliberate, strategies for presenting, displaying, and ultimately controlling their professional bodies. For Success, the professional body is one that emits appropriate signs. She says, "Body language is very, very important. I want people to read me as being confident. Um, they can read me, hopefully, through body language." Even sitting in a particular way is a sign of professionalism. Success explains that if she wants to show somebody she is very interested in communicating with them, then her "body language will come up forward." However, if she is relaxed, "then I'm sitting back. Basically, the way I cross my legs or don't cross my legs" is an external, embodied sign of her professionalism for her audience. For Success, appropriate nonverbal behavior demonstrates to others that she is a force to be reckoned with and taken seriously. The consequence of inappropriate nonverbal signals is a loss of credibility. Inappropriate nonverbal signals send a "message to the other party that there may be a way around this person, that somebody can take advantage of them," says Success.

Suzanne, an image consultant, also believes that professional women should learn to display appropriate nonverbal signs:

> I always recommend to my clients that, even though we are not the stronger [sex] and we do not have to be the stronger, we still need to have that firm handshake, but don't overdo it. . . . If we want to display confidence, then we need to have a confident posture. . . . I know that women fidget more than men, and I am definitely guilty of that. And men get nervous when women are fidgeting.

Suzanne suggests that women must be strong and confident, but not too strong and confident. Likewise, Sunshine believes that women must not present a "threatening" body: "I was very challenging and threatening to men, so I got softer." Sunshine "got softer" through her nonverbal behaviors. She explains,

> I would sit in a very female position with my legs crossed over, or I would relax into a chair instead of sitting real straight in a chair, or I would lean towards them when I talked to them instead of leaning back in my chair.

Women, it seems, must adopt just the right combination of "masculine" and "feminine" nonverbal behaviors.

For Sunshine, Suzanne, and Success, there are specific and learned ways of moving (or not moving) one's body that convey professionalism to an audience of body readers. If women are to be successful, they must learn to embody a particular set of professional signals. Indeed, Success suggests that women do whatever they can to develop professional comportment skills: "I don't care whether it's taking a modeling class, learning to walk, [or] learning to sit, [but women should] try to build self-confidence and self-esteem" through managing their bodies. In addition to learning the rules, the ropes, and the intricacies of their professions, professional women must also constantly attend to the details of sitting, walking, and moving professionally.

Female Body as Excess

The task of controlling and disciplining the female body is made even more difficult and complicated for women because the female body has a tendency to leak. Women never know when their bodies may display messages and meanings that were not intended. Thus, many interviewees seem to live in fear of losing hard-fought credibility as a result of their excessive or undisciplined bodies. In many ways, the female professionals described their own bodies and the bodies of other women in terms of spillage, slips, leaks, and excess. Nan, for example, said that the thought of putting her formerly 200-pound body on "display" at professional business gatherings was "unthinkable." Now that she has begun a regular exercise regimen, she feels more comfortable in public performances. An overweight body, for Nan, is simply too excessive to be in the public eye. An excessive body, however, is not just an overweight body; women's bodies may leak out through unruly clothing, menstrual bleeding, pregnancy, or emotional displays.[6] The excessive or undisciplined body draws attention to the otherness of the female, private body in the masculine, public sphere of work.

One story is particularly telling in this regard. Perhaps in contemporary Western culture, the most excessive display of a woman's "femaleness" is menstrual bleeding.[7] During the "embarrassing stories" portion of a conference and trade show I attended with the participants, one woman provided a horrific account of bleeding in front of a potential client. This young saleswoman described how she was wooing a multimillion-dollar account for her firm. The saleswoman and her potential client were out to lunch when "that particular time of the month" came early. She was wearing a cream-colored skirt. Upon her discovery, she was forced to ask her client if she could borrow his suit coat to cover herself while she went to "clean up." The potential client responded by saying, "If I'm going to let you borrow my suit coat, you have to show me the problem." The saleswoman told the client that he was a witness to the most embarrassing day of her life. Despite this horrible experience, she did end up getting the account. While the young salesperson told her story, the women in the audience were at once sympathetic and uncomfortable. They responded with sympathetic groans and hooded glances of disgust or shock at their neighbors.

This story may be interpreted as revelatory of the way that patriarchal culture responds to female desire in general and vaginas in particular. Patriarchal culture attempts to order or discipline female desire by harnessing it for male consumption (Turner, 1984). Within this troubling, largely visual or "scopic" logic, argues Irigaray (1991), a woman's body "finds itself thus eroticized, and called to a double movement of exhibition and chaste retreat in order to stimulate the [visually stimulated] drives of the [male] 'subject'" (p. 352). In a patriarchal culture, women's genitalia represent absence or "the *horror of nothing to see*" (p. 353). Menstrual blood, however, points directly to the vagina, making it available to see. In so doing, says Irigaray, it reminds us of the plurality and multiplicity of women's sex organs and desire (Cixous, 1991; Irigaray, 1991): "*[A] woman has sex organs, more or less, everywhere.* . . . The geography of her pleasure is far more diversified, more multiple in its differences, more complex, more subtle than is commonly imagined" (p. 353). Yet patriarchal culture rejects and represses this view of female desire and female bodies. As a result, a woman "experiences herself only fragmentarily . . . as waste, or excess" (Irigaray, 1991, p. 354). The narrator of the "bloody" story appears to experience herself and her body as excessively female, as do those around her. Some women later responded to her story by saying that it was not one that should be told in public. Making women's excessive bodies available to the public, whether it is through blood or narratives, is troublesome according to these professional women. Other indicators of women's excessive bodies were crying in public, embodying pregnancy, and wearing revealing clothing.

For these interviewees, the female body is always a potential professional liability. The response, therefore, is to keep the body in check, to prevent leaks, in short, to discipline and control the body. Although the women in this study did not use the term *discipline* to describe their own approaches and responses to bodies, the term is certainly fitting. Women go to great lengths to avoid appearing out of control or undisciplined. Women make very careful and considered choices regarding dress. Some women delay or avoid having children. Others guard their feelings carefully and strategically. In short, women discipline their corporeal selves in the name of professionalism (Bartky, 1988; Foucault, 1976/1990, 1979). If one can control her own body and self, despite its leaky and difficult-to-control "nature," then one may be well on the path to professional success. The assumption for these women seems to be that "control of the self can lead to control of the world" (Garsten & Gray, 1997, p. 218).

The Body's Disciplinarians

Bartky (1988) argues that women internalize the panoptic gaze of the male connoisseur. As a result, women live their bodies as "seen by another, by an anonymous patriarchal Other" (p. 72). That "other" disciplinarian can be either male or female. Many interviewees described the constant pressure they felt from the male gaze. They described the feelings of discomfort when men in professional settings stared at their breasts, commented on their clothing, touched them in inappropriate ways, or discussed other women in explicitly sexual terms. Moreover, these women expressed the belief that a male audience requires heightened vigilance and attention to bodily presentations of self. Suzanne explained that, when women are in the presence of a male audience, "you have to be a little more dressed up. You have to be a little more careful of the details. . . . Men just seem to be very aware, so you have to be really careful of that." Suzanne did not describe the powerful male gaze as a problematic phenomena; rather, it is simply a part of a woman's professional environment to which she must adapt. Cassie, an auto body shop owner, claimed, "When you're with a lot of men, it's more important to look good. I don't know why, but I just always feel that way, like I am always being judged." The male gaze requires women to be careful and reminds them that they are always being evaluated.

However, not all the interviewees simply accepted the male gaze as "normal." Lana, a saleswoman, was quite perturbed when a male colleague chided her for purchasing a candy bar.

> I know that if I were a man and I'm at the gift shop and I'm buying a Snickers bar that no one would walk up to me and say, "You're gonna get fat." Well, I don't care, you know. What's the difference? I want a Snickers bar.

Lana indicated that men believe that they are in the rightful position to comment on women's bodies and to discipline women when they think they need it.

Many women do expect men to be particularly judgmental and are willing to "internalize the panoptical gaze of the male connoisseur" (Bartky, 1988, p. 72). The interviewees are generally not surprised when men act as disciplinarians. What bothers the participants is when female colleagues and peers act as disciplinarians. The female gaze is an equally powerful (and complicitous) normalizing force, according to the interviewees. Beth contends that "women are much harsher on other women than men are." Nan notices that "women

judge each other a lot, like at the [women's association] meeting. I can tell."
Chris says that, when women are in the company of other women,

> they think they might be able to let their guards down, but I think women, um, are
> looked at [by women], and it all leads to the same thing. So even when we least
> expect it, you know, I do notice that women make comments about other women.

Susan suggests that she tries to keep her female customers happy by appearing
professional. "But," she says, "if you walk in there and everything is hanging
out, she ain't gonna be happy. She's going to think, 'Well, you're a little slut.'
You know how women are." Finally, Katie argues that women are more judgmental than men are. She says that, when she attends women's association
meetings and is dressed

> a little more flamboyant, I've felt the social pressure that I wasn't one of the group.
> It makes me sad, too. That's why I resist it. That's why I continue to not conform.
> But you have to force yourself not to. I find it real discouraging when women are
> judgmental of other women. You know, I think there's enough that we have to think
> about, [being concerned about how other women are judging you] shouldn't have
> to be a part of it.

Women actively discipline other women, perhaps even more so than men
do, according to the interviewees. When women evaluate and judge other
women using the problematic standards of masculine professionalism, there
are many potential flaws to be noticed, many potential mistakes to be examined. Rather than resisting patriarchal gendered and organizational discourses, women's more common response is to actively participate in and
perpetuate those normalizing discourses (Ashcraft & Pacanowsky, 1996;
Buzzanell, 1994; Mumby, 1997; Trethewey, 1999). Poststructuralist feminist
accounts of the body, like this one, make it clear that women experience their
bodies as on display, as available to the gaze of both male and female
disciplinarians. It is not surprising, then, that women routinely engage in self-
surveillance and work hard at getting their own bodies to behave by con-
forming to the contradictory (and seemingly impossible) dictates of both
professionalism and femininity.

The preceding discussion highlights the disciplinary techniques, including
dress, nonverbal comportment, fitness, and other forms of bodily control, that
constitute, enable, and constrain women's bodies at work. It is important to
remember that women's bodies are not mere facticities but discursive constructions. Organizational bodies, their topographies and boundaries, are constructed through subjects' identifications with normative and patriarchal
notions of gender that can, finally, never be achieved. The endless pursuit of
this normative and normalizing ideal ultimately inhibits women's collective

political action and adds yet another "shift" to working women's already difficult lives (Nadesan & Trethewey, 1998).

Experiencing, Enacting, and Resisting Embodied Identities

The preceding Foucauldian feminist conceptualization of women's professional bodies, however provocative, fails to account for the ways that different women (women of color, lesbian women, aging women, or maternal
women) experience, celebrate, and resist professional and gender discourses
through their own bodies. Foucault himself recognized the shortcomings of
conceiving of the body as simply a passive surface on which the discourses of
power are written. The gendered body should not be understood only as the
primary target of the techniques of disciplinary power, but also as the point at
which these techniques are resisted and thwarted (McNay, 1992). The body is,
after all, a site of struggle.

Following Deveaux (1994), I argue that we should conceptualize women's
relationships to their bodies as a reflection of both social constructions *and*
their own responses to (and mediation of) the cultural ideals of femininity.
According to McNay (1992), "Choosing one's gender, then, is a process, not
wholly conscious, but nevertheless accessible to consciousness. It is a certain
way of existing in one's own body which involves the individual's idiosyncratic interpretation of already established corporeal styles" (p. 72). In other
words, individual women can choose to embody and perform particular subject positions via corporeal styles. Although the socially constructed "ideal
body" is an organizing element, women may, in fact, adopt alternative corporeal styles or embodied identities in ways that produce a broader range of subject positions for women. Despite the fact that there are structures of domination and particular constructions of gender that contribute to the subordinate
position of women in society, we must not be blind to the ways that women
resist their subordination and act as agents in their organizational and life
worlds.

Melia's (1995) study of lesbian resistance as embodied practice, though
not necessarily written from an organizational perspective, does suggest that
women can resist gendered, heterosexist discourse through bodily displays,
namely through appearance and personal style. Lesbian women "use a conscious collage of bodily signifiers to resist the discourse of compulsory (het-
ero)sexuality" (Melia, 1995, p. 547). Although lesbian women may find it
unacceptable to display their sexuality as Queer activists in organizations,
some lesbians do play with conventions and expectations in their organizational lives. For example, when Fay was "forced" to wear a dress, she did so
without shaving her armpits. Similarly, if Diane goes to a meeting at work
where she is the only woman, she tends to dress in more "mannish" and

"stroppy" ways. For the women Melia (1995) interviewed, "playing with expectations and conventions, even whilst 'passing' within a heterosexual context was a significant part of lesbian identity" (p. 553). By "playing with" conventions, these women begin to revision normative expectations for gendered identity.

Murphy's (1998) analysis of flight attendants' forms of resistance in the face of disciplining discourses is precisely the sort of analysis that underscores the body politics of organizational life. Airline flight attendants work under panoptic conditions in which professional appearance, particularly for the female employees, is quite literally regulated. These women are surveilled by organizational disciplinarians, customers, and themselves. Specifically, female flight attendants are required to wear makeup and high heels and to conform to airline weight policies. However, flight attendants find a variety of "private" strategies to resist these constraining requirements. For example, one flight attendant wears the "required" makeup only during annual "appearance checks" (Murphy, 1998, p. 521). Flight attendants have also discovered "high-risk areas" where they are more susceptible to control and may be disciplined for breaking organizational rules. They "pass this information on to other flight attendants through their hidden transcripts, limiting the power of the panoptic gaze" (p. 522). Thus, attendants know to wear their high-heeled shoes only when they fly through a city in which supervisors are located. Finally, while many attendants appreciate and are compliant with the airlines' weight restrictions—because, as one woman explained, "without them I might blow up like a balloon"—others have learned how to "beat" the system by losing weight temporarily by ingesting laxatives and diuretics. The harmful consequences of this last resistance strategy notwithstanding, these women have found "private" ways to resist organizational gendered discourses and adopt alternative embodied identities. In so doing, "they enact fantasies of reversals, gain social support, and prepare themselves for possible entrance into the public realm" (p. 525). Indeed, the flight attendants' resistance ultimately led to a public challenge to and change in the airline's weight standard policy. Murphy's analysis suggests that embodied resistance practices can create a wider and broader range of subject positions available to professional women.

CONCLUSION

This chapter indicates that "I view our bodies as a site of struggle where we must work to keep our daily practices in the service of resistance to gender domination, not in the service of 'docility' and gender normalization" (Bordo, 1989, p. 28). A poststructuralist feminist analysis of women's embodied identities in organizational contexts works toward that goal by drawing attention to the ways in which women's bodies are inscribed with the often contradictory discourses of gender and professionalism. Women's professional bodies are a rich site at which important identity-forming yet contradictory experiences occur. Although women's bodies are often subordinated and devalued, individual women, through the appropriation of dress, style, and other signifying practices, can and do embody resistance to control, discipline, and normalization. How women take up and resist embodied identities in organizational contexts is an empirical question that demands investigation. Thus, the implications for organizational and managerial communication researchers are clear: We must empirically examine how women both take up and resist gendered and professional discourses in everyday organizational practices, and we must describe the constraining and enabling effects of those bodily displays for organizational actors. After all, it is only with a "knowledge of the complex political dimensions of discursive practices that we are able to cope with, understand, and facilitate our public and private lives" (Wendt, 1995, p. 292).

Poststructuralist feminist empirical investigations of women's embodied identities and the disciplinary regimes that attempt to contain and control them would contribute to organizational and managerial communication scholarship in three ways. First, such studies would articulate the ways in which the specific relationships between organizational discourses and their attendant micropractices create professional women's embodied identities as a means of organizational control and productivity (Mumby, 1993a). Second, they may suggest how women resist gendered discourses in professional contexts and, in so doing, offer alternative identity constructions of the "professional woman." Third, they would contribute to an important body of work in organizational communication that examines women's problematics from the perspective of women's experiences (Fine, 1993).[8] Empirical work is sorely needed in this area, and communication scholars are well positioned to address the disciplinary techniques of femininity, particularly in organizational contexts. Perhaps it is time for organizational and managerial communication scholars who are interested in and concerned about contemporary forms of control to work and struggle around a (revised) feminist rallying cry: "The body is political."

NOTES

1. Although certainly male bodies have long been the assumed "substance" on which control operates, the gendered implications of those forms of control have not often been explored.

2. Disciplinary practices operate on the body, but not exclusively so. The "body" is not, nor can it ever be, separated from the "mind." Indeed, the two are mutually constitutive. The disciplined body pulls the subject in its wake.

3. Despite these dangers, the relationship between the body and disciplinary power should not be conceived as simply a negative or repressive one. Rather, power (articulated in and through discourse) renders the body useful, productive, and "docile" (Foucault, 1979, p.138). The assembly line and the many contemporary organizational practices it spawned is an example of a disciplinary technique that calls for a regulated, efficient body. Historically, the assembly line extended the "collective bodies' capacity to produce. But it was also a new kind of tool. Rather than being subject to the body's rule, it subjugated the body into an extension of itself—a docile, useful body" (Deetz, 1992, p. 254). It is clear, then, that disciplinary power produces a particular kind of organizational identity, an always already embodied identity.

4. Though Young's (1990b) analysis is not a poststructuralist one, she does call for Foucauldian analyses of women's embodied practices that pay particular attention to the disciplinary regimes that position women's subjectivities in particular ways.

5. The 20 participants represented a variety of professions, including management consulting, mediation, auto repair, sales, banking, and human resources. All the women described themselves as professional. Nearly all the participants were Caucasian, with the exception of two Latina participants. Their ages ranged from early 20s to early 60s. The participants chose their own pseudonyms.

6. For a more complete discussion on women's "leakages," see Trethewey (1999).

7. I recognize that "femaleness" is a discursive construction. Femaleness or femininity has long been discursively linked with the body and nature. It is on biological differences, such as menstruation and reproductive labor, that the "edifice of gender inequality is built and legitimized" (McNay, 1992, p. 17).

8. The previous discussion has focused on women's embodied identities exclusively. I contend that the pressures to achieve and display the ideal gendered body affect women in more profound ways than the pressures that affect men. Although it is beyond the scope of this chapter, it is important to recognize that men's bodies are disciplined as well. Indeed, we see increasing evidence that marketers are making a deliberate effort to translate concern for personal appearance into a directly masculine context (in advertisements for skin creams, hair treatments, and even penile extensions). Success, achievement, physical fitness, efficiency, competition, and managing and controlling one's self-presentation are all themes used to make personal appearance a significant component of masculinity in advertisements for men's cosmetic products. To feel good about oneself, soon it will not be enough to be a successful achiever. A man will also have to look young, energetic, and healthy. What man will not find himself lacking when he measures himself against these new role models?

6

Walking the High Wire

Leadership Theorizing, Daily Acts, and Tensions

Marlene G. Fine
Patrice M. Buzzanell

Marlene's Final Diary Entry

I've accepted the new position. It's a wonderful opportunity for me—recognition of my academic work, a chance to spend more time at home with the boys (without giving up my salary and benefits), and a culture that values people. So why do I feel so conflicted? I think because I believe I failed here. I tried to lead by serving—and I failed. Failed—not to serve. I think I served well. But I failed to convince those above me that I was exercising leadership. I remained invisible to those above me. And, at the same time, I think I scared them. I suppose because they couldn't comprehend my way of leading—or, more accurately, my way of being. Powerless and powerful. The paradox of leadership as serving. Especially if you're a woman.

AUTHORS' NOTE: We would like to thank Beth Haslett and Marlene's reading group (Isolde Anderson, Lisa Cuklanz, Valeria Fabj, Lynn O'Brien Hallstein, Mary Marcel, and Anne Mattina) for their comments on this chapter.

Current organizational literature, both popular and academic, is rife with new conceptions of leadership. Although much of what is called new is simply old ideas presented in new language, several of these current conceptions do reflect a new vision of leadership, one that expands the leader's role beyond achieving the instrumental goals of the organization to achieving individual and/or community social ends. Each of these new conceptions contains elements of leadership as serving.

In this chapter, we describe and critique some current conceptions of leadership, offer a feminist revisioning of leadership as serving, and explore the tensions inherent in enacting leadership through serving others. Our analysis is based on our own experiences as academic administrators, managers, editors, and faculty members and is supported by diary entries that chronicle our daily lives. These diary entries reflect the essence rather than the details of our lives; people and events have been altered. We do not believe, however, that those alterations materially affect our analysis. The diary entries may not *be* true, but they *tell* the truth.

The original impetus for our analysis was Marlene's recent experience as an academic administrator. Our analysis, therefore, focuses on the exercise of leadership in an academic setting. Although the particular situations and roles vary in other organizational settings, we believe that the feminist revisioning we offer and the paradoxes inherent in it are applicable across male-defined organizations.

DEFINING LEADERSHIP

Traditionally, leadership, management, and administration are defined in mutually exclusive ways: *Leadership* is the process of externally articulating visions that challenge organizational identity and change; *management* is what translates that vision internally; and *administration* is the science of developing standardized and routine practices and constructs applicable to all members in every organization (Bryman, 1996; Clegg & Hardy, 1996; Frick & Spears, 1996; Kotter, 1990; Yukl, 1989; Zaleznik, 1977). Such role divisions are found throughout organizational literature, with the most telling division being that which bifurcates those who have the formal and/or informal power to lead, manage, and administer from those who do not. The conventional role of managers, administrators, and supervisors is to ensure conformance to established modes of doing work. Those who enact this role are named "enforcers of rules," and routine behavior is made into "a power game" in which various players and influencers seek to control organizational decisions and acts (Mintzberg, 1983), with adversarial interactions commonplace (Buzzanell, 1994). Leadership literature also has replicated divisiveness in organizational relationships by identifying leaders and followers, then concentrating research on the former (Burns, 1978; Sims & Manz, 1996).

Marlene's Diary Entry: February 15

Budget time again. I've decided to ask for a new budget line to provide internal grants for faculty development. I've had so many requests over the last two years, and there's no source of funding available on campus.

Marlene's Diary Entry: March 15

Met with Y to talk about my budget. I'm shocked—he approved most of what I requested. He didn't approve the faculty development funds, however. He's not opposed to having a pool of money available for faculty development projects. He just doesn't want to offer the funds. He said faculty development funds are a bargaining unit issue; let the faculty bargain for them—and, of course, give up something else in return. It's all a game to see how much control he (actually "we"— I think he thought he was instructing me on how to be a good administrator) can exert over the faculty. And I naively thought we were driven by our mission to educate students.

Numerous authors have described the gendered nature of organizations, organizational roles, and organizing processes (e.g., Acker, 1990, 1992; Buzzanell, 1994; Court, 1997; Ferguson, 1984; Fondas, 1997; Kanter, 1977; Mills & Tancred, 1992). These descriptions point to the organizational structures and practices that not only highlight men and marginalize women but also value male modes of thinking, feeling, acting, and forming identities while devaluing their female counterparts (Buzzanell, 1995; Fine, 1993; Kanter, 1977; Marshall, 1993). These gender identities are constructed out of a complex mix of experiences in the physical world, social relationships and activities in which men and women are engaged, and cultural stereotypes that are socially imposed and personally internalized. The research literature is divided on whether each gender constitutes its own culture (and speech community), with characteristic modes of thinking, feeling, and behaving (Gilligan, 1982; Johnson, 1989; Tannen, 1990, 1994; Wood, 1999), or whether people form relationships in which they, often unconsciously, replicate societal power struggles and gendered workplace interactions (Ashcraft, 1998; Ashcraft & Pacanowsky, 1996). Regardless of cause or rationale, however, hierarchical patterns of accomplishing work are replicated and valued in organizational communication and managerial constructs and practices such as management, administration, and leadership.

Although many writers distinguish among the terms, the boundaries between leadership, management, and administration have been blurred (Clegg & Hardy, 1996). Because there is overlap among the terms, we use leadership, management, and administration synonymously throughout this chapter but recognize that there are differences in communicative priorities among these processes.

Our goal is to revision administration, management, and leadership as serving through a revisionist/revalorist feminist analysis that recognizes that *both* feminine (e.g., care, nurture, interdependence, relationship, inclusion) and masculine (e.g., agency, autonomy, separation, instrumentality) approaches and ways of knowing have value depending on a given situation (Buzzanell, 1994; Marshall, 1993). Revisionist and poststructuralist feminists often rewrite traditional masculine passages to incorporate the missing half so that rationality, organizational goals, and autonomy do not supersede emotionality, relational priorities, and connection (e.g., Calás & Smircich, 1992). In these analyses, ways of maintaining tensions among differing values and approaches can be brought to the forefront of theorizing and practice.

We suggest that the role of the academic administrator (or manager) is more productively conceived of as serving the faculty and students (or multiple stakeholders, particularly employees). On the most basic level, serving means doing things for others that enable them to do their jobs; serving means taking obstacles out of employees' way rather than putting them up.

Marlene's Diary Entry: August 15

*J just returned from a conference in D.C. He met a FIPSE
(Fund for Post Secondary Education) funder who loved our
digital culture project; he said FIPSE has a call out
for proposals for training projects related to the use
of technology. The deadline is in one month. Don't know if
we can pull something together that fast, but we'll try.*

Marlene's Diary Entry: August 20

*We spent the last week brainstorming some ideas for a faculty
development project that would complement the digital culture
project. We've come up with an approach, but J is traveling
over the next two weeks—presenting papers at two conferences
and trying to finish his book manuscript. I'm going to do the
first draft of the proposal, and we'll work on editing via
e-mail.*

Marlene's Diary Entry: August 22

Went to talk with Y to tell him about the proposal and alert him that we'd need him to review it. I brought the budget for him to look at so we could see if we had any financial problems that we needed to work out before doing the final revisions. Y hit the ceiling. Wanted to know why we waited so long to get the proposal ready. I tried to explain that we just found out about the call for proposals, and we were working as quickly as we could to get it together. He refused to listen. Said he couldn't take the time on such short notice to review anything for us. I'm fuming.

Marlene's Diary Entry: August 24

I've been stewing over Y's refusal to review the proposal. That means he won't sign off on it either. Don't know what to do—it's a terrific idea and we need faculty development funds for new technology.

Marlene's Diary Entry: August 27

Have made an executive decision. I've reconfigured the budget so that nothing in it requires institutional support. Since I have the authority to sign off on grants that don't affect the institution's budget, I'm going to sign the proposal and not have Y review it. I'd much rather have everyone knowledgeable about the proposal—and I'd like to know that what we're proposing fits the institution's priorities—but I'm not going to let someone's attitude about hierarchy and deadlines stand in our way.

Serving means more than just enabling others; it is also an ethical vision that creates what is worthy in life, develops avenues for living the vision, and revisits this core vision continuously (see Haney, 1994; Mattson & Buzzanell, 1999). Like corporate visions, feminist organizational communication visions are images or ideas of more attractive organizational futures (Nanus, 1992). As such, serving encompasses different types of change: first order (incremental), second order (cognitive framework and shared schemas that give meaning to activities), and third order (transconceptual mode of understanding in which schemas are innovated and developed continuously; see Bartunek & Moch, 1994). By encompassing these three orders of change, serving provides a way to blur the boundaries between leadership, management, and administration. To serve is to articulate, translate, and implement organizational visions that challenge the gendered organizational values, beliefs, and behaviors that pervade organizational life.

To revision leadership as serving, we first discuss our feminist commitments and analytic method, then provide an overview of some leadership theories that incorporate different notions of serving, and finally offer our feminist revisioning as one (not the only) means of accomplishing transformational change and guiding leadership action.

FEMINIST COMMITMENTS AND ANALYTIC METHOD

Although feminisms vary along ideological positions and across academic disciplines, they share particular epistemological and methodological commitments: (a) ways of knowing, (b) feminist problematics, (c) feminist synalytics, and (d) revolutionary pragmatism (see Fine, 1993). Numerous feminist scholars have argued that women (and some men) come to understand the world in ways that are distinct from traditional *ways of knowing* (Belenky, Clinchy, Goldberger, & Tarule, 1986; Gilligan, 1982; Goldberger, Tarule, Clinchy, & Belenky, 1996; Keller, 1985). One of the most often acknowledged ways of knowing for women is subjective knowledge, which locates the place of truth within the individual and equates the scientific with the personal. Rather than looking to authority or theory for understanding, women learn through direct experience, personal relationships, subjectivity, and passion (Belenky et al., 1986).

Women's ways of knowing, particularly subjective knowing, often are at odds with the rationalistic approach to understanding and decision making that forms the foundation of U.S. management theory and practice. We use the term *rationalistic* rather than *rational* because the assumption that management theory and practice are rational (i.e., that the exercise of reason provides the only valid basis for action or belief) is not always realized. Decisions may be enacted in a rational style (e.g., impersonal, distant, or dispassionate), conveyed in rational or bureaucratic forms (e.g., argumentative discourse that provides a rationale for the decision or standardized written memos), or provided through expert or technical discourse (e.g., statistics or expert testimony), but these decisions still may not be rational when compared with members' lived experiences and values (see Clair, 1993a).

Personal experience in organizations, therefore, becomes valid and admissible data to use in understanding how organizing happens. Data can be presented in the form of a diary (i.e., personal recollections of people, events, feelings, and actions), as we do here. The epistolary form has long been associated with women's writing and historically has been marginalized as private musings rather than public rhetoric (Foss & Foss, 1991; Wertheimer, 1997). We chose this format to present our data to underscore the feminist nature of our inquiry.

Besides ways of knowing, feminist research also differs from other critical investigations by generating its *problematics*—conceptual schemes organized around central ideas—from the perspective of women's experiences (Harding, 1987). Problematics provide coherence in that researchers work on specific issues within core problems (Reed, 1992), such as women's trivialization and subordination in the workplace. Feminist organizational communication theory strives to understand how gender is constructed through discourse and practices so that traditional gender dynamics remain unchanged within contexts of messages, structures, policies, and procedures (i.e., the contexts in which gender is socially negotiated; Buzzanell, 1994).

Marlene's entries chronicle her dissatisfaction with administrators' responses to faculty and student needs, her presumed role as enforcer of rules, and faculty's and students' views that she should be a solver of problems (i.e., that she should find ways to negotiate the rules—and sometimes bend or skirt them—to accomplish their goals). She finds it more satisfying to help people solve their problems and believes that the university mission is better met when she solves problems rather than enforces rules without regard to the particular ends that students and faculty were trying to achieve.

Marlene's Diary Entry: November 10

T, a grad student who was awarded a prestigious fellowship when she was accepted, came by to see me yesterday. Apparently, she was led to believe by her department chair that the fellowship would pay her entire tuition for the length of her program. The financial aid office has informed her that the award is capped at a fixed amount each year; they've sent her a bill for $2,000. She doesn't have the money to pay it. If she doesn't pay immediately, they've threatened to withdraw her for nonpayment of fees. She's very upset. I promised to look into the situation.

Marlene's Diary Entry: November 11

As usual, no one has any answers. Financial aid says they got their instructions from the development office. The development office has no description of the fellowship available for students or faculty. They did promise to send me the legal documents that set up the endowment. I also talked with R, the department chair, who insists that the student is correct. The chair knew the individual who donated the money and said he intended to pay the full amount of the tuition. In any case, the chair confirmed that the student was told orally when she received the award, and before she decided to accept our offer, that her tuition would be fully paid.

Marlene's Diary Entry: November 13

T came by with a copy of a short note that R sent to financial aid when T was admitted. It does seem to imply that she was to receive full tuition. Of course, no one sent her an official award letter, so she has no direct evidence to support her allegation. I also received the legal documents from the development office today. What a jumbled mess. I don't have any idea what the donor intended or what the development office agreed to. My bottom line, however, is that the student shouldn't be penalized for our confusion and misinformation.

Marlene's Diary Entry: November 15

I've sent a memo to R and to President Z explaining the situation and saying that the student should not be penalized. I asked Z to have student accounts erase the bill so that the student's status would not be at risk. Then we could figure out who should cover the shortfall—the department or the development office. Of course, this is all complicated by the fact that Z and R can't stand each other.

Marlene's Diary Entry: November 17

No answer from anyone.

Marlene's Diary Entry: November 23

T came by again. She received another bill from student accounts. I called over to the student accounts office and talked with the director. Asked him to clear her account and explained that the president and I would find a way to cover the shortfall. He refused. Said he couldn't take the risk; his accounts had to balance. I sent another e-mail to Z asking for help.

Marlene's Diary Entry: November 25

Still no response.

Marlene's Diary Entry: December 5

Z came storming into my office today and shut the door. Wanted to know why I was supporting T against the institution; said T was out to get something from the college. Z is convinced that T and R are conspiring. I assured Z that T was an excellent student who appeared entirely trustworthy; I also said that T's story was plausible and the evidence she had, although not absolutely clear, did strongly suggest that her interpretation was warranted. Besides, weren't we supposed to serve students? Z was furious with me.

Marlene's Diary Entry: December 10

Still no resolution. T is about to graduate; she won't get her diploma unless this situation is resolved.

Marlene's Diary Entry: December 11

I called the director of student accounts today. Told him to clear T's bill; if Z or R doesn't pay, I'll transfer the money from my office and worry about the consequences later. What a ridiculous waste of time and effort. And we all look so foolish and inept to the student and her parents.

Marlene's diary also conveys her sense of unease with the assumption that, to be successful, women need to conform to masculine norms of behavior in their professional lives.

Marlene's Diary Entry: September 15

I was listening to a radio interview with the screen-writer and producer of GI Jane this morning. She was asked about the character played by Anne Bancroft in the film—a senior-ranking senator who does an abrupt about-face on her support for women in the Navy SEALS. In response to a question about whether a woman would behave as the character did, the screenwriter said that successful women have to play

*hardball. She later commented that women who want to join
the special forces should be held to the same performance
standards as men and be expected to endure the same training.
But that presumes that playing hardball and enduring
physical, verbal, and mental abuse are the way that we want
to conduct our lives. I don't want to play hardball—at
least not in the metaphorical sense—I enjoy playing when
I have my bat and glove.*

Patrice experienced similar conflicts and tensions about her purpose and the expectations for enacting her role when she was a credit manager.

Patrice's Diary Entry: June 13

*I'm reading Marlene's diary entries about contradictions,
ambivalences, doing something meaningful, wanting to be
recognized but also wanting to work behind the scenes by
helping others, believing that my work is teaching whether
I am acting as an editor, adviser, manager, or consultant.
I remember my work as a credit manager. I remember hearing
that I wouldn't make money on the collection desk even when
I had tracked down "deadbeats" and had a persistent debt
collection style. I was too nice, I didn't raise my voice,
I wasn't supposed to help "them." This was a business, and I
should get my head out of the clouds and down to real life.*

*But I viewed my work as twofold—I was supposed to
collect debts and I was supposed to listen and develop
connections with debtors and explain credit, collection
listings, finances, and credit bureau reports. I thought I
was supposed to assist and educate them. So no one expected
my desk to bring in money. I got a lot of pleasure when
reading my stats. But I felt ambivalence because my work
educating our customers should have been valued whether or
not it brought in money on a short-term basis. There was
something dissatisfying about demanding payment when these
people didn't have money for food and didn't know how to dig
themselves out of a bad financial situation. No one said
anything about my stats—I hadn't achieved these results the
"right" way.*

The ambivalences, tensions, and paradoxes of trying to meet stakeholder needs, especially in bureaucracies, are reflected in our work experiences and conversations. Marlene has shared her frustrations with other female senior administrators and has found that they, too, feel similarly constrained.

In addition to women's ways of knowing and problematics, our chapter is guided by *feminist synalytics,* the combining of analysis and synthesis to create new understandings and visions of phenomena that can replace traditional definitions (Fine, 1993). This movement from analysis through synthesis brings together the personal and the political. Feminist synalytics looks for the connections in women's experiences and breaks the artificial boundaries around personal, organizational, and cultural life. Organizational communication behaviors are analyzed and synthesized not just within the organization but within a sociopolitical framework that is external to the organization. In our case, personal experiences in organizations not only serve as the data on which the analyses of organizations rest; they are also contextualized in the larger world outside of the organization. In other words, this analytical frame extends beyond the structural and behavioral elements of the particular organizations in which we have worked to the social, political, and economic arrangements that constitute the cultural world in which organizations are situated. Key to understanding the power of using the metaphor of serving to (re)define administration is recognizing the gendered nature of organizations and the ways in which workplace gender relations both represent and reproduce gender dynamics and power distributions in the culture generally.

The final feminist commitment that underlies our analysis is *revolutionary pragmatism.* Feminist researchers study organizations so that they can create organizations that allow all people to fully express their human potential. Feminisms are committed to understanding women's subordination so that they can figure out how to change it (Gordon, 1979). Our commitment is revolutionary because it is about fundamental social change; our commitment is pragmatic because those changes are the everyday practices of our lives. Feminist organizational communication studies achieve revolutionary pragmatism through praxis, the synthesis of theory and practice in ways that transform personal experience and consciousness (Mumby & Stohl, 1996).

Reframing administration as serving is intended to redefine an organizational construct in a way that has immediate, concrete, and positive consequences for people in academic institutions. Although we use the context of administration in higher education, the image of serving cuts across organizational types and is consistent with contemporary management writings on leadership, management, teams, and change that encourage coaching, interdependence, and relationship formation as ways of accomplishing work and achieving multiple-stakeholder goals (Fondas, 1997). After providing an overview of leadership approaches that contain the idea of serving, we demonstrate the limits of traditional models of administration, management, and leadership to uncover the productive power of a feminist vision of serving.

OVERVIEW OF CURRENT APPROACHES
TO LEADERSHIP AND SERVING

The idea of serving others is embedded in several current theories of leadership, both mainstream and alternative. In this section, we briefly outline and critique several examples of each. Although some of these perspectives, especially gendered leadership and Greenleaf's (1977) servant leadership, approximate our feminist image of leadership, none fulfills it. No perspective deals adequately with the ethical issues that prompt women (and men) to infuse their careers and lives with images of serving. With the exception of discussions about double binds and paradoxes experienced by women leaders and female organizing processes (e.g., Jamieson, 1995; Sullivan & Turner, 1996; Wood & Conrad, 1983), these approaches cannot describe or resolve the contradictions, ambivalence, and tensions found in a feminist revisioning of serving.

Current Mainstream Approaches to Leadership

There are several streams of current theory and research that contain aspects of leadership as serving. In this section, we summarize the three that seem most consistent with notions of serving others: (a) adaptive leadership, (b) transformational leadership, and (c) self-leadership and SuperLeadership.

Adaptive Leadership

In adaptive leadership, leaders serve followers by assisting them through difficult times (Heifetz, 1994; Heifetz & Laurie, 1997). The adaptive challenge is to keep followers focused on key issues while regulating stress so that followers experience distress and uncertainty within bearable limits. Ultimately, leaders shift responsibility to followers and other stakeholders.

The primary question that drives a leader to assume adaptive leadership is *"Does making progress on this problem require changes in people's values, attitudes, or habits of behavior?"* (Heifetz, 1994, p. 87). Instead of providing solutions, leaders manage tensions so that followers realize that they need to adopt new roles, values, and approaches. These leaders are not omniscient and require assistance and support in making sense of complex situations (Weick, 1995). As its name suggests, adaptive leadership focuses on leaders' abilities and care in adapting information to specific contexts. Adaptive leadership assumes that leaders know what is best for followers, regulate information flow, and can be evaluated on whether interventions result in more effective processes and outcomes. In adaptive leadership, leaders "serve" followers by managing tensions and potential stressors *for* followers while building competencies in them so that they can direct their own lives in the future. This "serving" is problem- and information-centered.

Transformational Leadership

Transformational leadership is similar to adaptive leadership in that it is problem oriented. However, it focuses on the actions of leadership that create common aspirations geared toward performance enhancement (Bryman, 1996). Transformational leadership develops self and others in that it

> looks for potential motives in followers, seeks to satisfy higher needs, and engages the full person of the follower. The result of transforming leadership is a relationship of mutual stimulation and elevation that converts followers into leaders and may convert leaders into moral agents. (Burns, 1978, p. 4)

Transformational leaders generally are charismatic, inspiring, stimulating, and considerate (see Barge, 1994; Bryman, 1996). Because of these personal qualities, the transformational leader-follower relationship can be enabling or empowering because it capitalizes on enthusiasm for work and shifts wisdom, direction, risk taking, innovation, and involvement to followers (Manz & Sims, 1989; Sims & Manz, 1996). Empowerment means that followers feel as though they are doing something of significance, are developing competencies, and are joined with a community of others through a common purpose (Bennis & Nanus, 1985). However, "empowerment" is still influenced by leaders who use the relationship as a means of gaining greater productivity and of producing innovative ideas. Although workers' intrinsic rewards are developed by leaders who serve them, the vision is organizationally driven, not inner-, value-, or community-directed.

Self-Leadership and SuperLeadership

Building on ideas of leader-follower relationships that empower followers, Sims and Manz (1996) developed follower-centered approaches in their self-leadership and SuperLeadership constructs. Self-leadership is both a philosophy and a systematic set of behavioral and cognitive strategies for leading oneself to higher performance. Effective leaders direct the ways that they and others influence themselves so that both can shift from dependency on leadership to dependency on self and others. In other words, self-leaders serve themselves and others by advocating that followers become responsible for their actions and dependent on others only for assistance in their problem solving.

SuperLeaders teach ordinary people to be self-leaders through a set of skills for influencing behavior and thought and for structuring situations and rewards so that optimal performance can be achieved (Sims & Manz, 1996).

"Super" means both that leaders possess the strength and wisdom of many and that they oversee organizing processes (Sims & Manz, 1996). SuperLeaders capitalize on each person's potential and "devote significant effort to deliberately orchestrate an organizational culture for high performance and development of people" (Manz & Sims, 1989, p. 167). As are other managerial approximations of "serving," self-leadership and SuperLeadership are geared toward organizational ends, with leaders guiding others through processes that promise greater effectiveness.

Alternative Approaches to Leadership

In contrast to traditional approaches, alternative approaches that incorporate notions of serving either offer a gender-based leadership approach or focus on the solitary journey toward one's spirituality in the workplace (as well as ways to guide others in their search for wholeness). Neither approach encourages resistance to organizational practices nor managerial outcomes (see Buzzanell et al., 1997, for discussion and cases on alternative leadership). Instead, they suggest choices in ways to lead (gendered leadership) and work toward a more caring society (servant leadership).

Gendered Leadership

Gendered leadership focuses on leadership styles in terms of feminine and masculine stereotypical expectations. Because masculine is synonymous with leadership (i.e., qualities of being direct, assertive, commanding, and powerful), discussions about gendered leadership often describe feminine leadership and how this style contrasts with normative leadership. Theories of gendered leadership emerged out of early research on gender and language (e.g., Lakoff, 1975; Spender, 1980; Thorne, Kramarae, & Henley, 1983). This early work identified linguistic indicators (e.g., tag questions, the use of hedges, inclusionary phrasing, and indirect requests) that seemed to characterize (white, middle-class) women's speech. These characteristics were judged weaker than male linguistic patterns, and women who were in, or aspired to, managerial positions were encouraged to emulate the masculine business style of direct and decisive speech (Harragan, 1977). Likewise, in leadership contexts, the preferred behavioral style has been masculine.

When the business world became recognized as global, multicultural, and team structured, however, feminine speech community characteristics offered another tool for accomplishing organizational goals. Feminine speech community characteristics included support displays, conversational maintenance work, relational prioritization, inclusivity, and incorporation of details (for a summary, see Wood, 1999). These characteristics translated into leadership styles known as feminine leadership (Rosener, 1990) and women's styles of leadership (Helgesen, 1990; see also Borisoff & Merrill, 1998).

In feminine leadership, leaders see themselves [as centrally positioned] and others operating in a communicative web (Helgesen, 1990). The web metaphor implies that these leaders create structures characterized by the embeddedness of work and life aspects, spontaneity, emotion expression, and inclusion. Leaders situate themselves at the heart of the activity rather than at the top, and they view their strength as being derived from connection and information sharing.

Servant Leadership

As with gendered leadership, aspects of serving are also located in Greenleaf's (1977; see also Fraker & Spears, 1996; Frick & Spears, 1996) servant leadership. Greenleaf defines leadership broadly:

> Everyone who feels responsible, who feels some obligation to help some part of society function a little better, or whose own creative urges prompt him or her to want to build something anew, is a leader. . . . The leader is one who goes out ahead to show the way. (as cited in Fraker & Spears, 1996, p. 96)

People lead because failure to do so when there is an opportunity denies wholeness and creative fulfillment. Greenleaf believes that servant leaders must begin as servants; otherwise, their motives for becoming servant leaders have less to do with service and more to do with others' expectations.

Greenleaf calls leaders to start with their souls—to take an inner journey that can lead to understanding the lives of the institutions they lead and the members who work in them (Fraker & Spears, 1996). Servant leadership embodies the search for meaning in life. This journey is a spiritual journey that begins with oneself and is marked by increasing autonomy (Fraker & Spears, 1996). The quest for autonomy, wisdom, and authenticity drives servant leaders to transform society; that transformation, however, begins at the level of everyday practices. Greenleaf does not attempt to persuade others to become servant leaders. He believes that, if they are persuaded in their own hearts about the value of change, they can better serve the community and create a more caring future (Fraker & Spears, 1996; Frick & Spears, 1996; Greenleaf, 1977).

In short, servant leadership occurs when able, authentic individuals or institutions take the responsibility of nurturing others to create a more humane society (Frick & Spears, 1996). Servant leaders are autonomous and answer to their convictions. Both leaders and followers share in the ever-present and lonely search for wholeness. The aloneness of the journey to the humane society and to vision creation is expressed in Greenleaf's diaries and essays: "The search is a lonely affair. Beyond the few with whom I share individually, I have found it so" (as cited in Fraker & Spears, 1996, p. 291). This sense of aloneness also is evident in management writings on spirituality and trans-conceptual understanding in the workplace (see Bartunek & Moch, 1994; Ettore, 1996; Laabs, 1995; Mirvis, 1997; Neal, 1997).

Critique of Mainstream and Alternative Approaches to Leadership as "Serving"

Although each of these approaches represents, in some critical way, a departure from previous theories of leadership, each remains primarily male-centered. Each perspective characterizes leaders as agents directing action toward instrumental goals (e.g., to enhance productivity, to increase follow-ers' skills or potential, to share information for the development of the indi-vidual and/or project, and to actualize corporate or societal visions that lead-ers create). Even in feminine leadership, instrumental outcomes primarily determine the effectiveness and usefulness of the leadership style; relation-ship maintenance is a secondary goal. Each approach also focuses on the rela-tionship between leader and follower as the necessary link for effecting change. With the exception of gendered leadership, these approaches indicate that leaders move followers (and themselves) from dependence on leadership to greater autonomy under the guidance of and in the direction advocated by leaders.

The leadership approaches summarized in this chapter are "manstories" (see Gergen, 1990; Marshall, 1989); they involve often solitary searches for fulfillment and use service to others as a means of developing followers who can assist in achieving organizational or societal goals. Again, feminine lead-ership is the exception here. It does not present a solitary search, although the leader does guide information sharing. In all of these approaches, the leader is anyone willing and able to accept the leadership challenge.

These approaches also gloss over issues of gender differences (with the exception of gendered leadership). For example, Greenleaf (1977) universal-izes the experience of seeker, maintains organizational structures, and never questions the ways in which gender relations may make servant leadership a very different process for women and for men. On the other hand, although gendered leadership acknowledges gender as central to understanding leader-ship, it essentializes women (i.e., prescribes behaviors and expectations for all members) by implying that all women would use feminine leadership approaches similarly (see Wood, 1999).

Furthermore, gendered leadership discussions revolve around equality (i.e., females and males are more similar than different; females and males should be treated similarly) or difference (i.e., females and males have differ-ent styles, values, and approaches that often seem to operate as two separate cultures; females and males should be treated differently; Calás & Smircich, 1993; Lorber, 1994; Scott, 1988; Wood, 1999). Gendered leadership discussions do detail the difficulties that women have in navigating the contradictory directives imposed by others' (and, perhaps, their own) expectations, stereotypes, and judgments (e.g., Borisoff & Merrill, 1998; Haslett, Geis, & Carter, 1993). By being tied to feminine values and caught in equality-difference dualisms, however, feminine leadership lacks direction for the tensions, double binds, and paradoxes that women leaders face and that are described in Marlene's and Patrice's diary entries. The gendered leadership approach focuses on women's problematics but cannot offer a pragmatic approach for dealing with those problematics. Greenleaf (1977) also acknowledges tensions, albeit tensions that appear to grow out of male rather than female experience. He describes choices about whether and how to search and the beliefs in oneself that provide courage in times of doubt; he reflects on the certainty that grows through reflection and the growth in values and skills such as caring, self-development, and listening (Fraker & Spears, 1996).

Servant leadership and feminine leadership also fail to meet feminist commitments in that both have political implications but are not activist in the sense of a feminist leadership approach. Feminine leadership promotes stereotypical female values and ways of doing work as superior to more traditional values and behaviors, but it does not urge change for the betterment of women (and members of other traditionally underrepresented groups) as a feminist leadership approach would advocate. Similarly, servant leadership does not posit organizational transformation as a goal. Instead, Greenleaf (as cited in Fraker & Spears, 1996) defines the effectiveness of servant leadership in terms of the servant leader's ability to work within institutions as they are:

> The effectiveness of servants in nurturing the human spirit will be determined by how well they manage their lives and their serving under the constraints and opportunities of life in institutions as they are—all kinds and qualities of institutions. In order to serve, most of us will need to contend with bureaucratic inertia, as I did all of my active life. Yet on balance, I believe I was able to serve more effectively, working through institutions as they are, than if I had functioned alone and without such support as I had from the institutions through which I worked. (p. 186)

In sum, although each of the leadership approaches we have described, to a greater or lesser degree, contains some elements of the conception of leadership embodied in Patrice's and Marlene's experiences and reflections, none completely captures it. In our feminist revisioning of leadership as serving, we use previous writings as starting points and expand their boundaries. We first uncover the tensions inherent in a feminist revisioning and then use these tensions to create a vision of leadership that has the potential for radical organizational change that can benefit women and members of other marginalized groups.

FEMINIST REVISIONING OF SERVING

Marshall (1989) describes revisioning as "not rejecting the heritage we have but looking for the functions and creative potential of female and male patterns of being, especially drawing from archetypal understanding to go beyond the limits of social stereotypes" (p. 277). Revisioning begins with a critique of exclusionary underpinnings and male-centered assumptions within an approach, such as leadership as serving. It then rethinks constructs and linkages among conceptual elements by respecting aspects of women's lives that do not conform to traditional patterns and by acknowledging the "potentially destructive elements of the female principle" (Marshall, 1989, p. 278). In revisioning, nontraditional values are considered equally as important as some traditional values, so theorists could, for example, incorporate connectedness and individualism, caring and self-interest, intuition and reason, and female and male within a leadership approach. In revisioning, the limiting nature of traditional constructs and theories is challenged by redrawing boundaries—by enlarging, enriching, and complicating terms—in ways that adhere to visions grounded in feminist epistemological and methodological commitments (i.e., ways of knowing, feminist problematics, feminist synalytics, and revolutionary pragmatism). Through feminist visions, feminist revisionists look anew at phenomena and refuse to accept the destructive nature of male-centered approaches (Rich, 1979; Sullivan & Turner, 1996).

To revision leadership as serving, we reopen a discussion of conventional and alternative approaches to leadership. We scrutinize these perspectives to lay bare the ways that constructs and roles such as servant, leadership, and feminine restrict and enable behaviors. We transcend dualisms (either/or) that devalue the female component and pose paradoxical situations for women in management, administration, and leadership.

Servant, Leadership, and Feminine

At first glance, the metaphor of serving does not appear particularly feminist. In fact, it appears oxymoronic to feminism. According to the *Compact Edition of the Oxford English Dictionary* (1971), *serve* means to be a servant or a slave, to perform a term of service under a master, to wait on, to be a servant of God, to offer praise and prayer to, to gratify, to labor for, to benefit, to be subordinate, to be used by, to be a means to, to help fulfill, to prompt, to set food before, to give alms to, to support something requisite. This list is problematic. First, the definitions point to a hierarchical relationship—to perform under a master, to be subordinate, to be used by, and to be a servant or a slave. Hierarchy is antithetical to feminist beliefs; it is linked to women's oppression in patriarchal society (e.g., Ferguson, 1984). Second, the definitions reveal a constellation of "feminine" behaviors: to wait on, to minister to the comfort of, to labor for, to be used by, and to gratify. Although these behaviors reflect many women's real experiences as mothers and partners, they also are part of a stereotypic vision of women, a vision created by a patriarchal society that helps sustain its social arrangements.

A feminist analysis of *servant, leadership,* and *feminine* reveals that these terms are paradoxical for women. Paradoxical messages simultaneously prohibit action, comment verbally and/or nonverbally to negate or contradict that prohibition, and preclude the receiver from leaving the situation either psychologically or physically (Wood & Conrad, 1983). Feminine servant leadership contains four central paradoxes: (a) juxtapositions of subordinate/servant and superordinate/served gain power for males but fulfill traditional (unvalued) roles for women; (b) qualities built into the servant leadership role are evaluated according to their instrumental worth, making most feminine ways of enacting servant leadership devalued; (c) implications that leaders can change styles easily to suit situations do not fit with the commitment to "serving" as a lifelong ethical process; and (d) women who successfully enact leadership as "serving" threaten the status quo.

Paradox 1

The most fundamental way that *feminine servant leadership* is paradoxical is that these terms build on *juxtapositions of subordinate/servant and superordinate/served that gain power for males but fulfill traditional (devalued) roles for white women and women of color.* Servant leaders put their followers' needs first. Servant leaders perform duties for the served, who are then freed to pursue more worthy activities. In the case of academic institutions, administrators who serve clear away bureaucratic clutter, leaving faculty free to make curricular decisions, pursue their research agendas, teach their classes, and control their discretionary time. Paradoxically, therefore, women who attempt to enact leadership by serving are acting in ways that are consistent with stereotypic women's roles. In addition, their role enactment downplays aspects of power generally associated with leadership. For example, in traditional definitions of leadership, leaders have superior qualities and hierarchical position that give their goals priority over the goals of others. Thus, women servant leaders reinforce traditional feminine stereotypes through both the actions they choose and those they eschew.

This paradox presents a true double bind for women (Wood & Conrad, 1983). Women who act as traditional leaders are often perceived unfavorably because they violate others' gendered expectations of them (e.g., women who act tough are bitches) or because their behaviors, which are similar or identical to men's behaviors, are evaluated differently because of their sex (e.g., he's assertive and she's aggressive; Borisoff & Merrill, 1998; Haslett et al., 1993; Sullivan & Turner, 1996). By reinforcing the qualities of servant in women's organizational roles, servant leadership functions within conventional gendered work (work delegated to women) and gender work (work confirming beliefs about women's natural tendencies and abilities) that affirm gender ideologies (belief systems about what is natural and normal for the sexes; Rakow, 1992).

On the other hand, men who lead by serving violate gender expectations and disavow gender ideologies. Yet, by standing apart from the malestream, they ironically function to strengthen male power. In short, for a male businessperson, such as Greenleaf, servant leadership seems to offer a "legitimate" opportunity to engage in caring behaviors and to recommend organizational courses of action, but for a woman, enacting servant leadership is unremarkable. She is feminine and caring (i.e., not competent); she is silent or unassertive about her own self-interests (i.e., not selfish or promotable to critical positions; see double binds and women's roles: Jamieson, 1995; Kanter, 1977; Wood, 1994). Analogous figures to Greenleaf's (1977) servant leader are Jesus Christ or Ghandi; analogous figures to female servant leaders are traditional wives and mothers.

Paradox 2

The second paradox is that *only those stereotypical qualities useful for organizations are built into a servant leadership approach while other (feminine) ways of enacting servant leadership are devalued.* Qualities that are useful are those that build organizational members' competencies and further the corporate vision; feminine qualities are tolerated if they enhance (or do not detract from) the organizational mission (see Calás & Smircich, 1993). Greenleaf (1977) may be nurturing and caring, but he assists the corporation in developing a coherent organizational vision. Greenleaf still is the expert in the leader-follower relationship for he fulfills the role of the person who enables because he himself has started on his quest to achieve wholeness. When he experiences doubt, he can appeal to a higher knowledge source—the Christian God.

Unlike feminist works that prioritize personal knowledge, contradictions, and discontinuities as the everyday elements of women's lives that give meaning and coherence to their lives (Marshall, 1989, 1995), Greenleaf (1977) regrets that his theory derives from intuition and contradiction rather than from logical processes:

I am faced with two problems. First, I did not get the notion of the servant as leader from conscious logic. Rather it came to me as an intuitive insight.... [Second,] just as there may be a real contradiction in the servant as leader, so my perceptual world is full of contradictions.... My good society will have strong individualism amidst community. It will have elitism along with populism. . . . Reason and intuition, each in its own way, both comfort and dismay me. (pp. 12-13)

Greenleaf sees expert and personal ways of knowing as oppositions that "comfort and dismay" him. Although he questions himself, he does not display these tensions to others: "In other words, I have kept myself under tight rein" (as cited in Fraker & Spears, 1996, pp. 281-282). For many women, expressing contradictions, tensions, and emotions to themselves and others is the very way that they grow and challenge traditional notions.

Marlene's Diary Entry: October 26

I attended a dinner before a campus event. As I sat at the dinner surrounded by members of the board of trustees and their friends, I found myself stepping outside of myself and observing the interaction. I realized that, even though I was engaged in lively conversation with several people, I was largely invisible in the gathering. I've stayed on the periphery of the stage because I've defined my role as one who features others.

Marlene's Diary Entry: April 8

The deans have been asked to write up our ideas about the future of higher education; it's for an article in the alumni magazine. One week turnaround. I don't have to do this, but if something does get published, it will be the first time that I've been mentioned. It will be nice to get some recognition.

Marlene's Diary Entry: April 15

I have a "photo shoot" tomorrow—candid shots to accompany the alumni magazine article. I guess this means they plan to quote me. I have such a love/hate relationship with this. I don't want to spend time doing it and I'm kind of embarrassed (I don't want to see the pictures!), but I'm also attracted to the idea of being featured in a story, of being recognized for my role on the campus.

Marlene's Diary Entry: July 3

I live with a constant tension between my desire to serve and my desire to have others serve me, between wanting to play my role on the margins and wanting to be the center of attention, between denying my place in the organizational hierarchy and being resentful when students, secretaries, and strangers presume to call me by my first name.

The tensions we experience are not either/or dilemmas or insecurities with decision making. Rather, they are the times when we confront the "dark" places of our souls and think through possibilities in our lives. These tensions or dark places are the shadows that reveal one's true soul, "a quality brought into being when we must face the sometimes painful and contradictory nature of our own experience" (Briskin, 1998, p. 174). In uncertain times, individuals seek meaning (Briskin, 1998; Greenleaf, 1977). In our present age, when most of us spend more hours at work than at anywhere else and many of us identify our primary interpersonal relationships in the workplace, we seek meaning through our work. Briskin (1998) argues that the meaning we seek, we find in our souls. Finding soul, however, requires confronting the shadow in each of us:

> We learn that we can be both this and that, tyrannical and empowering, just and unjust, altruistic and controlling, compassionate and cruel. The experience of one-dimensionality can give way to a creative polarity that provides the tension necessary for new learning and new approaches to living a more differentiated and psychologically richer life. The confrontation with shadow is the first tentative step we make toward reclaiming wholeness. (pp. 58-59)

In short, servant leadership does not adequately value and incorporate *both* reason and intuition, thinking and emotions, masculine and feminine, and public and private. Greenleaf's suspicion of "feminine" sides of dualisms does not seem to have been fully resolved over his lifetime, although he does approach dialectic (both/and) possibilities closer to the end of his long life (Fraker & Spears, 1996; Frick & Spears, 1996). However, much of his servant leadership bifurcates understandings so that aspects of women's experiences still are trivialized.

Paradox 3

The third paradox is that most leadership approaches that contain elements of serving also carry at least implicit notions that *leaders can change a style to suit a situation, but serving is a way of life that is not easily discarded or modi-*

fied. One can learn to become a self-leader and SuperLeader by following steps supposedly applicable to all potential leaders (see Manz & Sims, 1987, 1989; Sims & Manz, 1996). Women are cautioned to be careful about using feminine (and masculine) styles (see Haslett et al., 1993). But leadership as serving in Greenleaf's work and in a feminist revisioning is a way of life that cannot be so easily discarded. Serving is a conviction that one person can make a difference in the world and that every day offers opportunities for growth and development of self and community.

Marlene's Diary Entry: March 11

Talked with Patrice today. She says I sound as if I'm trying to find a comfortable, stable definition of myself in my role as an administrator. But she also said it's not the definition I'm really having trouble with; it's the struggle inherent in defining myself.

Patrice's Diary Entry: March 11

Talked with Marlene on the phone today. She seems to be struggling with the desire to do what is worthy in life and what is recognized by others as worthy of acclaim. I think she's arguing that this uneasy tension between self- and other needs cannot be resolved simplistically but is an ongoing confrontation of the self. Besides, serving is worthwhile, despite the pejorative connotations to many white, middle-class feminists. If we do not serve others, then we expect that those lesser than we will serve. If we do not serve others, we lose the joy of doing something for its own sake, for ourselves. We become self-absorbed and less community- and other-focused. We also lose the relational connections that can save us in times of self-doubt and career trouble. Why should they serve or give of themselves in our times of need when we couldn't do so for them?

Patrice's Letter to Marlene: March 12

I see your way of administrating as a form of resistance. And this is very feminist!!! You are challenging what we consider to be a worthy life, a good use of our time and energy, and a legacy. As we confront what is of value in life, we probably need to conclude that much of what we do is not of value. It is in caring, serving, developing others, enabling their

*growth, standing beside them to assist their maturation
that we achieve our own immortality. This is a lifelong
perspective that doesn't hit some people until they are
in midlife and doesn't mesh well with the immediate
gratifications, me-orientation, and merit procedures in
most universities. But it certainly fits within many
women's moral and life development.*

Paradox 4

The final paradox is that *women who successfully enact leadership as "serving" are threatening to the status quo*. They guard their selves and their integrity—despite knowledge that selfishness is "a cardinal sin given prevailing images of women" (Wood, 1994, p. 25)—and are willing to live with the consequences. They choose to serve and accept the possibility that their calling to higher service ("serving" the community) may be antithetical to position security; they are threatening because the organization has no hold over them. They have the peace of mind and connections to others that can sustain them during times when they realize that they must leave either their positions or unhealthy relationships. As Marshall (1995) found repeatedly in her interviews with women managers, the act of "leaving," "resigning," or "failing" is reframed as "moving on," or as actions taken with the awareness that those who move on can no longer function in an environment that does not honor who they are and who they wish to be. Women who lead by "serving" are threatening because they are willing to subvert the "normal" gendered social order and to live with the daily tensions and self-questioning that are inherent in a life led from feminist ethical principles (see Mattson & Buzzanell, 1999).

Marlene's Final Diary Entry: Continued

*At the farewell party for me, one of my male colleagues said
he admired my courage in recognizing when it was time to
leave. He made me realize that I'm at peace with my decision.
And even though I continue to struggle with my doubts and
contradictions, I'm at peace with who I am.*

In sum, four main paradoxes become apparent when we examine *servant, leadership,* and *feminine* together. These double binds occur: when women attempt to fulfill the roles of servant and served in contemporary servant leadership writings; when women realize that their hope that feminine qualities in servant leadership roles will be valued for themselves and not for their instrumental worth is illusionary; when women realize that the notion of feminine style as easily changed (i.e., taken on and off) to suit situational needs is not isomorphic with their own experiences of "serving" as a lifelong process and goal; and when women recognize the power of "serving" to threaten the status quo by living the daily confrontations with the shadow (the hidden recesses of everyone's souls). The community in which they find the courage to confront the shadow is a dialectic process of valuing relationships and meeting self- and other needs simultaneously (Buzzanell, 1995).

Feminist "Serving"

As we reclaim *serving* as a feminist term, we are "websters": women whose work is to weave—weavers of worlds and world-webs (Daly, 1987, p. xiii). In a different constellation of meanings, service is an honorable term that suggests providing gifts from the self and giving of oneself for the good of others in the *service* of some greater good. Using the Greek root word for service, *diakoneo,* which includes the office of helper *and* helped as agent, we invest serving or service with the accoutrements of both agent and agency to displace the harmful feminine characteristics. Those who serve are no longer servants or slaves bereft of the freedom to choose what they do. Just as hooks (1990) positions housework as a source and manifestation of giving, pride, and self-sufficiency, we see serving as a gift to self and others.

Marlene's Diary Entry: September 26

> *I feel brain-dead because all I ever do is push paper*
> *and talk to people about processing their forms. I don't*
> *have intellectual connections. This is the hardest part of*
> *the transition from faculty to administration—the*
> *intellectual loneliness.*

Marlene's Diary Entry: October 26

> *I've decided to ask faculty to come join me for an informal*
> *lunch once a month and just talk to me. I sent a memo about*
> *this lunch—they can come and talk about last night's football*
> *scores or the latest paper they are working on. I'm going to*
> *call this "food for thought." I guess that's kind of corny.*

Furthermore, we envision *serving* as a form of resistance that operates through dialectic processes to creatively incorporate the multiple commitments to self, others, community, and principles so that we serve *ourselves* with and through our connections with others. The tensions within this form of resistance include: reassessing whose needs are served, reconsidering whether serving empowers or makes different stakeholders vulnerable, and rethinking whether actions create a more equitable world for women.

Managers, administrators, and leaders who serve in our feminist re-visioning of service find themselves filled with the uneasy and exciting tensions of hopefulness (for fundamental change), strength (in the feminist vision), watchfulness (lest service become servitude), humbleness (in knowledge that the server is an instrument of change), and wonderment (at the passages of self, other, community, and principle growth). Serving becomes an active process of engagement in which all who choose these relationships enact *coserving* with mutual respect and choice. Serving does *not* embody the idea of balancing competing needs (which can focus us inward; see Fondas, 1995) but of sustaining the healthy competition among needs, approaches, and values. Dialectic approaches subscribe to the belief that "social life is a dynamic knot of contradictions, a *ceaseless interplay* between contrary or opposing tendencies" (Baxter & Montgomery, 1996, p. 3; see also Fairhurst, in press). Strategic responses to contradictions within serving sustain intersections between poles (e.g., served and server) and reframe serving (as a verb) to transcend dualisms within potential power imbalances (see Baxter, 1988; Baxter & Montgomery, 1996; Weick, 1995).

As we revision serving, we accept our own (and others') humanness. We recognize that it is unethical *not* to be engaged in serving. If we turn away from the silencing, trivializing, and wearing away of the potential of women (and men), from the violence against them, from their removal of dignity and the diminishing of their community, then we act unethically (see Mattson & Buzzanell, 1999). If we do *not* engage in decision making about our service that considers the vulnerabilities of multiple stakeholders—the generalized and the concrete "others" and those made invisible by our language and business priorities (see Haas & Deetz, this volume)—then we act unethically. If we fail to consider ourselves worthy of the very service we give to others, then we act unethically. If we do *not* act against the privilege that many white women experience in choosing whom (and when) to serve and do not make visible the double binds and paradoxes that women of color experience in serving (see Bell, Denton, & Nkomo, 1993; Calás, 1992; Williams, 1991), then we act unethically. Serving means that we lay claim to our lives.

Patrice's Diary Entry: October 12 (Columbus Day)

I feel very torn. I have hidden away from others—I have not picked up voice mail, e-mail, or snail mail for days. I have not gone into my office—and I can manage to do so because of my Tuesday-Thursday teaching schedule, with meetings on

Tuesdays, Wednesdays, and Thursdays. So I am working on the journal I edit and on this book. Yet I also feel as though I should be accessible to my students and colleagues. I find great enjoyment and pride in helping my students develop and find their career paths. I could lose myself in service to them, my university, my profession, my family, and my community. So I feel guilty about pulling back—but I feel awful when my other (solitary) work isn't done and when I am not doing things for me.

As I am writing, I hear Lisette's friends and the twins (Sheridan and Ashlee) in the background. Annie wants one of her first-grade friends to come and play. I'm trying to talk to Marlene on the phone about our chapter while Teddy is barking outside (why won't someone else let him in?) and Stanley and Trevor are meowing at me for attention and treats. Thank God that Robyn is at day care, Steve commuted to Northwestern today, and Brendan skipped out of the house. In a few minutes, I'll do another load of laundry and make sure that Lisette cleaned out Leon's cage (gerbil). Call waiting beeps—a grad student needs help on her research project. . . . I say a quick goodbye to Marlene and talk to my graduate student, . . . then I shut my bedroom-office door.

But I don't return to the passage I am writing. Instead, I sit and reflect for a long time about whether I am doing enough with my life in service to others . . . not just to my family, students, colleagues, and profession. . .but to others whose voices are silenced through assaults on their bodies, talk, and dignity. . . . I can't close my door on these thoughts.

Administration, management, and leadership as serving is an unsettling tension between self- and other needs that cannot be resolved simplistically. We cannot simply assert that serving is worthy and therefore we engage in these actions (Kolb, 1992), nor can we resolve our dilemmas by deciding to act in a nonserving/caring/relational mode because it is antithetical to gaining recognition and job security (Huff, 1990). Serving is a struggle and ongoing confrontation with oneself to move toward feminist transformation.

> *Marlene's and Patrice's Joint Diary Entry:*
> *Meeting During the October Conference*
> *for the Organization for the Study of*
> *Communication, Language, and Gender*

We feel like such hypocrites. Here we are trying to talk about ethical "serving," and we both feel as though we fall so short of these ideals. We can't be everything to everyone. We have to make decisions that will help us as individuals. We are not saints—definitely not!!! We both feel all-too-human tensions, ambivalences, and resentments about our roles.

How hard we struggle with "serving" in our lives. But even though we can't achieve the ideal, it is worth the struggle. How else could we face ourselves? How else could we be at peace with our decisions and be certain that the people we care about will be proud of those decisions? Perhaps that is all any of us can hope to achieve in our lives. And that's not a bad legacy to leave our children.

CONCLUSION

Rich (1979) writes that revisioning is "the act of looking back, of seeing with fresh eyes, of entering an old text from a new critical direction" (p. 35). Revisioning is fundamental in women's lives as women (re)write their histories and develop theories from their own lives. Rich continues by saying that revisioning

> is an act of survival. Until we can understand the assumptions in which we are drenched we cannot know ourselves. And this drive to self-knowledge, for women, is more than a search for identity: it is part of our refusal of the self-destructiveness of male-dominated society. (p. 35)

Serving embodies the search for personal meaning. The search for personal meaning holds a significance beyond the individual; recent work in the literature on leadership suggests a relationship between soul and the efficacy of leadership. Daft and Lengel (1998) ask whether leaders act from a commitment to the good of the community or from their own "anger, greed, jealousy, insecurity, or fear of failure" (p. 188). They conclude that the answer is less important than the self-awareness of the internal conflict:

Self-awareness brings out higher potential in both the leader and the led. Becoming whole means uniting with your essential self, which enables you to touch the higher potential in others. Associates then trust the vision, love what they do, think independently, express their creativity, and maintain the highest standards of honesty. They and the organization thrive. (pp. 188-189)

Those who serve infuse their work with spirituality, with desires to create wholeness and a better life for all (see Mirvis, 1997). Serving is transformative in that the communicative process seeks to continuously question the very frameworks or schemas that guide our lives. Each movement in understanding destroys past partial illusions and insights to enlarge a worldview that can encompass contradictions by suggesting an overarching unity (see Bartunek & Moch, 1994).

Briskin (1998) says that "in serving, there lies dual purpose: to offer help to another and attend to our own need for learning and growth" (p. 269). Through serving, we affect the lives of the people with whom we work—students, faculty, staff, the university community, and others. In this way, the transformations in our own micropractices can lead to transformations in the micropractices of others. Our resistance to prevailing (competitive and community-diminishing) norms of behavior in organizations leads to resistance by others and, thus, to a weakening of those norms. Furthermore, our public self-reflections about organizational micropractices, both inside and outside the organization, have the potential to lead to self-reflection by others. Self-reflection throughout the organization creates an organizational consciousness raising that can even more directly challenge the prevailing norms and lead to the development of strategies and practices that initiate "micro-emancipation" (Alvesson & Wilmott, 1992) within the organization.

As feminists, we want to control the way in which *serving* is used and reframe the term to mean what we want. We want to eliminate the self-destructive hierarchical nature of leadership and the self-victimizing nature of "caring for" others. We revision leadership, management, and administration as "serving" to enlarge the boundaries of possibilities, to complicate our language, and to repaint a landscape conducive to women's development and tendencies to blur boundaries between female and male, heart and mind, and intuition and rationality.

7

A Feminist Reframing of Stress

Rose's Story

Marifran Mattson
Robin Patric Clair
Pamela A. Chapman Sanger
Adrianne Dennis Kunkel

Shinji Masami worked as a design engineer at Hino Motors. He was responsible for making sure that all the auto parts fit together properly during final assembly of trucks produced by Toyota. The pressing deadlines caused Masami to work . . . 25% above the average hours worked in Japan and 42% above the hours in the United States. Typically, Masami would leave his home before 7 a.m. and return home around midnight. Although he complained of severe headaches and stomach pains, he forced himself to go to work. At age 37, he died of a brain hemorrhage at his office. (Steers & Black, 1994, p. 599)

Stories of stress, like the one above, have drawn the attention of scholars, who have initiated rigorous research programs to explore the implications of work-

AUTHORS' NOTE: We would like to thank Beth Ellis and an anonymous reviewer for their feedback on this chapter.

place stress in our everyday lives. These research endeavors have led to the discovery of intriguing findings that in turn give way to prescriptive measures for reducing stress. For example, a recent study conducted by Mittleman (as cited in Haney, 1998) and presented to the American Heart Association concluded that bosses who must meet critical deadlines or who have to fire subordinates double their risk of experiencing a heart attack.[1] In turn, the prescriptions for reducing the chances of having a heart attack mentioned controlling weight, blood pressure, and cholesterol; getting enough exercise; and not smoking (Haney, 1998). Although these prescriptions are all logical bits of advice, they do not follow directly from the findings of the study. That is, none of the prescriptive measures suggests altering the way we "do business" so that we do not have "high-pressure deadlines," which evidenced the strongest effect in the study (as cited in Haney, 1998, p. A1). In addition, there were no suggestions for changing the hiring and firing practices that are so common to American-based organizations (but are not necessarily the case worldwide or common to all American companies).

In an equally alarming report, Restak (as cited in Peterson, 1998) claims that the strain of stress literally causes brain damage. He argues that the hippocampus region of the brain that deals with memory and learning can be damaged as a result of high-stress living. The prescriptions that follow from this study include reframing stress so that tough situations are seen more as challenges. Once again, the onus for change is placed on the individual rather than on the way we organize our work practices. Hank (1997) notes the tendency of organizations, especially the medical community, to frame the solution for illness as largely patient-oriented. In her study of breast cancer advertising programs, Hank found that responsibility was placed squarely on the shoulders of the women who had been diagnosed with breast cancer. Little, if any, attention was given to the economic, political, and social contingencies that place many women in situations of stress that contribute to health risks.

Stressful situations cannot always be controlled by rethinking them as challenges. Stressful situations also cannot necessarily be altered by exercise and healthy diet. Furthermore, not all stress-related situations can be connected to what is generally described as "the workplace," which tends to separate the private from the public and to marginalize work activities that do not fit neatly into the stereotypical description of work (see Clair, 1996). For example, the following poem speaks of the stressful interruptions of the work of *mothering* on the work of *writing:*

> a child with untamable curly blond hair. i call her kia,
> pine nut person, & her eyes so open as she watches me try
> to capture her, as I try to name her. . .
> . . .what of the lonely 7 year old (7½ mommy!) watching tv
> in the front room? what of her?

what of yesterday when she chased the baby into my room & I
screamed
OUT OUT GET OUT & she ran
right out but the baby stayed,
unafraid. what is it like to have
a child afraid of you, your own
child, your first child, the one
who must forgive you if either of you are to survive. . .
& how right is it to shut her out of the room so I can write about her?
how human, how loving? how can
I even try to
: name her.

Alta's Momma: A Start on All the Untold Stories,
1971 (as cited in Olsen, 1965/1978)

The stress written about in this poem speaks volumes. The interruptions and demands of mothering when juxtaposed with a second endeavor, such as writing, all too often result in a frustrating tension between the two. The poet struggles with the stress, and so does her daughter. The child faces a mother who both reaches out and pushes her away. The stress becomes relational, no longer an isolated, individual phenomenon.

Certainly, this woman is not alone. Others have experienced similar stress. And having children is not necessarily a prerequisite for being interrupted or having to deal with stress. Women, in general, face the consequences of constant interruptions, many of which evidence a direct impact on women's lives. As Katherine Anne Porter wrote,

> You're brought up with the curious idea of feminine availability in all spiritual ways, and in giving service to anyone who demands it. And I suppose that's why it has taken me twenty years to write this novel; it's been interrupted by just [about] anyone who could jimmy his way into my life. (as cited in Olsen, 1965/1978, p. 216)

Stories of stress should not be isolated as the stories of male managers at auto body plants. Women's stories are far too often neglected by researchers, or, if they are included, the focus is usually on women at "work," where work means a paying job. If we are to reframe stress, then we must reframe work and we need to be open to the sequestered stories, the marginalized stories, or the stories of stress that are labeled as categories other than stress. For example, Hazell (1997) provides a gripping narrative in his Associated Press release that highlights the stress of mothering under adverse conditions. Although it became a public story, it was never discussed as a story of stress. This narrative represents one woman's struggles with motherhood that led her to the brink of suicide.

A CALL FOR HELP

A desperate "quivering voice" sent chills into the homes of the New Yorkers who had tuned in to listen to WCBS radio's *Ask the Mayor* call-in radio program. The audience was expecting to hear the usual discussions of such fairly mundane matters as the size of "potholes." Instead, to their surprise, they listened as the distraught voice of a young mother pleaded for help.

Rose, the mother of 2-year-old twins, had recently given birth to a set of triplets. Now with five children under the age of 3, she has had barely enough sleep to function. She explains that her husband, a teacher, has been working 16-hour days to support the family and that she is left with the child care—an enormous undertaking.

"I can't take the kids to get some . . .," Rose said, briefly choking up. "They have to get shots. I can't even take them to the doctor."

How could she? How could she even hold three infants and two toddlers? The desperation with which she lived escalated daily. The simplest chores were now beyond her capabilities. She had tried to get help from city agencies but had failed, she told Mayor Giuliani. Social services, for whatever reason, were unable to help her.

> "Sometimes I do feel like I'm going to jump off a bridge," she told the mayor.
>
> "No, no you're not going to jump off a bridge," Giuliani responded emphatically. "We're going to help you. OK? Do you believe me? Hello? Answer me back. Do you believe me?" After a few seconds of silence, . . . Rose responded, "If you say you're going to help me . . ."
>
> "I'm going to help you," insisted Giuliani. . . . "We're going to make sure that you have the help that you need. You know, I have children myself," [Mayor Giuliani assured her.] Within a half hour, members of Giuliani's community assistance team arrived at the woman's home. Neighbors who had heard the broadcast were already there. (Hazell, 1997)

This story ran under the subject heading of "domestic"—not stress, not suicide, not social services, not public policy, and most certainly not work (Hazell, 1997). It received brief attention from *USA Today* and other media sources. It captures our attention: five children under the age of 3; a young woman threatening to jump off a bridge; the mayor to the rescue; and a community that responds. But, generally speaking, academic research on the topic of stress would probably not label this incident as work-related stress. This woman's story probably would be labeled a *domestic issue,* an *interpersonal issue,* or a *women's issue,* as it was by the Associated Press.

The reasons for this labeling may, in large part, be the result of traditional framings of stress as "work" related, as an individual problem, and as an outcome variable of certain situations and/or certain types or styles of communication. To expand our conceptualizations of stress, we need to recognize stress as a sociopolitical concern, as a discursive and material practice, and as a phenomenon that transcends the public-versus-private dichotomy. However, before we reframe stress, we provide an overview of the traditional approaches to the study of stress.

TRADITIONAL OVERVIEW OF STRESS

Traditionally, stress has been equated with physical and/or emotional strain. Left unchecked, stress leads to burnout or the *wearing out* of the individual over time (Freudenberger, 1974). The *American Heritage Dictionary* (1992) provides the following definition of stress:

> A mentally or emotionally disruptive or upsetting condition occurring in response to adverse external influences and capable of affecting physical health, usually characterized by increased heart rate, a rise in blood pressure, muscular tension, irritability, and depression. A stimulus or circumstance causing such a condition. A state of extreme difficulty, pressure, or strain.

This denotation of stress captures the traditional emphases of stress literature—the individualized experience of stress and the physical and mental manifestations of too much stress. This perspective also implies a continuum of stress, with one extreme representing an optimal level of stress that is positive and motivating and the other extreme representing too much stress, which causes harm. Organizational literature on stress tends to be grounded in this traditional perspective of stress.

Although one of the few researchers with a positive view of stress in the workplace, Owens (1987) argues that the stress imposed by deadlines is necessary and invigorating to the workplace. She states that deadlines serve the following purposes: "They provide an objective measurement of accomplishments; they promote excitement and cooperation; they add zest to endless tasks; they give management greater control; and they encourage autonomy and delegation" (p. 16). When interviewing managers who were required to "manage faster" because of downsizing, Sobkowski (1994) found that setting deadlines and imposing stress were critical to efforts designed to curb wasted time.

More often, however, business and management research conceptualizes stress as an outcome variable to be avoided in the workplace. Organizations will not be productive and financially successful if employees are subjected to stress that leads to dysfunctional work performance and/or job turnover (Cordes & Dougherty, 1993; Guaspari, 1995; Krinsky, 1984). Therefore, the literature emphasizes how to manage employees to achieve maximum output while minimizing their feelings of stress (Golembiewski, Munzenrider, & Stevenson, 1986; Lee, 1993; Markels, 1996; Quick, 1984; Sutton, 1991).

Acknowledging that prolonged stress often gives rise to a number of counter-productive behaviors, including turnover, absenteeism, alcoholism, drug abuse, aggression, and sabotage, managerial literature often suggests creating and promoting "moderator variables that buffer the effects of potential stress-ors on individuals" (Steers & Black, 1994, p. 606). These buffers are intended to reduce the incidence of the aforementioned counterproductive behaviors by reducing perceived stress. Although implicating the role of the individual employee in reducing stress (through the use of such strategies as time man-agement, developing outside interests, increasing physical exercise, and adopting new cognitive perspectives), the current business perspective tends to emphasize the role of management in reducing work-related stress.

In addition, other researchers have identified several antecedent factors that affect employee stress through the imposition of demands and deadlines. Specifically, role overload, role conflict, and role ambiguity are frequently identified workplace stressors (Miller, Ellis, Zook, & Lyles, 1990) that involve demands and deadlines that have become ambiguous, overwhelming, and problematic. For example, *role overload* typically is defined as a "condi-tion in which individuals feel they are being asked to do more than time or ability permits" (Steers & Black, 1994, p. 597). Implicit in this definition is that overload results when roles or tasks "place competing *demands* [italics added] on available money, time, information, goods, and skills" (Kaufman, Lane, & Lindquist, 1991, p. 393). Steers and Black (1994) define *role conflict* as "the simultaneous occurrence of two (or more) sets of pressures or ex-pectations" and continue with an example: "A secretary who reports to several supervisors may face a conflict over whose work to do first" (p. 596). Like role conflict, role ambiguity in conjunction with demands and deadlines may result in a stressful situation. Matteson and Ivancevich (1982) define *role ambiguity* as existing when there is uncertainty regarding work requirements or expectations. Thus, just as too many demands on an employee can cause stress through overload, demands that are unclear (i.e., role conflict and role ambiguity) can also cause stress.

Stress: Demands and Deadlines

Demands are related to *deadlines* in that deadlines are treated as objective limits on the time in which the demand may be completed. In this way, dead-lines become demands because deadlines serve as time requirements that must be met. These time limits, framed as deadlines, become yet another factor affecting the levels of stress experienced by employees. Because deadlines are common and because of the intensity of their impact on stress levels, they are often thought of as real phenomena that must be satisfied. For example, operations researchers Posner (1985) and Tautenhahn (1994) present algo-rithms designed to allow for the effective completion of manufacturing jobs when a specific number of jobs need to be processed on a given number of machines by a certain deadline. Deadlines are treated as objective features that constrain the manufacturing process by requiring that work be accomplished in a limited amount of time.

In addition to how deadlines affect the work process, researchers have also explored the ways in which deadlines affect group development. Lim and Murninghan (1994) test four models of group development, each of which posits various ways that group members attempt to complete a task in a fixed amount of time. Using a bargaining task, the authors' laboratory experiments conclude that impending deadlines in mixed-motive tasks (i.e., tasks characterized by both individualistic and cooperative elements, actions, and goals) lead to individualistic, as opposed to group, action prior to the deadline. Consistent with the studies of manufacturing operations, this research on group development assumes and perpetuates the notion that organizational members recognize deadlines as *real* demands on their time and allow deadlines to shape activity.

Currently, there is popular interest in individualized strategies for meeting demands and deadlines based on the idea that meeting demands and deadlines will buffer the potential for or alleviate induced stress. This body of literature from scholars and practitioners, known broadly as *time management,* is rooted in the assumption that deadlines are objective facts of life and that time can be managed and planned to satisfy such deadlines (Wheeler, 1994). Pollock (1991) champions a common belief about satisfying deadlines: "People with a future invariably have a healthy respect for the time at their disposal. They are organized, have devised routine ways to dispose of routine chores and almost never miss a deadline" (p. 24). Meeting deadlines is equated with "having a future," so it is no surprise that Hartley (1991) claims, "We all want to be organized. We all want to be able to remember every deadline, every payment date, and every meeting" (p. 40). Recent technological advances have yielded a slew of computer programs and handheld organizers to facilitate this ideal (Harris, 1994; Hartley, 1991). A review of a survey of executives indicates that, in addition to computer organizers, there are several ways that executives can manage and *keep track of* their time: They can use traditional and contemporary calendars, date books, and written notes or employ someone as a *time manager* (Crispell, 1995).

Owens (1987) suggests that deadlines can best be met by "dividing the project into subtasks with mini-deadlines [that] not only relieves stress, but allows for time delays" (p. 16). In contrast to assumptions that deadlines lead to stress, this strategy of creating many smaller deadlines is posited as a means of alleviating stress. Similarly, Douglass and Douglass (1994) advise that the first step in completing a project should be establishing a step-by-step timeline. They suggest that, "by knowing how long an activity will take and when it has to be finished, we can calculate when it has to begin" (p. 7). Furthermore, these authors offer the idea of creating a "tickler file":

a set of 43 file folders: one for each day of the month and one for each month of the year. . . . We file each highlighted activity sheet in the tickler file under the date when the activity must be started. This ensures that no key activity will ever be forgotten. (p. 7)

Likewise, Pollock (1992), Towler (1991), and Wright (1985) offer ways of self-organizing that include making plans and lists of tasks to accomplish in specific time periods. Implicit in such approaches is the notion that deadlines imposed by others are effectively met when time is compartmentalized into finite blocks defined by *mini deadlines* that are self-created. Although these strategies focus on individual employee behaviors, they are often mandated by organizations. In addition to these individualized approaches to stress reduction, the management literature discusses both the importance of and procedures for managing employees to reduce stress.

Reducing employee stress is a bottom-line issue for many corporations. This fact is heightened in tight labor markets, where recruiting and retaining skilled employees can be increasingly difficult. According to Steers and Black (1994), some of the managerial imperatives suggested to reduce the effects of stress are personnel selection and placement designed to ensure that employees are prepared to meet the demands of their jobs; skills training; job redesign (Hackman & Oldham, 1976); company-sponsored counseling programs; increased personal control and participation; improved communication; and health promotion programs (Roberts & Harris, 1989). Even though a number of these efforts require a variety of corporate commitments, including financial support, many companies see a return on their investments because of increased productivity and reduced absenteeism and stress-related illness (Roberts & Harris, 1989).

Stress: Social Interaction and Social Support

Outside of business, management, and popular literature, scholars in social psychology are also studying stress and its concomitant effects. Maslach (1982) and Maslach and Jackson (1982) were among the first researchers to recognize that being overwhelmed by stress is not simply a result of job design. More than a decade ago, they suggested that burnout is especially acute among human service workers because of their constant contact or interaction with people. Stress from prolonged interpersonal contact can lead to burnout. Furthermore, the authors delineated the outcome variables of emotional exhaustion, depersonalization, and a reduced sense of personal accomplishment. *Emotional exhaustion* refers to a depletion of emotional resources and the feeling that one has nothing left to give to those who make demands in the workplace. Based on this sense of emotional exhaustion, *depersonalization,* or the development of a callous and negative attitude about the people with whom one works, can ensue. Another psychological aspect of stress and burnout is a perceived sense of *reduced personal accomplishment,* which is characterized by a feeling that accomplishments fall short of expectations. These three dimensions of stress and burnout can ultimately lead to decreased quality of work, job dissatisfaction, personal dysfunction, and employee turn-over (Maslach, 1982; Maslach & Jackson, 1982). Here, the outcomes of stress are seen as specific to the employee rather than as detrimental conditions for the organization (with the exception of employee turnover, which may be seen in either way).

Other researchers in social psychology are concerned with the ways that stress is managed through social support. Cassel (1974) proposed the stress-buffering hypothesis, which has been widely tested (Cohen & Wills, 1985; Lin, Woelfel, & Light, 1986; Wilcox, 1981). This hypothesis is based on the assumption that social support operates as a buffer against the harmful effects of stressful life events. Social support can intervene between the stressor and the stress response in one of two ways. First, support may intercede between the stressful event and the distressed response by diminishing or preventing the stress reaction (see also Cutrona & Russell, 1990, for a discussion of their related model of optimal matching between stress and social support). In other words, support by others redefines and decreases the potentially harmful impact of the stressor or bolsters one's ability to cope, thus decreasing the possibility that the event is perceived as stressful. Second, social support may mediate between the experience of the stressful event and the onset of pathology by eliminating the stressful situation or influencing a positive psychological or physical response to the stressful event. This perspective conceptualizes social support as having a buffering influence, rather than a main effect, on the strain of an organizational stressor.

Stress: Communication and Connectedness

Organizational and managerial communication scholars who employ a traditional perspective focus on the idea that working conditions, including environmental factors and interaction with others, can cause stress and burnout. For example, K. Miller and her colleagues (Miller, Birkholt, Scott, & Stage, 1995; Miller et al. 1990; Miller, Stiff, & Ellis, 1988; Miller, Zook, & Ellis, 1989) found that certain forms of communication mediate or offset the impact of stress on burnout. In addition, Miller et al. (1988) proposed and tested the empathic communication model of burnout. This framework specifies dimensions of emotional communication and from these dimensions predicts employee levels of communicative responsiveness. Two dimensions of emotional communication are suggested: emotional contagion and empathic concern. *Emotional contagion* refers to a parallel response to the support recipient or *feeling with* another, whereas *empathic concern* refers to a general concern for the welfare of another or *feeling for* another (see also Pines, 1982). Although the term, empathic concern, generally denotes feeling with the other person, these authors use a different conceptualization—more along the lines of sympathy rather than empathy. Miller et al. (1988) suggest that empathic concern should be the communicative response of choice to avoid stress and burnout. On the other hand, the authors point out that, when negatively valanced in the direction of emotional contagion, communicative responsiveness can lead to emotional exhaustion, depersonalization, and reduced personal accomplishment.

Since its initial conception, this general empathic model of communication, stress, and burnout has been refined to include other aspects of the work environment, including role stress and workload. Recent research (Miller et al., 1990; Miller et al., 1989; Starnaman & Miller, 1992) reveals that participation in decision making and social support from supervisors and coworkers have an inverse impact on stress and burnout, a positive relationship with job satisfaction, and commitment to the job for both human service workers and support staff.

Several researchers have extended the investigation of communication and stress by exploring interpersonal connectedness. For example, Ray (1991; see also Ray, 1987) examined the role of informal networks in the alleviation of job stress and burnout through supportive communication. Each role within the network experienced a different level of stress. Isolates, for example, reported significantly less stress and burnout than dyad members, group members, and network linkers (for a notable exception, see Ray, 1990). Other studies suggest that group members report significantly less burnout than network linkers (e.g., Albrecht, Irey, & Mundy, 1982). In addition, Starnaman and Miller (1992) found that structural variables and perceptions of social support in the workplace influence levels of stress and burnout. The implications of this research suggest not only that the existence of supportive communication is important (Thoits, 1995; Zimmermann & Applegate, 1994) but that the depth, breadth, and shared definition of network roles are key to understanding the relationships between network positions and stress and burnout.

Various attributes of workers have also been examined in models of stress and burnout. Ellis and Miller (1993, 1994) proposed and tested a model of worker participation in which nurses' involvement and communicative assertiveness were predictor variables of the outcome variables of emotional exhaustion, job commitment, and intent to remain with the organization. Personal control was used as the moderating variable that predicted the outcome variables. Results of this research suggest that personal control in the workplace is an important factor to consider in addition to other aspects of organizational structure and working conditions. On the basis of the previous models, Miller et al. (1995) recently developed and tested an integrated model of stress and burnout that includes the factors of job involvement, organizational roles, and attitudes toward service recipients (i.e., clients and customers) as predictors of stress, burnout, and related organizational outcomes. The revised model replicated earlier findings that emphasize the influence of contextual variables, such as workload, job involvement, role conflict, and role ambiguity, on moderating the processes of burnout and organizational commitment. However, these authors call for further studies that address the complicated nature of stress in organizations.

Although we have learned a great deal from these traditional studies of stress, much remains to be explored. In the following section, we suggest that, by rethinking or reframing a phenomenon, an alternative perspective that can further illuminate the subject of study may surface. Furthermore, and more specifically, we believe that a feminist approach has much to offer on the topic of stress.

RETHINKING AND REFRAMING

Framing is a well-developed concept that refers to how people organize and interpret communicative behavior. Anthropologist Gregory Bateson has been credited with the development of framing (Goffman, 1974). In turn, Bateson (1972) credits such renowned scholars as Whitehead, Russell, and Whorf for influencing his development of framing. Bateson conceived of the frame as a form of *metacommunication.* Specifically, for Bateson (1972), "The frame is involved in the evaluation of the message. . . . As such the frame is metacommunicative" (p. 188). Simply put, we communicate about our communication in the act of communicating. Thus, as communication communicates about itself, be it in a subtle or obvious manner, a metalevel of meanings appears. Drawing an example from Bateson's work might make this philosophy of framing more clear. Bateson's observations of animal communication suggest that animals initiate playful fighting with each other that can be distinguished from aggressive fighting. This observation led Bateson to surmise that humans hold an equal or more sophisticated ability to comment on their own communicative acts. This commentary is called *metacommunication,* and the variety of ways that we comment on our communication is called *framing.*

Definitions of framing are multiple and diverse, yet they carry within them Bateson's original premise. For example, Goffman (1974) purports,

My point is to try to isolate some of the basic frameworks of understanding available in our society for making sense out of events and to analyze the special vulnerabilities to which these frames of reference are subject. I start with the fact that from an individual's particular point of view, while one thing may momentarily appear to be what is really going on, in fact what is actually happening is plainly a joke, or a dream, or an accident, or a mistake, or a misunderstanding, or a deception, or a theatrical performance, and so forth. And attention will be directed to what it is about our sense of what is going on that makes it so vulnerable to the need of these various readings. (p. 10)

The vulnerability that Goffman discusses creates a space for a specific reading of the events. According to Goffman, interactions are organized through frames, which help people to make sense of the world. Other scholars conceptualize frames as rhetorical practices. For example, both Stahl (1989) and Clair (1991, 1993b) rely on the discursive and rhetorical aspects of narrative to ground their definitions of framing. Specifically, Clair (1993b) conceives of frames as persuasive "devices [that] are rhetorical/discursive practices that define or assign interpretation to the social event" (p. 118). Putnam and Holmer (1992) contribute to the rhetorical and persuasion focus on framing by exploring conflict and negotiation episodes as ways of establishing lines of argument concerning boundaries around issues that occur during interaction. Similarly, Fairhurst and Sarr (1996) define framing in leadership as "a quality of communication that causes others to accept one meaning over another" (p. xi). Thus, researchers often conceive of frames as rhetorically persuasive commentaries, with interpretation open to debate. However, just how open this debate is raises questions about power, oppression, resistance, challenge, and the possibilities for change. Who assigns meaning to an event or how a frame comes to hold suasion is not so easily determined. As such, framing or reframing constitutes a sociopolitical practice that defines reality and assigns meaning(s) to our social relations.

The persuasiveness of a frame may range from being so strong that one would never think to question the interpretation of events to being an obvious decoy for other intentions. When a frame is solidified by society, it is deemed reified. Reified or not, frames, as discursive practices, are open to challenge and debate, even though, at times, they seem immutable. At other times, they may be openly accepted while they are being secretly challenged. For example, Clair (1993b, 1998) provides several examples related to sexual harassment in which women say that men want them to think of it as a joke; the women may laugh and "blow it off," but they also report knowing that it is not a joke.

Over the years, researchers have employed the concept of framing across a variety of social situations. Several scholars have taken advantage of the precept that discourses are challengeable by providing alternative frames to understand social practices. As Clair (1993b) points out,

> Several scholars have used the concept of framing to understand such concepts as interpersonal relations (Rawlins, 1987), leader-member exchange (Fairhurst & Chandler, 1989), conflict and negotiation (Putnam & Holmer, 1992), the paradox of professional women (Wood & Conrad, 1983), and sexual harassment (Clair, 1991, 1993[b]; Clair, McGoun, & Spirek, 1993). (p. 151)

Studies that employ framing as a way of understanding how social relations are created and sustained, or challenged and changed, help to shed light on problems that people face every day. In addition to being considered rhetorical political practices, frames can be characterized as both an active practice and an outcome. The following artistic analogy is intended to provide clarification of this position.

Imagine an artist who is standing before a collection of objects (e.g., a pitcher, a few wooden spoons, and a variety of fruits) that are cushioned in the folds of a soft terry cloth towel on top of a table. An artist might stand before a still life such as this with two small cardboard pieces, each cut into the shape of an "L." He or she might use the L shapes to create a frame around the still life. By placing the Ls together, the artist can elongate the frame, move the frame from left to right or right to left, crop out the table legs from view, or reduce the amount of background that is visible. The L helps to frame the still life in the artist's image before painting begins.

Some artists throw away the L shapes altogether; instead, they look inside the pitcher, taste the fruit, lift the wooden spoons, or touch the towel before embarking on an artistic rendering that may be more surrealistic than realistic. The way they *frame* the composition may be drastically different from an artist who uses the traditional L shape. Approaches to painting a still life may range from realistic renderings to surreal illusions, from impressionist statements to abstract cubist commentaries.

In our metaphorical image of framing, we remove the term *frame* from its more common referent as the material pieces that are fitted around a finished product (e.g., a painting, photograph, or bas relief) to give it borders and to limit its meaning to a certain space; instead, we draw on the active framing an artist enacts as part of the creative process. In short, we reframed the concept of framing. Framing contributes to the ways in which the statements will be created and viewed in the above example: One is more directly associated with the final product, and the other is more related to the process. Each frame contributes to the way that we see things and come to know the world. Frames are persuasive. Framing can be a powerful means of creating and interpreting reality. Furthermore, a realistic interpretation of the still life is no more correct than the abstract or surrealist interpretation. They are persuasions, discourses, and renderings (see Clair, 1998, for a discussion of aesthetic theory and organizational communication).

However, this is not to say that the paintings or framings are value free. Bias is inherently a *part of the picture* whether one is referring to art or research or both: "Every way of seeing is a way of not seeing" (Burke, 1935, p. 70). As Langer (1951) points out, the ways of seeing influence both the questions we ask and the answers we derive. Every representation has implications. At times, those implications may be most profound for women. As Flax suggests, "How gender relations are constituted and experienced and how we think or, equally important, do not think about them may have a profound impact on our lives" (as cited in Buzzanell, 1994, p. 341).

In the following sections of this chapter, we reframe stress by discussing the possibilities for a feminist framing of the phenomenon. By placing women's needs at the center of our discussion, we hope to highlight some aspects of stress that have received less attention from scholars. But first we present an overview of what is meant by a feminist framing.

A FEMINIST FRAMING OF STRESS

To suggest that a framing can be feminist is to suggest that feminism can be characterized by certain principles. In general, this may be true, but because various feminist theories exist (see Buzzanell, 1993, 1994; Tong, 1989), both complementary and competing feminist views could color any interpretation of stress. Rather than single out a specific feminist theory, we draw from the general tenets of feminism that argue that "women's issues" have been marginalized, devalued, and sequestered to the private realm. Furthermore, what constitutes "women's issues" are likely to be issues of concern to society as a whole, even though they have been disguised as solely women's concerns. With regard to stress, a complicated set of conceptualizations leads to a deception that perpetuates the current sociopolitical arrangement. A feminist rethinking or reframing of stress holds a number of hopes for organizational and managerial communication scholars: to highlight stressful situations that may not have received the same legitimation as current "workplace" conceptualizations of stress; to advance a more holistic understanding of stress as a sociopolitical phenomenon; to point out the discursive as well as the material aspects of stress; and to expose the ways in which women's work-related stress is far too often privatized. We discuss each of these "reframings" in the subsequent four sections of this chapter.

Legitimating Marginalized Forms of Stress

Images of stress that highlight overworked managers who are struggling to meet corporate deadlines legitimize a specific conceptualization of stress. In doing so, images of stress become associated with certain people or particular jobs. Research that draws its subject pool from a wider array of possibilities (of both people and jobs) contributes to a more balanced conceptualization of stress. For example, Ray (1991) studies elementary school teachers; K. Miller and her colleagues (Miller et al., 1988, 1995) study human service workers; and Albrecht and Ropp (1982) and Ellis and Miller (1993, 1994) observe nurses. Each of these studies contributes to a feminist rethinking of stress by including women and occupations that are female dominated and by exploring workplaces that are generally ignored because they lack big-business interests.

The story of Rose (which appears earlier in this chapter), the mother of five children under the age of 3, provides another avenue for extending our studies of stress. Rose's work as a mother and homemaker has been delegitimated in society by capitalist standards. What to do about this kind of delegitimation has been debated by numerous feminists (e.g., Clair & Thompson, 1996; Delphy, 1984; Lopate, 1974; MacKinnon, 1989). Nevertheless, little attention has been given to mothering and homemaking as legitimate sources of work-related stress. Thus, even less attention has been given to how this form of stress is related to the macroorganization of society. The work itself must be legitimated as valuable in order for the related stress to be given serious attention. Too often, marginalized jobs are perceived as *supporting* real work rather than *being* real work (see Clair, 1996). The study of stress related to undervalued jobs (e.g., support staff, servers, service personnel, part-time and temporary workers, or marginalized jobs such as baby-sitting, day care, or unskilled labor) is deserving of further research.

Stress as a Sociopolitical Concern

Although studying individual-level stress based on work-related demands and deadlines (e.g., Shinji Masami's story of stress that was presented at the opening of this chapter) is important, it cannot provide a full picture of stress in society. First, some jobs (e.g., mothering) are so marginalized that they are not even granted the legitimacy to be included in studies of work-related stress. Second, the focus on individual outcomes isolates the relational aspects of stress. Finally, by focusing on job demands and stressful outcomes at the microlevel, researchers neglect to see that the micro is the macro (see Giddens, 1979, 1984) or that one woman's story is an articulation of the gender structuring of society.

Traditional views of stress far too often leave the sociopolitical aspects of stress unmentioned and unchallenged. To incorporate a microlevel and macrolevel understanding of stress, we as researchers need to rethink and reframe definitions and conceptualizations of stress. We need to explore individuals as more than workers; we need to investigate the connections between a marginalized status and stress at work; we need to redefine what constitutes "work"; and we need to question how "legitimate" organizations interact with each other to secure a "workforce" that rarely challenges the everyday organization of society or the stress that undergirds the current organization of society. We need to ask questions: Why is stress treated as though only the individual can remedy the situation (see Hank, 1997)? Why are certain issues relegated to the personal when they are political? When will we allow these micromanaged problems to be addressed by social thought and policy?

The existence of an undercurrent of stress in our society needs to be explored, not just as a "work-related" phenomenon but as waves that spread outward engaging a broader and more complex life experience. Rose's telephone call for help not only came from the personal stress experience of her individual situation; it was a call rooted in sociopolitical tensions. Rose's stress spawned not only from her work as the mother, wife, and caretaker of the home and family but also from her position as a politically marginalized and isolated woman in society because of her work. Although earlier on she sought help to relieve her stress through social service agencies, the dominant political powers that organize society denied the very existence of her stress and refused her the much-needed assistance that she requested. In this way, her microlevel stress experience speaks to larger, macrolevel societal structures that denied her assistance. Was it because the source of her stress was not seen as legitimate? Was her position in society not seen as deserving? Not until she called the mayor and challenged the system in a profoundly dramatic way did she receive prompt attention. Whether intentional or not, the call makes an overtly political statement. Although the mayor's immediate response curbed one woman's experience of stress, it did not begin to champion social reform that would recognize the gender and work biases that limit our notions of stress in general. On the whole, stress is seen as an individual concern rather than a sociopolitical one.

Ironically, once the issue is supposedly remedied, yet another concern surrounding stress is raised. The very people who are assigned the social task of assisting Rose suffer incredibly high levels of stress themselves. Social work is a female-dominated occupation, which is generally considered low status (Aldridge, 1990; Davenport & Davenport, 1997) and is characterized by low pay (Gibelman & Schervish, 1997; U.S. Department of Labor, 1998) and a high rate of burnout (Gummer, 1996; Poulin & Walter, 1993; Siefert, Jayaratne, & Chess, 1991; Soderfeldt, Soderfeldt, & Warg, 1995). In addition, these marginalized members of society are placed in the uncomfortable position of either controlling or caring for other marginalized members of society (Tancred-Sheriff, 1989). In essence, those who are under stress are called on to care for others who are stressed. Stress has a rippling effect.

Stress as a Discursive and Material Practice

Although studying stress as an outcome variable has generated important studies and useful findings, this approach does not develop the communicative aspects of stress itself. Stress is an expression of the sociopolitical organization of society. Stress articulates the tensions created by a capitalist patriarchal order. It announces the anger and the frustrations people find themselves with when trying to live an impossible reality. And yet this articulation ebbs and flows, it waxes and wanes. Life cannot be impossible at all times or people would give up. There must be just enough "give" in the system to allow for the expression of accomplishment, of a job well done, of the joys of creation, and the satisfaction of success. Furthermore, stress as a discursive practice that promotes the current capitalist and patriarchal characteristics of society must name itself as a normalized function. It is to be expected. Just as deadlines are to be expected (see Clair & Kunkel, 1998),[2] stress is normalized to maintain and even escalate production and privilege. From students to managers, people are expected to be *stressed out*. Normalization or reification of any phenomenon is achieved through discursive practices (Foucault, 1976/ 1990; see also Giddens, 1979, 1984; MacKinnon, 1989). Stress is no exception; stress is a discursive practice. However, stress is also a material practice. Stress is physically performed. It acts on the body. And the body reacts. To forget the materiality of stress would create a postmodern fiction. Indeed, the fiction does exist. Stress is created for us and by us. Stress is a narrative by which we often live, but that narrative has physicality.

The story of Rose demonstrates the discursive and material aspects of stress. Rose both tells a story and is a story. Her own story depicts the intense emotional and physical aspects of stress that drive her to the brink of suicide. At the same time, her story becomes a collective narrative—a story that speaks on behalf of a whole group of people (Richardson, 1995). In this case, parents—and more specifically, mothers—with few resources available to them are the collective being named. What mother would not feel that she had lived at least a small portion of Rose's narrative? All mothers become contained within Rose's narrative. Their stress is captured and reflected in her stress. More than a collective narrative, Rose's story is an open secret like so many stories that women live. Rose's experiences are sequestered, unnamed, and virtually invisible. Sequestered stories deserve critical feminist attention (Clair, 1993b). Researchers need to explore the turning point in the narratives that force the sequestered story into public view as well as the ways in which the stories are silenced. Stress, then, is both an outcome and an expression, both physical and discursive, both oppression and resistance. Stress is the body screaming out the silence.

Stress Transcends the Public-Versus-Private Dichotomy

Marxist feminists provided a significant contribution in their efforts to revive and revise Fredrich Engel's work on the private labor of women (see Tong, 1989). Although much has been done to highlight "women's work" over the last few decades, more needs to be done. Women still occupy the largest percentage of employees in the lowest-paying jobs (see Clair & Thompson, 1996). Their work as mothers, baby-sitters, and the general caregivers (Wood, 1994) is often marginalized as unimportant to a capitalist patriarchal society and is relegated to a private, individual concern. Fraser (1989) suggests that privatizing issues imprints them with an image of incontestability. If an issue is not contestable, then it is unlikely to reach the public forum. This effectively keeps the issue from being addressed through public policy.

Rose's story dramatically demonstrates a moment when a once-privatized concern is forced into a public arena. By calling the mayor's radio talk show, Rose effectively questions the way in which society has relegated her concerns to a private matter. She is quickly assisted by public social service agencies as well as by her concerned neighbors (i.e., both public and private sources of help). But will public policy change? The reasons Rose could not get public assistance earlier are not clear, but it is clear that she was in desperate need. Her story as a public story will help to deprivatize the stress associated with mothering and may contribute to public policy change.

REFLECTING ON A
FEMINIST REFRAMING OF STRESS

Stress, a serious social concern, has received attention from scholars representing a variety of disciplines. However, a feminist framing of stress has not been well developed in past literature. In this chapter, our goal was to introduce the possibilities of a feminist reframing of stress. We recognize that it is still in need of further development. Nevertheless, after reviewing traditional approaches to the study of stress, we suggested that four areas were in specific need of attention. First, undervalued jobs need to be legitimated in order to bring to light stress that has been hidden from public view. Second, stress needs to be conceptualized as a sociopolitical concern that has an impact on both micro- and macrolevels of society. Third, the study of the discursive and material aspects of stress should provide new insights regarding the physical, political, and social construction of reality. Fourth, transcending the bifurcated view of public and private issues would allow for a feminist reframing of stress as a more holistic concern.

It was Rose's story that helped us to see stress in a new light. And it is stories like hers that deserve the attention of further study.

NOTES

1. The stress of being fired was not directly investigated in the study because the number of patients admitted to the emergency room who reported having been fired the previous day was not high enough to make statistical generalizations. Although we report that having to fire someone is stressful, it also should be noted that being fired is greatly, if not more, stressful.

2. According to Clair and Kunkel (1995),

> The origin of deadline has been traced to the Civil War practice of drawing a line around an area partitioned off to contain prisoners of war. Any prisoner crossing the line was shot. We would like to thank Susan Whalen for pointing out the origin of the term deadline to us. This historical definition can be found in the Oxford English Dictionary. (p. 34)

PART III

AUTHORING OUR FUTURE

AUTHORING OUR FUTURE

8

"Learning the Ropes"

A Black Feminist Standpoint Analysis

Brenda J. Allen

Anyone who has assumed a new role in an organization has experienced organizational socialization, the process by which an individual enters and becomes integrated into organizational settings. Often referred to as "learning the ropes," socialization is an inherently communicative process because newcomers rely on formal and informal communication to help them make sense of their job and their work environment (Jablin, 1987). To reduce uncertainty about their role, newcomers acquire information and insight from numerous sources (e.g., supervisors, coworkers, orientation programs, employee manuals, clients, managers, training sessions, and staff) within the organization.

Studies on these information sources and socialization in general date back to the 1950s when researchers studied ways to transform a new employee into a responsible organizational citizen (e.g., Berlew & Hall, 1966; Hughes, 1958; Van Maanen, 1976). Most of these works reflect a strong managerial as well as patriarchal bias because they sought to predict and control employees' behaviors for the sake of the organization. The following quote captures this sentiment: "Put bluntly, new members must be taught to see the organiza-

AUTHOR'S NOTE: I would like to express my appreciation to Connie Bullis and Karen Dace, who reviewed an earlier draft of this chapter.

tional world as do their more experienced colleagues if the traditions of the organization are to survive" (Van Maanen & Schein, 1979, p. 211).

When communication scholars began to study socialization, they also worked for the benefit of the organization. Similar to organizational scientists, they sought to explain how the organization could mold or transform individuals to meet the needs of the organization (Bullis, 1993; Deetz, 1992; Jablin, 1987). Although this body of research highlights communication as a fundamental aspect of socialization, some organizational communication scholars believe that we have yet to render a complete, authentic picture of socialization processes. For example, they cite a need for more projects that study process instead of focusing on outcomes; that examine socialization from newcomers' perspectives rather than from the viewpoint of organizations and managers; and that abandon the tendency to view socialization as linear and rational (e.g., B. Allen, 1996; Bullis, 1993; Cheney, 1991; Clair, 1996; Deetz, 1992; Louis, 1980; McPhee, 1986). Research that attends to these issues will help organizational communication scholars to develop more holistic theories about socialization and communication. Equally as important, we might offer practical guidance to members of organizations who not only face the persistent demands of socializing new employees but also must contend with contemporary challenges such as a multicultural workforce, globalization, teams, temporary workers, downsizing, mergers, and telecommuting.

The purpose of this chapter is to apply a black feminist standpoint approach to analyzing organizational socialization processes and to offer suggestions for practice that the analysis implies. First, I briefly explain feminist standpoint theory and offer a rationale for why it is appropriate for reassessing "learning the ropes" practices. Next, I provide an overview of organizational socialization research. Then, I offer deeper or alternative perspectives on organizational socialization, based primarily on experiences of black women. I focus mainly on U.S. academe, although I believe that the analyses and discussion apply to numerous organizational contexts (e.g., corporations, nonprofit agencies, and manufacturing companies). I conclude with implications for research and practice.

FEMINIST STANDPOINT THEORY

Standpoint theory is based on the idea that the world looks different depending on one's social location. Socialist feminists borrowed this concept from Marxian work on the standpoint of the proletariat (see P. Collins, 1991, 1997; Flax, 1990; Harding, 1991, 1997; Hartsock, 1983a, 1997; Hekman, 1997; Hennesey, 1993; Rose, 1983; Smith, 1987a, 1997; Wood, 1992a). These writers contend that women's lives in Western capitalist society provide valuable resources for criticizing prevailing knowledge claims, which tend to be based on the lives of men in dominant races, classes, and cultures (Harding, 1991, 1997; Rixecker, 1994). These knowledge claims usually depict women and other marginalized persons (e.g., men of color) as "other" or "outsider."

Feminist standpoint theory endorses allowing women, as "others," to speak from and about their everyday experiences in order to discover aspects of the social order that have not been brought to light. Like all feminist efforts, standpoint theory demands that we identify instances of domination and patriarchy. For example, we can scrutinize women's lives for instances of oppression and exploitation. We then can see how hegemony pervades social relations, and we can make recommendations for changing these conditions. Hegemony refers to taken-for-granted societal assumptions that lead people to believe that hierarchical relationships are normal and natural (Conrad & Poole, 1998). Conrad and Poole explain,

> As people *internalize* the values and assumptions of their societies they also internalize its class, race, gender, and ethnicity-based hierarchical relationships. In contemporary Western societies educated Anglo, middle- and upper-class men traditionally have been (and often still are) assumed to be superior to everyone else. (p. 349)

Members of organizations (including those who are oppressed and exploited) tend to behave (consciously and unconsciously) in ways that perpetuate these patriarchal assumptions and hierarchies.

Feminist standpoint theory does not essentialize the category "woman." Rather, it advocates incorporating viewpoints of a variety of women across the multiple contexts that women occupy or encounter (Harding, 1991). Thus, it responds positively to lingering criticisms that feminist projects focus mainly on white, middle-class women without considering other women's experiences. Moreover, standpoint theory places primacy on the role of context in building theory: "Context matters because it shapes the way we construct reality" (Rixecker, 1994, p. 124). Therefore, as they construct theory, researchers should consider the impact of political and historical contexts because efforts to create knowledge are never apolitical or ahistorical. For instance, as Rixecker (1994) points out, "Race, sex, gender construction, class, and sexuality all play a role in the creation of epistemological [ways of knowing] stances" (p. 128).

Standpoint theory "refers to historically shared, *group* experiences . . . [and] places less emphasis on individual experiences within socially constructed groups than on the social conditions that construct such groups" (P. Collins, 1997, p. 375; see also Wood, 1992a). As it requires researchers to seek women's accounts of their everyday lives, it compels them to contextualize their studies and to seek commonalities among group members' experiences.

Feminist standpoint helps us to accomplish feminist goals of emancipation and social change. For example, we can identify acts of resistance. As we study women's ways of knowing and being, we can provide insight for where, what, and how to change existing practices. Equally important, this type of work validates experiences and feelings of similar "others." When we invite marginalized others to tell their stories, we can help them to free themselves, to raise their consciousness.

I focus on the standpoint of black women. However, I advocate studying any group of persons that society tends to marginalize. I concentrate on black women because I am a member of that group and therefore can offer personal reflections. I believe that we need to detect distinctions among various racial and ethnic groups of women, as opposed to viewing them as monolithic. Because they are simultaneously members of two traditionally disenfranchised groups, black women may enact the role of "outsider" differently than white women (Bell, 1992; Higginbotham & Weber, 1992; hooks, 1989, Houston, 1997). They may experience power and domination based on their gender, their race, or both of these socially constructed aspects of their identity. Their unique social position allows them to identify patterns and behaviors that dominant members cannot readily discern (B. Allen, 1996).

As more women and men of color and white women enter the workforce and ascend organizational ranks, we need to study how they learn the ropes in order to understand what succeeds and what fails. Studying black women in academe might provide insight about how to develop practices that welcome persons of color and empower them and value their contributions. We also can provide examples of resistance and emancipation to black women and other marginalized persons.

ORGANIZATIONAL SOCIALIZATION

In this section, I provide a historical overview of literature on organizational socialization. Because this area of study abounds with essays and research projects, I cannot offer a comprehensive review (see Jablin, 1987). Rather, I highlight work that relates explicitly to this chapter.

As I noted earlier, research about organizational socialization originated in the organizational sciences when investigators studied how organizations could transform newcomers into productive employees (e.g., Van Maanen & Schein, 1979). These projects tended to view newcomers as passive, blank slates on whom organizations could write whatever script they desired. They relied on an anthropological model that analyzed organizational newcomers similarly to how one might study infants in societies (Bullis & Bach, 1989b).

They viewed socialization as a linear, one-way transfer of information from the organization to the employee. Moreover, they concentrated on socialization outcomes, such as employee commitment, communication competence, job satisfaction, absenteeism, and turnover. Thus, early investigations tended to be prescriptive and biased toward management.

Jablin (1987) presents an overview of socialization literature that focuses on communication. He portrays socialization as a developmental, ongoing process. Following the tradition of early writers, he divides the process into stages that he labels anticipatory socialization, assimilation, and exit (Bullis, 1993). According to this model, vocational anticipatory socialization occurs throughout childhood as we receive messages about occupations and careers from various sources (e.g., family members, teachers, peers, and the media). The next stage, organizational anticipatory socialization, occurs immediately prior to assuming a new organizational role and includes recruitment and interviewing. Within the assimilation stage, Jablin distinguishes between socialization (i.e., how the organization attempts to influence newcomers) and individualization (i.e., ways that newcomers adapt to their roles).

According to the literature, upon entry into a new role, a newcomer experiences an encounter, or "breaking in," period and "metamorphosis" (Jablin, 1987). During the encounter period, incumbent members send the newcomer ambient (implicit, indirect) and discretionary (explicit, direct) messages about job-related role skills as well as organizational and group norms and values (Comer, 1991; Jablin, 1987; Louis, 1980). In addition, the newcomer seeks information or feedback about his or her performance or about unclear or ambiguous information or events. The newcomer may encounter surprise if his or her expectations fail to correspond with reality (Louis, 1980). He or she may also experience role ambiguity (i.e., confusion about job requirements or lack of information regarding his or her role; Katz, 1977).

The literature characterizes metamorphosis as a time when the individual tries to become an accepted, participating member of the organization. The newcomer "acquires organizationally 'appropriate' attitudes and behaviors, resolves intra- and extra-organizational role conflicts, and commences efforts to individualize his or her organizational role" (Jablin, 1987, p. 694). He or she begins to use, accept, and internalize organizational rules and norms. During this time, a newcomer may try to modify others' expectations of him or her. In addition, the newcomer may attempt to change informally accepted values and norms (Jablin, 1987; Miller & Jablin, 1991).

Many scholars have criticized aspects of Jablin's model and the work that he reviews (e.g., B. Allen, 1996; Bullis, 1993; Bullis & Stout, 1996; Clair, 1996; Smith & Turner, 1995). For instance, the literature tends to assume a universal experience of organizational socialization. As Bullis and Stout (1996) observe, this act of universalizing privileges white men's experiences and positions. Jablin's model also implies that all newcomers have access to similar information sources. On the contrary, women and other marginalized persons often are excluded from formal and informal networks that comprise important, powerful socialization resources.

Critics also note that the literature continues to be biased toward organizations (B. Allen, 1996; Bullis & Bach, 1989b; Clair, 1996; McPhee, 1986; Smith & Turner, 1995). Consequently, although projects increasingly turn to newcomers for insight about socialization, a need persists to examine socialization from the individual's perspective. Organizational socialization literature also is biased toward dominant cultural constructions of reality. The literature does not explicitly acknowledge the inherent hegemony that pervades socialization processes (B. Allen, 1996; McPhee, 1986). Regardless of newcomers' gender and racial identities, power distinctions obviously influence socialization processes as organizational actors contend with systems of hierarchy, competition, authority, and territoriality. Rarely do researchers seem to recognize that organizational settings usually reflect the dominant culture's norms, attitudes, and values. Yet, as a black woman professor of organizational behavior observes, "Organizational cultures—large scale, hierarchical, white, and male-dominated—have their own set of norms, traditions, and values and, in the extreme, are prototypes of the Anglo-Saxon tradition and the Protestant Ethic" (Bell, 1990, p. 465). Therefore, the "appropriate" socialization attitudes and behaviors that researchers study usually parallel those of the dominant culture.

Moreover, the literature does not give adequate attention to contextual variables that may affect socialization processes. Research usually does not address historical, political, or local circumstances that might influence newcomers' realities. For instance, empirical studies usually provide only cursory information about research sites and participants, rarely identifying respondents by gender and/or race (e.g., Bullis & Bach, 1989b; Miller, 1996; Miller & Jablin, 1991; Morrison, 1993; Stohl, 1986). In addition, theoretical essays seem to refer to a monolithic, universal "organization" (e.g., Jablin, 1987; Van Maanen & Schein, 1979). A need exists to situate and analyze socialization studies according to historical, societal, and organizational/institutional factors that may influence how organizational members interact with one another. As one example, we need to consider sociohistorical factors such as sexism and racism that reflect historical power relations in Western societies.

To conclude, even though recent socialization studies have sought to understand the newcomer's perspective and experiences, several needs persist. Research needs to delve more deeply into individuals' experiences; to study the socialization experiences of marginalized persons; to identify instances of patriarchy and domination; and to assess the influences of sociohistorical and organizational contexts on socialization practices. This chapter addresses these needs. As I discuss next, the everyday experiences of black women faculty in predominantly white universities demonstrate alternative or deeper issues regarding socialization processes.

BLACK FEMINIST STANDPOINT ANALYSIS
OF LEARNING THE ROPES

The newcomers to whom I refer are black women in occupational roles historically reserved for white males. Although I focus primarily on black women faculty or graduate students at white universities, the discussion also applies to other situations in which black women and other marginalized persons assume nontraditional positions (e.g., top-level corporate executives or high-ranking administrators). These types of hires depart from traditional practices in which recruiters sought an employee who fit the "ideal" of the vacant position. Employers usually based their ideals on race-, sex-, and class-derived prototypes of who "belonged" in which types of jobs. Thus, employers placed white men in high-level positions of power, while they relegated black women to more subservient roles. As one consequence, black women are among the lowest-paid workers in the United States (Parker & Ogilvie, 1996).

However, contemporary organizations are increasingly hiring black women for nontraditional roles, in part as a result of affirmative action initiatives (or other laws and institutional mandates). Consequently, black women frequently enter workplace roles where they previously have not been welcome and where governing ideologies generally have ignored their existence or have viewed them pejoratively. These and other sociohistorical factors place black women in a distinct social location that may affect socialization processes in ways that most researchers do not seem to have considered.

To explore how sociohistorical and contextual factors influence socialization processes, I describe and analyze "micropractices"—daily, mundane occurrences in organizational life (Mumby, 1993b). Rather than attempt to cover the range and complexity of socialization processes, I focus on assimilation, or what happens *after* an individual enters a new role.[1] In addition, I discuss newcomers' interactions with significant others in their immediate work environment, as opposed to organization-based initiatives (e.g., orientation programs or employee manuals, newsletters, and memoranda). Interpersonal interactions with others (e.g., coworkers, supervisors, clients, students, and clerical staff) provide the primary means by which newcomers attempt to learn their role and to reduce uncertainty (Jablin, 1987; D. Katz & Kahn, 1978; R. Katz, 1980). Other persons provide cues that give an individual a sense of achievement and competence (or failure and incompetence; Van Maanen & Schein, 1979).

I concentrate on two broad aspects of assimilation: newcomer treatment (how others interact with the newcomer) and newcomer sense making (the ways that the newcomer attempts to cope with the challenges that she faces). I refer to *role-sending* and *role-taking* concepts that Katz and Kahn (1978) describe in their model of an organization as a system of roles:

> Each person in an organization is linked to some set of other members by virtue of the functional requirements of the system that are heavily implemented through the expectations those members have of the person; he or she is the focal person for that set. An organization can be viewed as consisting of a number of such sets, one for each person in the organization. (p. 220)

Within this system, *role-set* members communicate to the newcomer their expectations regarding the newcomer's role. As the newcomer processes these messages, she engages in role taking.

To portray everyday micropractices, I refer to a variety of sources, including my experiences; data from my research projects on women of color faculty and graduate students of color; essays and research projects by and/or about black women or other women of color; and anecdotal data from some of my friends and acquaintances. To adhere to an important tenet of feminist standpoint theory, I offer examples from numerous individual women to tell a *collective* story, to describe common experiences for members of this particular group.

First, however, to further contextualize the discussion, I offer a bit of autobiographical data (see also B. Allen, 1995b, 1996, 1998a). I am a black, heterosexual, middle-aged woman who was born and raised by my mother in a single-parent home in a working-class black community in Ohio. Currently, I am an associate professor of communication at a large, predominantly white, Western research university. I have worked at this institution since 1989, when the university hired me as a tenure-track assistant professor. Prior to that, I was an instructor in the Comprehensive Sciences Department of the School of Liberal Arts at a black university in the eastern United States. At that time, my area of study was computer-mediated organizational communication. A couple of years ago, I added race, ethnicity, and feminism to my research interests. I am the first and only person of color faculty member in my department, along with only one graduate student of color, a Chicana. The university recruited me based partially on state and institutional directives to hire minorities, as well as concern about public image and funding. I believe that members of my department also valued my expertise in computer-mediated communication. When I came to the university, I was one of only three black women faculty who were tenured or in the tenure track.

Newcomer Treatment

When a newcomer enters her role, numerous sources within the organization provide information about job-related skills as well as organizational and group norms and values (Comer, 1991; Jablin, 1987; Louis, 1980, 1990). In addition, members of her role set consciously and unconsciously convey their expectations of her (Katz & Kahn, 1978; Miller & Jablin, 1991). During formal and informal communication, other persons transmit discretionary (explicit, direct, intentional) and ambient (implicit, indirect, pervasive) messages to the newcomer (Jablin, 1987). Miller and Jablin (1991) state that, "These messages to newcomers constitute efforts to engender (1) a sense of competence in the task role and (2) a sense of acceptance into the work group/organization" (p. 92). Members of the role set transmit prescriptions and proscriptions that reveal what they expect of the newcomer (Katz & Kahn, 1978).

Although the literature tends to presume relatively equal treatment for newcomers, one's identity as a black woman in a nontraditional role can influence her interactions with veteran members of the organization. Members of her role set may not interact with her based strictly on their expectations of her position, or role, as the literature implies (see Katz & Kahn, 1978). Prejudiced individuals who do not welcome a black woman's presence and who want her to fail may give her erroneous or misleading information, if any. Because of institutional sexism and/or racism, white people may apply different standards for evaluating a woman of color. As one consequence, they may provide nonproductive feedback. For instance, they might be more concerned with her personality than with how well she does her job (Cox & Nkomo, 1986). Or, because of fear that the black woman may think that they are patronizing, sexist, and/or racist, white people may refrain from sharing useful information or productive criticism.

In general, the white people with whom she interacts (e.g., coworkers, administrators, supervisors, managers, clients, students, staff, and community members) will have had fewer experiences with blacks than she has had with whites. They will be unaccustomed to dealing with black women in positions of authority. Because many whites do not have a "socially cognitive framework based on authentic contacts with black women, they can easily base their perceptions of them on negative stereotypes and assumptions" (Dumas, 1979, p. 124). These perceptions can influence communication processes.

Prevailing stereotypes and assumptions frequently emanate from various sociohistorical images of black women, some of which I describe and discuss below. White people (and persons of color) may rely on centuries-old pejorative images of black women as blueprints for interacting with us (Dumas, 1979; Hoke, 1997; Orbe, 1998; Parker & Ogilvie, 1996). Although I refer to these stereotypes under separate headings, they can occur simultaneously. Furthermore, some of the examples can apply to more than one stereotype.

Stereotypes

Beneficiary of Affirmative Action. Organizational members often perceive a black woman to be an affirmative action hire, someone recruited strictly to meet policy requirements (Hine, 1997). Sometimes they view minority women as "twofers" because they can be counted for their gender and for their race or ethnicity (Benjamin, 1991). This perception frequently accompanies a belief that the newcomer is not competent. When they enter academe, black women confront the long-standing presumption of white male intellectual superiority and its accompanying belief that blacks are intellectually inferior. Assuming that black women are affirmative action hires fuels this conviction. A. Allen (1994) explains, "Black women, like black men, often are presumed to be at the bottom of the intellectual heap. Employing us is perceived as stepping over the deserving in favor of the least able" (p. 192). Research reveals that white faculty and students often assume that faculty of color are underqualified and/or were hired to meet quotas (James, 1994; Kossek & Zonia, 1994). These false perceptions may restrict whites from accurately perceiving black women as competent colleagues or teachers. They also might induce hostility and distrust, as well as opposition (Essed, 1991).

Through subtle and blatant communication, other persons display these attitudes toward black women. For instance, when I was first hired, a faculty member in my department was overheard telling a group of students that I was not qualified, that I had been hired only to meet a quota. In addition, a black male faculty member from another department told me (during a reception for new faculty of color) that someone in my department said I was not a good writer (see B. Allen, 1995b). A black woman law professor recounts her experience as a graduate student preparing to enter the job market: "A white male professor told me that as a black woman I would have to 'pee on the floor' at job interviews not to get hired" (A. Allen, 1994, p. 186). Black women research participants report comparable experiences. One participant stated, "My appointment was seen as an affirmative action hire. People did not expect me to be successful. But I was. Some were actually rude enough to tell me so—thinking it was a compliment" (as cited in Moses, 1989, p. 14). A second woman said,

> I was treated most graciously when I came to campus—many people in my department breathed a sigh of relief that they had "gotten one." So the pressure was off. But on the other hand, I have been insulted, treated with arrogance and a sense of superiority, especially by white males. (as cited in Moses, 1989, p. 14)

Thus, wherever a black woman turns on campus, she may receive messages from (or endure interactions with) colleagues, students, and staff that implicitly or explicitly question her right to be in her new role. As one writer observes, "Black women have their credentials tested over and over again" (Moses, 1989, p. 11).

Some persons may challenge her based on her chosen area of study. People often assume that a black woman's scholarship focuses on race and/or gender. This stereotype probably stems from the notions that people of color are responsible for studying these topics and that we are not qualified to study other disciplines. If she does focus on such issues, a black woman may endure disparaging and discouraging interactions because others may view her work as inconsequential and marginal (B. Allen, 1995a; Benjamin, 1991; Burgess, 1997; Cox & Nkomo, 1990). If she has chosen a more "mainstream" discipline, people question and negate her capabilities to succeed. Black women in the life and physical sciences are particularly vulnerable to these types of attacks (Essien, 1997; Henry, 1994).

Black women faculty report that their white students (especially males) frequently challenge and disrespect them, thereby ignoring the hierarchy of the teacher-student relationship in favor of white/male dominance over black/female (Benjamin, 1991; Burgess, 1997; Moses, 1989; Pope & Joseph, 1997). One of my friends who teaches at a predominantly white university explains,

> I experience students ignoring their own cultural hierarchy [for authority] when it comes to me as an African American woman with a Ph.D. They feel they can follow the dictates of white superiority when it comes to me. They are always the supreme authority and are always worthy of being in control.

For example, when one black faculty member first began teaching college in 1976, a young white male student asked her, "What gives you the right to teach this class?" (A. Allen, 1994, p. 183). Unfortunately, contemporary students also engage in such disrespectful behaviors. A research participant reported that a student said to her, "You are here because of affirmative action" (Pope & Joseph, 1997, p. 256). Another respondent indicated that a student told her that he did not want a "colored" teacher (Pope & Joseph, 1997).

Black women graduate students have described situations in which professors seem to acknowledge them and value their input only during discussion of diversity issues; otherwise, they feel silenced and invisible during classroom discussions (B. Allen, 1998b; Sandler, 1986; Zappert & Stansbury, 1987). For instance, teachers exhibit negative nonverbal cues such as rolling their eyes or sighing when students of color speak about their concerns (e.g., course materials and topics that do not reflect their cultural ideologies or their existence). Graduate students experience other forms of ethnocentrism and patriarchy: A black woman in her early 40s told me that one of her white male graduate professors told her that she was inarticulate, that he could not understand her speech. Yet this woman is an independent consultant who is much in demand for motivational speaking. Proud of her hard work on a challenging project in an engineering graduate program, a young black woman I know was crushed when her instructor chided, "You should do your own work."

Staff members sometimes display prejudicial attitudes and behaviors toward black women (Benjamin, 1991). A new assistant professor of history told me that several white men in her department would not speak to her when she encountered them in the hallway or on campus. In addition, they showed favoritism to her white male office mate, who also was a new assistant professor. He could give the office staff work (e.g., tests to be typed) at the last minute, and they immediately would complete it. The staff members told her, however, that she had to turn in her work at least 3 days in advance. It seems that the office staff took their cues about discriminatory treatment from faculty and administrators.

Token. Organizational actors enact stereotypes when they seem to regard a black woman as a token, someone who represents her social category. They identify her as a symbol rather than as an individual. Tokenism can lead to performance pressures because organizational members evaluate the person more closely than they do nontokens and then generalize to other persons in the same category (Kanter, 1977). For example, one research participant—a black professional woman—recounts an interaction with her white supervisor:

> "I hope *you* make it." Emphasis on *you*. And I told my new supervisor right then and there. I stopped her in her tracks and I said, "What do you mean? I detect some sort of implication here regarding the pronoun *you*. I don't feel that you're addressing it singularly, but plural. And there's nobody here but me and you." (St. John & Feagin, 1997, p. 193)

The supervisor replied that a black person had never "made it" in the role.

Tokenism also can elicit role encapsulation, in which dominants distort the token's characteristics to fit stereotypes, thereby limiting the number and types of roles that the token may assume (Kanter, 1977). Viewing a woman of color as an expert on race and/or gender relations represents a common example of this mind-set. This may produce limited opportunities for career development (S. Collins, 1989, 1997; Ilgen & Youtz, 1986). For instance, in corporate settings, executives often restrict blacks to human resources jobs or relegate them to cultural attaché roles (e.g., community liaison or urban affairs) as opposed to more powerful positions (S. Collins, 1989, 1997; Tucker, 1994).

In academe, other people routinely and frequently consult black women faculty members on racial or gender issues (Hoke, 1997; McKay, 1997; Moses, 1989, 1997). When I was first hired, some of my colleagues consulted me for advice about how to handle black students in the classroom, and they requested me to give guest lectures about race and gender (even though my area of study at that time was computer-mediated organizational communication). Although service is a defined component of my academic role, I received many more requests to serve on university committees than my two white female peers did. I believe that I was invited to serve on these committees to be the spokesperson for blacks, people of color, women of color, and/or white women. Often, chairpersons from other departments invite me to lunches or dinners with minority faculty job applicants. Once, the university president invited me to accompany her to a meeting with minority community leaders in the nearby big city (see B. Allen, 1995b, for additional examples).

Members of an organization may believe that a black woman's *only* role is to be an expert on issues of race. Once, a white male student dropped my introduction to organizational communication class after the first session because, he said, he had already fulfilled the college's ethnic studies requirement. I had made no references to ethnicity during my opening remarks (see B. Allen, 1998a). Similarly, as I noted earlier, graduate students report that their professors and classmates expect them to provide *the* minority perspective on course materials, even as they question the students' intellectual capacities (see Baraka, 1997).

Mammy. In addition to regarding black women as tokens, members of organizations often expect them to assume nurturing, caretaking roles that are reminiscent of the black woman's role as mammy in early U.S. history (Dumas, 1979; Hoke, 1997; Mullings, 1994; Omolade, 1994).

> Whether she likes it or not, the black woman has come to represent the kind of person, a style of life, a set of attitudes and behaviors through which individuals and groups seek to fulfill their own socio-emotional needs in organizations. (Dumas, 1979, p. 123)

Consequently, members of the organization may expect her to be a mother confessor, to provide comfort, and to advocate for the oppressed. Moses (1989) reports that black women often seem to spend more time than their white counterparts discussing personal issues with students (see also Benjamin, 1991; Burgess, 1997; Hoke, 1997; McKay, 1997; Moses, 1997). As McKay (1997) points out, "Students (even white ones) in need of counseling on academic issues as well as psychological ones continually appear on the doorstep of the black mother, the great bosom of the world" (p. 21).

My experiences strongly support the preceding points. Students in my department, as well as students of color and women students from other departments, frequently seek my advice and comfort regarding their concerns about discrimination or other personal problems. Some of my white colleagues have asked me how to deal with problematic black students. When I first arrived at the university, a member of the Black Student Alliance asked me to be their adviser.

Matriarch. Black women also may face the stereotype of matriarch, an aggressive, overbearing individual. Sociological studies by Frasier (1939) and Moynihan (1965) spawned this caricature by offering the derisive label of matriarch to a society that devalues powerful women or blacks (Mullings, 1994; Parker & Ogilvie, 1996). Research shows that some persons may believe this stereotype. For example, white college students rated black women as more confrontational than white women (Weitz & Gordon, 1993). Similarly, white professional women viewed black women's conflict-management styles as more confrontational than white women's (Shuter & Turner, 1997). A tall, soft-spoken black woman graduate teaching assistant whom I know received negative evaluations from a couple of white males in her class; they described her as intimidating and loud.

Power Plays

Although power dynamics thread through the examples that I have already described, I include this separate section to depict blatant exemplars of the ways that incumbents wield power over black women newcomers. These interactions reflect historical relations of group power and dominance.

When I was hired, the chair of my department at that time (three men have chaired the department during my 9 years here) warned me that I would be asked to "sit on every damned committee." He knew that many members of the university actively were trying to address "diversity" issues and that they would view me as an "expert." He gave me an "out" by telling them that he did not *allow* me to sit on external committees. I appreciate that he was looking out for my welfare, but I believe that he was demonstrating a patriarchal attitude. In a protective father role, he did not seem to consider that I was an adult who had her own ideas about service. One of the reasons that I accepted the position was because I saw the dire need for more women and people of color at the university, and I wanted to be an active agent for social change (see B. Allen, 1998a). I wish that he had invited me to discuss how I felt about service and then advised me about how to negotiate service roles so that I could accomplish my personal goals as well as meet the department's expectations regarding research and teaching.[2] Given the university's mission to increase and value diversity, such a discussion might have been productive for both of us.

Power dynamics also arose when a couple of department chairs, the dean of my school, the chancellor, and the president of the university "invited" me to be a member of a variety of university committees.[3] These committees ranged from those that specifically dealt with diversity issues to others for which I believe I often was expected to fulfill the role of token. From their positions of power, these persons probably did not stop to consider that I might be overwhelmed with requests to serve or even that I might not have been qualified to provide the perspective that they desired. This tendency among persons in power positions to expect oppressed people to shoulder the burden of addressing diversity symbolizes their privilege and status:

> Whenever the need for some pretense of communication arises, those who profit from our oppression call upon us to share our knowledge with them. In other words, it is the responsibility of the oppressed to teach the oppressors their mistakes. . . . The oppressors maintain their position and evade responsibility for their actions. (Lorde, 1984, p. 114)

As my tenure case worked its way up the university hierarchy, the chair of my department at that time asked to meet with me. Speaking on behalf of the dean, he offered me 2 more years to "prove myself," because, he said, the dean doubted that my case would succeed. It seems that he did not think that evaluators would view my research record favorably. He thought that I had spent too much time on service, perhaps to the detriment of my research endeavors. Thus, they would grant me 2 additional years to redeem myself. I refused the offer.

Like this chairperson, the white people that a black woman encounters probably do not even think twice about how they interact with her: "The power imbalance is reinforced, as blacks tread lightly, carefully, and whites comfortably go about their business. The powerful can choose what they wish to ignore" (Thomas, 1989, p. 284). The powerful also can choose how they behave toward the powerless, as the following example from a black woman faculty member illustrates: "An eminent white scholar with whom I was dining suddenly took my chin into his hand to inspect my face. He told me, approvingly, that I resembled his family's former maid" (A. Allen, 1994, p. 187). The fact that he was comfortable touching her face without her permission reveals his patriarchal position as starkly as his patronizing comment does. White persons often feel comfortable touching a black woman's hair (particularly when it is in braids or some other nonmainstream style). In addition, white men routinely invade black women's office spaces or interrupt their conversations (see McKay, 1997, p. 14).

Students also engage in power plays, as the following anecdote illustrates:

> A white male student informed me that at the beginning of the course he had often been angry at many of the things I had said, and that he had considered confronting me and "punching" me in the nose several times. When he told me the story he was congratulating himself on not having taken such drastic action. (A. Allen, 1994, p. 146)

This woman's story is not an isolated incident. A research project on black women and student harassment reveals that the typical harasser was a white male (Pope & Joseph, 1997). Students' behaviors ranged from verbal comments (e.g., "Bitch, go back to Africa") to physical attacks. One woman shared the following:

> After reading his grade, the student lunged out of his seat, threw the chair on its side, and shouted very loudly, "I don't want that grade. You can't teach. You black women are not qualified; you are here because of affirmative action. I'm going to see that you don't get tenure." He then stormed out of the room. (as cited in Pope & Joseph, 1997, p. 252)

Another professor reported that a white female student tried to persuade her peers to write negative evaluations of her teaching. A friend told me about a black woman faculty member who was asked by a white male student, during class, "How would you feel if someone called you a 'black bitch'?"

A final way that dominants engage in power plays is through sexual harassment. One woman reports that her adviser kissed her on the mouth (A. Allen, 1994). When a professor friend of mine wore a T-shirt decorated with figures of African women, a white male professor commented, in front of staff members, "If you shake your breasts, it would look like those women were dancing." Other black women report that white male students made sexual advances toward them (McKay, 1997; Moses, 1989; Pope & Joseph, 1997).

Insensitive or Patronizing Comments or Requests

This final category encompasses types of comments that others make to black women. On top of the interactions that I have described, these add insult to injury. The following incidents typify others' assumptions about black women and their lives. A graduate student I know described her interaction with a white male professor during an orientation session:

> [The professor said,] "Wow! To be black *and* a woman getting your Ph.D." Then I believe he commented that my family must be proud. . . . Not only did he lack political correctness and social grace, but he also (1) had no concept of the fact that I had just come from a university where seeing a black woman with a Ph.D. goes completely unnoticed because that is just the way it is (and is supposed to be) and (2)

had no way of knowing whether every person, both male and female, in my family held a Ph.D.

An attorney friend of mine cannot count the number of times that a white person has said, "Why did *you* decide to become a lawyer?" Similarly, people often tell a young black woman graduate student I mentor, "You don't look like an engineer." A white male asked a black woman branch bank manager (the only person of color among 12 managers) to wear a blond wig (i.e., play the part of the buffoon) in a skit. A white woman faculty member told a black woman that she might be happier if she "returned" to a historically black college: "My Ivy League graduate training, my colleague told me, would make me a 'queen' at a historically black college" (McKay, 1997, p. 14). Another black graduate student describes her first meeting with her temporary adviser:

> After telling him that my interest was in African American women, ethnic identity, and organizational communication, the discussion moved to issues of career planning and life in academia in general. He proceeded to tell me that because that I was (1) black, (2) female, (3) had interest in feminism, and (4) tall in stature, that I might have a hard time in the field because people (translation—white folks) would be intimidated by me!

Houston (1997) discusses three types of insensitive statements that white people sometimes make to black women: "I never even notice that you're black"; "You're different . . . "; and "I understand your experience as a black woman because . . . sexism is as bad as racism, I watch 'The Cosby Show,' [or] I'm also a member of a minority group" (p. 192). As Houston explains, these types of statements erase or diminish a black woman's ethnic cultural experience.

To summarize, a black woman newcomer endures a complex variety of treatment from incumbent members, many of whom may interact with her based on stereotypes, from positions of power, or both. As a result, a black woman may find herself responding to a series of stereotypical projections rather than being able to establish herself as a vital member in the organization. On the one hand, members of the organization seem to value her for nurturing behaviors and for representing the "minority" voice, but only when they ask for her perspectives and advice. On the other hand, they may question whether she is competent to be an intellectual, a scholar. Consequently, black women may experience a type of role ambiguity (confusion about requirements or lack of information regarding the role) that the literature does not describe (e.g., D. Katz & Kahn, 1978; R. Katz, 1977).

As she endures all sorts of subtle and blatant forms of prejudice, sexism, and racism, and provides a variety of services that her job description does not include, a black woman tries to make sense of the multiple and sometimes conflicting messages that bombard her. In their discussion of role taking, Katz and Kahn (1978) propose the concept of *received role,* the newcomer's "perceptions and cognitions" of what members of her role set have communicated to her. This received role strongly influences how the member performs her role and how she perceives her competence and value to the organization. Next, I discuss potential sources of stress regarding their received role that confront black women as they engage in making sense of their socialization experiences.

Newcomer Sense Making

Socialization researchers have acknowledged that newcomers experience conflict and stress as they attempt to assume their new role (Katz & Kahn, 1978; Miller & Jablin, 1991). As Van Maanen and Schein (1979) observe, "Individuals undergoing any organizational transition are in an anxiety-producing situation" (p. 214). Newcomers usually try to reduce this anxiety by learning the functional and social requirements of their new role as quickly as possible. They work actively to make sense of the situation and information that they receive or elicit (Weick, 1995).

The naturally stressful position of newcomer probably is more pronounced for black women. Many of them undergo constant inner struggles as they endure the types of interactions I described earlier, as they try to learn their role, as they conduct job-related tasks, and as they fulfill external obligations. Next, I describe some of the major sources of stress and conflict that black women may experience as they receive role information and engage in the role-taking process. Again, although I divide these into topical headings, the issues may overlap.

Potential Stressors

Seeking Information. A primary way that newcomers strive to reduce uncertainty about job-related skills and group norms and values is by seeking information rather than waiting for others to provide it (Conrad & Poole, 1998; Katz, 1985; Miller & Jablin, 1991). Therefore, socialization researchers often study newcomer information-seeking behaviors (Ashford, 1986; Ashford & Cummings, 1985; Comer, 1991; Louis, 1990; Miller & Jablin, 1991; Morrison, 1993; Van Maanen & Schein, 1979). These researchers report that newcomers employ a variety of strategies to obtain information from such sources as the organization itself (e.g., employee manuals or training sessions), coworkers, managers and supervisors, social networks, or mentors.

Miller and Jablin (1991) offer a theoretical model of factors that affect newcomers' information-seeking tactics. They describe some of these tactics (e.g., direct questions, indirect questions, disguising intent, surveillance, observation, and disclosure), and they provide propositions about how newcomers enact them. They contend that newcomers often are aware of costs or social exchanges that embed information-seeking behaviors. For instance, newcomers express concern about "bugging" coworkers or eliciting social disapproval. Miller and Jablin further posit that newcomers are more likely to ask direct questions when they feel comfortable approaching a source or when they feel that little chance exists for "losing face" or being embarrassed. They hypothesize that the higher the level of uncertainty, the more a newcomer engages in information-seeking behavior. In addition, they argue that individual differences (e.g., self-esteem and tolerance for ambiguity) may influence newcomer behaviors. Finally, they note that contextual factors, such as the type of socialization program, can also affect newcomers' information-seeking behaviors (see also Miller, 1996).

Social conditions also might influence black women's information-seeking behaviors.

> Acquiring role information is particularly challenging for many black women, because, in general, they have limited career opportunities, experiences, and interactions in high-status positions through which to learn role requirements sufficiently well. They are particularly vulnerable at work when entering newly acquired positions where they feel pressured to perform, in order to compensate for both their race and gender, before learning adequately the formal and informal roles. (Bell, 1990, p. 475)

Aware that others might use stereotypes to perceive and evaluate her behaviors, a black woman may hesitate to seek information directly, not only because of how others might judge her but also because she feels responsible for representing others like herself. A senior vice president of a large finance firm explains, "When they put you in a job, you feel as if you are carrying the future of any black person or any woman in this role forever" (as cited in Tucker, 1994, p. 62). A black woman may fear that others might offer her misinformation because they want her to fail. Her white coworkers may feel competitive and threatened by her presence because they believe that she will reap benefits that they will not because of her perceived "twofer" status (Benjamin, 1991). Thus, a black woman may be especially conscientious and cautious about whom to ask, what to ask, and when to ask for information.

When I became a tenure-track professor, I did not anticipate the complexities of the role. Accustomed to reading a situation and quickly assimilating, I felt frustrated and confused as the intricacies of my role emerged. In previous job situations, my information-seeking behaviors paralleled those that Miller and Jablin (1991) predict of a newcomer (e.g., as a person with high self-esteem, I was likely to ask questions directly). However, in this new context, I proceeded cautiously. Acutely aware of my "first and only" status, I rarely asked direct questions or sought help. Instead, I paid close attention to my colleagues and how they enacted their roles. Although I was friendly with my colleagues, I rarely consulted with them about how to do my job (even though some of them routinely approached me for advice about race or gender issues or computers).

Mentors and sponsors are particularly important sources for learning the ropes in complex roles such as faculty or executive positions. Some research shows that black women often are not involved in mentoring relationships (Benjamin, 1991; Justus, Freitag, & Parker, 1987; Moses, 1989). However, Thomas (1989) found that black women frequently participate in developmental relationships with other women, but rarely with white men. In most contemporary university settings, as well as in the corporate world, white men usually are the main persons positioned to mentor black women newcomers. Because of homophily (a tendency to develop relationships with others like oneself), white men and black women might not easily develop mentoring or apprentice relationships with one another (Burgess, 1997; Ibarra, 1993). The mentor-protégé relationship seems to work best when the two parties highly identify with one another (Thomas, 1990).

Research shows that white mentors find it difficult to build sharing relationships with black women. Thomas (1989) contends that the U.S. history of race relations and racial taboos influences cross-sex/cross-race mentoring relationships (see also Conrad & Poole, 1998). Black women in career-enhancing relationships with white men may encounter pressures and negative attributions. For instance, their coworkers may accuse them of having sex with their mentor. In addition, white men's coworkers might accuse them of betraying other white people, of being disloyal (Moses, 1989). Intergroup dynamics may occur when a black woman feels pressure to avoid contact with other blacks to seem loyal to the dominant group (Benjamin, 1991; Ibarra, 1993). Similarly, she may experience intragroup sanctions from black people for interacting with white men (Ibarra, 1993).

White men may not believe that they understand black women's needs (Hall & Sandler, 1983; Moses, 1989). Research reveals that cross-sex or cross-race/ethnicity mentoring relationships seem to focus more on task-related issues than same-sex and same-race/ethnicity relationships do (Conrad & Poole, 1998). When I first became an assistant professor, I took advantage of a program at the university that matched minority faculty with professors outside of their own departments. My mentor was a white man from a sister discipline of communication. We met once for coffee, and I enjoyed our conversation. A few months later, I called him when I was feeling stressed. I disclosed that I was feeling bewildered and confused. He seemed to want to help, but the relationship fizzled. He did not contact me again. I ran into him on campus some months later, and he seemed uncomfortable. I never figured out what happened.

Newcomers can also obtain important information and insight from social networks. However, black women may experience restricted access to informal networks because of exclusion or self-imposed isolation (Benjamin, 1991; Denton, 1990; Greenhaus, Parasuraman, & Wormley, 1990). Their white colleagues may not invite them to participate because of outright discrimination or boundary-heightening effects (e.g., misgivings about interacting with an "other" outside of the job context). In addition, black women may decline to involve themselves in social events. Some may isolate themselves because they "interpret invitations to participate in informal relationships as bids to behave according to stereotypes" (Dumas, 1979, p. 125). Once, a white woman at a faculty gathering asked me to sing a Negro spiritual (B. Allen, 1995a).

Many black women have other obligations (e.g., family responsibilities or community work) that preclude their spending time on extracurricular activities that often characterize social interaction (e.g., happy hour, golf, or other sports). Some black women may choose not to interact much with whites beyond performing the assigned tasks of their jobs (Bell, 1990). Or some of us may want to avoid yet another situation in which we have to suppress our own cultural preferences in favor of the dominant culture.

Bicultural Identity. Many black women may face the challenge of negotiating a bicultural life structure (i.e., attempts to balance professional and personal lives) and experience the emotional strains of walking a line between two worlds (Bell, 1990, 1992; Denton, 1990). They also have to respond to demands from their job and from the black community (Locke, 1997). A research participant explains,

> You have double demands placed on you; you have a choice to ignore one and go with the other or try to satisfy both. I try to satisfy both. I don't believe I would be here without the support of the community. . . . I feel I have an obligation and debt to pay to my community. (as cited in Benjamin, 1991, p. 130)

In addition, a black woman may be "torn between the expectations and demands born of her mythical image and those that are inherent in her official status and task in the formal organizations" (Dumas, 1979, p. 123; see also B. Allen, 1995b; Omolade, 1994). I often struggle with the dilemma of trying to refute others' stereotyped expectations of me (e.g., to be a "mammy") while feeling an ingrained sense of obligation (based on how I have been socialized as black and as a woman) to be a caretaker, to look out for others (see Collins, 1991).

Black women must negotiate the paradox of being expected to check their race and gender at the door at the same time that organizational members solicit their insight for dealing with race and gender issues (Bowman, 1991). Baraka (1997) explains, "The Eurocentric academy most readily embraces those African Americans who divest themselves of their culture and heritage to become more acceptably European and limit their interests to 'black' or 'gender' issues" (p. 242).

In addition, black women sometimes must negotiate conflicts related to the two stigmatized aspects of their identity (B. Allen, 1995b; Collins, 1991; Dill, 1979). In an article titled "Black Woman Professor—White University," McKay (1983) asserts,

> One constantly feels the pressure of a double-edged sword: simultaneously, a perverse visibility and a convenient invisibility. We are treated as blacks, on one hand, as women, on the other. We are left constantly taking stock of the landscape as different issues arise and we have to determine which side, women, or non-white we wish to be identified [with]. (p. 144)

Thus, black women may "experience pressure to choose between their racial identity and their womanhood" (Moses, 1989, p. 1). When one of my former students (a black man) faced rape charges, some members of the black community wanted me to support the student, while women's groups wanted me to support their position. I responded by avoiding everyone (see B. Allen, 1998a). Trying to negotiate these aspects of bicultural identity can contribute to role ambiguity, role overload, or role conflict (i.e., "the inability to conform to the expectations of a particular role," Denton, 1990, p. 456; see also Benjamin, 1991; Katz & Kahn, 1978).

Isolation and Alienation. Sometimes black women feel frustrated because "people around them are likely to be insensitive to their needs for socio-psychological support, reassurance, or some relief from the heavy demands on their time and energy" (Dumas, 1979, pp. 124-125; see also Benjamin, 1991). Believing the stereotype of matriarch, other people may assume that a black woman is emotionally strong and capable of taking care of herself (Moses, 1989). Her white colleagues may seem to be oblivious to her plight as an "outsider within" (see B. Allen, 1998a, p. 578; Collins, 1991). One woman explains,

> No one ever stopped to think that this might be [an] uncomfortable or difficult situation [being the only and/or first black woman in her role]. It's not an issue for them [white people]. You just have to learn how to deal with it. But I don't think you ever stop being uncomfortable. (as cited in Tucker, 1994, p. 61)

In meetings or classrooms, I sometimes get the strangest feeling when I realize that, once again, I am the only person of color (and sometimes also the only woman) present.

Black women who study race and/or gender may feel alienated or isolated because their white colleagues marginalize their area of study (Benjamin, 1991; Henry, 1994; Hoke, 1997; James & Farmer, 1993; McKay, 1997). Black women who study a mainstream topic may feel alienated because other scholars question their credibility (as I discussed earlier). These women also may feel physically isolated and alienated when the community surrounding the university is predominantly white (Locke, 1997). Besides alienation from colleagues and community, some black women's spouses, family, and friends also may not understand their situations. For instance, I do not have many friends or family members who understand the life of an academic. Many of them believe that I have it made because I teach *only* two classes a semester and, as they put it, I "don't work" in the summer.

To summarize, as they attempt to learn the ropes, black women newcomers encounter numerous potential stressors that may arise from socially constructed aspects of their identity (i.e., their race and/or their gender). As I discuss next, black women respond in a variety of ways to these and other sources of stress.

Responding to Sources of Stress

Before I describe responses and strategies, I must note that many black women expend a lot of energy trying to make sense of our experiences. Often, I find myself second-guessing: Was that remark racist, sexist, both, or neither? I also wonder if I am being paranoid or too sensitive. These thoughts may scurry across my mind, or they may consume minutes or hours of my time. In addition, double-bind situations often arise in which I feel "damned if I do, damned if I don't."

Consider, for instance, the numerous times that I had to decide whether to accept invitations to serve. If I provided the service, I might perpetuate the notion that minority persons should shoulder the burden. If I did not, other minority persons might feel that I betrayed them or that I did not care about the issues.

In response to double binds and other issues, many black women faculty members decide to exit their jobs. Some of them transfer to other institutions of higher education. Others join corporate America. Sometimes they become entrepreneurs. Sadly, whether we leave or we stay in nontraditional roles, many black women endure physiological and psychological consequences of our first and/or only status. We may suffer chronic physical ailments or burnout. We may have nervous breakdowns and even commit suicide.

McKay (1997) recounts an interaction with a colleague who asked her, if things are so bad, why do black women stay in the academy? She replied, "We choose to remain in these contested spaces because as black women (and men) we know that we have a right to occupy them and will not be driven out by those who would gladly see us go" (p. 15). When they choose to remain in their roles, black women employ a variety of strategies to negotiate the impacts of racism and sexism and other sources of stress. They may avoid discriminatory work environments or alter or lower their career goals (Parker & Ogilvie, 1996). They may assimilate (Locke, 1997), or they may employ proactive strategies such as networking/mentoring or compartmentalizing (Parker & Ogilvie, 1996). To fill the gap formed by limited access to mentors or social networks, some newcomers form relationships and networks with individuals (women and men from varying racial or ethnic backgrounds) from other departments or universities who specialize in similar areas of research. We communicate through phone calls or electronic mail, and we interact at social gatherings or conferences.

Black women also develop social support systems with other black women or women of color who may or may not be academics. For instance, one of my friends has developed a group of black women scholars on her campus called the Brown Sugar Brigade. On my campus, women of color faculty have formed a Sister Scholars group that meets once a month at one of their homes. In addition to offering task-related information, these sources provide a type of psychosocial support that our white peers cannot. As Denton (1990) observes, "Black women's bonds provide direct confirmation and validation for experiences that others might not readily understand" (p. 448). She elaborates,

> For black women, who must consider whether an incident was motivated by their race, their sex, or both (Smith & Stewart, 1983), support from significant black female friends can clarify the source of discrimination and help them select pertinent coping behaviors. (p. 448)

These social networks help to make black women feel less isolated and alienated. For example, I am a member of a couple of electronic mail groups that provide support and information.

I also have developed productive mentoring relationships with two white men in my department. One of them was instrumental in my being hired, and he always has respected and supported me. He has played a critical role in my advancement as an organizational communication scholar by assisting and advising me regarding publications, by introducing me to other academicians in the field, and by helping me to present a strong case for my tenure and promotion review. The second person recently joined our faculty. I scheduled a meeting with him and asked him to be one of my mentors. He agreed, and he already has provided useful information and guidance. I meet with him regularly, and I am comfortable seeking information from him. My research and writing on the socialization of people of color have helped me to become more proactive in my own career advancement.

Some black women compartmentalize their roles by drawing sharp boundaries among them (Bell, 1990; Parker & Ogilvie, 1996). This can prove advantageous, as Parker and Ogilvie (1996) observe: "Having multiple, compartmentalized roles gives them perspectives on a setback or problem in one role because it is only one part of their identity" (p. 204). My colleagues seemed skeptical about my attitude when I told them that I would not be devastated if I did not earn tenure. However, I meant what I said; just like I got that job, I knew I could get another one. I know better than to limit my identity to my job as a university professor.

In a study about black women executives, Bell (1990) concludes, "They are extremely vigilant in their work environments, and they take pain in not revealing parts of their true selves" (p. 474). Thus, one way that many black women respond to the threat of stereotyping is by monitoring themselves. For instance, some black women may pay special attention to their appearance. Participants in a research project reported that they intentionally manage their dress to appear professional (B. Allen, 1998b). One woman said,

> I feel like people look at Black bodies more. . . . I try to represent Black women in a very positive way no matter where I go because often I am the only one . . . and I want my colleagues to have a good impression. I think there is a stereotype of black women being "sex pots." (p. 9)

Another research participant told me, "There have been times when I wanted to dress in a more ethnically appealing manner [e.g., mud cloth, head wrap], but I shy away from doing this because . . . I do not want to appear too militant" (p. 12).

An awareness of stereotypes also might influence the ways that black women display their feelings (B. Allen, 1996; Tucker, 1994). I rarely display emotions such as anger, frustration, or disappointment because I do not want to perpetuate stereotypes of being overbearing, militant, or hypersensitive.

Because of consciousness raising (i.e., studying, thinking, writing, and talking about feminism and black women's lives), I realize that black women sometimes are complicit in hegemonic practices. For instance, I sometimes reinforce stereotypes or remain silent in the face of oppression (mine and others'). In addition, I used to say "yes" to all requests for service because I felt obligated. I rarely questioned the process or the system. Furthermore, I continue to struggle with identity issues related to scholarship. I used to be offended and defensive when someone asked me if I studied race and/or gender. I would reply proudly that I study computers, thus attempting to establish that I am intelligent (because I am expert in a white-male-dominated area of study). I liked the positive (and usually surprised) way that people would respond to me. Now that I conduct research on race and gender, I sometimes hesitate to admit it. I believe that my reticence stems largely from internalized racism and sexism. I also struggle with the irony that I am fulfilling the stereotype that a black woman scholar should study race and/or gender. I will continue to raise my consciousness and free myself from those hegemonic shackles.

Although the literature implies that persons who remain in the organization have been metamorphosed (i.e., transformed into the ideal employee), that is not always the case. In fact, "newcomers may stay but not become identified with the organization" (Bullis & Bach, 1989b, p. 287). In addition, newcomers may try to change the groups to accommodate their needs (Jablin, 1987). Indeed, black women may work for their personal needs, but many of us also work to effect social change for others. We may speak out against stereotyping and discriminatory behaviors. We take advantage of situations in which others ask for our opinions about diversity issues by being straightforward and by helping to develop and implement policy.

Related to this work to influence change, many black women in university settings engage in acts of resistance. As I reported earlier, I did not allow administrators to postpone my tenure case for 2 years. I told the chair of my department that either the university valued me and would give me what I earned or I could move on. Although I know that I can offer beneficial insight and perspective to my department, I have learned to refuse to shoulder the entire responsibility. I encourage my colleagues to refer to other sources and resources and to share responsibility. To negotiate constant demands from others, I have learned how and when to say "no." I carefully consider the pros and cons of accepting an invitation to serve, and I feel less guilty than I used to when I decline. When I say "no" to community activities, I explain that I need to concentrate on research and writing so that I can retain my position in the university (and therefore continue to be available to assist the community). The inviting party usually seems to understand and support my position. At the university, I try to serve only on committees that engage in making decisions, solving problems, or developing policy.

I also enact hooks's (1989) definition of resistance by actively shaping a new identity of myself, rather than allowing other forces to shape me (see also Etter-Lewis, 1993). Therefore, adding black feminism to my area of research represents a significant act of resistance. Following Collins's (1991) counsel, I am using my "outsider within" status to help create black feminist thought, the self-knowledge that can help black women break glass ceilings (Locke, 1997). To cope with stressors related to bicultural identity, I have learned to value how I have been socialized as a black woman academic. I am proud of the fact that I can move fluidly from one "cultural" context to another. I refuse to be stigmatized, even as I am aware of oppression. I try not to operate from a "victim" mentality (B. Allen, 1995b, 1996, 1998a; Buzzanell, 1994).

I am proud of my heritage, and I infuse elements of my black woman cultural experience into my work. In the classroom, I sometimes use a "call and response" teaching style reminiscent of some black preachers who interact with their congregation by actively eliciting responses (e.g., "Can I get an 'amen'?"; B. Allen, 1998a). I intersperse anecdotes about my life into lecture and discussion material to give my white students positive perspectives on "the black experience." In addition, I view my concern for others as an "ethic of caring" that adds value to how I interact with colleagues, staff, administrators, and students (see Collins, 1991).

To address my sense of physical isolation and alienation, I moved to a suburb 40 miles away from campus that is more diverse in terms of race and ethnicity, class, and age. I have developed a diverse group of friends and acquaintances, and I engage in a variety of activities that allow me to honor and nurture many facets of my multicultural identity.

Summary

Viewing socialization practices from a black feminist standpoint illuminates issues that previous research has not broached. Therefore, the analysis contributes to our understanding and analyses of "learning the ropes" processes. This discussion supports feminist standpoint theory's argument for assessing contextual influences on social practices. The examples demonstrate that the unique social location of black women in contemporary U.S. society affects their socialization experiences. Moreover, the specific context of black women in nontraditional occupational roles exposes numerous ways that members of organizations enact hegemony.

Black women's experiences demonstrate that socialization processes may not be based solely on the expectations inherent in one's occupational role, as the literature implies. Rather, organizational members may project onto the newcomer expectations that arise from sociohistorical stereotypes. The job description of assistant professor did not align with the expectations that members of my role set conveyed to me. Furthermore, it did not correspond with the expectations that my role-set members seemed to have for my two white female peers (hired at the same time that I was). Socialization does not encompass a universal experience for newcomers. The particular social location of a black woman affects interpersonal interactions when she assumes occupational roles that women like her previously have not occupied. I must introduce a caveat: Because I write from a black feminist standpoint, this discussion refers only to black women's impressions and perceptions. Consequently, the examples provide insight about newcomers' received roles rather than sent roles (see Katz & Kahn, 1978). Future research might assess incumbents' experiences and accounts.

This analysis underscores the primacy of communication and interpersonal interactions in socialization micropractices. Moreover, it reveals the complexity and some of the nuances of "learning the ropes" practices. For instance, a black feminist standpoint demonstrates that organizational socialization is not entirely rational. Rather, emotions permeate "learning the ropes" processes. In addition, the examples indicate that this naturally stressful situation holds particular sources of stress for black women. Finally, black women's experiences show how domination and patriarchy pervade socialization practices. They also illuminate the multiplicity of ways that black women respond to micropractices, including acts of compliance and resistance.

This analysis is nowhere near exhaustive. I could have written *much* more about this complicated topic. I hope that the discussion provides insight and direction for future research on women of color and organizational socialization. As scholars theorize about learning the ropes, they might consider revelations that this chapter provides. More relevant to my goals for this essay, this depiction yields numerous implications for everyday practices, as I discuss next.

IMPLICATIONS FOR
ORGANIZATIONAL SOCIALIZATION PRACTICES

In this section, I offer recommendations for social practices that arise from the discussion. I provide suggestions for persons who interact with black women or other historically disenfranchised persons, then offer guidelines for newcomers. Although I focus on black women, these suggestions also apply to other newcomers. As a black woman historian observes, "In many ways the experiences of black women professors serve as a window into the issues, problems, and frustrations most marginalized groups and women in general daily encounter in the academy" (Hine, 1997, p. 337). The recommendations might benefit newcomers in organizational contexts other than academia.

Members of the Newcomer's Role Set

Although macrolevel societal and institutional/organizational forces influence how people interact with one another, as an individual, you can facilitate a newcomer's socialization experiences. First, realize that you can help to effect positive change. Try to be sensitive to the plight of black women (and other traditionally disenfranchised persons) in white institutions. Do not dismiss, discount, or dilute our experiences by engaging in "me-tooism." Sometimes when I describe my experiences, a white person will observe that he or she has had similar experiences. This type of claim may support the argument that using a black feminist standpoint helps us to render more accurate depictions of everyday socialization processes; it may demonstrate how persons (not just black women) can experience oppression based on various aspects of identity. Moreover, this type of response may indicate a genuine attempt to empathize and to engage in dialogue. I wholeheartedly welcome such discussions. However, sometimes such reactions may reflect denial, a refusal among some white persons to see or try to understand the experiences of oppressed and disenfranchised people. Occasionally, I get the feeling that white people think that I am paranoid or hypersensitive. This impression occasionally may be true, but black women often endure pressures that others do not based on the physically salient cues of race and gender. Please try to understand that not only do the micropractices I describe count, they also accumulate and take their toll.

Second, recognize that, contrary to what many persons seem to believe, racism, sexism, prejudice, and discrimination are not limited to blatant, overt behaviors, as I hope this chapter demonstrates. Although you may believe that you are not guilty of any of the behaviors and attitudes that I describe, I encourage you to monitor yourself. Try not to reinforce negative stereotypes and expectations as you interact with black women. Understand that black women are individuals, but we are also members of a collective that other people often treat in predictable, discriminatory ways. We may or may not be affirmative action hires; regardless, we probably are qualified to perform our roles. Most of us have paid (and continue to pay) prices that you might not imagine to reach our current positions. If you consider inviting a black woman to perform a service, ask yourself if your request is reasonable. You probably are not the only person making demands on her. Respect and honor her time as well as her specific skills and interests.

Third, be an advocate for valuing difference. Do not place the burden of addressing social issues such as sexism, racism, and diversity on the newcomer's shoulders. Rather, make everyone responsible. For instance, identify and use resources on campus and elsewhere. Challenge or question colleagues or students who make racist and/or sexist remarks. If the newcomer conducts traditionally marginalized research, develop strategies to publicize and value her work and accomplishments.

Fourth, so that no one feels slighted or favored, develop inclusive policies and programs for *all* newcomers. For example, create and maintain a formal mentoring program based on tested models and/or with specific evaluation strategies in place. In other words, do not take a slipshod, superficial approach to mentoring; mentoring is a critical aspect of any newcomer's socialization.

If you wish to encourage same-sex and same-gender mentoring, do not require or coerce potential mentors to participate. However, if they agree, compensate them appropriately (e.g., through release time).

Fifth, take an active role in providing task-related information to newcomers. Volunteer to create a developmental relationship with a newcomer. Routinely offer information and insight to all newcomers. This will help to create a collegial climate in which everyone works to help all newcomers (regardless of their race or ethnicity and gender) succeed. In addition, include black women in informal networks and activities.

Finally, try to establish a climate of trust, openness, and inclusiveness. Listen attentively when a newcomer talks during meetings. Solicit and consider her input on a variety of topics (not just race and/or gender). Try to develop a setting in which you and the newcomer feel comfortable discussing sensitive or taboo topics. For instance, my department recently instituted a "mentioning" policy that encourages us to talk privately with someone who says something that seems offensive or insensitive. On the basis of what I have disclosed, you may feel more apprehensive about how to behave because you do not want to be perceived as patriarchal, racist, and/or sexist. If you feel awkward, tell the person. If you seem genuine, I believe that most of us will meet you halfway.

Newcomers

McKay (1997) observes that "black women must always weigh the cost of their choices against the balance of energy, will, and the determination to survive with human dignity. Each woman must learn to identify her own limits" (p. 15). I agree. Try to weigh the costs and rewards for anything you might consider doing in your role as a newcomer (e.g., asking for information, feedback, or advice; providing service that your job description does not require; or confronting a colleague regarding a questionable comment). In addition, be extremely proactive in your own socialization.

Alfred (1996) offers several recommendations for black women academics, including "know who you are" (p. 8). Do not allow someone else to define you. Create a positive self-image, and do not buy into the stereotypes (see also hooks, 1989). Recognize the value that you add to your organization. Remind yourself often of what you have accomplished and what you intend to achieve.

Alfred (1996) also tells black women, "Know what you want and how to get it" (p. 8). Develop and follow a game plan. If you aspire to ascend the ranks of an organization, find out exactly what that entails. Try to get expectations and requirements in writing. Do not hesitate to ask colleagues whom you trust questions about your role, and invite them to be mentors. Select individuals to assist you in various ways, according to their strengths and your needs. For example, ask an excellent teacher to help you become more proficient, and solicit advice about research and writing from someone who has published a lot of research. Develop relationships with other marginalized persons to acquire insight about socioemotional as well as task-related aspects of your role. Actively solicit feedback on your scholarly work from persons whom you respect and trust. I told my two mentors not to hold back, and I meant it. This facilitated and expedited the socialization process for me.

Protect and manage your time and energy. Realize that there will always be battles to wage. Opportunities to serve, if that is one of your goals, will always exist. Keep your priorities in mind. Sometimes you may have to postpone working with a student or community group to concentrate on a research or teaching project. Therefore, choose carefully depending on your time commitments, your emotional and physical states, and your sense of whether or not your efforts will pay off. As a minor example, when a white male student said he was going to drop my class, I did not try to dissuade him of his misconception that the course was about ethnicity. Do not feel obliged to edify someone every time a "teachable moment" occurs (see Orbe, 1998).

Find or create constructive outlets for stress, and learn how to cope with isolation and alienation. Develop support networks that allow you to discuss challenges and victories (Hine, 1997). Celebrate and savor your successes with people who care about you. If you have not already done so, consider trying to explain your career and job concerns to your loved ones who are not in similar situations. If you tend to fulfill the stereotype of trying to take care of everyone else but yourself, try to break out of that habit. Let significant others know when you need tender loving care or time alone.

Try to recognize when you are being complicit, and consciously decide whether to comply or resist. If someone invites you to provide a service that you believe is inappropriate for your role, ask him or her to explain why he or she selected you. Regarding offensive comments and jokes, Alfred (1996) recommends that you confront offenders privately and discuss the offense calmly, walk away, or consult a trusted colleague to process your feelings.

Finally, strive to raise your consciousness about marginalized people; learn about our challenges and our victories in the face of oppression and exploitation. Share your stories and insight with others. As Hine (1997) observes, "The surest way to a productive and fulfilling future for black women in any profession is paved with understanding of the experiences of those who went before" (p. 327). Make time for mentoring marginalized newcomers. These developmental relationships can be personally rewarding, and they will help to build a larger, more diverse group of persons in nontraditional occupational roles. Basically, we must empower and support one another (Baraka, 1997; Hine, 1997; Locke, 1997).

CONCLUSION

Learning the ropes is a complex and stressful communicative process that presents distinctive conflicts and challenges for marginalized persons who assume jobs traditionally reserved for dominant males. I hope that this black feminist standpoint analysis of learning the ropes provides insight and information that will help newcomers and incumbents to enact socialization processes that allow marginalized persons not only to survive but also to flourish.

NOTES

1. See B. Allen (1996) for a discussion of the ways that patriarchy and hegemony pervade anticipatory socialization processes. For instance, as a "smart" black female growing up in a lower-class neighborhood in the 1950s, I received messages that my only occupational choices were to become a nurse or a teacher.

2. The tenure and promotion process entails a complex set of requirements and expectations. At the university where I work, personnel committees at several levels of the institution evaluate a faculty member according to research, teaching, and service. The evaluations are weighted 40%, 40%, and 20%, respectively, usually after the first 6 years in the tenure track. To achieve tenure and promotion, a faculty member needs to demonstrate excellence in either teaching or research (including publications in mainstream journals or by prestigious publishing houses) and meritorious performance in both teaching and research. Although service counts for 20%, committees do not seem to penalize a faculty member for not providing an adequate amount of service. During a personnel evaluation meeting, a couple of my colleagues admitted that they were uncertain about criteria we should use to judge faculty service.

3. I say "invited" because I believe that these requests were actually directives. I think that few persons in subordinate positions will say "no" to persons in high positions of power.

9

The Promise and Practice of the New Career and Social Contract

Illusions Exposed and Suggestions for Reform

Patrice M. Buzzanell

Career research and advice have traditionally focused on the advancement of white males within one company through executive development programs and sponsorship (Arthur, Hall, & Lawrence, 1989; Buzzanell, 1987; Vicere & Graham, 1990). *Career* was defined as a time-bound sequence of corporate positions with increasing compensation, status, and privilege. This notion of career corresponded with *social contracts,* or societal (normative) expectations for employee-employer relationships, in which employees felt entitled to intergenerational upward mobility and lifelong employment and employers counted on worker loyalty and productivity (e.g., Altman & Post, 1996; Bennett, 1990; Chilton & Weidenbaum, 1994; Heckscher, 1995; Rousseau, 1995).

AUTHOR'S NOTE: I would like to express my appreciation to the following individuals who read and commented on an earlier chapter draft: Linn Van Dyne, Cynthia Stohl, and Suzyn Ornstein.

Careers and social contracts were interrelated in that the social contracts coincided with idealized career forms such as the American dream (e.g., Buzzanell & Goldzwig, 1991). The American dream promoted not only societal beliefs in competition, meritocracy, and individual determinism but also individuals' hopes for better times through hard work, education, loyalty, competence, and organizational commitment (see Bennett, 1990; Buzzanell & Goldzwig, 1991; Mumby, 1988; Newman, 1988, 1993). These beliefs were operationalized in corporate structures and practices such as internal labor markets, early (fast-track) identification programs, and firm-specific training. The American dream and retirement from one company were so embedded in career mythology and discourse that many did not realize how few people, even within the white middle-class, educated male workforce segment, actually advanced to top corporate levels and had secure positions within single companies (see Buzzanell & Goldzwig, 1991; Heckscher, 1995).

Over the last couple of decades, a new career and social contract have become newsworthy because managers and professionals have joined the ranks of those who were unemployed, displaced, and underemployed. This *new career* can be defined structurally as a series of work contracts over the course of a lifetime. It can be applied to contingent, volunteer, virtual, and unpaid home-work relationships (e.g., Byron, 1995; Rousseau, 1996). This new career coincides with a revised social contract in which "partnership," exchange, and "survival of the fittest" images are prominent (e.g., Chilton & Weidenbaum, 1994; Stroh, Brett, & Reilly, 1994) and with revised psychological contracts in which temporary terms of exchange are stipulated.

Whereas social contracts are generalizable structures for thinking about, talking about, and enacting employment as well as other social obligations, psychological contracts are individual perceptions about employment. Specifically, *psychological contracts* are sets of "individual beliefs, shaped by the organization, regarding terms of an exchange agreement between individuals and their organization" (Rousseau, 1995, p. 9). Psychological contracts may be explicit or implicit, but they measure employee-organization relationships in terms of "money, benefits, training, working conditions, advancement opportunities, and prospects of employment continuity in exchange for the time, energy, commitment, loyalty, and skills of the individual" (Sugalski, Manzo, & Meadows, 1995, pp. 389-390). Psychological and social contracts are inherently conflictual because they operate as "mixed-level phenomena" linking micro-macro practices and person-organization-society interactions (Rousseau & McLean Parks, 1993, p. 3).

This chapter focuses on writings about career and social contracts in general but recognizes that these contracts are manifest in the discourse and practices of specific person-organization relationships. Two interrelated goals inform the structure and content of my analysis. My first goal is to expose how the language of the "new" career and social contract may create a system even more insidious and detrimental to most workforce members, particularly to marginalized members of society (i.e., people of color, white women, poor and lower class, and the less educated), than the "old" career. To accomplish this goal, I examine discourse, discursive practices, and thinking about the new career using organizational communication problematics as a framework. Problematics are issues or possibilities that organizational communication theorists and researchers address implicitly and explicitly by what and how organizational phenomena are studied (Mumby & Stohl, 1996). My initial argument is that the new career and contract are presented as equitable and economically necessary systems that correct the faulty assumptions and power imbalances of the old career, but they do not deliver on these promises.

My second goal is to develop feminist career conceptualizations that, when enacted, can address underlying concerns about the new career and transform person-organization-community relations. I use poststructuralist feminism as a means of analysis (see Weedon, 1987). In general, postmodern feminisms allow us to question: Who is served by the new career? Why we are lulled into believing that this new career is the only reasonable response to a changing workplace? and How can we use this questioning to undermine and alter the underlying power distributions represented by the new career? By substituting nontraditional language and feminist ethical bases for those embedded in the new career conceptualization, I hope to enlarge the notion of career so that we can challenge material practices, such as pay inequity and worker displacement. My argument in this second half is that feminist careers and social contracts are socially constructed and negotiated. Through feminist analyses, careers and social contracts can be reconceptualized.

PROBLEMATIC ISSUES IN THE
NEW CAREER AND SOCIAL CONTRACT

Like the old career, the new career is simply one of numerous ways to socially construct "career." Both manifestations of career have been presented as commonsense, necessary, and normal ways of working. There are several commonalities between the language and practices in the old and the new careers. First, both career forms are "masculine" in the sense that they center on one true version of reality, focus on instrumental values, and enforce the contract by disparaging other views of career (see Buzzanell, 1994; Buzzanell & Goldzwig, 1991). As one example, Arthur and Rousseau's (1996) discussion of the new boundaryless career does not admit alternatives because the boundaryless career still focuses on person-organization linkages (although these attachments are not "bound" to a single company as in the old career). Another commonality in the old and new conceptualizations of career is that, if someone "fails," the individual is responsible rather than the social structure, practices, or situational constraints. Beyond these similarities, the careers differ in terms of career sites, contract forms, and workers who can identify with the career (i.e., managerial/professional in the old career vs. universal worker in the new career; see Table 9.1).

On the surface, what is different about the new career and social contract is that "everyone" (worldwide) is affected by changes in the ways that work is being done and organizations are being reconfigured (Rifkin, 1995). In the past, managers were those who benefited from job security and career development; in the present, presumably anyone who can foresee work changes and acquire requisite skills can benefit. Likewise, everyone, including managerial and professional employees, can suffer unemployment, underemployment, and uncertainties consistent with temporary work contracts (see Heckscher, 1995; London, 1998; Newman, 1993; Rifkin, 1995).

On a deeper level, what is different about the new career and social contract is that the assumptions in the new career language may operate to institutionalize power imbalances and to benefit managerial ideology in much more sophisticated ways than ever before. Although social contract language promises a fair exchange based *both* on contributions by either side and on corporate survival, the discourse actually accomplishes three corporate objectives: disenfranchising workforce members; benefiting managerial ideology; and curtailing discussions of underlying premises and alternative solutions. Through an organizational communication problematics framework and a poststructuralist feminist analysis, I display how the uncritical adoption of the new career and social contract may prove detrimental to many people, particularly to certain segments of the global workforce, by enabling the organization to fulfill these three corporate objectives. These assumptions, language choices, and related practices of the new career and social contract have not been examined systematically except in economic terms.

To organize my analysis of the new career, I use the four problematics inherent in the study of organizational communication: rationality, voice, organization, and organization-society relationship (Mumby & Stohl, 1996). The first part of each problematics discussion identifies concerns about the new career discourse and practices (see the left column of Table 9.2), and the second part of each section explores possibilities for change when career is reconsidered from feminist perspectives (see the right column of Table 9.2).

Rationality: Economic Rationality of the New Career Versus Multiple Ways of Knowing

The problematic of rationality argues that different rationalities are needed to uncover knowledges without privileging one way of knowing over others. Current career literature elevates economic and technical rationality (i.e., the "orientation toward knowledge that privileges a concern with prediction, con-

TABLE 9.1 Comparison of the "Old" and the "New" Social Contract and Career

Old Social Contract and Career	New Social Contract and Career
Employment Relationship	*Employment Relationship*
Family	Transactional exchange
Individual's duties and responsibilities: competence, loyalty, work as a priority, adaptation to organizational needs	Individual's duties and responsibilities: continuously update skills and add value to business efforts
Act as "organization man"	Act as "free agent"/contractor
Managers are experts who make decisions for and about employees.	Individual makes own decisions and directs own career.
Organization's duties and responsibilities: lifetime employment except for extreme business conditions or individual behavior, entitlement, benefits	Organization's duties and responsibilities: provide training and retraining
Individual's Emotions	*Individual's Emotions*
Trust, security, acceptance of corporate paternalism	Range of (mixed) feelings, including fear, betrayal, wariness, cynicism, abandonment, and confusion; acceptance of new contract and career as a fact of life; opportunities for growth
Career Definitions	*Career Definition*
Time-bound sequence of positions progressing toward greater compensation, status, and privilege; lifelong series of work-related experiences	Series of employee-employer relationships over the course of one's lifetime
Career goals: advancement or some sort of progression (e.g., in experiences, competencies, and/or personal growth)	Career goal: employability security
Organization Image	*Organization Image*
Family, marriage, religion, team, partner, associate, benefactor	Current employment "site" (can be virtual "site")

SOURCES: Altman & Post (1996); Buzzanell & Goldzwig (1991); Byron (1995); Csoka (1995); Hall (1996); Hall & Mirvis (1996); Hirsch (1987); Kanter (1992); McKendall & Margulis (1995).

trol, and teleological forms of behavior") over practical rationality (i.e., "a form of knowledge grounded in the human interest in interpreting and experiencing the world as meaningful and intersubjectively constructed"; Mumby & Stohl, 1996, p. 59; see also Deetz, 1992). These rationalities are tensions between managerially defined processes or outcomes and socially constructed realities.

In the new career, the problematic of rationality involves the career theme, or semantic issue, of economic or technical knowledge and the image of contracts as exchange relationships (see the left column of Table 9.2). In the new

TABLE 9.2 Organizational Communication Problematics as a Framework for
Identifying New Career Discourse and Issues

Problematics Within the New Career	Feminist Rethinking of Career
Rationality: Economic Rationality	*Rationality: Ways of Knowing*
Economic/pragmatic/dispassionate language	Humanistic/idealistic/emotional language
One-sided construction of contract/career	Mutual contracting/career
Transactional exchange	Relational exchange
Short-term focus (quick fix)	Long-term focus
Clear cause-effect relationship	Complex interconnected dynamics
Technical rationality	Practical rationality
Instrumental ways of knowing	Feminist/women's ways of knowing
Voice: Managerial Voice	*Voice: Tensions Between and Within Voices of "Others"*
Managerial voice	Other voices
Corporate imperative	Transformation imperative
Subordinates individuals to good of the corporation	Empowers individuals to challenge the corporation
People should adapt to the new career	People should reevaluate and change the new career
Organization: Organization as "Container"	*Organization: Social Construction of Relationships/Community in Organizing*
Construction of organization as site for transaction exchange	Organizing as processes of developing and enhancing relationships, connection, and community
Individualism, self-"survival of the fit-test," and separation of the organization from relational and community interests	Boundary permeability
Organization-Society Relationship: Distinct Competing Entities	*Organization-Society Relationship: Blurring Boundaries*
Distinct boundaries between corporation and society	Corporate commitment to society at large; blurring boundaries between organization and society; stakeholder concepts
Organization is rootless	Organization is embedded in community
Corporate commitment to itself	Corporate responsibility to justice
Competitive ethic	Collaborative ethic

contract, desirable organizational outcomes include lower operating costs,
higher profits, and streamlined organizations that facilitate quick responses to
clients and to environmental threats. Desirable individual outcomes include
employability, training for the next job, adequate notice of contract termination, honesty about membership possibilities, and severance packages

(Hirsch, 1987; Kanter, 1992). Organizational members are expected to prioritize these sets of outcomes. Within the new contract, mutual usefulness justifies the continuance—or termination—of the employment exchange. The new career, then, becomes a series of transactional relationships in which workers are temporary partners acting as free agents. Although employees are encouraged to develop ties to their professions and work rather than to their organizations (Stroh et al., 1994), they often are rewarded (or at least not punished) for their time commitment to current firms and for their suppression of objections to psychological contract violations (Turnley & Feldman, 1998). Employees are informed that these careers are the only realistic response to turbulent global environments; indeed, the old career "is dead" (Hall & Associates, 1996). To question the economic, dispassionate language and practices of the new contract and career is to be deficient, naive, and weak, because such questioning deviates from common sense.

Advice about careers, social contracts, and psychological contracts affirms the inevitability of and single-minded attachment to the "new" career and contracts. In his study of the American work ethic, Bernstein (1997) concludes that, in this world "where labor might be viewed as a 'disposable commodity,' it is not likely that businesses will give up immediate bottom-line gain for the possible benefits of long-term employment. For better or worse 'contingent labor' is here to stay" (p. 246). Employees are advised to "look out for [themselves] because there are no promises" (Blancero, Marron, & Keller, 1997, p. 1; see also Hirsch, 1987) and to accept the "new reality" that everyone is temporary (Chilton & Weidenbaum, 1994, p. 31) or "self-employed" (Csoka, 1995, p. 25). Employers are instructed not to backtrack ("We cannot go back" to old contracts; Csoka, 1995, p. 29) or send mixed messages (about possible rewards for loyalty) but to construct a consistent unequivocal message about changed contracts (Blancero et al., 1997, p. 6; Rousseau, 1996). Indeed, discussions for employers often describe how the contract should be communicated without any consideration of alternative contract and career forms (e.g., Rousseau, 1996).

Changes in careers and contracts are described as "a sign of the times," with both parties regarding "the exit mentality as symptomatic of a new and acceptable way of corporate life. Both sides should plan for it. Employers should encourage it" (Byron, 1995, pp. 9, 11). Strategic human resource management plays a critical role in establishing and developing new arrangements (Singh, 1998). Articles affirm that employers are the prime beneficiaries of the new contract and career (Csoka, 1995; see also Lehrer, 1996), but they also list advantages that the new career and contract have for both parties (i.e., no illusions about job security and lifetime employment; e.g., Byron, 1995; Chilton & Weidenbaum, 1994).

In other words, the new career is presented as a "fact of life." As such, it is consistent with routine business practices that include periodic downsizing, the use of cheaper labor markets, and technological replacements of humans; it also is consistent with a lack of real gains in corporate earnings (see Cascio, 1993; Chilton & Weidenbaum, 1994; Pfeffer, 1994, 1995). Instead of questioning the new career language and practices, organizational members and researchers perpetuate the illusion that the new career is an unalterable response to economic imperatives.

When feminist approaches are applied to the new career and social contract, the arbitrary privileging of technical knowledge over practical rationality is shown to hinder individual and collective development. Poststructuralist feminists point out that unexamined discourse curtails discussion of who we want to be, of what different kinds of knowing contribute to individual and collective development, and of how we can challenge systematic disadvantages and inequitable material practices. Without examining the language and practices of the new career and contract, we unwittingly subscribe to a uniform way of conducting organizational lives (involving series of temporary contracts for the "survival of the fittest") that fails to recognize how growth through and within relationships and situated knowing is valuable in and of itself.[1]

When the new career is presented as a "fact of life," organizational members rely on expert knowledge rather than challenging the assumptive bases of this knowledge. This privileging of technical knowledge and economic outcomes is gendered because it enables firms to better control people and processes and it silences dissent. By eliminating the use of practical rationality, the new career and contracts weaken the emergence of transformational values that are consistent with (women's) ways of knowing and with valuing noneconomic outcomes.

Practical rationality is consistent with ways of knowing that are manifest in humanistic/idealistic/emotional language, mutual career discussions, relational exchange, and complex interconnected dynamics (see the right column of Table 9.2). Although labeled "women's ways of knowing," alternative epistemologies are used by both women and men (Belenky, Clinchy, Goldberger, & Tarule, 1986; Goldberger, Tarule, Clinchy, & Belenky, 1996). As people rely less on experts for knowledge (i.e., silence and expert knowing), they begin to deal with contextual complexities and their own emotional responses to situations. They think through and evaluate claims by using themselves and others as knowledge bases in career discussions (i.e., procedural ways of knowing, discussion of self- and other needs), and they maintain understandings of knowledge as tentative, situated, and socially constructed. They would recognize that the new career and social contract are not concrete realities but temporary constructions created by those who can benefit most and who have the power to elevate this text version over other possible texts. They also would acknowledge that emotions are needed sources of information. They would not disregard the anguish, sadness, helplessness, disillusionment, betrayal, and anger felt by many members of the U.S. and global workforce who are confused by changes in their work lives and who are unable to earn a living wage (e.g., Hall & Associates, 1996; Heckscher, 1995; London, 1998; Rifkin, 1995; Stearns, 1995). Rather than viewing these emotions as symptomatic of change and as problems to be remedied, feminist career and contract reconceptualizations would use these emotions (as well as the more positive responses to career changes) to revise careers and contracts. Emotions would inform decision making about what is fair and about ways to enhance workers' dignity, voice, and connections with others (see Mattson & Buzzanell, 1999).

In sum, as long as the new career and social contract are the only versions considered realistic and informed by technical rationalities, then any other versions of career, social contract, and organizational life will be trivialized and silenced.[2] The use of different rationalities generates choice among transactional and relational (i.e., socioemotional, evolving sets of mutual obligations) contracts and various career forms over the course of workers' lifetimes (see Buzzanell & Goldzwig, 1991; Rousseau & McLean Parks, 1993). Poststructuralist feminists urge us to maintain tensions within and between multiple career and contract forms so that our career understandings and practices are neither limiting nor exclusionary.

Voice: Managerial Voice and Tensions Between and Within Voices of "Others"

The problematic of voice argues that organizational communication theorists and researchers should not focus solely on the management voice but infuse discussion with multiple voices, including managerial concerns, while identifying whose perspective is being presented (Mumby & Stohl, 1996). This dualism for career is labeled as the tension between managerial voice and the voices of "others." In this section, I first discuss how the managerial voice operates within the corporate imperative. Then I outline how new career and contract discussions are exclusionary and, finally, describe how feminist reconceptualizations might enlarge our discourse about (and practices concerning) careers and contracts.

In the corporate imperative, survival of the organization and returns for stockholders are the most important priorities (see the left column of Table 9.2). For employees, this imperative translates into one primary role— believer in the corporate imperative—and two interrelated and mutually reinforcing roles—job role (obligation to contribute to organizational effectiveness as a worker) and leisure role (consumer obligation to use salary to purchase products; consumption enhances organizational stability; Rifkin, 1995; Scott & Hart, 1989). Employees enact these roles unconsciously. The tasks of management and of boards of directors are to make decisions in the organization's best interests. Employers operate under two assumptions: that the individual, in comparison with the organization, is insignificant and disposable; and that human nature is malleable (Scott & Hart, 1989; see also Cheney & Carroll, 1997). Scott and Hart (1989) state that organizational members, particularly those in power, often fail to challenge the supremacy of corporate goals because this act would force them to question the values they live by. However, they also may not question the ethics of corporate imperatives not only because organizational contexts are complex but also because the pace at which decisions are made militates against the kind of reflection needed to challenge taken-for-granted imperatives.

So who are these "others" whose voices are unheard in the new career and social contract? In the past, only blue-collar and temporary workers suffered layoffs, but now managerial and professional employees worldwide experience downsizing and underemployment (Heckscher, 1995; Rifkin, 1995; Sloan, 1996). Managers and professionals have been among the last groups to undergo job loss, but U.S. and global labor forecasts predict continuing downsizing and employment insecurity for managers and professionals as well as other organizational cohorts (O'Connell, 1990; Rifkin, 1995; Schwartz, 1990; Taylor & Giannantonio, 1993). In a hearing before the Joint Economic Committee (1993) of the U.S. Congress, Greenberg, the research and survey director of the American Management Association, said that middle management is "hardest hit" by downsizing because of economic reasons (salary and benefits), technology, and the flattening of organizational structure.

Even so, white male professionals and managers are still privileged over other workforce groups. Not only are these men recipients of education, corporate training and development, mentors, and networks, but they also start with higher earnings prior to job loss and often have working partners who can buffer the financial constraints (Graham, 1995). In addition, Silvestri (1995; see also Kutscher, 1995), an economist in the U.S. Office of Employment Projections, found that managers work in a projected growth occupation. Gittleman and Joyce (1995), economists in the Office of Labor Projections of the U.S. Bureau of Labor Statistics, found that higher-earning white males were more likely to be employed in managerial or professional occupations, which have more stable earnings, and more than half of white men left the bottom quintile of earnings for consecutive time periods. In contrast, Fullerton (1995, Office of Labor Projections) reports that the labor force participation rates of African Americans, Hispanics, Asian Americans, and Native Americans are projected to decrease from 1994 to 2005. Even if the outlook for white men did worsen, white managers have the resources to create career insurance, such as executive job search database memberships, including Exec-U-Net, to which they subscribe while still employed (Graham, 1995).

In short, the new career and social contract have caught media and researchers' attention because these contracts presumably affect the security and entitlements of white middle- and upper-class America. In blue- and white-collar RIFs (reductions in force), the managerial voice continues to operate under the assumptions that the individual is, and should be, subordinated to the greater good (i.e., corporate interests) and that people should adapt to the corporate agenda. Management is presented as fair, rather than as paternalistic or discriminatory, because everyone is affected by economic necessities. Supposedly, all people are equal in the eyes of cost cutters, meaning that if someone does not add value, then that person is terminated.

Because most contemporary career and contract discussions primarily focus on managerial and professional employees (e.g., Hirsch, 1987; Rousseau, 1995, 1996; Rousseau & McLean Parks, 1993; Stroh et al., 1994; Sugalski et al., 1995), questions about voice must address the ways in which these discussions are exclusionary by (a) essentializing employees; (b) systematically excluding demographic groups; and (c) adhering to white middle-class values.

First, these discussions about new contracts and careers essentialize employees because they create an illusion that all workforce groups have had equal access to employability. To essentialize means that all members of a particular group (e.g., workers) are treated as similar so that variations within groups (e.g., Hispanic and European American *textile workers*) and variations between groups (e.g., displaced workers in *manufacturing* and in *advanced information technology* industries) are erased. By promoting equal employability access, essentialist career arguments neglect the point that there are particular workforce segments that are less able to enter the new career "survival of the fittest" contests. For instance, individuals without basic skills, without the resources to acquire additional training, and without mobility cannot compete (Bunning, 1990; Hall, 1996; Lehrer, 1996). They are members of the approximately 32 million people in the U.S. workforce who are contingent workers employed in work situations with few hours, little security, and no benefits (U.S. Labor Force estimates, in Schellenbarger, 1995). Most of these contingent workers are young, female, and in support roles (Jarratt & Coates, 1995). Males and females who lack high school and higher education are the least able to pursue jobs in growth occupations (see Kutscher, 1995; Silvestri, 1995). Displaced workers with high job tenure, less education, and blue-collar occupational classification incur higher than average losses in terms of wages (Hamermesh, 1989). Outside of the United States, those most vulnerable to labor force declines and unemployment are the poor in underdeveloped nations who have relied on single economies that are disappearing rapidly (see Rifkin, 1995). In short, essentialization means that career and contract discussions treat all employees in a similar fashion, as if all employees have the same opportunities to construct careers and contracts. Yet, on the basis of sex and gender, race, and educational level, individuals and groups are more or less able to construct careers guaranteeing employability.

Second, the new career and social contract are exclusionary demographically. Glass-ceiling, "mommy track," racial and ethnic, and gay and lesbian career studies indicate that these contracts, career developmental support, and programs to create equality in the workplace are not and never were similar to the "normal" development of and career possibilities available to white managers (Bell, Denton, & Nkomo, 1993; Buzzanell, 1995; Buzzanell & Goldzwig, 1991; Hayes, 1995; hooks, 1984; Kaufman, 1995; Morrison & Von Glinow, 1990; Morrison, White, Van Velsor, & the Center for Creative Leadership, 1987; Nkomo, 1992; Roberts, 1995; Williamson, 1993). In short, there are differential treatment and different outcomes in career paths and employability for diverse workforce members and for members of the worldwide (poor) underclass (see Rifkin, 1995).

With regard to gender and race ethnicity, Gittleman and Joyce (1995) examined individual earnings patterns from the annual demographic files of the Current Population Survey (CPS) from 1968 to 1992. In consecutive periods of work, they found that women are more likely to stay at the bottom quintile than men (72% compared with 51%) despite hours of work; blacks have more earnings instability than those who are older, more educated, or white; women are less likely to remain in the top quintile of the overall earnings distribution than men; and blacks are more likely to remain in the bottom quintile than whites. Moreover, according to a report of the U.S. General Accounting Office (1994; see also Sharpe, 1993), average African American wage rates are consistently below those of whites; African Americans were 15% more likely to lose their jobs than whites during the 1990-1991 recession even after accounting for occupational and industrial affiliations, worker age, and educational levels; and African Americans are unemployed slightly longer than other racial groups. In postdisplacement situations (i.e., being rehired after the loss of a job to which the individual had significant labor force attachment), blacks and Hispanic Americans incurred greater earnings and hierarchical level losses than Anglos (Ong, 1991), and blacks were less likely to be rehired, particularly for white-collar jobs (Mar & Ong, 1994). In case there was any doubt that racial prejudice still exists in corporate America, the Texaco tape "has revealed a great divide between blacks and whites—this one in the workplace" and has confirmed what black employees say that they have long suspected, namely that "racism and prejudice are endemic in corporations" (Kaufman & Markels, 1996, p. B1). The *Wall Street Journal* reported Brookings Institution economic evidence that the current "surging economy [not only] bypasses black men" and women but disadvantages black blue-collar workers in particular (Duff, 1997, p. A2; see also Rifkin, 1995). In short, the new career and social contract thinking systematically disadvantages certain groups of workers. The new career obscures these patterns by establishing premises and discourses of equity so that individual deficiencies—not systemic biases displayed in employment patterns—account for unemployability, underemployment, and displacement.

Third, not only are the new career and social contract exclusionary demographically; they are exclusionary attitudinally as well. Both old and new contracts assume that employees want to invest their identities in careers, an assumption biased toward white middle-class achievement orientations and managerial/professional occupations. The attitudes that the new career and social contract reinforce are job and organizational involvement, along with feelings of deficiency if employees cannot live up to the ideals of "temporary employment" and short-term thinking. Heckscher (1995) reports that, even when managers have survived massive downsizings, they still demonstrate loyalty.

Commitment and temporary employment place workers in a double bind. Double binds operate when there is no satisfactory resolution to an issue and when concerns are approached in an either/or fashion (Watzlawick, Beavin, & Jackson, 1967). Workers are not in positions of power in which they can ask for direction. Instead, workers' continued employability may depend on *both* time commitment and demonstrated loyalty *and* behaviors and attitudes consistent with temporary or free-agent mentalities. Time commitment and demonstrated loyalty lessen the opportunities to develop support systems and interests outside of the organization that can buffer the devastating effects of job loss (e.g., Heckscher, 1995; Leana & Feldman, 1990; Rifkin, 1995). When organizations bind managers and professionals (and others) to the corporation through company-specific training, promises of career movement, and frequent relocations that prevent developing ties to local communities, then the sole attachment—except to the corporation—that individuals exhibit is to their families (Heckscher, 1995). Time commitment also benefits full-time and tenure-track employees, who already are at an advantage because they do not need to work multiple jobs to compensate for inadequate income and benefits. A seemingly inescapable two-tiered system between "haves" and "have nots" exists that favors, and even enhances, career prospects and rewards for core workers over unpromotable hires (Barnett & Miner, 1992; Rifkin, 1995). Thus, the new career and contract encourage individuals to maintain employability and positive attitudes about temporary employment contracts while simultaneously encouraging them to invest time and energy in their corporations. Individuals who have difficulty handling these double-bind tensions will not fare well under the new career and social and psychological contracts.

In sum, the new career promises an equitable and attainable model for all workers. While describing a "universal worker" who can develop employment sequences congruent with the new career model and contract, the discourse and discursive practices privilege corporate interests. There certainly are some workers for whom the new career is advantageous (e.g., mostly white educated men in managerial or professional occupations who have careerist and/or entrepreneurial inclinations). However, differences in occupations, race, sex and gender, class, age, and educational level may increase or decrease individuals' abilities to sustain employment. Listening to the voices and situated experiences of "others" may help to convince those who believe that there is no option other than the new career and social contract that inequity demands revision of assumptions, language, expectations, and practices relating to the new career contract.

Specifically, tensions between and within voices of "others" encourage us to engage in feminist transformational imperatives that fundamentally alter the nature of inequitable relationships (see the right column of Table 9.2). Transformational imperatives urge individuals to reevaluate the ways in which the language of the new career further disenfranchises individuals and groups who already are disadvantaged in material practices (e.g., pay inequity, lack of jobs, lower rehiring rates and pay, and fewer opportunities for formal education and training). Transformational imperatives require democratic dialogue that promotes participation in discussion; recognition of the uniqueness of persons; acceptance of responsibility for nondemocratic communication; and the development of skills and sites for resistance and expression without censure (Deetz, 1992). Through democratic dialogue, workforce members can reclaim "the choices against all forms of domination or privileging of any arbitrary social formation" (Deetz, 1992, p. 233). Heckscher (1995) states that workers and managers must discuss change but have not found a way to do so.

Although we cannot empower others, organizational and managerial communication researchers and practitioners can help establish conditions for empowerment. Empowerment can be assisted by confirming disenfranchised groups' versions of inequitable realities, verifying the accuracy of their observations through communication, and recognizing that others' definitions for work and careers are valid. Empowerment also can be aided by valuing and emulating the looser connections between work and organization that some workforce members maintain (e.g., some African, Hispanic, and Native Americans). If organizational commitment is less important, then familial and friendship relationships with others, volunteer activities, and ethnic identities could become more important in these individuals' lives (see Heckscher, 1995; Rifkin, 1995). Lesser importance of organizational commitment could be quite liberating and allow or encourage a more diverse set of personal relationships; lesser importance of organizational commitment could remove some of the bases for power imbalances currently seen in abusive organizations (when fear of job loss overrides home considerations; see Powell, 1998). Society could be viewed as sanctioning multiple foundations of self-esteem and identities rather than just self-esteem based on work identities. In short, a feminist communication approach to the new career and social contract would advocate the dissemination of information through multiple communication channels and sites that unequivocally display who does and does not benefit by transactional exchanges.

Organization: Organization as "Container" Versus Organization as a Social Construction of Relationships/Community in Organizing

In the third problematic of organization, organizational communication theorists and researchers attempt to conceptualize organization by questioning the metaphors, spatial location, and social construction of organizing (Mumby & Stohl, 1996). In the new career and social contract, the organization is the site of transactions in which there is short-term exchange of benefits and services (see the left column of Table 9.2). Whether the organization is "virtual" or situated in a physical location, it functions as a "container," or context, in which this exchange takes place. Using the image of organizations as transient or interim sites for exchange, it is easy to understand how people can behave as dispassionate free agents who have no ties to anyone, anything, or any place. The work "site" can be moved anywhere, and the specific organization as a place for displaying skills and earning a living is irrelevant. In theory, employees, employers, and the community owe each other nothing except a temporarily satisfying economic agreement.

Taken to logical extremes, the transactional exchange produces no ties, except mutually economically advantageous relationships. The disintegration of former linkages determined by loyalty and more centralized organizing processes produces varying emotional responses in employees, but consistently managers feel "more isolated, more cautious, [and] less able to enter into informal and spontaneous agreements" (Heckscher, 1995, p. 76). If sustaining employability and assessing cost benefits for current and potential employment are beneficial strategies for employee movement from one employment exchange site to another, then the employee needs to focus inward. Workers should, logically, disengage or fail to create or engage in long-term proximal relationships with individuals and groups, especially if the loss of such attachments would prove painful and if there is no apparent connection to the time-consuming task of maintaining marketability. Employees also should not engage in activities, such as good citizen or peacemaker interactions, that do not produce an observable and immediate return on investment (see Huff, 1990; Kolb, 1992). Employees manage their own careers, view themselves as commodities to be bartered, and are vigilant for changes that could affect them. Through these behaviors, workers gain the "freedom" from attachments and organizational investment to transfer to other employment sites.

One consequence of the new career and social contract may be a renewed emphasis on individualism. The new career and contract literature focuses on how the *individual* can survive, sustain employability, recuperate from job loss, and avoid underemployment and downward mobility (e.g., Byron, 1995; London, 1998; Stearns, 1995). The new career promotes individual postures that alternate between a defensive self-survival mentality and an assertive push for opportunities to maximize employability. Bernstein (1997) advises that workers need

> the foresight to seek out new job opportunities before short product-life cycles, restructuring, and obsolescence overtake them. They will need . . . to wait for the grim reaper of unemployment to provide them with the impetus to change. In a market economy job security will never be a realistic goal. No amount of hard work, dedication, and loyalty will overcome the cold hand of rationality if people must be laid off. To be prepared by continuous learning and a mind set that "nothing is forever" is the best defense. (p. 247)

In the new career and contracts, there is minimal corporate responsibility since the onus for employability relies on the watchfulness of the employee.

A second implication and consequence of the new career and contract language may involve the isolation and alienation of employees from themselves and from work and nonwork activities. Workers may increasingly view themselves as factors in production and as potentially disposable commodities, and they may assess their marketability in a dispassionate manner (see Altman & Post, 1996; Cheney & Carroll, 1997). As they work to develop skills valuable for exchange, they may reduce opportunities to foster the gratification gained from doing activities they find inherently enjoyable (i.e., intrinsic rewards; Csikszentmihalyi, 1978, 1997).

Besides their potential alienation from themselves and from work and nonwork activities, organizational members may also become isolated from relationships with family and friends. Managers and professionals subscribing to the corporate imperative forgo relationships and devote their lives to organizational maintenance "even though such behavior incurs broader social costs too vast to calculate" (Scott & Hart, 1989, p. 6; see also Deetz, 1992; Newman, 1988, 1993). They may lose themselves, their families, and their homes. Individuals may fear that, if they do not comply with organizational demands, they could be replaced by a more dedicated worker (Heckscher, 1995; Powell, 1998). Suicide rates for laid-off workers are 30 times the national average (Bunning, 1990). Children of parents who have been laid off or underemployed report little faith in government or in industry and little hope for a good life (Newman, 1988, 1993).

Families are affected by cost cutting and downsizing as well as by the organizational and geographic mobility potentially required by the new career.

When pressed to locate work quickly because of family needs and other financial demands, industrial workers who were unsatisfactorily reemployed experienced substantially lower life satisfaction, which can be detrimental to well-being (Leana & Feldman, 1995). Individuals who lose their jobs because of downsizing may display increased domestic problems, lose their homes (15% lose their homes), and suffer long-term negative effects on employee earnings (Bunning, 1990). Violence against others is exacerbated by unemployment, underemployment, and hopelessness (Krugman, Lenherr, Betz, & Fryer, 1986; Rifkin, 1995). Yet the new career and social contract subscribe to organization-as-container thinking. Taken to extremes, this thinking fosters a myopic view in that outcomes and processes not connected with employability, productivity, and competitiveness within the temporary employment context simply are irrelevant.

When we reexamine the problematic of organization from feminist approaches, we can envision different processes and outcomes for organizational members (see the right column of Table 9.2). Because organizations are ongoing processes and products of communication practices, they are constructed through connections and are changeable through these same processes. For the career and social contract, the problematic of organization involves issues of connection, relationships, and community and of boundary permeability.

The new career and contract language displays container, self-interest, and temporary employment security images. This same language could be linked to the opposing characteristics and images of connection, community interest, and stable relational security. If the individual member does not turn to the free-agent mentality, then the new career and contract can initiate the development of self-reliant individuals who become proactive in maintaining professional and personal relationships that give tangible and intangible personal support. Indeed, Heckscher's (1995) interview data indicate that organizational members desperately want to belong to a community and desire the kinds of bonds and support that they believe they previously had with specific firms in the old career and social contract. To enable individuals to develop security within uncertain ties, researchers recommend the enlargement and enrichment of work roles, the reduction of work hours to create more time for third-sector (volunteer and community-based organizational) activities, downshifting from work-oriented lifestyles, and the creation of contexts for the types of dialogue and social support needed for sense making (Deetz, 1992, 1995b; Heckscher, 1995; Hochschild, 1997; Rifkin, 1995; Saltzman, 1991; Weick, 1995).

The paradox of the new career and social contract language is that, as individuals are encouraged to be more self-reliant, mobile, and self-sufficient, they also need to be more connected to family, friends, work and professional networks, and community. The paradox is that "individuals are only capable of being fully self-reliant when they experience themselves as supported by and attached to trusted others" who may or may not be connected to the organization (Kahn, 1996, p. 161). Some of the new career and social contract changes can be liberating and allow for more personal and collectivist connections (see Mirvis & Hall, 1996).

As organizational and managerial communication researchers and practitioners, we can alter the discourse, practices, and values that promote isolation. We can shape language to be consistent with feminist values (see the right column of Table 9.2). Career and contract writings are filled with advice focused on action, doing, the individual as agent, and work (i.e., masculine values), yet relational development is long term, reflective, social, mutually constructed, contextual, and situated in life rhythms (i.e., feminine/feminist values; see Marshall, 1989). An alternative career development process begins with relationships as an impetus for and continued source of development (Gallos, 1989). Rather than working toward development characterized by an increasingly differentiated sense of self in relation to others, we can position maturity and growth from perspectives emphasizing interdependence (Fletcher, 1996; Gallos, 1989; Marshall, 1989, 1993). This means that the goal of feminist career and social contract language is to shift the context from containers to growth through interdependence, as displayed in women's identity, career, and moral development models (see Gallos, 1989; Gilligan, 1982; Wood, 1999). Interactions characterized by interdependence, mutuality (expecting to grow and to benefit from growth), and reciprocity (feeling responsible to be both teacher and learner; Fletcher, 1996) offer opportunities for personal learning within work (Kahn, 1996; Kram, 1996) and nonwork (Parker, 1996).

Besides issues of connection, relationships, and community, organizational and managerial communication researchers and practitioners could foster thinking, language, and practices conducive to boundary permeability. Unlike the "boundaryless" new career that breaks the individual's ties to a single organization (see Arthur & Rousseau, 1996), a career marked by boundary permeability would recognize overlaps in many life dimensions. Boundary permeability would require that individuals explore their career anchors (abilities, needs, and values; see Schein, 1978) and develop career resilience and hardiness to handle challenges (see London, 1998) as their motives and interests unfold over time and space. Boundary permeability would embrace the feminist career value of change seeking as central in lifelong career, identity, and work processes (see Marshall, 1989, 1993).

The boundary permeability approach requires integrating different aspects of life, creating identities and feelings of success through relationships and interdependencies, and adopting a sense of wonderment when developing new capabilities and "selves" through change. As such, it differs from the protean boundaryless career that is centered on the individual: "The locus of career development responsibility will shift even more so to the individual in part because boundaryless organizations will not be able to meaningfully plan an employee's career" (Mirvis & Hall, 1994, p. 369). The protean boundaryless career is based on cyclical periods of reskilling, lateral career moves, and possible role conflict and overload as individuals pass across home-work boundaries (see Mirvis & Hall, 1994). In contrast, boundary permeability connotes more than interfirm careers and individual career success development. Boundary permeability means that distinctions between home, work, self-responsibilities, others' contributions, and community interests are fluid or merged (Buzzanell, 1997; Chester & Grossman, 1990; Grossman & Stewart, 1990). The language fosters less emphasis on "I" and "you" and more on "us" or how "we" can meet our self- and other (stakeholder) needs and desires over time. Communication skills are essential in developing the authentic dialogue that boundary permeability would require. The organization as container simply could not exist in a boundary permeability approach.

Although the feminist directions for change in this organizational communication problematic may appear idealistic and unfeasible, we already have models for transforming careers and social contracts away from the organization-as-container images found in the new career and social contract literature. We can look for models of relational interdependence growth in women's career and identity development literature (e.g., Gallos, 1989; Marshall, 1989) and for models of boundary permeability in work-family and dual-career couple research (e.g., Buzzanell, 1997).

Organization-Society Relationship:
Distinct Competing Entities Versus Blurring Boundaries

The problematic of the organization-society linkage involves an exploration of the interdependent relationship between context and organizational practices (see the left column of Table 9.2). The new career and social contract foster competitive environmental orientations. Organizations search for: new technologies to replace human capital; ways of creating advantages for stockholders, top corporate officers, and information specialists ("haves" vs. "have nots" in a two-tiered global market); means of aggressively recruiting or retaining the most marketable workers; and ways of shedding responsibilities for health care, pensions, insurances, and family support (see Perrow, 1996; Rifkin, 1995; Wysocki, 1997). Increasingly, benefits that are cast off by organizational society are not being absorbed by civil (U.S. citizenship) society (Perrow, 1996). In his review of historic career and social contract changes, Perrow (1996) asserts that, "in the world's history, no elites have had such a productive, economical, and safe means of domination" (p. 307). This domination in the United States endangers "our egalitarian and democratic culture" (Perrow, 1996, p. 310).

The new career and social contract have real and potentially negative effects for U.S. and global society. Rifkin (1995) reports that, "After centuries of defining human worth in strictly 'productive' terms, the wholesale replacement of human labor with machine labor leaves the mass worker without self-definition or societal function" (p. 236) or a means of earning a living wage. Some researchers project that diminishing work, less secure futures, and underemployment might decrease standards of living (affecting primarily women and people of color in the United States and the poor in less industrialized societies throughout the world), might strain resources as individuals retire, and might prompt increasing trends of worldwide violence and hopelessness (Altman & Post, 1996; B. Harrison, 1994; Newman, 1988, 1993; Rifkin, 1995). Other potential social costs include fundamental shifts in social relations (i.e., "Workers do not enter jobs confident that they will be able to build meaningful lives around them"); long-term cultural costs (i.e., "Many of the social bonds and personal loyalties that traditionally sustained businesses, families, and local communities are being rapidly pared away"); and less caregiving (i.e., "One consequence of the rise of Lean America is a marked decline in our once-strong spirit of cooperation"; Winner, 1993, p. 68). Pollsters indicate that a major concern is job insecurity, resulting in feelings of vulnerability and powerlessness when corporations make cuts (Lehrer, 1996). Lehrer NewsHour focus group participants assert that ordinary persons have neither the bargaining power nor the highly marketable skills to reshape the new career in their own image (Lehrer, 1996). They look to the government for assistance but feel that the government has not been helpful in addressing their concerns (i.e., their needs for portable health care and pensions, education, and training; see Lehrer, 1996). Disillusionment and cynicism about political and corporate leaders can compound feelings of hopelessness about the new social contract (Deetz, 1995b; Kouzes & Posner, 1993).

The corporate imperative mandates that costs be cut no matter what the human cost. Yet we have models that "prove" that human layoffs are not the best response for the economy as a whole or for individual firms.[3] In the new career, there is limited corporate responsibility—although some responsibility is dictated by local, state, and federal laws (see Note 3). At a time when corporations need to invest more heavily in remedial education and retraining, McKendall and Margulis (1995) report that, "to become less encumbered, many [companies] have chosen to invest less in human capital" (p. 21). Except in situations in which low unemployment necessitates drastic corporate training efforts, firms can choose if and where to spend money for education (see Wessel, 1997). When corporate and government programs fund education, some writers question whether the future workforce will have the skills needed for employability (Altman & Post, 1996).

A feminist career and social contract perspective can serve as one road map for affecting change (see the right column of Table 9.2). The feminist approach admits that there are no easy answers to bridging organizational-environmental boundaries. One possibility, European models of worker participation in state decision making, probably is not transferable to the United States or to other parts of the world (Perrow, 1996). However, without adequate transferable benefits, government-sponsored initiatives, and corporate recognition of community responsibilities, workers cannot fulfill the promise of a feminist career and social contract. A feminist approach to these issues asks who is most vulnerable and how we, as organizational and managerial communication researchers and practitioners, can assist individuals and groups in empowering themselves (see Mattson & Buzzanell, 1999). A feminist career and social contract approach recognizes that not all individuals or groups are disadvantaged. Indeed, for the better educated and the professionals, this time of multiple careers, flexible options, and opportunities can be exciting (e.g., top executive rebounds from failure; see Bennett & Lublin, 1995).

One way of blurring the boundaries between organization and society is to approach the organization-society relationship from a feminist stakeholder perspective. The language of the current business environment describes interdependencies among parties who have a "stake" in or are connected to the organization (e.g., workers, stockholders, clients, and communities in which organizations are embedded). Wicks, Gilbert, and Freeman (1994; see also Deetz, 1995b) describe how stakeholder concepts have masculine orientations focusing on autonomy and separateness, control of the external environment, the language of competition and conflict, objective strategies, and hierarchical power structures. We can reframe stakeholder concepts to better "articulate the meaning of the corporation and the sense of responsibility that businesses feel to those both inside and outside the walls of the firm in a more useful and compelling manner" (Wicks et al., 1994, p. 477). To uncover how we think about corporate responsibilities and blurred organizational-environmental boundaries, we can revise the gendered language and practices that shape stakeholder thinking. Using postmodern feminisms, Wicks et al. suggest that we not only envision corporations as webs of stakeholder relationships but also explicitly direct a moral agenda centered on community embeddedness and responsibility for future communities and environments.

As organizational-environmental boundaries blur through a moral commitment to be responsive to and responsible for potential problems (or vulnerabilities) presented by the temporariness of the new career and contract, some processes can be encouraged: (a) participatory decision making and (b) governmental assistance in the form of third-sector commitments.

Firms with internal processes encouraging workforce participation (i.e., participatory firms) often avoid laying off employees and forgo short-term gains for long-term outcomes and processes such as commitment, return on training and socialization investment, and innovation (Levine & Parkin, 1994). Levine and Parkin (1994) display how workforce participation in decision making can have macroeconomic spillovers that affect multiple stakeholders:

> Plant X lays off workers whenever there is a downturn in demand. Plant Y . . . avoids layoffs during downturns by retraining workers, transferring workers within the firm, and hoarding excess labor. The Y plant's no-layoff pledge is relatively expensive when recessions are frequent and deep. . . .
>   There is feedback from the firm's employment system to the macroeconomy. Recessions are deeper when many companies have layoffs (X style). Layoffs lead to lower spending by X workers, resulting in further layoffs at other companies. On the other hand, recessions are shallower when many firms avoid layoffs (Y style). Since the costs of running participatory systems increase as the variability of product demand increases, policies that reduce demand variability encourage participatory systems. Because Y firms are not rewarded by the market as an automatic stabilizer, the economy under-provides employers that avoid layoffs. (p. 253)

In short, although Levine and Parkin (1994) recognize that onetime shocks can necessitate layoffs, they argue that macroeconomic evidence does not support ongoing downsizing as a beneficial cost-reduction strategy.

Additional gains from workforce participation in decision making and from greater employment certainty include workers' willingness to innovate, cooperate with corporate goals, fulfill consumer roles, and develop work communities in which disagreements can occur without fear of job loss (see Levine & Parkin, 1994; Yovovich, 1995). Even in companies that do not promise employment security, employee involvement in the development and implementation of temporary strategic goals can foster the confidence needed to face uncertain employment (see Heckscher, 1995). Moreover, workforce participation in decision-making processes can spill over into increased community action and caregiving attitudes as past performance (of gaining a voice in matters that affect our own lives) predicts future performance (see Deetz, 1992). In a feminist stakeholder model, these participatory firms should obtain governmental tax incentives for their roles as economy stabilizers and as models for citizens' participation in a civil society.[4]

Levine and Parkin (1994) caution that simple government subsidies for workforce participation are inadequate because firms can go through the motions of enacting participatory systems without fully incorporating the designs. They advocate tax subsidies contingent on training, employee stock ownership, and other policies. The government also could grant partial unemployment insurance for partial layoffs, release Jobs Training Partnership Pact funds for workers who have not yet been laid off, and encourage work sharing and workforce training (Levine & Parkin, 1994). Levine and Parkin argue that these and other policy interventions can become self-sustaining over time.

With regard to governmental assistance in the form of third-sector commitments, federal tax incentives for education and for third-sector participation would provide better chances for more people to find employability security and meaningful work. While the government can offer tax incentives to individuals and organizations for taking and delivering training, corporations should pay workers for the time to take in-house and needs-based training and earn traditional degrees. Years of traditional schooling are predictive of earnings mobility patterns (Gittleman & Joyce, 1995). Even if less-educated workers (in years of schooling) move into higher earnings brackets and display mobility stability, earnings patterns indicate that this advantage is temporary (Gittleman & Joyce, 1995). Similarly, company-sponsored and skills training has only temporary benefits, because individuals may not find similar work in other firms and skills become obsolete. A sustained and comprehensive corporate educational plan, along with an educational system conducive to lifelong learning, could lessen some disparities between workers and managers and those with less and more formal schooling (Jarratt & Coates, 1995).

In addition, the independent, volunteer third sector of the economy could be expanded. Community activities already offer social services for the handicapped, disadvantaged youth, homeless, patients, victims of abuse, and countless others in need of temporary or permanent assistance (see Rifkin, 1995). Not only does third-sector activity provide tangible and intangible assistance, it also fosters caregiving attitudes: "Community service stems from a deep understanding of the interconnectedness of all things and is motivated by a personal sense of indebtedness" (Rifkin, 1995, p. 242). Rifkin calls the third sector the "social glue that helps unite the diverse interests of the American people into a comprehensive social identity" (p. 245). Rifkin suggests that the government provide tax incentives for every hour an individual gives to a legally certified tax-exempt organization. There could be a shadow wage with a standardized tax form (similar to a W-2 generated for those already employed) and a social wage as an alternative to welfare payments for unemployed American workers. Nongovernmental organizations (NGOs) already model ways to accomplish third-sector activities on national and international levels.

In sum, by working toward increasingly blurred boundaries between organization and society using a feminist revision of stakeholder concepts, we can negotiate careers and social contracts for long-term beneficial individual, societal, and global results. Deetz (1992) notes that there are inadequate forums for the kinds of dialogue needed to resolve stakeholder conflicts. But democratic communicative linkages must be fostered to achieve the promise of stakeholder models: "Stakeholder theorists have stripped away the facade of such constructs as agency relationships and efficiency calculations, to remind us that the most fundamental questions about economic activity are unavoidably and profoundly moral" (Wicks et al., 1994, p. 476). Through democratic communication processes, corporations can be responsive to and responsible for different stakeholder concerns grounded in productivity and morality (Deetz, 1995b).

A FEMINIST ORGANIZATIONAL COMMUNICATION RECONCEPTUALIZATION OF THE NEW CAREER

Whereas the new career and social contract trivialize the concerns of those ill prepared to enact free-agent activities in an uncertain workplace with few—if any—safety nets, the feminist career and social contract are temporary, inclusionary, relationally oriented, and responsive to multiple-stakeholder needs. The discourse and related practices of the feminist career and social contract promote multiple courses of action and reconceptualize the relations and responsibilities of organizations and communities and environments. Perhaps continued modification of the feminist career and social contract will resemble models from other cultures in which the organization's purpose is to serve the community and create or sustain social stability (e.g., Germany, Japan).

The four organizational communication problematics enable us to develop a framework for questioning the political, pragmatic, and moral consequences of the new career and social contract discourse. When we fail to question career language, our silence sustains technical over practical rationality, managerial over cooperative imperatives, organizations as sites of temporary exchange contracts over organizations (re)constructed for the good of employees and families, and corporations as autonomous entities over blurred organizational-environmental responsibilities for multiple stakeholders. When we use poststructuralist feminist approaches, we analyze social organizations, meanings, power, and individual consciousness through language to display how the business text is privileged over the worker/community text. According to Weedon (1987), language is the site of self- and organizational construction, power struggles, and the transformation of society. Language creates our commonsense meanings about inequitable micro- and institutional practices and processes (Weedon, 1987).

Through new career discourse, we constitute understandings of people's identities that maintain corporate imperatives and deny participation to employees. Because individuals are both the subjects and agents of dominant ideologies (Weedon, 1987), discourse can oppress as well as emancipate people. The basis for an ethical, moral caregiving view of career and social contracts lies in micropractices and macroprocesses of communication. Through communication that does not suppress conflicting interests (see Deetz, 1992,

1995b; Littlejohn, 1995; Sullivan & Goldzwig, 1995), we can select alternative and broadened interpretations of the career and social contract text.

These alternatives can be organized according to the directions presented by the examination of organizational communication problematics (see the right column of Table 9.2). First, elaborating on the *rationality problematic* suggests that we devise career models, definitions, and language that systematically promote feminine/feminist values of relationship, interconnectedness, collaboration, and long-term focus. We can do this by questioning the new social contract and career in our research and practices rather than simply accepting them as the only sensible models and by deriving best practices for communicating downsizing more clearly. Although cost cutting through layoffs and downsizing may appear necessary, other avenues for corporate survival and other outcomes should be promoted in our case studies, textbooks, and research articles (for instructional suggestions, see Buzzanell, 1993). We can expand thinking by asking students and others to apply their creativity to and incorporate different ways of knowing in the very real issues of corporate survival. What is reasonable, moral, and fair from these different perspectives? How can these different knowledges inform pragmatic problem solving? How can we be caring and compassionate even if employment is temporary?

Second, the *problematic of voice* demands that we publicize repeatedly in social scientific, interpretive, and critical reports the ways that the new career and social contract disadvantage white women, people of color, the lower class, and less-educated members of the workforce who are both female and male. Each of us has a forum for exposing corporate imperatives and managerial voice in our classrooms, our everyday conversations, and our writings (for ways to incorporate messages in everyday conversation and practices, see Fairhurst & Sarr, 1996).

Third, the *problematic of organization* mandates that we channel human behavior and broaden possibilities through values. Weick (1995) states that, in times and conditions of equivocality, there are numerous plausibilities from which we can direct thinking and behavior *if* we have the courage to act on our values and beliefs. To do otherwise means that we allow others to choose for us what our lives look like. Maintaining organizations as self-contained temporary employment sites does not assist any of us in developing integrated lives. Weick (1995) recommends authoring new texts, telling stories, creating occasions for interaction, and constituting identities consistent with values.

Caregiving values can lend security: "The experience of feeling cared about in the context of role-related work interactions allows people to experience security in organizational contexts that are (particularly under the terms of the new contract) insecure" (Kahn, 1996, p. 163). In addition, growth-enhancing relationships outside work can bridge work and nonwork life dimensions (Parker, 1996) that benefit individuals and communities besides the work organization. Finally, educators, communication practitioners, and human resource professionals can assist others by normalizing feelings of insecurity through conversations and by helping us learn to read ourselves so that we can begin to realize when we need to move into self-reflective safe havens (Louis, 1996). This means that we can foster our abilities to recognize our feelings as normal in these unsettling times, and we can prioritize self-knowledge or insight through reflection so that we can proactively produce positive experiences even when feeling insecure and worried.

Finally, *the problematic of organization-society relationships* requires that we bring a more diverse cross-section of people into the conversations and negotiations about contracts and career and, hopefully, treat all stakeholders as legitimate contributors to discussions about blurred boundaries and moral responses to corporate environments and community concerns (see Deetz, 1992, 1995b).

In conclusion, my thesis is that the new career and social contract are continuations of organizational trends toward greater corporate self-interest and workforce disposability that are unhealthy not only for the workers but for global society as a whole (see Cheney & Carroll, 1997; Rifkin, 1995). Yet because of the language and the masculine premises embedded in the ways we discuss career and contracts, we fail to see alternative ways of thinking about and enacting these contracts. Through a poststructuralist feminist analysis of rationality, voice, organization, and organization-society boundaries, we can find different ways of talking about and enacting careers and social contracts.

NOTES

1. Although many career, management, and organizational experts portray relationships and feminine values as essential to effective business processes and career outcomes, these experts often do not challenge the underlying instrumental orientation of organizational practices (see Calás & Smircich, 1993; Fondas, 1997).

2. Reactions are so hostile against women's ways of knowing and the use of nontechnical rationalities that corporate leaders' battles against noninstrumental business concerns can make the front page of the *Wall Street Journal* and gain reader support in subsequent editorials (e.g., Pollock, 1996). Fondas (1997) notes that admission of feminine approaches must always have a "hard" instrumental edge or they will be discounted by managers and other organizational members.

3. There are numerous popular and academic articles offering advice about best practices for downsizing (e.g., Blaxill & Hout, 1991; Bobo, 1994; Greengard, 1993; Rich & Bailey, 1993; Schmenner & Lackey, 1994). Some articles present cases in which downsizing worked well to streamline the organization, to handle some of the trauma experienced by individuals who had been laid off and by survivors, and to act as responsible community members (e.g., HealthSpan, see Greengard, 1993). However, American

Management Association (AMA) surveys of 7,000 corporate members report dismal effects:

> Fewer than half—43%—report that operating profits improved after cuts were made; 24 percent said that profits fell after the downsizing. While 31 percent said that worker productivity increased after the cuts were made, nearly as many, 28 percent, said that productivity declined. Community relations tended to suffer; 27 percent reported a decline in the quality of their relations with the wider community of stakeholders. And one thing that happens for sure in the wake of a work force reduction is that morale plummets: 22 percent of the companies reporting cuts said that morale declined severely and an additional 52 percent said that morale declined somewhat. (Joint Economic Committee, 1993, p. 5)

Moreover, almost two thirds of the AMA-surveyed companies that made cuts in a given year also made cuts in the following year (Joint Economic Committee, 1993). Other articles emphasize that downsizing can do more harm than good (Rolfe, 1993) and can incur heavy legal penalties from the lack of strict compliance with local, state, and federal laws (Banham, 1995; Edmonston, 1994; Elliott, 1994). For example, Digital saved money from downsizing but lost credibility with clients and sales support. The short-term savings did not equal the loss of expertise, image, and clients (Markels & Murray, 1996). Some firms have found workers to be so "traumatized" by a decade of downsizing that the companies have returned to longer-term contracts for union and non-union, blue- and white-collar workers. These organizations include Ford Motor Company, Boeing Company, UAL Corporation (parent of United Airlines), Monsanto, and American West Airlines (Markels & Murray, 1996; White & Lublin, 1996).

4. In the United States, there are precedents for governmental action and increased responsibility for change. Newman (1993) describes past social engineering (i.e., governmental action to promote beneficial economic outcomes for large portions of the U.S. population). Work projects during the depression built bridges, highways, and suburban areas that enabled the millions of families qualifying for low-interest mortgages after World War II to commute into urban areas for work. State and local governments supplemented federal investments with funds for sewers, schools, police, and fire departments. Newman (1993) claims that "federal involvement in the creation of the mass middle class of the 1950s and 1960s was every bit as much an intrusion into the 'natural' dynamics of the market as any poverty initiatives taken since that time have been" (p. 161).

10

Chaos Theory and the Glass Ceiling

Cindy Reuther
Gail T. Fairhurst

If we keep on doin' what we always done, we'll keep on gettin' what we always got.

Barbara Lyons
(as cited in Warner, 1992, p. 48)

The complexities of race and gender relationships are a continuous struggle for white women and men and women of color who attempt to climb organizational hierarchies only to be shut out of top management positions. In a recent article in *Working Woman,* Dunkel (1996) explored what it would take for a woman to become the first woman CEO without having to create her own corporation. Only two women made the Fortune 1000 list of CEOs, and both owned their own businesses. It was not until 1997 that a white woman reached the top in the traditional way—by climbing the corporate ladder—ironically succeeding in the Barbie division of Mattel (Dobrzynski, 1996).

AUTHORS' NOTE: We would like to thank Alice Adams, Patrice Buzzanell, Noshir Contractor, Katherine Miller, and Anne Nicotera for their many helpful comments on earlier drafts of this chapter.

A 3-year study commissioned by the U.S. government and reported in the *New York Times* in November 1995 also reported bleak statistics for white women and women and men of color trying to make it to the top. The study reported that 97% of senior managers of Fortune 1000 Industrial and Fortune 500 companies were white, and 95% to 97% were men. In Fortune 2000 industrial and service companies, 5% of senior managers were women, and only four tenths of 1% of managers were Hispanic, even though they made up 8% of the working population. Although white women and people of color make up 57% of workers, white males continue to occupy positions of power and privilege in disproportionate numbers.

Many refer to the exclusion of women at senior levels as the "glass ceiling" (Bell, 1994; Buzzanell, 1995; Holliday, 1995; Kilborn, 1995; Wood, 1999). The "invisible barrier" created by this exclusion implies a static structure, one that blocks opportunities for white women and people of color (Holliday, 1995). Whereas traditional definitions of the glass ceiling focus on disproportionate representations in the upper echelons (i.e., glass-ceiling outcomes) as a result of this invisible structure, Buzzanell (1995) defines glass-ceiling processes as "language and interaction patterns associated with gender ideologies in which women are devalued overtly and subtly" (p. 333). We adopt her definition by focusing on ideologies, language patterns, and organizing practices that establish and reify this invisible barrier. However, we expand the definition of glass-ceiling processes to include racist ideologies and practices that devalue people of color. This addition suggests that women of color are most at risk and likely to be constructed as invisible in organizational settings because they disappear into the gap between "women" (often considered white) and "minorities" (often considered male). To ensure visibility, we employ language throughout this chapter that explicitly marks both race and gender.[1]

Years of studying the glass ceiling have culminated in programs and procedures that offer quick fixes rather than systemic change. For example, training programs often attempt to help white women and women of color develop communication behaviors stereotypically defined as masculine. Policy mandates such as affirmative action, instituted to increase the representation of women and men of color and white women in organizations, have not succeeded in enabling these groups to break through the glass ceiling and are currently being questioned. Although companies such as Avon, Colgate-Palmolive, Motorola, and Dow Chemical are pursuing some aggressive strategies to attract and promote more women, and companies such as Mattel and Avon have women in the senior ranks, their numbers still are relatively small (Morris, 1998).

The glass ceiling is just one of many complex issues that have surfaced as more white women and women and men of color have begun competing for white-collar jobs in today's organizations. Organizational diversity initiatives, racial and sexual harassment, office romance, child care issues, mentoring, and the "mommy track" are a few of the recent phenomena that we have seen with social, cultural, political, and legal consequences for organizations. Taken separately or together, these phenomena contribute to the already turbulent environments that today's organizations face as a result of globalization, technology, and changing market conditions.

Chaos science and related approaches offer a means for understanding how organizations weather turbulence in chaotic environments to maintain a sense of balance (Stacey, 1992, 1996; Wheatley, 1992, 1993). These approaches, also known as the new sciences, have been used by organizational theorists to glean lessons in leadership (Blank, 1995; Wheatley, 1992, 1993), dialogue (Shelton, 1993), creativity (Klein, 1993), and embracing instability (Miller, 1998; Stacey, 1992, 1996). In this chapter, we make a case for using the new sciences' perspectives on chaos to explore the complex processes that create and sustain glass ceilings. Because of the dynamic and complex nature of language and social interaction, chaos concepts can offer another perspective for understanding the glass ceiling. In this sense, we are following the lead of many within the field of organizational development who believe that the new sciences are beneficial for understanding complex organizational dynamics. However, although many organizational chaos theorists take a positive view of the inherent order that is found in chaos, we intend to show that this order can actually perpetuate discriminatory ideologies and practices. We will also show that feminist theories of resistance can suggest new ways that women and men of color and white women may evoke chaotic dynamics. Chaos can lead to self-organizing processes that replace discriminatory practices with processes that dismantle the glass ceiling. We begin with an introduction to the new sciences and its relevance for organizational processes.

THE NEW SCIENCES

> The only thing that makes life possible is permanent, intolerable uncertainty; not knowing what comes next.
>
> Ursula K. Le Guin
> (as cited in Warner, 1992, p. 225)

A collection of theories from the hard sciences such as physics and chemistry constitutes the new sciences. These theories are referred to as chaos theory, complexity theory, and self-organizing systems theory. Although they are different in many ways, all share a common emphasis on complex, nonlinear systems and organizational science applications that tend to group the concepts from each theory into one perspective (e.g., Miller, 1998; Stacey, 1992, 1996; Wheatley, 1992).

The new sciences represent a significant departure from Newtonian physics and classical systems theory. For example, the interplay between order and disorder and the ability of systems to renew themselves is central to the new sciences but antithetical to Newtonian laws of equilibrium, entropy, and linearity for natural and social systems. Straightforward links between cause and effect disappear in the new sciences, in part because large and unforeseen effects can be the outcome of very small causes, referred to as the "butterfly effect" (Cohen & Stewart, 1994). In contrast, a Newtonian worldview presumes a correlation between the size of the cause and the size of the effect. Finally, the famous "double slit" experiments from quantum physics demonstrate the principle that observation affects the observed in significant ways. This finding runs counter to the long-cherished notions of objectivity and the separation of the knower from the known in scientific inquiry in a Newtonian and classical systems theory worldview (see also Miller, 1998).

A new sciences approach offers several possibilities for changing the ways that organizing practices have been conceived. Eoyang (1993a) suggests such possibilities:

> Chaos science and its related areas of investigation use mathematical, objective, scientific strategies to describe systemic behavior that defies the reductionist strategies of the past. In the same way, it is possible that a chaotic paradigm might lend cohesion to the plethora of organizational and management models that are driving organizational change today. (p. 17)

To apply the benefits of new sciences concepts, some translation to the realm of organizations is necessary. Described in organizational terms, complex nonlinearity implies that all components of a system are dependent on each other and that interdependence can lead to complex change. Thus, line workers may change because of information received from management, but management also changes based on information from line workers (Eoyang, 1993a). In chaotic systems, the changes are complex. For example, a supervisor who tells racist jokes may encourage racist language patterns among some line employees. If other line workers feel offended by this behavior, they might challenge these jokes, write up a complaint, or sue the company for a hostile work environment. The effect of any of these actions may be inconsequential or significant, especially as legal outcomes reverberate to the rest of the organization or beyond. In some cases, causal links may be clear. In other cases, the sequence of causal links gets lost in the complexity of the system's interactions (Stacey, 1996). These dynamics form interdependent nonlinear relationships that generate complex "chaotic" organizing behaviors.

Eoyang (1993a) describes the complexity and interdependency displayed among chaotic systems' components and the unpredictability and emergent behaviors that arise as a result. Complexity and interdependency are two fea-

tures of chaotic systems that are readily apparent in language patterns and discriminatory practices that uphold the glass ceiling. For example, in today's
politically correct environment, discrimination of all kinds has become more
covert. Often unconsciously, language carries and reinforces a managerialist
ideology, one outcome of which is the dominance of corporations in modern
life—and the white males who run them (Deetz, 1992). Gender politics in
organizations is also intertwined with the often unarticulated influences of
race, social class, education, age, and sexual orientation, especially as they
influence leader-member relationships and executive succession (Fairhurst,
1993, in press). Combined with Tutzauer's (1997) observation that chaos may
be lurking anywhere, there is discontinuity in organizations. For this reason,
executive succession (including hirings and firings) is an ideal circumstance
in which to examine processes that sustain the glass ceiling.

In our analysis of the glass ceiling, we assume that organizations are nonlinear, chaotic systems, in which a "system" refers to any pattern of activity
(Priesmeyer, 1992). Two branches of chaos theory from the new sciences, the
strange-attractor and order-out-of-chaos branches, are pertinent because they
are used by organizational theorists to explicate organizational phenomena
(e.g., leadership, instability, or dialogue). We highlight the differences between the branches by first introducing the strange-attractor branch to illustrate how organizational policies, behaviors, and practices are produced and
reproduced. We then examine the order-out-of-chaos branch and feminist
resistance approaches to suggest methods for disrupting racist, sexist,
classist, and heterosexist practices.

Strange Attractors and Fractals

Chaos theorist Katherine Hayles (1990) writes about two branches of chaos
theory, referring to the first as the strange-attractor branch. In this branch of
chaos theory, theorists are interested in the hidden order that exists within
chaotic systems, called "strange attractors" (see Table 10.1). The hidden
order is a shape that emerges over time, suggesting that a system can be chaotic but still have a structure. A strange attractor is the unpredictable shape
contained within certain boundaries that emerges when tracking the movement of a system. For example, computer graphics can simulate and chart a
system's fluid movement at a particular moment in time (Gleick, 1987).
Despite the unpredictability and evolution of the system's chaotic movement,
order emerges. Wheatley (1992) explains, "The most chaotic of systems never
goes beyond certain boundaries; it stays contained within a shape that we recognize as the system's strange attractor" (p. 21). As the chaotic movement of
the system forms into a pattern revealing order within disorder, the "basins of
attraction" function as the boundaries within which the system stays.

TABLE 10.1 Chaos Theory Terms and Glass-Ceiling Applications

Chaos Theory Term	Definition	Organizational Applications	Glass-Ceiling Applications
The Strange-Attractor Branch			
Fractal	The order created by a strange attractor	Fractal organizations: Strong vision and values with a diverse expression of roles	Replication of white males at senior levels through stereotyping and the suppression of individual differences
The Order-Out-of-Chaos Branch			
Self-organizing systems	Order emerging out of chaos	The promotion of innovation through instability brought on by conflict and questioning attitudes	The promotion of a new social order through instability brought on by feminist resistance approaches

A "fractal" is the order created by a strange attractor. Mandelbrot (as cited in Gleick, 1987) introduced the scientific community to fractals when he found similar patterns within patterns across different scales of magnification. As one example, the basic shape of a broccoli plant is a floret. As florets are repeated at different levels of scale, the complex broccoli plant is created.

Organizational theorists use the strange-attractor and fractal metaphors to describe patterns of behavior that provide order in times of turbulence. According to Wheatley (1992), in a fractal organization, there are patterns of behavior representing the organization's vision and values that can be seen in employees throughout the organization. She states, "The potent force that shapes behavior in these fractal organizations, as in all natural systems, is the combination of simply expressed expectations of acceptable behavior and the freedom available to individuals to assert themselves in non-deterministic ways" (p. 132). Miller (1998) found just this combination among nurses at a medical center. Group leadership with a vision and high expectations combined with the freedom of nurses to creatively enact their roles in ways that embodied those principles.

However, what is problematic about Wheatley's (1992) fractal organization is that no one questions *whose* values and visions are being asserted in fractal patterns (see also Jantsch, 1980). The replication of white men at senior levels of the organization, often signifying the replication of patriarchal values and a managerialist ideology, forms a pattern of order that also offers an excellent example of a fractal. Without using chaos theory terminology, former secretary of labor Robert B. Reich said as much in a recent *New York Times* article: "It is often easier for white males to simply replicate themselves in deciding who is going to be partner or a manager of a management team or get a tenure track position" (as cited in Kilborn, 1995). The replication of white men at senior levels promotes interaction patterns and behaviors that maintain the glass ceiling. This is achieved through the qualitatively different experiences that the sexes and/or races have in mentoring, career counseling, and development opportunities. When these vehicles give white males the advantage, they are put on a career path to the upper echelons created by the impression that they are better suited to jobs at this level.

The practices leading to the replication of white males in senior levels are based in ideology. In often subtle and unconscious ways (e.g., in language, dress, and work rituals), white women and men and women of color are pressured to commit to patriarchal and white interests and value systems. The upshot is that replication promotes conformity rather than a pluralistic system in which individuals can interact and work according to personal principles.

The suppression of individual differences and stereotypes are two mechanisms that promote fractal-like self-similarity. Bell, Denton, and Nkomo (1993) describe the first, showing how the suppression of identity creates a bicultural lifestyle for many white women and people of color:

> A bicultural life structure requires a woman of color manager to shape her professional world in a male-dominated white culture, while her personal world often remains embedded in her racial/ethnic community. At the workplace, she may be forced to sacrifice the racial/ethnic part of her identity in favor of what is normal in the dominant culture. The suppression of her identity can happen at the superficial level of dress, hairstyle, and language patterns and at much more substantive levels of social, personal, and political values. (p. 18)

The suppression of different identities facilitates the replication of white males at senior levels by favoring sameness rather than diversity. The suppression of individual differences creates a mirror for white men. The combined effects of race and sex privilege mean that a white man can see himself (i.e., his values and beliefs) rather than the various women who represent pluralistic identities, values, and beliefs. A woman of color describes her experience of this suppression:

> He made some interesting comments at different times, such as: "Being Hispanic here is not going to help you," and "You do not want to be known as the in-house Hispanic." He advised me to hide my calls from people with Hispanic surnames, and my Spanish newspaper. (as cited in Bell et al., 1993, p. 119)

Whether intolerance toward difference is reflected in overt or covert behaviors, suppression serves to replicate dominant value systems that protect and promote white patriarchal traditions. This becomes especially true for women and men of color and white women who move up the corporate ladder, stay with an organization for a long period of time, and transform their identities in the process. Deetz (1992) argues that such success often comes at the cost of giving up one's voice and assuming the ownership of problems not of one's own making. White women are often asked to take responsibility for not "fitting in," not going along with the "joke," or not enjoying the playful "come on." When the burden is placed on a woman to endure others' offensive language and discriminatory practices, her social interaction needs are denied and suppressed. The same is true for each ethnic, racial, and class distinction in the United States whose members end up suppressing their individuality in the pursuit of staying employed.

Stereotypes are the second mechanism that promote fractal-like self-similarity by confining women of color and white women to a narrow range of roles and identities. Wood (1999) elaborates on four organizational stereotypes of women first proposed by Kanter (1977). These stereotypical roles, which include the sex object, mother, child, and iron maiden, maintain familiar forms of interaction between men and women, formalizing the woman's place in a group and forcing her to live up to this very limiting image.

The *sex object* stereotype defines women in terms of their sex and/or sexuality and expects their actions and dress to conform to traditional views of femininity. Women who support others or bring a nurturing quality to their work often are expected to assume a *mother* role. Kilbourne and England (1996) describe the social and nurturing skills required in occupations represented by high numbers of women (e.g., teachers, social workers, counselors, service providers, clerical and administrative support personnel, and administrators and managers). This skill, also referred to as emotional labor (Hochschild, 1983), requires the ability to deal with one's own and other people's emotions to negotiate interpersonal encounters. Regardless of job type, this skill is required of most women. Moreover, it is also devalued in the workplace and results in lower pay for those jobs requiring the skill. Women are thus segregated into "women's work," disproportionately occupying low-paying, low-status positions (Kilbourne & England, 1996; Wood, 1999).

Stereotypes that characterize women as *childlike* limit women's advancement opportunities and also lead to pay inequities. When women are perceived as less mature or less competent than men, they are often protected in the workplace and may not be given demanding projects that would strengthen their promotional opportunities.

Finally, the *iron maiden* is viewed as being unfeminine. This stereotype leads to discrimination based on the idea that a woman should not be aggressive, tough, direct, or competitive. Wood (1999) describes a 1990 sex discrimination suit that suggests the iron maiden stereotype:

> Ms. Hopkins brought in more money in new accounts than any of her 87 male peers, yet 47 of the men were made partner while Ms. Hopkins was not. Executives refused to promote Ms. Hopkins because they perceived her as unfeminine. Describing her as authoritative and too tough, they suggested she could improve her chances for promotion if she wore more jewelry and dressed and behaved more femininely. (p. 263)

In this case, a federal district court ruled gender stereotyping an aspect of sex discrimination, and thus illegal. Unfortunately, many such cases never get to court. Whether it is the iron maiden, sex object, mother, or child, stereotypes place white women and women of color in restrictive roles and limit their potential contributions to the organization. Stereotypes also help to define interactions and promote sexist and racist behaviors.

In summary, from the strange-attractor branch of chaos theory, we can see how patterns of interactions reify over time and become part of the inherent order in an organizational system. When interactions replicate at different levels in an organization, the inherent order gives stability and security to the system. Some organizational chaos theorists take a positive view of the inherent order that is found in chaos by focusing on the integrity of the organization (e.g., Jantsch, 1980; Wheatley, 1992). We argue, however, that this inherent order can serve to replicate patriarchal and racist patterns of interaction that continue to reinforce the glass ceiling. Although the strange-attractor paradigm offers a timely analysis for researchers exploring the effects of the glass ceiling, it offers little hope for change. To challenge interactions that are guided by the suppression of individual differences and stereotyping, we need to explore the order-out-of-chaos branch.

Order-Out-of-Chaos

The order-out-of-chaos branch sets itself apart from the strange-attractor branch through the concept of "new order" (see Table 10.1). In the order-out-of-chaos branch, self-organizing systems and dissipative structures arise in systems far from equilibrium. The process of self-organization occurs when a complex system is open to its environment, moves far from equilibrium, and reorganizes into a new structure (Jantsch, 1980; Prigogine & Stengers, 1984). A dissipative structure emerges spontaneously when the system interacts with its environment (Eoyang, 1993b). When a system is at equilibrium, energy is equally distributed throughout the system, and differentiation is low. When a system is far from equilibrium, there is high differentiation and a continual transfer of information (energy) between the divergent parts of the system.

For example, when water is heated, some parts of the water are affected more than others, increasing the differentiation in the system and moving the system far from equilibrium. The system adjusts by self-organizing and creating a dissipative structure, resulting in an adaptation of the whole system (Eoyang, 1993b).

Referring to systems composed of human interactions, Stacey (1992) suggests that self-organizing occurs when specific conditions are present. According to Stacey, continual sharing of new information between various groups can push systems far from equilibrium. During these transitions, the system moves through patterns of instability where order and symmetry are broken. At these critical points, the system confronts a series of choices. The process of spontaneous self-organization occurs when communication and cooperation among the components of the system produce a new order or structure (Stacey, 1992). More recently, Stacey (1996) defined self-organization in terms of agents' own local rules of behavior versus a blueprint that specifies how they must act. To facilitate self-organizing, individuals in organizations should stay on the edge of chaos by doing everything they can to avoid complacency while making sure that they contain the anxiety that this inevitably produces. Strong relationships, high-quality leadership, and honest self-reflection that can promote double-loop learning (in which dominant schemas are changed) are the keys to this process (Stacey, 1996).

Nonaka's (1988) study of Japanese companies illustrates how organizations promote innovation through instability. Honda has a culture that encourages confrontation among employees and the hiring of new employees with diverse specialties to help form countercultures. Honda wants new hires to oppose existing values and for those challenges to be met with productive conflict. When instability is viewed positively, the politics of power take on a different perspective because it functions as "an amplifying feedback loop whose purpose is to encourage conflict and spread questioning attitudes" (Stacey, 1992, p. 86). Instability provides a context in which existing patterns of behavior can be disrupted, allowing new perceptions to emerge.

We apply the order-out-of-chaos lens as a framework for exploring how organizations can "unlearn" old repetitive patterns and learn new behaviors. New patterns of interaction can emerge from self-organizing that provides opportunities for people of color and white women to succeed in positions that mostly white men occupy today. Stacey's (1992, 1996) work, in particular, offers exciting opportunities for challenging oppressive beliefs and behaviors through his emphasis on questioning attitudes, the expression of difference, and productive conflict. In addition, Stacey's (1996) concern for double-loop learning, which results in replacing the dominant schemas that groups or organizations may hold, signals the potential at least to replace the arcane belief systems that keep glass-ceiling outcomes in place. Double-loop learning can create second-order change that results in the transformation of a system

(Watzlawick, Weakland, & Fisch, 1974). Single-loop learning produces only a first-order change in which some behaviors and interactions may be challenged but there is no significant change to the system. To prevent the production of glass ceilings, a second-order change is clearly required.

But Stacey's (1992, 1996) perspective, too, has its problems. For example, Miller's (1998) study of nurses trained in chaos principles found them hoping that order would emerge spontaneously from the complexity they faced. Unfortunately, they lacked strategies for facilitating and participating in that emerging new order. Miller raised the crucial questions: What if order does not emerge? What are the costs that result from the cacophony of effort when order does not emerge? How does one deal with the indeterminacy while living it? Miller (1998) writes,

> A number of theorists have used "good jazz" as a metaphor for a self-organizing system. However, the fact remains that *good* jazz is hard to find and that *bad* jazz is among the worst music to endure. An old colleague of mine defined jazz fusion as "five guys playing whatever they want at the same time." And, this is one of the dangers in applying ideas from the new sciences to social systems. (p. 125)

Miller's questions are not easily answered—especially when they are applied to the glass ceiling. What happens if the outcome of conflict over racist and sexist practices is only more chaos and not the hoped-for new order of equal opportunity? Even Stacey (1996) acknowledges that the self-reflection that the chaos sciences promote is not a guarantee of success, only a vehicle for making sense of experiences and *potentially* designing more effective outcomes.

Another problem with self-organizing systems concerns the nature of the conflicts that result from living on the edge of chaos. Some conflicts are socially approved by management because they are about the distribution of money and power within the system (Deetz, 1992). Others go much deeper because they are ideology based. Management does not sanction these conflicts because they are about the system of distribution itself. Will an organization embracing self-organizing principles embrace the deep-seated ideological conflicts that tend to be group based, structural, and perpetual? Will they go beyond the conflicts that tend to be individual centered, situational, and seeking only technical solutions (Deetz, 1992)? For white women and women and men of color to excel and be seen in all aspects of organizational life, chaos dynamics and double-loop learning have to flourish both within and outside of management's control, with both approved and unapproved conflicts.

By implication, if self-organizing systems theory and related approaches are to be used as self-reflexive tools by organizational researchers and practitioners, the applications must be socially—not just organizationally—relevant. That is, these approaches must take up the issues of gender, race, class, age, and sexual orientation to understand how glass ceilings are sustained. Feminist resistance approaches encourage us to analyze traditional ideologies and interactions and how these practices lead to gender-, race-, and class-based discrimination.

Feminist Resistances

Western culture or society has a system of thought that has evolved from ancient history (Bohm, 1994; Calás & Smircich, 1991). Thoughts are reproduced over time, maintaining a cultural structure that helps us describe and define the world. According to Bohm (1994), thought has a systemic fault. It is part of the system and, therefore, always part of the problem. Because thought is part of the system, if an idea or new concept gets repeated several times, it begins to change to fit the system. To use a chaos metaphor, it begins to develop a pattern like the fractal. Therefore, if we try to create new insights and learnings about race and gender relationships, we must first examine the patterns that are part of the system to better know the pattern of self-similarity that needs to be broken.

Crawford (1995) argues that men have had more public power in most societies and thus more access to the creation of discourse and thought. Buzzanell (1995) proposes that "our language and discourse practices often recreate stereotypic masculine and feminine divisions of family, work activities, and occupations" (p. 327). Bhavnani (1993) argues that "an important consequence of these histories is that racialised, gendered, and class-based inequalities are embedded into the creation of knowledge" (p. 96). This supports Foucauldian notions that certain power bases can produce organizing practices and discourses that our culture defines as knowledge (Calás & Smircich, 1991).

These researchers span multiple feminist perspectives (e.g., social constructionist, cultural, socialist, and poststructuralist). They suggest that claims of knowledge that govern our system of thought may protect and enforce the views of those who have access to public discourse (e.g., academics, government, or law) while repressing the views of those who do not have such power. When select individuals have more access to the creation of knowledge, that knowledge has significant limitations within the organization and in the larger society in which the organization interacts. Feminism challenges us to pay attention to power dynamics in knowledge creation and the complex interdependencies of gender, race, sex, and class as we seek to create new organizing practices. Tong (1989) describes feminist thought as a kaleidoscope, writing,

The reader's preliminary impression may be one of chaos and confusion, of dissension and disagreement, of fragmentation and splintering. But a closer inspection will always reveal new visions, new structures, and new relationships for personal and political life, all of which will be different tomorrow than today. (p. 238)

Consistent with Tong (1989), feminist resistance can encourage women and men of color and white women to challenge existing patterns of knowledge, creating chaotic dynamics that can potentially remove the glass ceiling. Sotirin and Gottfried (1996) focus on resistance as crucial to feminist studies of women and work, "both as an organizing concept for rereading women's histories and as a mode of action creating possibilities for the transformation of the conditions of women's oppressions" (p. 367). Forms of resistance often include educating organizational members in feminist principles, praxis, and the deconstruction of oppositions in ways that prevent or remedy the marginalization of white women and women and men of color (Buzzanell, 1995, 1999; Calás & Smircich, 1996; Tong, 1989).

Feminist education might begin by helping individuals understand how prejudice is socially constructed over time and can be changed. Stereotyping and prejudicial views are often the result of seeing the world too simply (Buzzanell, 1999). When people challenge current thinking about gender, race, class, age, and sexual orientation, more frameworks for interacting can open up. When individuals understand that they might be able to change the social processes that create and maintain prejudice, they are more likely to take action. Rosa Parks modeled this kind of action when she refused to give up her seat to a white passenger on a Montgomery, Alabama, bus during the U.S. civil rights era.

Feminist principles, combined with the chaos sciences' concept of the butterfly effect, help individuals locate the relationships between organizing practices and community health or destruction. The butterfly effect refers to a system's sensitive dependence on initial conditions that can lead to large and unforeseen outcomes (Cohen & Stewart, 1994; Miller, 1998; Stacey, 1996). With such effects, even small organizational initiatives have the potential to trigger complex change, just as a corporation's decision to open a plant in Mexico can have far-reaching effects. As individuals, we must learn to ask what the connections are between corporate business decisions, Third World famine, local unemployment, and poverty. What corporate processes prevent individuals from accessing well-paid positions? What corporate practices allow some workers to be paid exorbitant wages while other workers struggle to pay for food and housing? These practices are linked to language and behavior patterns that continue to sustain the glass ceiling and other discriminatory practices. Education can help individuals understand patterns of prejudice, make connections between often ambiguous and contradictory practices, and take action to resist.

Larger acts of resistance, involving organized opposition to discriminatory practices and policies, may also trigger complex change. However, as with butterfly effects, their impact is not easily predicted. For example, when women were found to be leaving a large Fortune 500 firm at eight times the rate of men, a remaining group of women from across the corporation became extremely concerned (Berryman-Fink, personal communication, July 13, 1998). Since this company promoted only from within, this meant that fewer numbers of women would be candidates for senior-level positions and management positions in general. The women also believed that a critical mass of women throughout the company would be needed to change a traditional male-dominated culture, a position reminiscent of Kanter's (1977) theory of numerical proportions. As a result of the women's organized effort to this problem, senior management provided a large amount of money to support renewed training efforts and organizational development to make the existing culture more hospitable to white women and men and women of color. However, the outcome of this effort is still unknown some 5 years after it began.

Finally, acts of resistance created out of women's everyday experiences also may trigger complex change. For example, women's resistance in the workplace often emerges from the multiple interpretations of oppression rooted in women's everyday lives (Sotirin & Gottfried, 1996). Thus, feminist analyses may attempt to blur conventional dichotomies that establish the social context for power and resistance. One example of a culturally influential dichotomy is the private-public divide that characterizes Western culture, constructing traditionally female and male spheres (Cirksena & Cuklanz, 1992). Responding to the fallacies inherent in dichotomous thinking, Collins (1991) suggests that "dichotomous oppositional differences invariably imply relationships of superiority and inferiority, hierarchical relationships that mesh with political economies of domination and subordination" (p. 42). However, practices in the workplace that integrate home and work blur traditional distinctions like the private-public divide. Sotirin and Gottfried (1996) note that "women often weave domestic rituals and celebrations of women-centered events (such as marriage or the birth of a child) into an ensemble of practices, thereby constituting an oppositional culture to resist management control" (p. 368). But calling certain celebrations "women-centered" tends to reinforce stereotypical and heterosexist notions of gender, illustrating how difficult it is to open up possibilities for communicating and behaving without reifying existing stereotypes. Nevertheless, as a resistance strategy, challenging traditional dichotomies such as private-public opens up possibilities for different kinds of workplace communication and behavior that may directly or indirectly (e.g., through child care provisions and sexual harassment policies) affect glass-ceiling outcomes.

Not all feminist resistance strategies are accompanied by reflection, but it seems necessary to break away from the grip of existing stereotypes to ensure double-loop learning. Reflection requires an individual to concentrate on an experience by bringing the experience to the forefront of the mind, while making connections to other experiences (Daudelin, 1996). During this process, the experience is being filtered through unexamined biases and attitudes. When these assumptions are recognized, the individual initiates a new phase in the reflection process, coming close to the edge of chaos, where new thought patterns can be created. Reflection can also be used at the group level to create spaces for self-organizing to occur. For instance, support groups within organizations can serve as a catalyst for resistance, encouraging groups of people to embrace their full identities, reflect on and resist suppressive workplace values, and replace them with values and visions that emerge from pluralism. Pluralism refers to accessing a variety of different opinions, values, and beliefs to create processes that can significantly alter the system's core identity. Although many groups disband after making initial, surface-level connections, groups that remain intact can provide much-needed support and protection to individuals who risk alienation, demotion, or termination as a result of the chaos introduced by their resistance.

Feminist praxis encourages individuals and groups to reflect on those ideologies and behaviors that uphold the glass ceiling. Consistent with this transformation strategy, the experiences of white women and women of color need to be contextualized because women's oppression and resistance do not occupy one universal category. The many and varied relations between race, age, class, gender, sexual orientation, and religion need to be better understood (Sotirin & Gottfried, 1996). For instance, black women often are fighting what Clarke (1995) describes as plantation protocol, when white people in the contemporary United States assume that their birthright is privilege and power. In confronting plantation protocol, women of color resist both race and gender oppression. Diversity initiatives in organizations and groups working to eliminate racism, sexism, and heterosexism can challenge traditional patterns and facilitate chaotic dynamics. Research that explores two or more layers of relations (e.g., race, class, sexual orientation, age, and religion) will provide more complex and heuristic information.

In summary, we have shown how feminist resistance approaches can make organizational chaos theory more socially relevant as a tool for explicating the practices that produce the glass ceiling. In turn, organizational chaos theory offers new hope for feminist resistance approaches that can introduce even a small amount of chaos into organizational life. Drawing on lessons from chaos theory and feminist epistemologies, we conclude by offering several suggestions for creating environments that offer the potential to disrupt discriminatory practices.

CONCLUSION

> For difference must be not merely tolerated, but seen as a fund of necessary polarities between which our creativity can spark like a dialectic. Only then does the necessity for interdependency become unthreatening. Only within that interdependency of different strengths, acknowledged and equal, can the power to seek new ways to actively "be" in the world generate, as well as the courage and sustenance to act where there are no charters.
>
> Within the interdependence of mutual (non-dominant) differences lies that security which enables us to descend into the chaos of knowledge and return with true visions of our future, along with the concomitant power to effect those changes which can bring that future into being. Difference is that raw and powerful connection from which our personal power is forged.
>
> (Lorde, 1983, p. 99)

Many organizational theorists are extolling the virtues of embracing concepts from the new sciences, such as fractal organizations and self-organizing systems. In this chapter, we have tried to show some of the problems with and opportunities for applying these ideas to the glass ceiling. With respect to fractal organizations, individuals who continue to reinforce visions and values that are part of a homogeneous status quo will continue to replicate systems that encourage and continue the almost exclusive occupation of top positions by white men. Elements of chaos may flourish, but inevitably organizational members will repeat traditional ways of interacting based on core visions and values that are fundamentally flawed. Stereotyping and suppressing individual differences will proceed as the norm, and power bases and structures that continue to keep women and men of color and white women from accessing their full potentials will be replicated. Organizations will suffer as a consequence.

Self-organizing systems theory, especially when combined with feminist resistance approaches, offers more promise for changing racist, classist, sexist, and heterosexist patterns because of the potential to create new order through instability. Also promising is the emphasis placed on small acts of resistance as a trigger of complex change. This bodes well for individuals, not just organized groups, who hope to make a difference in affecting glass-ceiling outcomes.

Finally, it is not just organizational insiders who have the potential to introduce chaos that leads to new self-organizing behaviors. Organizational researchers and consultants also can ask new questions about the kinds of chaos that might be introduced into organizations that lead to new self-organizing behaviors. A new research agenda might include the following:

1. Exploring structures that are highly susceptible to chaos and thus capable of shifting power dynamics

2. Looking for chaotic dynamics in interactions and behaviors that give white women and women and men of color voice and opportunity to redefine dominant values, visions, and paradigms

3. Locating behaviors that continue to perpetuate gendered and racialized work and suggesting methods for change

4. Identifying spaces "at the edge of chaos" where self-organizing can occur

5. Analyzing language patterns in research and theorizing that promote racist, classist, sexist, and heterosexist ideologies that lead to the replication of white, Western, and patriarchal thought

A feminist chaos agenda for organizational development might include the following:

1. Hiring consultants to identify fractal patterns in organizations

2. Exploring structures that are highly susceptible to chaos and thus capable of shifting power dynamics

3. Designing training programs from a wide theoretical base, emphasizing how work has been defined by gender and race and is maintained through sexist and racist behavior

4. Seeing the connections between
   - the lack of retention of women and men of color and white women and the replication of white, patriarchal visions and value systems
   - lawsuits and the suppression of individual differences
   - lack of advancement opportunities and stereotyping
   - employee conflicts, low morale, and racist, sexist, heterosexist, and classist ideologies

5. Creating the potential for self-organization to occur by
   - challenging and redefining definitions of *vision, values, mission,* and *leadership* to include alternative and marginalized perspectives
   - seeking a diversity of individuals to work in the organization
   - encouraging marginalized individuals to form subgroups to get necessary support and resources for maintaining their beliefs, values, and identities
   - creating forums for employees to study, analyze, and discuss behaviors at all levels of the organization
   - analyzing and developing new processes for embracing differences among employees

The systems that emerge from self-organization are based on the needs, values, and visions of those involved in the process of chaos and creation. Through these new insights, current practices that impose silence and invisibility on many women and men of color and white women can be resisted and changed. Many different voices and visions can erupt from the depths of organizational chaos viewed through a feminist lens.

NOTE

1. In marking the race of white women, we resist collaborating in the phenomenon Haraway (1997) terms the "race of no race." She identifies a typical effect of unexamined race privilege as the tendency for individuals associated with a dominant racial category to freely ignore their privilege. Unexamined ideological assumptions of race privilege are embedded in organizational cultures; these assumptions inform language patterns and policies, producing race-based discrimination.

CONCLUDING
CHAPTER

11

Dialoguing . . .

Patrice M. Buzzanell

Dialoguing . . . is to continue discussion, to value instability, and to temporarily resolve issues with a willingness to reopen conversation. "Dialoguing . . ." seems to be an appropriate title for our last chapter because we cannot provide closure on the themes represented by the work in this book or in other contemporary feminist organizational and managerial writings. Because we are engaged in critiquing ongoing feminist concerns, this chapter simply highlights some interrelated issues that require further attention: (a) sustaining tensions between binary oppositions; (b) exploring resistance; and (c) promoting participatory discourse and alternative organizing.

SUSTAINING TENSIONS
BETWEEN BINARY OPPOSITIONS

One issue that requires the sustained attention of communication scholars is learning how to maintain tensions between dualisms. As a feminist third wave emerges, a primary characteristic of this phase is learning to live with and navigate contradictions and ambiguities (Bailey, 1997; Orr, 1997). Contemporary feminist work opposes either/or thinking and behaving by revaluing the missing half of oppositions and promoting both/and thinking. Of particular importance to feminist organizational and managerial communication research is our continuing critique of sameness/difference and inclusion/exclusion, among other dualisms.

Sameness/difference typically refers to claims about the similarity or uniqueness of women and men. When women are presumed to be identical to men in all aspects except some biological characteristics, then advocates argue for equality. Equality arguments run into trouble when they neglect the disparate life experiences of women and men, the worldwide devaluation of the feminine, and the different expectations and consequences for identical behaviors enacted by women or men. However, when women are considered to be different from men, then two-culture arguments surface; the sexes' ways of knowing, relating, leading, making moral decisions, and viewing their organizational lives presumably are so different that women and men could come from different planets (e.g., Gray, 1992). Difference is problematic because of essentialist assumptions; namely, all women and all men are assumed to behave in certain sex stereotypical ways. The variations within and between the sexes are considered inconsequential. The complexities in work that seeks to understand women's and men's lives are obscured by pressures to simplify and arrange hierarchically.[1]

In addition to sameness/difference divides between the sexes, we also can look at sameness/difference with regard to race and ethnicity and sexual-social orientation. Expectations and consequences for similar behaviors enacted by whites or people of color and by heterosexuals or gays and lesbians are vastly different. Women of color may find themselves second-guessing or questioning what they know to be true or being subjected to others' assessments that they have been hired or promoted as "twofers" (see Allen, this volume). Gays and lesbians may situate themselves in an uneasy space in conversations and decision making about their lifestyle preferences when they are unsure about whether they will be accepted by others (see Spradlin, 1998; Woods, 1994). Sameness/difference arguments come into play at sites where identities are challenged and our responses cannot address the complexities of the situation. If we assume sameness, then we lose the diversity in human existence that enriches our experiences and thinking. If we take the argument about difference to the extreme, then we lose sight of the underlying similarity that unites all of us—our humanness and desires to be treated with dignity and respect.

The issue of *inclusion/exclusion* takes a number of forms in this book. We have included multiple feminisms as analytic methods and lenses, varied evidence types, different chapter presentational formats (e.g., narratives, poems, diary entries, personal experiences as moments for challenging theory), and numerous organizational topics and theories. We often use our personal experiences and identities to question and construct theorizing. Chapter authors struggle with definitional boundaries that defy inclusion of what they know to be part of organizational constructs. For examples, see Allen's descriptions of black women's experiences as "outsiders within"; Mattson, Clair, Sanger, and Kunkel's exploration of women's everyday stressors that are not identified as organizationally related; Fine and Buzzanell's paradoxical experiences when enacting leadership as serving; or Bullis and Stout's revisions of earlier socialization research to incorporate traditionally underrepresented members of society. The authors in this volume question the ways in which women (and men) subscribe to singular career forms that cannot lead to greater equity for the sexes, classes, and races or ethnicities (Buzzanell) and the ways in which they fail to deal with the self-organizing repetitive structures inherent in workplace inequity (Reuther & Fairhurst).

In general, although feminist communication research still does not adequately publicize the different concerns of women of color (Aldoory & Toth, in press), our chapters have attempted to develop some understandings of what organizational life looks like from marginalized standpoints. It should be a source of embarrassment and a call to action that "the situation of younger middle-class [white] women today seems to be better than that of their mothers a generation ago. . . . By contrast, the situation of many working-class women, including many women of color, has deteriorated" (Jaggar, 1994, p. 5). Indeed, Bailey's (1997) analysis of emerging third-wave feminist issues indicates that "if there is one message that screams from the pages of . . . [third-wave] books, it is that despite the efforts of older feminists, racism within feminism is alive and well" (p. 26).

Although we have attempted to bring alternative insights to each organizational and managerial construct or theory, there are other issues of inclusion/exclusion, such as masculinities in gender relations and transnational feminist concerns, that are not represented in this volume. The incorporation of masculinities is a logical outgrowth of a contemporary feminist agenda that prioritizes inclusion of difference in theorizing. Feminism is "not *just* about women, but about oppression, and ways to create life and work experiences that are honest, sensitive and open to all types of voices (*including* men's)" (Aldoory & Toth, in press, emphasis in original). Mumby (1998) illustrates how masculinities consist of variations that are infrequently accounted for in the ways writers describe gender. Spitzack (1998) reasons,

> Researchers have sought avenues for the empowerment of women by encouraging a disruption of the hierarchical and often essentialized opposition of masculine and feminine. In this process the cultural purchase of the feminine is often interrogated in relation to a relatively stable and monolithic notion of masculinity. Such an imbalance not only endorses an agenda of unilateral change, thereby preserving the normative power of the masculine, but it also forecloses the need for sustained conversations in which gender is figured as a cultural production. (p. 141)

To understand gender in organizational life means to critique femininities, masculinities, and the intersections within and between the genders.

Likewise, Hegde (1998) calls for a postcolonial move "to account for the interplay between the local and global, the minority and hegemonic culture" (p. 282). This move reflects a growing disenchantment that feminisms have lessened discriminatory treatment of white women but have either not helped or further disenfranchised women of color and Third World women by neglecting economic class structures (Aldoory & Toth, in press). Hegde (1998) recommends that one way to represent political interests in the social community is to consider theory from the standpoint of feminist resistance and within a transnational (shifting) context. She sees the emerging global critique of Eurocentric assumptions in feminist thinking as third-wave feminism.

EXPLORING RESISTANCE

As we describe resistance to unjust situations, we need to move away from typologies that describe strategies of resistance and focus more on the ways that people incorporate resistant thinking and behaving into their identities and interactions. Resistance takes many forms. Organizational members may resist through hidden transcripts (Murphy, 1998), through retelling and revising the stories of their lives (Marshall, 1995), through the use of different strategies to preserve identities within cocultural (dominant/nondominant) exchanges (Orbe, 1998), and through expression in silence and/or in voice (Clair, 1998).

In some cases, resistance can mean living in an intolerable situation while laying plans to leave. Calás and Smircich (1996) note that forms of resistance in a transnational feminist perspective may not correspond with First World understandings, such as cases in which female workers become "possessed by spirits and disrupt the work situation" (p. 242). Moreover, in personal relationships dominated by violence and in ethnic cleansing that destroys those most vulnerable in a given society, resistance can mean death. Resistance can mean that women "steal time" for what they would need to do. They overtly comply with traditional gendered activities and priorities while finding time in their daily routines for other activities (Buzzanell, 1997). They both comply with and challenge temporal gendered orderings. Our chapters show that resistance can range from the deliberate alteration of daily micropolitics (see Allen; Fine & Buzzanell) to the small gestures that emerge—unanticipated—as major systemic changes (see Reuther & Fairhurst). We also see resistance to standard negotiation scripts through the development of alternative negotiation and bargaining processes (see Putnam & Kolb, this volume).

At first, women may not resist stereotypical gender expectations. Trethewey (this volume) shows how they may subscribe to and discipline themselves to conform to masculine ideals of professional behavior or looks without challenging the double binds such complicity incurs. However, over time, women may emerge as resistant and may enact both resistance and complicity simultaneously. What makes action a form of resistance is that the individuals engage in thinking and behaving that preserves dignity and identities that normally are trivialized, denied, or oppressed.

Because of the situated understandings, unfolding nature, and simultaneous enactment of resistance and complicity, typologies cannot fully capture the complexities underlying resistance. We need to contextualize thinking (and behaving) about resistance within broader themes such as ethical organizational communication. By insisting that all organizational stakeholders have a responsibility to develop awareness of and responsiveness to practices that undermine authentic relationships and identities, communication specialists can create organizational systems centered in the daily enactment of a value transformation vision (i.e., equitable power sharing and decision making; Mattson & Buzzanell, 1999). Unethical behavior from a feminist organizational communication perspective is defined as "communicative actions and processes that attempt to marginalize, silence, and disempower individuals or groups and prohibit development of voice" (Mattson & Buzzanell, 1999, p. 62). Conversely, ethical messages, practices, and structures support and enable individuals or groups in ways that challenge power imbalances and include participatory discourse.

PROMOTING PARTICIPATORY DISCOURSE AND ALTERNATIVE ORGANIZING

In our chapters, feminisms are used not only to probe issues considered pertinent to the lives of white women and women of color but also to explore participatory discourse. Our chapters describe the creation of participatory systems in stakeholder relations (Haas & Deetz); permeable boundaries between (public and private) spheres that admit discourses previously relegated to one sphere into the other (Mumby); and co-constructed negotiation processes (Putnam & Kolb). These chapters are consistent with current feminist trends to delve into alternative ways of reconceptualizing organizing and organizational structure (see Calás & Smircich, 1996). By examining how gender operates within struggles for control over organizing processes, we may further challenge commonsense notions of legitimate structure, work processes, and workplace identities, including hierarchy and career (Buzzanell & Goldzwig, 1991; Ferguson, 1984; Mumby, 1998). We also may lessen managerialist tendencies to appropriate aspects of feminine working and leading that promote organizational effectiveness and efficiency but do not transform the power dynamics that disenfranchise most workers (see Calás & Smircich, 1993; Fine, 1993; Fondas, 1997).

In general, alternative organizing either is resistant to traditional bureaucratic structures and thinking or offers a different kind of structure aligned with values of choice, relationship, inclusion, caregiving, information sharing, community, and membership ownership and decision making (Buzzanell et al., 1997). We see growing attention to processes of representation and advocacy for change, as displayed in writings on workplace democracy and feminist organizing. Cheney (1995) defines workplace democracy as

> a system of governance which truly values individual goals and feelings (e.g., equitable enumeration, the pursuit of enriching work and the right to express oneself) as well as typical organizational objectives (e.g., effectiveness and efficiency, reflectively conceived), which actively fosters the connection between those two sets of concerns by encouraging individual contributions to important organizational choices, and which allows for the ongoing modification of the organization's activities by the group. (pp. 170-171)

Cheney et al. (1998) encourage additional research into issues of democracy not only because our disciplinary roots and important questions in varied communicative contexts relate to influence processes but also because our field has ethical and practical interests in promoting democratic organizations and illuminating the processes of representation. Democracy operates as a "form of social relations that aims simultaneously at developmental individualization and the collective good" (Deetz, 1992, p. 5).

Democracy can prioritize organizational goals and participatory structures, whereas feminist organizing consists of processes that are enacted within different types of organizational structures but conform to core feminist principles (Bate & Taylor, 1988; Ferree & Martin, 1995; Martin, 1990). Buzzanell (1994, 1995) portrays feminist organizing as the openness to different ways of working, the incorporation of holistic human beings (with regard to needs, values, and work outcomes), and collaborative work environments. These are not all-or-nothing elements in organizing, and they are difficult to achieve. However, according to Riger (1994), "Creating organizations that serve and advocate for women has been an outstanding achievement of the feminist movement in the United States during the past two decades" (p. 275). Because these organizations serve as means of promoting feminist values, their structures can have a variety of forms, including bureaucratic, participatory, and compound, or can combine "elements of more than one pure feminist practice" (Gottfried & Weiss, 1994, p. 24). Thus, the "critical choice facing members of a newly formed feminist organization is how far to deviate from mainstream principles and practices" (Riger, 1994, p. 280).

The critical dilemma for communication researchers and practitioners is how to enlarge the understanding of stakeholder concerns (Haas & Deetz, this volume), negotiation parties' interests (Putnam & Kolb, this volume), and evidence admissibility (Mumby, this volume) in organizational decision making while developing pragmatic arguments about the needs and means for transformation. Of interest to researchers and advocates of both democratic and feminist organizing is how members communicatively evolve structures that can deal with ideological tensions and changes in size or purpose and promote participatory and feminist values (see Bate & Taylor, 1988; Buzzanell et al., 1997; Cheney et al., 1998). A continuing challenge for feminist organizational and managerial communication researchers and practitioners is to locate sites in which members replicate, resist, and transform traditionally gendered organizing processes.

CONCLUSION

This book is just one attempt to generate further feminist organizational and managerial communication theory, research, and practice so that our work is inclusive, representative, and diverse. As Calás and Smircich (1996) conclude, "It's not only about 'gender' any more, as both women and men, from both First and Third Worlds, employed and unemployed, with and without families, struggle with inequality, injustice, inequity and intolerance" (p. 242). It is about presenting and publicizing the voices of those who are silenced, ignored, and misunderstood because of either taken-for-granted practices or deliberate attempts to squelch resistance. Through the tensions between the voices of those centrally located within and those inadequately represented by communication theorizing, we hope to call into question the very theoretical elements and frameworks that we have taken as the bases of our discipline.

Our responsibility as feminist organizational and managerial communication researchers is to articulate feminist issues in such a way that makes these concerns so compelling that others cannot help but see their importance in everyday interactions. Feminist communication scholarship can stretch the boundaries of what is possible in our research and practice. Our scholarship in these chapters reflects and develops emerging feminist concerns. At present, a third-wave feminist movement is not fully developed, but it seems to include and extend many of the themes we discuss in our chapters: living with contradictions, dissolving dualisms that threaten equality and difference, developing contexts for participatory practices and decision making, using the personal narrative to produce knowledge and theorizing, and critiquing and remedying the paucity of solutions and political strategies inherited from earlier feminist work (Bailey, 1997; Heyes, 1997; Siegel, 1997). The work of emerging feminism has to do with a stance and practice:

Regardless of how, when, and under what circumstances one becomes a part of the current wave of feminist activism and scholarship, what unites practitioners in a third wave of praxis is a pledge to expand on the groundwork laid during waves one and two; a commitment to continue the feminist legacy of assessing foundational concepts, particularly the category "woman"; and the courage to embrace the challenge of moving feminism, as a political movement without the fixity of a single feminist agenda in view, into the next millennium. (Siegel, 1997, p. 56)

NOTE

1. Simplification and hierarchical arrangement are conditions that prompt essentialist thinking. Heyes (1997) describes the antiessentialism work of contemporary feminists as reactions to second-wave feminists' "lack of intellectual rigor" (p. 145). This second-wave work often erased salient differences among women by using broad categories and generalizations. However, Heyes acknowledges that some difference arguments, such as those developed by Gilligan (1982) in her earliest and subsequent publications, helped rally support for the ways gender operated uniquely as an oppressive social construction:

> The challenge facing third wave feminist theory lies in the observation that neither interminable deconstruction nor uncritical reification of the category "women" is adequate to the demands of feminist practice. The task we have inherited [from second wave feminists] is to take seriously the commitments entailed in anti-essentialism but to find ways effectively to incorporate them into resistive political projects. (p. 146)

One way of accomplishing this goal is to "examine how generalizations are used; not to reject the use of generality altogether, but to ask what is enabled and what is excluded in the context in question" (p. 149). Generalizations can have emancipatory potential depending on how they are used and whether they can develop exploratory inquiries into underdeveloped aspects of women's lives.

References

Acker, J. (1990). Hierarchies, jobs, bodies: A theory of gendered organizations. *Gender & Society, 4,* 139-158.

Acker, J. (1992). Gendering organizational theory. In A. J. Mills & P. Tancred (Eds.), *Gendering organizational analysis* (pp. 248-260). Newbury Park, CA: Sage.

Adams, C. (1990). *The sexual politics of meat: A feminist-vegetarian critical theory.* New York: Continuum.

Adams, C. (1997). "Mad cow" disease and the animal industrial complex: An eco-feminist analysis. *Organization and Environment, 10,* 26-51.

Adler, G. S., & Tompkins, P. K. (1997). Electronic performance monitoring: An organizational justice and concertive control perspective. *Management Communication Quarterly, 10,* 259-288.

Adorno, T. (1973). *Negative dialectics* (F. Ashton, Trans.). New York: Continuum.

Albrecht, T. L., Irey, K. V., & Mundy, A. K. (1982). Integration in a communication network as a mediator of stress. *Social Work, 27,* 229-234.

Albrecht, T. L., & Ropp, V. A. (1982). The study of network structuring in organizations through the use of method triangulation. *Western Journal of Speech Communication, 46,* 162-178.

Aldoory, L., & Toth, E. L. (in press). Two feminists, six opinions: The complexities of feminism in communication scholarship today. In W. Gudykunst (Ed.), *Communication yearbook 24.* Thousand Oaks, CA: Sage.

Aldridge, M. (1990). Social work and the news media: A hopeless case? *British Journal of Social Work, 20,* 611-625.

Alfred, M. V. (1996). Tenured black women survive the white research academy. *Women in Higher Education, 2,* 8-9.

Allen, A. L. (1994). On being a role model. In D. T. Goldberg (Ed.), *Multiculturalism: A critical reader* (pp. 180-199). Boston: Blackwell.

Allen, B. J. (1995a). "Diversity" and organizational communication. *Journal of Applied Communication Research, 3,* 143-155.

Allen, B. J. (1995b, November). *Twice blessed, doubly oppressed: Women of color in the academy.* Paper presented at the meeting of the Speech Communication Association, New Orleans, LA.

Allen, B. J. (1996). Feminist standpoint theory: A black woman's (re)view of organizational socialization. *Communication Studies, 47,* 257-271.

Allen, B. J. (1998a). Black womanhood and feminist standpoints. *Management Communication Quarterly, 11,* 575-586.

Allen, B. J. (1998b). *Pejorative representations of black women: Implications for organizational communication.* Unpublished manuscript.

Allen, B. J., & Sandine, B. (1996, February). *Surprise and sense-making: Socialization experiences of graduate students of color.* Paper presented at the meeting of the Speech Communication Association, San Diego, CA.

Allen, N. J., & Meyer, J. P. (1990). Organizational socialization tactics: A longitudinal analysis of links to newcomers, commitment, and role orientation. *Academy of Management Journal, 33,* 847-858.

Altman, B. W., & Post, J. E. (1996). Beyond the "social contract": An analysis of the executive view at twenty-five large companies. In D. T. Hall & Associates (Eds.), *The career is dead, long live the career: A relational approach to careers* (pp. 46-71). San Francisco: Jossey-Bass.

Alvesson, M., & Wilmott, H. (1992). On the idea of emancipation in management and organization studies. *Academy of Management Review, 17,* 432-464.

American heritage dictionary of the English language (3rd ed.). (1992). Boston: Houghton Mifflin.

Anderson, N., & Thomas, H. (1996). Work group socialization. In M. A. West (Ed.), *Handbook of work group psychology* (pp. 423-450). Chichester, UK: Wiley.

Arendt, H. (1961). *Between past and future: Six essays in political thought.* New York: Meridian.

Arthur, M. B., Hall, D. T., & Lawrence, B. S. (1989). Generating new directions in career theory: The case for a transdisciplinary approach. In M. B. Arthur, D. T. Hall, & B. S. Lawrence (Eds.), *Handbook of career theory* (pp. 7-25). Cambridge, UK: Cambridge University Press.

Arthur, M. B., & Rousseau, D. M. (1996). A career lexicon for the 21st century. *Academy of Management Executive, 10*(4), 28-39.

Ashcraft, K. L. (1998). "I wouldn't say I'm a *feminist,* but . . .": Organizational micropractices and gender identity. *Management Communication Quarterly, 11,* 587-597.

Ashcraft, K. L., & Pacanowsky, M. E. (1996). "A woman's worst enemy": Reflections on a narrative of organizational life and female identity. *Journal of Applied Communication Research, 24,* 217-239.

Ashford, S. J. (1986). The role of feedback seeking in individual adaptation: A resource perspective. *Academy of Management Journal, 29,* 465-487.

Ashford, S. J., & Cummings, L. L. (1985). Proactive feedback seeking: The instrumental use of the information environment. *Journal of Occupational Psychology, 58,* 67-79.

Bach, B. (1990a, April). *Making a difference by doing differently: A response to Putnam.* Paper presented at the Arizona State University Conference on Organizational Communication: Perspectives for the 90s, Tempe, AZ.

Bach, B. (1990b). "Moving up" on campus: A qualitative examination of organizational socialization. *Journal of the Northwest Communication Association, 18,* 53-71.

Bailey, C. (1997). Making waves and drawing lines: The politics of defining the vicissitudes of feminism. *Hypatia, 12*(3), 17-28.

Bakhtin, M. M. (1981). *The dialogic imagination: Four essays* (M. Holquist, Ed.; C. Emerson & M. Holquist, Trans.). Austin: University of Texas Press.

Balsamo, A. (1996). *Technologies of the gendered body: Reading cyborg women.* Durham, NC: Duke University Press.

Banham, R. (1995, January). The downside of downsizing. *Risk Management, 42,* 18-27.

Baraka, J. N. (1997). Collegiality in the academy: Where does the black woman fit? In L. Benjamin (Ed.), *Black women in the academy: Promises and perils* (pp. 235-245). Gainesville: University Press of Florida.

Barge, J. K. (1994). *Leadership: Communication skills for organizations and groups.* New York: St. Martin's.

Barker, J. R. (1993). Tightening the iron cage: Concertive control in self-managing teams. *Administrative Science Quarterly, 38,* 408-437.

Barker, J. R., & Cheney, G. (1994). The concept of discipline in contemporary organizational life. *Communication Monographs, 61,* 19-43.

Barker, J. R., & Tompkins, P. K. (1994). Identification in the self-managing organization. *Human Communication Research, 21,* 223-240.

Barnard, C. (1968). *The functions of the executive.* Cambridge, MA: Harvard University Press. (Original work published 1938)

Barnett, W. P., & Miner, A. S. (1992). Standing on the shoulders of others: Career interdependence in job mobility. *Administrative Science Quarterly, 37,* 262-281.

Baron, R. A. (1989). Impression management by applicants during employment interviews: The "too much of a good thing" effect. In R. W. Eder & G. R. Ferris (Eds.), *The employment interview: Theory, research, and practice* (pp. 204-215). Newbury Park, CA: Sage.

Barrentine, P. (1993). *When the canary stops singing: Women's perspectives on transforming business.* San Francisco: Berrett-Koehler.

Barrett, F. J. (1995). Creating appreciative learning cultures. *Organizational Dynamics, 24*(2), 36-49.

Barrett, F. J., & Cooperrider, D. L. (1990). Generative metaphor intervention: A new approach for working with systems divided by conflict and caught in defensive perception. *Journal of Applied Behavioral Science, 26,* 219-239.

Bartky, S. (1988). Foucault, femininity, and the modernization of patriarchal power. In I. Diamond & L. Quinby (Eds.), *Feminism and Foucault: Reflections on resistance* (pp. 61-86). Boston: Northeastern University Press.

Bartlett, K. T. (1994). Only nice girls wear barrettes: Dress and appearance standards, community norms, and workplace equity. *Michigan Law Review, 92,* 2541-2582.

Bartos, O. (1970). Determinants and consequences of toughness. In P. Swingle (Ed.), *The structure of conflict* (pp. 45-68). New York: Academic Press.

Bartunek, J. M. (1988). The dynamics of personal and organizational reframing. In R. E. Quinn & K. S. Cameron (Eds.), *Paradox and transformation* (pp. 137-162). Cambridge, MA: Ballinger.

Bartunek, J. M., & Moch, M. K. (1994). Third-order organizational change and the mystical tradition. *Journal of Organizational Change Management, 7,* 24-41.

Baruch Bush, R. A., & Folger, J. P. (1994). *The promise of mediation: Responding to conflict through empowerment and recognition.* San Francisco: Jossey-Bass.

Bate, B., & Taylor, A. (Eds.). (1988). *Women communicating: Studies of women's talk.* Norwood, NJ: Ablex.

Bateson, G. (1972). *Steps to an ecology of the mind.* New York: Ballantine.

Bateson, M. C. (1989). *Composing a life.* New York: Plume.

Baxter, L. A. (1988). A dialectical perspective on communication strategies in relationship development. In S. W. Duck (Ed.), *A handbook of personal relationships* (pp. 257-273). New York: John Wiley.

Baxter, L., & Montgomery, B. M. (1996). *Relating: Dialogues and dialectics.* New York: Guilford.

Becker, C., Chasin, L., Chasin, R., Heraiz, M., & Roth, S. (1995). From stuck debate to new conversation on controversial issues: A report from the Public Conversations Project. In K. Weingarten (Ed.), *Cultural resistance: Challenging beliefs about men, women, and therapy.* Binghamton, NY: Haworth.

Belenky, M. F., Clinchy, B. M., Goldberger, N. R., & Tarule, J. M. (1986). *Women's ways of knowing: The development of self, voice, and mind.* New York: Basic Books.

Bell, E. L. (1990). The bicultural life experience of career-oriented black women. *Journal of Organizational Behavior, 11,* 459-477.

Bell, E. L. (1992). Myths, stereotypes, and realities of black women: A personal reflection. *Journal of Applied Behavioral Science, 28,* 363-376.

Bell, E. L., Denton, T. C., & Nkomo, S. (1993). Women of color in management: Toward an inclusive analysis. In E. A. Fagenson (Ed.), *Women in management: Trends, issues, and challenges in managerial diversity* (pp. 105-130). Newbury Park, CA: Sage.

Bell, L. M. (1994). *Looking for passages through the glass ceiling: An empirical field investigation into the effects of gender, age, and leader-member exchange relationships on the career progress and career perceptions of working professionals.* Unpublished doctoral dissertation, University of Cincinnati, OH.

Benhabib, S. (1985). The utopian dimension in communicative ethics. *New German Critique, 35,* 83-96.

Benhabib, S. (1986). *Critique, norm, and utopia: A study of the foundations of critical theory.* New York: Columbia University Press.

Benhabib, S. (1987). The generalized and the concrete other. In S. Benhabib & D. Cornell (Eds.), *Feminism as critique: On the politics of gender* (pp. 77-95). Minneapolis: University of Minnesota Press.

Benhabib, S. (1990). Afterword: Communicative ethics and current controversies in practical philosophy. In S. Benhabib & F. Dallmayr (Eds.), *The communicative ethics controversy* (pp. 330-369). Cambridge: MIT Press.

Benhabib, S. (1992). *Situating the self: Gender, community, and postmodernism in contemporary ethics.* New York: Routledge.

Benjamin, L. (1991). *The black elite: Facing the color line in the twilight of the twentieth century.* Chicago: Nelson-Hall.

Bennett, A. (1990). *The death of the organization man.* New York: William Morrow.

Bennett, A., & Lublin, J. S. (1995, March 31). Teflon big shots: Failure doesn't always damage the careers of top executives. *Wall Street Journal,* pp. A1, A6.

Bennis, W., & Nanus, B. (1985). *Leaders: The strategies for taking charge.* Cambridge, MA: Harper & Row.

Benson, S. (1992). "The clerking sisterhood": Rationalization and the work culture of saleswomen in American department stores, 1890-1960. In A. J. Mills & P. Tancred (Eds.), *Gendering organizational analysis* (pp. 167-184). Newbury Park, CA: Sage.

Berlew, D. E., & Hall, D. T. (1966). The socialization of managers: Effects of expectations on performance. *Administrative Science Quarterly, 11,* 207-233.

Bernstein, P. (1997). *American work values: Their origin and development.* Albany: SUNY.

Bernstein, R. J. (1983). *Beyond objectivism and relativism: Science, hermeneutics, and praxis.* Philadelphia: University of Pennsylvania Press.

Bhavnani, K. (1993). Tracing the contours: Feminist research and feminist objectivity. *Women's Studies International Forum, 16,* 95-104.

Bitzer, L. (1987). Rhetorical public communication. *Critical Studies in Mass Communication, 4,* 425-428.

Blancero, D., Marron, G., & Keller, T. (1997). Managing psychological contracts. *Employment Relations Today, 24*(2), 1-10.

Blank, W. (1995). *The nine natural laws of leadership.* New York: Amacon.

Blau, P. M. (1964). *Exchange and power in social life.* New York: John Wiley.

Blaxill, M. F., & Hout, T. M. (1991). The fallacy of the overhead quick fix. *Harvard Business Review, 69*(4), 93-101.

Bobo, J. (1994, January 17). The dark side of downsizing. *National Underwriter, 98,* p. 19.

Bohm, D. (1994). *Thought as a system.* New York: Routledge.

Bohm, D. (1996). *On dialogue* (L. Nichol, Ed.). London: Routledge.

Bordo, S. (1989). The body and the reproduction of femininity. In A. Jaggar & S. Bordo (Eds.), *Gender, body, knowledge* (pp. 13-33). New Brunswick, NJ: Rutgers University Press.

Bordo, S. (1993). *Unbearable weight: Feminism, Western culture, and the body.* Berkeley: University of California Press.

Borisoff, D., & Merrill, L. (1998). *The power to communicate: Gender differences as barriers* (3rd ed.). Prospect Heights, IL: Waveland.

Botan, C. (1996). Communication work and electronic surveillance: A model for predicting panoptic effects. *Communication Monographs, 63,* 293-313.

Bowen, S. P., & Wyatt, N. (Eds.). (1993). *Transforming visions: Feminist critiques in communication studies.* Cresskill, NJ: Hampton.

Bowman, P. J. (1991). Organizational psychology: African American perspectives. In R. L. Jones (Ed.), *Black psychology* (pp. 509-531). Berkeley, CA: Cobb & Henry.

Braverman, H. (1974). *Labor and monopoly capital: The degradation of work in the twentieth century.* New York: Monthly Review Press.

Brett, J. M., Shapiro, D. L., & Lytle, A. L. (1998). Breaking the bonds of reciprocity in negotiations. *Academy of Management Journal, 41,* 410-424.

Briskin, A. (1998). *The stirring of soul in the workplace.* San Francisco: Berrett-Koehler.

Brown, M. H. (1985). That reminds me of a story: Speech action in organizational social-ization. *Western Journal of Speech Communication, 49,* 27-42.

Bryman, A. (1996). Leadership in organizations. In S. R. Clegg, C. Hardy, & W. R. Nord (Eds.), *Handbook of organization studies* (pp. 276-292). London: Sage.

Buber, M. (1958). *I and thou* (2nd ed.; R. G. Smith, Trans.). New York: Scribner. (Original work published 1923)

Buchanan, B. (1974). Building organizational commitment: The socialization of managers of work organizations. *Administrative Science Quarterly, 19,* 533-546.

Bullis, C. (1984). *A report to the Forest Service: Summary of findings.* Unpublished manuscript.

Bullis, C. (1991). Communication practices as unobtrusive control: An observational study. *Communication Studies, 42,* 254-271.

Bullis, C. (1993). Organizational socialization research: Enabling, constraining, and shifting perspectives. *Communication Monographs, 60,* 10-17.

Bullis, C., & Bach, B. W. (1989a). Are mentor relationships helping organizations? An exploration of developing mentee-mentor organizational identifications using turning point analysis. *Communication Quarterly, 37,* 199-213.

Bullis, C., & Bach, B. W. (1989b). Socialization turning points: An examination of change in organizational identification. *Western Journal of Speech Communication, 53,* 273-293.

Bullis, C., & Bach, B. W. (1991). An explication and test of communication network content and multiplexity as predictors of organizational identification. *Western Journal of Speech Communication, 55,* 180-197.

Bullis, C., & Bach, B. W. (1996). Feminism and the disenfranchised: Going beyond the other. In E. B. Ray (Ed.), *Communication and the disenfranchised* (pp. 3-28). Hillsdale, NJ: Lawrence Erlbaum.

Bullis, C., & Stout, K. (1996, November). *Organizational socialization: A feminist standpoint approach.* Paper presented at the meeting of the Speech Communication Association, San Diego, CA.

Bunning, R. L. (1990). The dynamics of downsizing. *Personnel Journal, 69*(9), 69-75.

Buono, A. F., & Kamm, J. B. (1983). Marginality and the organizational socialization of female managers. *Human Relations, 36,* 1125-1140.

Burawoy, M. (1979). *Manufacturing consent: Changes in the labor process under monopoly capitalism.* Chicago: University of Chicago Press.

Burgess, N. J. (1997). Tenure and promotion among African American women in the academy: Issues and strategies. In L. Benjamin (Ed.), *Black women in the academy: Promises and perils* (pp. 227-234). Gainesville: University Press of Florida.

Burke, K. (1935). *Permanence and change.* New York: New Republic.

Burns, J. M. (1978). *Leadership.* New York: Harper & Row.

Burton, B., & Dunn, C. (1996). Feminist ethics as moral grounding for stakeholder theory. *Business Ethics Quarterly, 6,* 133-147.

Butler, J. (1988). Performative acts and gender constitution: An essay in phenomenology and feminist theory. *Theatre Journal, 40,* 519-531.

Butler, J. (1990). *Gender trouble: Feminism and the subversion of identity.* New York: Routledge.

Buzzanell, P. M. (1987). *An information acquisition and use approach to perceived career uncertainty, career track, and transitional career events.* Unpublished doctoral dissertation, Purdue University, West Lafayette, IN.

Buzzanell, P. M. (1993). Feminist approaches to organizational communication instruction. In C. Berryman-Fink, D. Ballard-Reisch, & L. H. Newman (Eds.), *Communication and sex role socialization* (pp. 525-553). New York: Garland.

Buzzanell, P. M. (1994). Gaining a voice: Feminist perspectives in organizational communication. *Management Communication Quarterly, 7,* 339-383.

Buzzanell, P. M. (1995). Reframing the glass ceiling as a socially constructed process: Implications for understanding and change. *Communication Monographs, 62,* 327-354.

Buzzanell, P. M. (1997). Toward an emotion-centered feminist framework for research on dual career couples. *Women & Language, 20*(2), 39-47.

Buzzanell, P. M. (1999). *A feminist sensemaking approach to organizational communication theorizing and change.* Unpublished manuscript.

Buzzanell, P. M., Ellingson, L., Silvio, C., Pasch, V., Dale, B., Mauro, G., Smith, E., Weir, N., & Martin, C. (1997). Leadership processes in alternative organizations: Invitational and dramaturgical leadership. *Communication Studies, 48,* 285-310.

Buzzanell, P. M., & Goldzwig, S. R. (1991). Linear and nonlinear career models: Metaphors, paradigms, and ideologies. *Management Communication Quarterly, 4,* 466-505.

Byron, W. J. (1995). Coming to terms with the new corporate contract. *Business Horizons, 38*(1), 8-15.

Calás, M. B. (1992). An/Other silent voice? Representing "Hispanic woman" in organizational texts. In A. J. Mills & P. Tancred (Eds.), *Gendering organizational analysis* (pp. 201-221). Newbury Park, CA: Sage.

Calás, M. B., & Smircich, L. (1991). Voicing seduction to silence leadership. *Organization Studies, 12,* 567-602.

Calás, M. B., & Smircich, L. (1992). Using the "F" word: Feminist theories and the social consequences of organizational research. In A. J. Mills & P. Tancred (Eds.), *Gendering organizational analysis* (pp. 222-234). Newbury Park, CA: Sage.

Calás, M. B., & Smircich, L. (1993). Dangerous liaisons: The "feminine-in-management" meets "globalization." *Business Horizons, 36*(2), 71-81.

Calás, M. B., & Smircich, L. (1996). From "the woman's" point of view: Feminist approaches to organization studies. In S. R. Clegg, C. Hardy, & W. R. Nord (Eds.), *Handbook of organization studies* (pp. 218-257). London: Sage.

Calhoun, C. (1986). Computer technology, large-scale social integration, and the local community. *Urban Affairs Quarterly, 22,* 329-349.

Calhoun, C. (1988). Populist politics, communications media, and large scale social integration. *Sociological Theory, 6,* 219-241.

Calhoun, C. (1991). Indirect relationships and imagined communities: Large-scale social integration and the transformation of everyday life. In J. Coleman & P. Bourdieu (Eds.), *Social theory in a changing society* (pp. 95-120). Boulder, CO: Westview.

Calhoun, C. (1992). The infrastructure of modernity: Indirect relationships, information technology, and social integration. In N. Smelser & H. Haferkamp (Eds.), *Social change and modernity* (pp. 205-236). Berkeley: University of California Press.

Calhoun, C. (1995). *Critical social theory: Culture, history, and the challenge of difference*. Oxford, UK: Basil Blackwell.

Carnevale, P. J. D., & Isen, A. M. (1986). The influence of positive affect and visual access on the discovery of integrative solutions in bilateral negotiation. *Organizational Behavior and Human Decision Process, 37,* 1-13.

Carroll, A. (1989). *Business and society: Ethics and stakeholder management.* Cincinnati, OH: South Western.

Cascio, W. F. (1993). Downsizing: What do we know? What have we learned? *Academy of Management Executive, 7*(1), 95-104.

Cassel, J. (1974). Psychosocial processes and "stress": Theoretical formulation. *International Journal of Health Services, 6,* 471-482.

Chao, G. T., O'Leary-Kelly, A., Wolf, S., Klein, H., & Gardner, P. (1994). Organizational socialization: Its content and consequences. *Journal of Applied Psychology, 79,* 730-743.

Cheney, G. (1983a). On the various and changing meanings of organizational memberships: A field study of organizational identification. *Communication Monographs, 50,* 342-362.

Cheney, G. (1983b). The rhetoric of identification and the study of organizational communication. *Quarterly Journal of Speech, 69,* 143-158.

Cheney, G. (1991). *Rhetoric in an organizational society: Managing multiple identities.* Columbia: University of South Carolina Press.

Cheney, G. (1995). Democracy in the workplace: Theory and practice from the perspective of communication. *Journal of Applied Communication Research, 23,* 167-200.

Cheney, G., & Carroll, G. (1997). The person as object in discourses in and around organizations. *Communication Research, 24,* 593-630.

Cheney, G., Straub, J., Speirs-Glebe, L., Stohl, C., DeGooyer, D., Jr., Whalen, S., Garvin-Doxas, K., & Carlone, D. (1998). Democracy, participation, and communication at work: A multidisciplinary review. In M. E. Roloff (Ed.), *Communication yearbook 21* (pp. 35-91). Thousand Oaks, CA: Sage.

Chernik, A. F. (1995). The body politic. In B. Findlen (Ed.), *Listen up: Voices from the next feminist generation* (pp. 75-84). Seattle, WA: Seal.

Chester, N. L., & Grossman, H. Y. (1990). Introduction: Learning about women and their work through their own accounts. In H. Y. Grossman & N. L. Chester (Eds.), *The experience and meaning of work in women's lives* (pp. 1-9). Hillsdale, NJ: Lawrence Erlbaum.

Chilton, K., & Weidenbaum, M. (1994). *A new social contract for the American workplace: From paternalism to partnering.* St. Louis, MO: Washington University, Center for the Study of American Business.

Cirksena, K., & Cuklanz, L. (1992). Male is to female as _____ is to _____: A guided tour of five feminist frameworks for communication studies. In L. F. Rakow (Ed.), *Women making meaning: New feminist directions in communication* (pp. 18-44). New York: Routledge.

Cixous, H. (1991). The laugh of the medusa. In R. R. Warhol & D. P. Herndl (Eds.), *Feminisms: An anthology of literary theory and criticism* (pp. 334-339). New Brunswick, NJ: Rutgers University Press.

Clair, R. P. (1991, November). *The use of framing devices to sequester organizational narratives: Hegemony and harassment.* Paper presented at the meeting of the Speech Communication Association, Atlanta, GA.

Clair, R. P. (1993a). The bureaucratization, commodification, and privatization of sexual harassment through institutional discourse: A study of the Big Ten universities. *Management Communication Quarterly, 7,* 123-157.

Clair, R. P. (1993b). The use of framing devices to sequester organizational narratives: Hegemony and harassment. *Communication Monographs, 60,* 113-136.

Clair, R. P. (1996). The political nature of the colloquialism, "a real job": Implications for organizational socialization. *Communication Monographs, 63,* 249-267.

Clair, R. P. (1998). *Organizing silence: A world of possibilities.* Albany: SUNY.

Clair, R. P., & Kunkel, A. W. (1995, May). *An organizational communication analysis of "unrealistic realities": Child abuse and the aesthetic resolution.* Paper presented at the annual meeting of the International Communication Association, Albuquerque, NM.

Clair, R. P., & Kunkel, A. W. (1998). "Unrealistic realities": Child abuse and the aesthetic resolution. *Communication Monographs, 65,* 24-46.

Clair, R. P., McGoun, M. J., & Spirek, M. M. (1993). Sexual harassment responses of working women: An assessment of current communication oriented typologies and perceived effectiveness of the response. In G. L. Kreps (Ed.), *Communication and sexual harassment in the workplace* (pp. 209-233). Cresskill, NJ: Hampton.

Clair, R. P., & Thompson, K. (1996). Pay discrimination as a discursive and material practice: A case concerning extended housework. *Journal of Applied Communication Research, 24,* 1-20.

Clark, C., & Bullis, C. (1992, February). *Socialization turning points: A test.* Paper presented at the meeting of the Western States Communication Association, Boise, ID.

Clark, S. M., & Corcoran, M. (1986). Perspectives on the professional socialization of women faculty. *Journal of Higher Education, 57,* 20-43.

Clarke, T. S. (1995, November/December). The invisible woman: Plantation protocol in contemporary America. *Colors,* pp. 15-16.

Clegg, S. R., & Hardy, C. (1996). Conclusion: Representations. In S. R. Clegg, C. Hardy, & W. R. Nord (Eds.), *Handbook of organization studies* (pp. 676-708). London: Sage.

Cobb, S. (1993). Empowerment and mediation: A narrative perspective. *Negotiation Journal, 9,* 245-259.

Cobb, S. (1994). A narrative perspective on mediation: Toward the materialization of the "storytelling" metaphor. In J. P. Folger & T. S. Jones (Eds.), *New directions in mediation: Communication research and perspectives* (pp. 48-63). Thousand Oaks, CA: Sage.

Code, L. (1991). *What can she know?* Ithaca, NY: Cornell University Press.

Cohen, J., & Stewart, I. (1994). *The collapse of chaos: Discovering simplicity in a complex world.* New York: Viking.

Cohen, S., & Wills, T. A. (1985). Stress, social support, and the buffering hypothesis. *Psychological Bulletin, 98,* 310-357.

Collins, P. H. (1986). Learning from the outsider within: The sociological significance of black feminist thought. *Social Problems, 33*(6), 14-32.

Collins, P. H. (1991). *Black feminist thought: Knowledge, consciousness, and the politics of empowerment.* New York: Routledge.

Collins, P. H. (1997). Comment on Hekman's "Truth and method: Feminist standpoint theory revisited": Where's the power? *Signs: Journal of Women in Culture and Society, 22,* 375-381.

Collins, S. M. (1989). The marginalization of black executives. *Social Problems, 36,* 317-331.

Collins, S. M. (1997). Black mobility in white corporations: Up the corporate ladder but out on a limb. *Social Problems, 44,* 55-67.

Collinson, D. (1988). "Engineering humor": Masculinity, joking, and conflict in shop-floor relations. *Organization Studies, 9,* 181-199.

Collinson, D. (1992). *Managing the shop floor: Subjectivity, masculinity, and workplace culture.* New York: De Gruyter.

Comer, D. R. (1991). Organizational newcomers' acquisition of information from peers. *Management Communication Quarterly, 5,* 64-89.

Compact edition of the Oxford English dictionary. (1971). Oxford, UK: Oxford University Press.

Conrad, C., & Poole, M. S. (1998). *Strategic communication: Toward the twenty-first century* (4th ed.). Fort Worth, TX: Harcourt, Brace & Jovanovich.

Cordes, C. L., & Dougherty, T. W. (1993). A review and an integration of research on job burnout. *Academy of Management Review, 18,* 621-656.

Corey, F. C. (1996). Personal narratives and young men in prison: Labeling the outside inside. *Western Journal of Communication, 60,* 57-75.

Cornelius, S. (1998). *Sexual harassment: Legal standards versus individual experiences.* Unpublished doctoral dissertation, University of Utah.

Cotton, J. (1993). *Employee involvement: Methods for improving performance and work attitudes.* Newbury Park, CA: Sage.

Court, M. (1997). Removing macho management: Lessons from the field of education. In D. Dunn (Ed.), *Workplace/women's place: An anthology* (pp. 198-219). Los Angeles: Roxbury.

Cox, S. (1997, May). Communication and the employee exit decision: A social exchange model. In J. Hollowitz (Chair), *Workplace socialization: Perspectives on organizational entry, training, and exit.* Symposium conducted at the fifth meeting of the A. F. Jacobson symposium, Omaha, NE.

Cox, S., & Kramer, M. (1995). Communication during employee dismissals: Social exchange principles and group influences on employee exit. *Management Communication Quarterly, 9,* 156-190.

Cox, T., & Nkomo, S. (1986). Differential performance appraisal criteria: A field study of black and white managers. *Group and Organizational Studies, 11,* 101-119.

Cox, T., & Nkomo, S. (1990). Invisible men and women: A status report on race as a variable in organization behavior research. *Journal of Organizational Behavior, 11,* 419-431.

Crawford, M. (1995). *Talking difference: On gender and language.* London: Sage.

Crispell, D. (1995, January). How executives manage time pressure. *American Demographics, 17,* 38.

Crow, G. M., & Glascock, C. (1995). Socialization to a new conception of the principalship. *Journal of Educational Administration, 33*(1), 22-43.

Csikszentmihalyi, M. (1978). Intrinsic reward and emergent motivation. In M. R. Lepper & D. Greene (Eds.), *The hidden costs of rewards: New perspectives on the psychology of human motivation* (pp. 205-216). Hillsdale, NJ: Lawrence Erlbaum.

Csikszentmihalyi, M. (1997). *Finding flow: The psychology of engagement with everyday life.* New York: Basic Books.

Csoka, L. S. (1995, Summer). A new employer-employee contract? *Employment Relations Today, 22*(2), 21-31.

Cutcher-Gershenfeld, J. E. (1994). Bargaining over how to bargain in labor-management negotiations. *Negotiation Journal, 10,* 323-335.

Cutcher-Gershenfeld, J. E., McKersie, R. B., & Walton, R. E. (1995). *Pathways to change: Case studies of strategic negotiations.* Kalamazoo, MI: W. E. Upjohn Institute for Employment Research.

Cutrona, C. E., & Russell, D. W. (1990). Type of social support and specific stress: Toward a theory of optimal matching. In B. R. Sarason, I. G. Sarason, & G. R. Pierce (Eds.), *Social support: An interactional view* (pp. 319-366). New York: John Wiley.

Daft, R. L., & Lengel, R. H. (1998). *Fusion leadership: Unlocking the subtle forces that change people and organizations.* San Francisco: Berrett-Koehler.

Dahl, R. (1961). *Who governs? Democracy and power in an American city.* New Haven, CT: Yale University Press.

Daly, J. P. (1991). The effects of anger on negotiations over mergers and acquisitions. *Negotiation Journal, 7,* 31-39.

Daly, M. (with Caputi, J.). (1987). *Webster's first new intergalactic wickedary of the English language.* Boston: Beacon.

Danielson, M. (1997, May). At-risk youths' organizational entry experiences: A taxonomic analysis. In J. Hollowitz (Chair), *Workplace socialization: Perspectives on organizational entry, training, and exit.* Symposium conducted at the fifth meeting of the A. F. Jacobson Symposium, Omaha, NE.

Daudelin, M. W. (1996). Learning from experience through reflection. *Organizational Dynamics, 24*(3), 36-48.

Davenport, J. A., & Davenport, J. (1997). Social workers: Fad-chasing jackasses or still on the side of the angels? *New Social Worker, 4,* 11-12.

Deal, T., & Kennedy, A. (1982). *Corporate cultures: The rites and rituals of corporate life.* Reading, MA: Addison-Wesley.

Deetz, S. (1992). *Democracy in an age of corporate colonization: Developments in communication and the politics of everyday life.* Albany: SUNY.

Deetz, S. (1995a, November). *Discursive formations, strategized subordination, and self-surveillance: An empirical case.* Paper presented at the meeting of the Speech Communication Association, San Antonio, TX.

Deetz, S. (1995b). *Transforming communication, transforming business: Building responsive and responsible workplaces.* Cresskill, NJ: Hampton.

Delphy, C. (1984). *Clonist Studies, 20,* 223-247.

Diamond, I. (1994). *Fertile ground.* Boston: Beacon.

Dill, B. T. (1979). The dialectics of black womanhood. *Signs: Journal of Women in Culture and Society, 4,* 543-557.

DiSanza, J. R. (1993). Shared meaning as a sales inducement strategy: Bank teller responses to frames, reinforcements, and quotas. *Journal of Business Communication, 30,* 133-160.

DiSanza, J. R. (1995). Bank teller organizational assimilation in a system of contradictory practices. *Management Communication Quarterly, 9,* 191-218.

Dobrzynski, J. H. (1996, November). The first woman to buy and head a Fortune 1000 company. *Working Woman,* pp. 107-108.

Donohue, W. A., & Diez, M. E. (1985). Directive use in negotiation interaction. *Communication Monographs, 52,* 305-318.

Donohue, W. A., Diez, M. E., & Hamilton, M. (1984). Coding naturalistic negotiation interaction. *Human Communication Research, 10,* 403-425.

Douglass, M. E., & Douglass, D. N. (1994, November). Planning work and time. *Supervisory Management, 39,* p. 7.

Duff, C. (1997, June 3). Surging economy bypasses black men: Blue-collar workers face particularly daunting odds. *Wall Street Journal,* pp. A2, A4.

Dumas, R. G. (1979). Dilemmas of black females in leadership. *Journal of Personality and Social Systems, 2,* 120-129.

Dunkel, T. (1996, April). The front runners. *Working Woman,* pp. 31-33, 72-75.

Eastland, L. (1991). *Communication, organization, and change within a feminist context.* Lewiston, NY: Edwin Mellen Press.

Edmonston, J. (1994, February). Experience can't be measured in dollars. *Business Marketing, 78,* p. 34.

Edwards, R. (1979). *Contested terrain: The transformation of the workplace in the twentieth century.* New York: Basic Books.

Egdorf, K. (1994, November). *The vanishing social support network: A study of job elimination.* Paper presented at the meeting of the Speech Communication Association, New Orleans, LA.

Eisnitz, G. (1997). *Slaughterhouse.* Amherst, NY: Prometheus Books.

Ellinor, L., & Gerard, G. (1998). *Dialogue: Discovering the transforming power of conversation.* New York: John Wiley.

Elliott, J. R. (1994, April). Risks and opportunities in downsizing the work force. *Risk Management, 41,* 101-110.

Ellis, B. H., & Miller, K. I. (1993). The role of assertiveness, personal control, and participation in the prediction of nurse burnout. *Journal of Applied Communication Research, 21,* 327-342.

Ellis, B. H., & Miller, K. I. (1994). Supportive communication among nurses: Effects on commitment, burnout, and retention. *Health Communication, 6,* 77-96.

Englebrecht, A. R. (1994, March). *A feminist perspective of organizational socialization: A game of blindman's bluff.* Paper presented at the Western Academy of Management, Santa Fe, NM.

Eoyang, G. H. (1993a). Introduction to the chaos network conference. *Third Annual Chaos Network Conference,* 15-23.

Eoyang, G. H. (1993b). Patterns: An algorithm for complex interactions. *Third Annual Chaos Network Conference,* 154-160.

Essed, P. (1991). *Understanding everyday racism: An interdisciplinary theory.* Newbury Park, CA: Sage.

Essien, F. (1997). Black women in the sciences: Challenges along the pipeline in the academy. In L. Benjamin (Ed.), *Black women in the academy: Promises and perils* (pp. 91-102). Gainesville: University Press of Florida.

Etter-Lewis, G. (1993). *My soul is my own: Oral narratives of African American women in the professions.* New York: Routledge.

Ettore, B. (1996). Religion in the workplace: Implications for managers. *Management Review, 85*(12), 15-18.

Evered, R., & Tannenbaum, B. (1992). A dialog on dialog. *Journal of Management Inquiry, 1,* 43-55.

Fairhurst, G. T. (1993). The leader-member exchange patterns of women leaders in industry: A discourse analysis. *Communication Monographs, 60,* 321-351.

Fairhurst, G. T. (in press). Dualisms in leadership communication research. In F. M. Jablin & L. L. Putnam (Eds.), *The new handbook of organizational communication.* Thousand Oaks, CA: Sage.

Fairhurst, G. T., & Chandler, T. A. (1989). Social structure in leader-member interaction. *Communication Monographs, 56,* 215-232.

Fairhurst, G. T., & Sarr, R. A. (1996). *The art of framing: Managing the language of leadership.* San Francisco: Jossey-Bass.

Falcione, R. L., & Wilson, C. E. (1988). Socialization processes in organizations. In G. M. Goldhaber & G. A. Barnett (Eds.), *Handbook of organizational communication* (pp. 151-169). Norwood, NJ: Ablex.

Feldman, D. C. (1976). A contingency theory of socialization. *Administrative Science Quarterly, 21,* 433-452.

Feldman, D. C. (1989). Socialization, resocialization, and training: Reframing the research agenda. In I. Goldstein & Associates (Eds.), *Training and development in organizations* (pp. 376-415). San Francisco: Jossey-Bass.

Ferber, M. A., & Nelson, J. A. (Eds.). (1993). *Beyond economic man: Feminist theory and economics.* Chicago: University of Chicago Press.

Ferguson, K. (1984). *The feminist case against bureaucracy.* Philadelphia: Temple University Press.

Ferraris, C., Carveth, R., & Parrish-Sprowl, J. (1993). Interface Precision Benchworks: A case study in organizational identification. *Journal of Applied Communication Research, 21,* 343-357.

Ferree, M. M., & Martin, P. Y. (Eds.). (1995). *Feminist organizations: Harvest of the new women's movement.* Philadelphia: Temple University Press.

Fine, M. (1994). Working the hyphens. In N. Denzin & Y. Lincoln (Eds.), *Handbook of qualitative research* (pp. 70-82). Thousand Oaks, CA: Sage.

Fine, M. G. (1993). New voices in organizational communication: A feminist commentary and critique. In S. Perlmutter Bowen & N. Wyatt (Eds.), *Transforming visions: Feminist critiques in communication studies* (pp. 125-166). Cresskill, NJ: Hampton.

Fisher, R., Ury, W., & Patton, B. (1991). *Getting to yes* (2nd ed.). Boston: Houghton Mifflin.

Flax, J. (1990). *Thinking fragments: Psychoanalysis, feminism, and postmodernism in the contemporary West.* Berkeley: University of California Press.

Fletcher, J. K. (1996). A relational approach to the protean worker. In D. T. Hall & Associates (Eds.), *The career is dead, long live the career: A relational approach to careers* (pp. 105-131). San Francisco: Jossey-Bass.

Fletcher, J. K. (1998). Relational practice: A feminist reconstruction of work. *Journal of Management Inquiry, 7*(2), 164-186.

Fleuridas, C., Nelson, T., & Rosenthal, C. (1986). The evolution of circular questions. *Journal of Marriage and Family Therapy, 12*(2), 113-127.

Fondas, N. (1995). The biological clock confronts complex organizations: Women's ambivalence about work and implications for feminist management research. *Journal of Management Inquiry, 4,* 57-65.

Fondas, N. (1997). Feminization unveiled: Management qualities in contemporary writings. *Academy of Management Review, 22,* 257-282.

Forward, G., & Scheerhorn, D. (1996). Identities and the assimilation process in the modern organization. In H. Mokros (Ed.), *Interaction and identity: Vol. 5. Information and behavior* (pp. 371-391). New Brunswick, NJ: Transaction Publishing.

Foss, K. A., & Foss, S. K. (1991). *Women speak: The eloquence of women's lives.* Prospect Heights, IL: Waveland.

Foss, K. A., & Foss, S. K. (1994). Personal experiences as evidence in feminist scholarship. *Western Journal of Communication, 58,* 39-43.

Foss, S. K., & Griffin, C. L. (1995). Beyond persuasion: A proposal for an invitational rhetoric. *Communication Monographs, 62,* 2-18.

Foucault, M. (1979). *Discipline and punish: The birth of the prison* (A. Sheridan, Trans.). New York: Vintage.

Foucault, M. (1980). *Power/knowledge: Selected interviews and other writings 1972-1977* (C. Gordon, L. Marshall, J. Mepham, & K. Soper, Trans.). New York: Pantheon.

Foucault, M. (1990). *The history of sexuality: An introduction* (Vol. 1; R. Hurley, Trans.). New York: Random House. (Original work published 1976)

Fox-Genovese, E. (1991). *Feminism without illusions: A critique of individualism.* Chapel Hill: University of North Carolina Press.

Fraker, A. T., & Spears, L. C. (Eds.). (1996). *Seeker and servant: Reflections on religious leadership.* San Francisco: Jossey-Bass.

Fraser, N. (1989). *Unruly practices: Power, discourse, and gender in contemporary social theory.* Minneapolis: University of Minnesota Press.

Fraser, N. (1990-1991). Rethinking the public sphere: A contribution to the critique of actually existing democracy. *Social Text, 25/26,* 56-80.

Frasier, E. F. (1939). *The Negro family in the United States.* Chicago: University of Chicago Press.

Freeman, R. (1984). *Strategic management: A stakeholder approach.* Boston: Pitman.

Freeman, R., & Gilbert, D. (1988). *Corporate strategy and the search for ethics.* Englewood Cliffs, NJ: Prentice Hall.

Freeman, R., & Gilbert, D. (1992). Business, ethics, and society: A critical agenda. *Business and Society, 31,* 9-17.

Freudenberger, H. J. (1974). Staff burn-out. *Journal of Social Issues, 30,* 159-165.

Frick, D. M., & Spears, L. C. (Eds.). (1996). *The private writings of Robert K. Greenleaf: On becoming a servant leader.* San Francisco: Jossey-Bass.

Friedman, R. A. (1992). From theory to practice: Critical choices for mutual gains' training. *Negotiation Journal, 8,* 91-98.

Friedman, S. (1995). Beyond white and other: Relationality and narratives of race in feminist discourse. *Signs: Journal of Women in Culture and Society, 21,* 1-49.

Fullerton, H. N., Jr. (1995). The 2005 labor force: Growing, but slowly. *Monthly Labor Review: Bureau of Labor Statistics, 118*(11), 29-44.

Gadamer, H. (1975). *Truth and method* (G. Barden & J. Cumming, Trans.). New York: Seabury.

Gallos, J. V. (1989). Exploring women's development: Implications for career theory, practice, and research. In M. B. Arthur, D. T. Hall, & B. S. Lawrence (Eds.), *Handbook of career theory* (pp. 110-132). Cambridge, UK: Cambridge University Press.

Garber, M. (1992). *Vested interests: Cross dressing and cultural anxiety.* New York: Routledge.

Garsten, C., & Gray, C. (1997). How to become oneself: Discourses of subjectivity in post-bureaucratic organizations. *Organization, 4,* 211-228.

Gearhart, S. (1982). Womanpower: Energy re-sourcement. In C. Spretank (Ed.), *The politics of women's spirituality: Essays on the rise of spiritual power within the feminist movement* (pp. 194-206). Garden City, NY: Anchor.

Gergen, M. (Ed.). (1988). *Feminist thought and the structure of knowledge.* New York: New York University Press.

Gergen, M. (1990). Baskets of reed and arrows of steel: Stories of chaos and continuity. In S. Srivastva (Ed.), *Symposium: Executive and organizational continuity.* Cleveland, OH: Case Western Reserve University, Weatherhead School of Management, Department of Organizational Behavior.

Gibelman, M., & Schervish, P. H. (1997). *Who we are: Second look.* Washington, DC: National Association of Social Workers Press.

Giddens, A. (1979). *Central problems in social theory: Action, structure, and contradiction in social analysis.* Berkeley: University of California Press.

Giddens, A. (1984). *The constitution of society: Outline of the theory of structuration.* Berkeley: University of California Press.

Gilligan, C. (1982). *In a different voice: Psychological theory and women's development.* Cambridge, MA: Harvard University Press.

Gittleman, M., & Joyce, M. (1995). Earnings mobility in the United States, 1967-1991. *Monthly Labor Review: Bureau of Labor Statistics, 118*(9), 3-13.

Gleick, J. (1987). *Chaos: Making a new science.* New York: Viking.

Goffman, E. (1974). *Frame analysis: An essay on the organization of experience.* Cambridge, MA: Harvard University Press.

Goldberger, N., Tarule, J., Clinchy, B., & Belenky, M. (Eds.). (1996). *Knowledge, difference, and power: Essays inspired by* Women's Ways of Knowing. New York: Basic Books.

Golembiewski, R. T., Munzenrider, R. F., & Stevenson, J. G. (1986). *Stress in organizations: Toward a phase model of burnout.* New York: Praeger.

Goodnight, G. T. (1981). The personal, technical, and public spheres of argument: A speculative inquiry. *Journal of the American Forensic Association, 18,* 214-227.

Goodnight, G. T. (1987). Public discourse. *Critical Studies in Mass Communication, 4,* 428-432.

Goodnight, G. T. (1997). Opening up "the spaces of public dissension." *Communication Monographs, 64,* 270-274.

Gordon, L. (1979). The struggle for reproductive freedom: Three stages of feminism. In Z. Eisenstein (Ed.), *Capitalist patriarchy and the case for socialist feminism* (pp. 107-132). New York: Monthly Review Press.

Gorz, A. (1987). *Critique of economic reason* (G. Handyside & C. Turner, Trans.). London: Verso.

Gottfried, H., & Weiss, P. (1994). A compound feminist organization: Purdue University's Council on the Status of Women. *Women & Politics, 14*(2), 23-44.

Graham, E. (1995, October 31). The baby boom hits 50: Their careers: Count on nothing and work like a demon. *Wall Street Journal,* pp. B1, B7.

Gramsci, A. (1971). *Selections from the prison notebooks* (Q. Hoare & G. Nowell-Smith, Trans.). New York: International.

Gray, B. (1994). The gender-based foundations of negotiation theory. In R. J. Lewicki, B. H. Sheppard, & R. Bies (Eds.), *Research on negotiation in organizations* (Vol. 4, pp. 3-36). Greenwich, CT: JAI.

Gray, J. (1992). *Men are from Mars, women are from Venus: A practical guide for improving communication and getting what you want in your relationships.* New York: HarperCollins.

Greengard, S. (1993, November). Don't rush downsizing: Plan, plan, plan. *Personnel Journal, 72,* 64-70.

Greenhaus, J. H., Parasuraman, S., & Wormley, W. M. (1990). Effects of race on organizational experiences, job performance evaluations, and career outcomes. *Academy of Management Journal, 33,* 64-86.

Greenleaf, R. K. (1977). *Servant leadership: A journey into the nature of legitimate power and greatness.* New York: Paulist.

Grossman, H. Y., & Stewart, A. J. (1990). Women's experience of power over others: Case studies of psychotherapists and professors. In H. Y. Grossman & N. L. Chester (Eds.), *The experience and meaning of work in women's lives* (pp. 11-33). Hillsdale, NJ: Lawrence Erlbaum.

Guaspari, J. (1995). A cure for "initiative burnout." *Management Review, 84,* 45-49.

Gulliver, P. H. (1979). *Disputes and negotiations: A cross-cultural perspective.* New York: Academic Press.

Gummer, B. (1996). Stress in the workplace: Looking bad, telling lies, and burning out. *Administration in Social Work, 21,* 73-88.

Gwartney-Gibbs, P. A., & Lach, D. H. (1994). Gender and workplace dispute resolution: A conceptual and theoretical model. *Law & Society Review, 28,* 265-296.

Habermas, J. (1970). On systematically distorted communication. *Inquiry, 13,* 205-218.

Habermas, J. (1973). *Wahrheitstheorien.* In H. Fahrtenbach (Ed.), *Wirklichkeit und reflexion: Walter Schultz zum 60* (pp. 211-263). Pfullingen: Neske.

Habermas, J. (1974). The public sphere: An encyclopedia article. *New German Critique, 1*(3), 49-55.

Habermas, J. (1984). *The theory of communicative action: Vol. 1. Reason and the rationalization of society* (T. McCarthy, Trans.). Boston: Beacon.

Habermas, J. (1987). *The theory of communicative action: Vol. 2. Lifeworld and system* (T. McCarthy, Trans.). Boston: Beacon.

Habermas, J. (1989). *The structural transformation of the public sphere: An inquiry into a category of bourgeois society* (T. Burger, Trans.). Cambridge: MIT Press.

Habermas, J. (1990). *Moral consciousness and communicative action* (C. Lenhardt & S. Nicholsen, Trans.). Cambridge: MIT Press.

Habermas, J. (1993). *Justification and application: Remarks on discourse ethics* (C. Cronin, Trans.). Cambridge: MIT Press.

Hackett, R. D., Bycio, P., & Hausdorf, P. A. (1994). Further assessments of Meyer and Allen's (1991) three-component model of organizational commitment. *Journal of Applied Psychology, 79,* 15-23.

Hackman, J. R., & Oldham, G. R. (1976). Motivation through the design of work. *Organizational Behavior and Human Performance, 16,* 250-279.

Hall, D. T. (1996). Long live the career: A relational approach. In D. T. Hall & Associates (Eds.), *The career is dead, long live the career: A relational approach to careers* (pp. 1-14). San Francisco: Jossey-Bass.

Hall, D. T., & Associates. (Eds.). (1996). *The career is dead, long live the career: A relational approach to careers.* San Francisco: Jossey-Bass.

Hall, D. T., & Mirvis, P. H. (1996). The new protean career: Psychological success and the path with a heart. In D. T. Hall & Associates (Eds.), *The career is dead, long live the career: A relational approach to careers* (pp. 15-45). San Francisco: Jossey-Bass.

Hall, R. M., & Sandler, B. R. (1983). *Academic mentoring for women students and faculty: A new look at an old way to get ahead.* Washington, DC: AAC/PSEW.

Hamermesh, D. S. (1989). What do we know about worker displacement in the U.S.? *Industrial Relations, 28,* 51-59.

Haney, D. Q. (1998, March 20). "This will hurt me worse than you: You're fired": Study of heart attacks says stress on bosses can't be dismissed. *Journal and Courier,* p. A1.

Hank, H. (1997, April). *"Sellabrating" women: Women's health promotion.* Paper presented at the annual meeting of the Central States Communication Association, St. Louis, MO.

Haraway, D. (1997). *Modest_witness @ second millennium. Female Man meets Onco Mouse.* New York: Routledge.

Harding, S. (1986). *The science question in feminism.* Ithaca, NY: Cornell University Press.

Harding, S. (1987). *Feminism and methodology.* Bloomington: Indiana University Press.

Harding, S. (1991). *Whose science? Whose knowledge?* Ithaca, NY: Cornell University Press.

Harding, S. (1997). Comment on Hekman's "Truth and method: Feminist standpoint theory revisited": Whose standpoint needs the regimes of truth and reality? *Signs: Journal of Women in Culture and Society, 22,* 382-391.

Harragan, B. L. (1977). *Games mother never taught you: Corporate gamesmanship for women.* New York: Warner.

Harris, L. (1994, January/February). Use technology to manage time wisely. *Executive Female, 17,* pp. 14-15.

Harrison, B. (1994, January). The costs of lean and mean. *Technology Review, 97,* p. 64.

Harrison, T. (1994). Communication and interdependence in democratic organizations. In S. Deetz (Ed.), *Communication yearbook 17* (pp. 247-274). Thousand Oaks, CA: Sage.

Hart, A. (1991). *Principal succession: Establishing leadership in schools.* Albany: SUNY.

Hartley, J. (1991, July/August). Keeping one step ahead of your deadlines. *Business Credit, 93,* p. 40.

Hartmann, K. (1997, May). Socialization tactics as related to the commitment of volunteer. In J. Hollowitz (Chair), *Workplace socialization: Perspectives on organizational entry, training, and exit.* Symposium conducted at the fifth meeting of the A. F. Jacobson Symposium, Omaha, NE.

Hartsock, N. (1983a). The feminist standpoint: Developing the ground for a specifically feminist historical materialism. In S. Harding & M. Hintikka (Eds.), *Discovering reality: Feminist perspectives on epistemology, metaphysics, methodology, and philosophy of science* (pp. 283-311). Hingham, MA: Kluwer Boston.

Hartsock, N. (1983b). *Money, sex, and power: An essay on domination and community.* New York: Longman.

Hartsock, N. (1985). Exchange theory: Critique from a feminist standpoint. In S. G. MacNall (Ed.), *Current perspectives in social theory* (Vol. 6, pp. 57-70). Greenwich, CT: JAI.

Hartsock, N. (1987). The feminist standpoint: Developing the ground for a specifically feminist historical materialism. In S. Harding (Ed.), *Feminism and methodology* (pp. 181-190). Bloomington: Indiana University Press.

Hartsock, N. (1997). Comment on Hekman's "Truth and method: Feminist standpoint theory revisited": Truth or justice? *Signs: Journal of Women in Culture and Society, 22,* 367-374.

Haslett, B., Geis, F. L., & Carter, M. R. (1993). *The organizational woman: Power and paradox.* Norwood, NJ: Ablex.

Hauser, G. A. (1997). On publics and public spheres: A response to Phillips. *Communication Monographs, 64,* 275-279.

Hayes, E. L. (1995, August). *It's not what you know, it's who you know: The effects of human and social capital on race differences in promotion and support.* Paper presented in the careers division of the Academy of Management conference, Vancouver, BC, Canada.

Hayles, K. N. (1990). *Chaos bound: Orderly disorder in contemporary literature and science.* Ithaca, NY: Cornell University Press.

Hazell, D. (1997, November 7). *Mayor responds to overwhelmed mom's pleas for help.* Associated Press.

Hearn, J., Sheppard, D., Tancred-Sheriff, P., & Burrell, G. (Eds.). (1989). *The sexuality of organization.* Newbury Park, CA: Sage.

Heckscher, C. (1995). *White-collar blues: Management loyalties in an age of corporate restructuring.* New York: Basic Books.

Heckscher, C., & Hall, L. (1994). Mutual gains and beyond: Two levels of intervention. *Negotiation Journal, 10,* 235-248.

Hegde, R. S. (1998). A view from elsewhere: Locating difference and the politics of representation from a transnational feminist perspective. *Communication Theory, 8,* 271-297.

Hegel, G. W. F. (1967). *The phenomenology of mind* (J. B. Baillie, Trans.). New York: Harper & Row. (Original work published 1807)

Heifetz, R. A. (1994). *Leadership without easy answers*. Cambridge, MA: Belknap.

Heifetz, R. A., & Laurie, D. L. (1997). The work of leadership. *Harvard Business Review, 75*(1), 124-134.

Hekman, S. (1990). *Gender and knowledge: Elements of a postmodern feminism.* Boston: Northeastern University Press.

Hekman, S. (1997). Truth and method: Feminist standpoint theory revisited. *Signs: Journal of Women in Culture and Society, 22,* 341-365.

Helgesen, S. (1990). *The female advantage: Women's ways of leadership.* Garden City, NY: Doubleday.

Hennesey, R. (1993). Women's lives/feminist knowledge: Feminist standpoint as ideology critique. *Hypatia, 8,* 14-34.

Henry, M. (1994). Ivory towers and ebony women: The experiences of black women in higher education. In S. Davies, C. Lubelska, & J. Quinn (Eds.), *Changing the subject: Women in higher education* (pp. 48-95). London: Taylor & Francis.

Hess, J. A. (1993). Assimilating newcomers into an organization: A cultural perspective. *Journal of Applied Communication Research, 21,* 189-210.

Heyes, C. J. (1997). Anti-essentialism in practice: Carol Gilligan and feminist philosophy. *Hypatia, 12*(3), 142-163.

Higginbotham, E., & Weber, L. (1992). Moving up with kin and community: Upward social mobility for black and white women. *Gender & Society, 6,* 416-440.

Hine, D. C. (1997). The future of black women in the academy: Reflections on struggle. In L. Benjamin (Ed.), *Black women in the academy: Promises and perils* (pp. 327-339). Gainesville: University Press of Florida.

Hirsch, P. (1987). *Pack your own parachute: How to survive mergers, takeovers, and other corporate disasters.* Reading, MA: Addison-Wesley.

Hochschild, A. (1983). *The managed heart: Commercialization of human feelings.* Berkeley: University of California Press.

Hochschild, A. (1997). *The time bind: When work becomes home and home becomes work.* New York: Metropolitan Books.

Hocker, J. L., & Wilmot, W. W. (1995). *Interpersonal conflict* (4th ed.). Madison, WI: Brown & Benchmark.

Hoke, B. (1997). Women's colleges: The intersection of race, class, and gender. In L. Benjamin (Ed.), *Black women in the academy: Promises and perils* (pp. 291-301). Gainesville: University Press of Florida.

Holliday, K. K. (1995, June). Bankers break through the glass ceiling. *Bank Marketing,* pp. 11-16.

hooks, b. (1981). *Ain't I a woman: Black women and feminism.* Boston: South End.

hooks, b. (1984). *Feminist theory: From margin to center.* Boston: South End.

hooks, b. (1989). *Talking back: Thinking feminist, thinking black.* Boston: South End.

hooks, b. (1990). *Yearning: Race, gender, and cultural politics.* Boston: South End.

Houston, M. (1997). When black women talk with white women: Why dialogues are difficult. In A. Gonzalez, M. Houston, & V. Chen (Eds.), *Our voices: Essays in culture, ethnicity, and communication* (2nd ed., pp. 187-194). Los Angeles: Roxbury.

Howard, J. A., & Hollander, J. A. (1997). *Gendered situations, gendered selves: A gender lens on social psychology.* Thousand Oaks, CA: Sage.

Huff, A. S. (1990, May). *Wives—of the organization*. Paper presented at the Woman and Work Conference, Arlington, TX.

Hughes, E. C. (1958). *Men and their work*. New York: Free Press.

Hunter, F. (1953). *Community power structure*. Chapel Hill: University of North Carolina Press.

Huspek, M. (1994). Critical and nonfoundational analyses: Are they contradictory or complementary? In B. Kovacic (Ed.), *New approaches to organizational communication* (pp. 191-210). Albany: SUNY.

Iannello, K. (1993). *Decisions without hierarchy: Feminist interventions in organizational theory and practice*. London: Routledge.

Ibarra, H. (1992). Homophily and differential returns: Sex differences in network structure and access in an advertising firm. *Administrative Science Quarterly, 37,* 422-447.

Ibarra, H. (1993). Personal networks of women and minorities in management: A conceptual framework. *Academy of Management Review, 18,* 56-87.

Ibarra, H. (1995). Race, opportunity, and diversity of social circles in managerial networks. *Academy of Management Journal, 38,* 673-703.

Ilgen, D. R., & Youtz, M. A. (1986). Factors affecting the evaluation and development of minorities in organizations. In K. Rowland & G. Ferris (Eds.), *Research in personnel and human resource management: A research annual* (pp. 307-337). Greenwich, CT: JAI.

Ingersoll, V., & Adams, G. (1986). Beyond organizational boundaries: Exploring the managerial myth. *Administration and Society, 18,* 360-381.

Irigaray, L. (1991). The sex which is not one. In R. R. Warhol & D. P. Herndl (Eds.), *Feminisms: An anthology of literary theory and criticism* (pp. 350-356). New Brunswick, NJ: Rutgers University Press.

Isaacs, W. N. (1993). Taking flight: Dialogue, collective thinking, and organizational learning. *Organizational Dynamics, 22*(2), 24-39.

Isen, A. M., Daubman, K. A., & Nowicki, G. P. (1987). Positive affect facilitates creative problem solving. *Journal of Personality and Social Psychology, 52,* 1122-1131.

Jablin, F. M. (1982). Organizational communication: An assimilation approach. In M. E. Roloff & C. R. Berger (Eds.), *Social cognition and communication* (pp. 255-286). Newbury Park, CA: Sage.

Jablin, F. M. (1984). Assimilating new members into organizations. In R. N. Bostrom (Ed.), *Communication yearbook 8* (pp. 594-626). Beverly Hills, CA: Sage.

Jablin, F. M. (1987). Organizational entry, assimilation, and exit. In F. M. Jablin, L. L. Putnam, K. H. Roberts, & L. H. Porter (Eds.), *Handbook of organizational communication* (pp. 679-740). Newbury Park, CA: Sage.

Jablin, F. M., Grady, D., & Parker, P. (1994, November). *Organizational disengagement: A review and integration of the literature*. Paper presented at the meeting of the Speech Communication Association, New Orleans, LA.

Jablin, F. M., & Krone, K. J. (1987). Organizational assimilation. In C. Berger & S. Chaffee (Eds.), *Handbook of communication science* (pp. 711-746). Newbury Park, CA: Sage.

Jablin, F. M., & Putnam, L. L. (Eds.). (in press). *The new handbook of organizational communication*. Thousand Oaks, CA: Sage.

Jackson, S. E., Stone, V. K., & Alvarez, E. B. (1992). Socialization amidst diversity: The impact of demographics on work team oldtimers and newcomers. *Research in Organizational Behavior, 14,* 45-109.

Jaggar, A. M. (1994). Introduction: Living with contradictions. In A. M. Jaggar (Ed.), *Living with contradictions: Controversies in feminist social ethics* (pp. 1-12). Boulder, CO: Westview.

James, C. E. (1994). The paradox of power and privilege: Race, gender, and occupational position. *Canadian Women's Studies, 14,* 47-51.

James, J., & Farmer, R. (1993). *Spirit, space, and survival: African American women in (white) academe.* New York: Routledge.

Jamieson, K. H. (1995). *Beyond the double bind: Women and leadership.* New York: Oxford University Press.

Jantsch, E. (1980). *The self-organizing universe: Scientific and human implications of the emerging paradigm of evolution.* Elmsford, NY: Pergamon.

Jarratt, J., & Coates, J. F. (1995). Employee development and job creation: Trends, problems, opportunities. In M. London (Ed.), *Employees, careers, and job creation: Developing growth-oriented human resource strategies and programs* (pp. 1-30). San Francisco: Jossey-Bass.

Jasinski, J. (1987). Perspectives on mass communication. *Critical Studies in Mass Communication, 4,* 423-424.

Johannesen, R. L. (1971). The emerging concept of communication as dialogue. *Quarterly Journal of Speech, 57,* 373-382.

Johannesen, R. L. (1996). *Ethics in human communication* (4th ed.). Prospect Heights, IL: Waveland.

Johnson, F. L. (1989). Women's culture and communication: An analytical perspective. In C. M. Lont & S. A. Friedley (Eds.), *Beyond boundaries: Sex and gender diversity in communication* (pp. 301-316). Fairfax, VA: George Mason University Press.

Joint Economic Committee. (1993). *The outlook for jobs and the economy: Hearing before the Joint Economic Committee* (102d Cong., 2d Sess., held on Nov. 6, 1992). Washington, DC: Government Printing Office.

Jones, G. (1986). Socialization tactics, self-efficacy, and newcomers' adjustments to organizations. *Academy of Management Journal, 29,* 262-279.

Jorgensen-Earp, C. R., & Staton, A. Q. (1993). Student metaphors for the college freshman experience. *Communication Education, 42,* 123-141.

Justus, J. B., Freitag, S., & Parker, L. L. (1987). *The University of California in the 21st century: Successful approaches to faculty diversity.* Berkeley: University of California Press.

Kahn, W. A. (1996). Secure base relationships at work. In D. T. Hall & Associates (Eds.), *The career is dead, long live the career: A relational approach to careers* (pp. 158-179). San Francisco: Jossey-Bass.

Kanter, R. M. (1977). *Men and women of the corporation.* New York: Basic Books.

Kanter, R. M. (1992, October). Creating a habitat for the migrant manager. *Personnel Management, 24,* 38-40.

Katz, D., & Kahn, R. L. (1978). *The social psychology of organizations* (2nd ed.). New York: John Wiley.

Katz, R. (1977). Job enrichment: Some career considerations. In J. Van Maanen (Ed.), *Organizational careers: Some new perspectives* (pp. 133-147). New York: John Wiley.

Katz, R. (1980). Time and work: Toward an integrative perspective. In B. M. Staw & L. Cummings (Eds.), *Research in organizational behavior* (Vol. 2, pp. 81-121). Greenwich, CT: JAI.

Katz, R. (1985). Organizational stress and early socialization experiences. In T. Beehr & R. Bhagat (Eds.), *Human stress and cognition in organization: An integrative perspective* (pp. 117-139). New York: John Wiley.

Kaufman, C. F., Lane, P. M., & Lindquist, J. D. (1991). Exploring more than 24 hours a day: A preliminary investigation of polychronic time use. *Journal of Consumer Research, 18,* 392-401.

Kaufman, J. (1995, March 20). How workplaces may look without affirmative action. *Wall Street Journal,* pp. A1, A2.

Kaufman, J., & Markels, A. (1996, November 18). Blacks, whites differ on lesson of Texaco tape. *Wall Street Journal,* pp. B1, B7.

Keller, E. F. (1985). *Reflections on gender and science.* New Haven, CT: Yale University Press.

Keough, C. M. (1992). Bargaining arguments and argumentative bargainers. In L. L. Putnam & M. E. Roloff (Eds.), *Communication and negotiation* (pp. 109-127). Newbury Park, CA: Sage.

Kilborn, P. T. (1995, March 16). For many in work force, "glass ceiling" still exists. *New York Times,* p. A22.

Kilbourne, B. S., & England, P. (1996). Occupational skill, gender, and earnings. In P. J. Dubeck & K. Borman (Eds.), *Women and work* (pp. 68-71). New York: Garland.

Kimle, P. A., & Damhorst, M. L. (1997). A grounded theory model of the ideal business image for women. *Symbolic Interaction, 20,* 45-68.

Kirk, D., & Todd-Mancillas, W. R. (1991). Turning points in graduate student socialization: Implications for recruiting future faculty. *Review of Higher Education, 14,* 407-422.

Klein, B. (1993). Novelty and confirmation: The creative coevolution on the edge of chaos. *Third Annual Chaos Network Conference,* 161-168.

Kohlberg, L. (1981). *Essays on moral development: Vol. 1. The philosophy of moral development.* San Francisco: Harper & Row.

Kohlberg, L. (1984). *Essays on moral development: Vol. 2. The psychology of moral development.* San Francisco: Harper & Row.

Kolb, D. M. (1992). Women's work: Peacemaking in organizations. In D. M. Kolb & J. M. Bartunek (Eds.), *Hidden conflict in organizations* (pp. 63-91). Newbury Park, CA: Sage.

Kolb, D. M., & Coolidge, G. (1991). Her place at the table. In J. Z. Rubin & J. W. Breslin (Eds.), *Negotiation theory and practice* (pp. 261-277). Cambridge, MA: Harvard Law Program on Negotiation.

Kolb, D. M., & Putnam, L. L. (1997). Through the looking glass: Negotiation theory refracted through the lens of gender. In S. E. Gleason (Ed.), *Workplace dispute resolution: Directions for the twenty-first century* (pp. 231-257). East Lansing: Michigan State University Press.

Kolb, D. M., & Williams, J. (1999). *Tough enough: Gender in the shadow of negotiations.* New York: Simon & Schuster.

Kossek, E. E., & Zonia, S. D. (1994). The effects of race and ethnicity on perceptions of human resource policies and climate regarding diversity. *Journal of Business and Technical Communication, 8,* 319-334.

Kotter, J. P. (1990). What leaders really do. *Harvard Business Review, 68*(3), 103-111.

Kouzes, J. M., & Posner, B. Z. (1993). *Credibility: How leaders gain and lose it, why people demand it.* San Francisco: Jossey-Bass.

Kram, K. E. (1996). A relational approach to career development. In D. T. Hall & Associates (Eds.), *The career is dead, long live the career: A relational approach to careers* (pp. 132-157). San Francisco: Jossey-Bass.

Kram, K. E., & Isabella, L. A. (1985). Mentoring alternatives: The role of peer relationships in career development. *Academy of Management Journal, 28,* 110-132.

Kramer, M. W. (1989). Communication during intraorganization job transfers. *Management Communication Quarterly, 3,* 219-248.

Kramer, M. W. (1993). Communication and uncertainty reduction during job transfers: Leaving and joining processes. *Communication Monographs, 60,* 178-198.

Kramer, M. W. (1994). Uncertainty reduction during job transitions. *Management Communication Quarterly, 7,* 384-412.

Kramer, M. W. (1995). A longitudinal study of superior-subordinate communication during job transfers. *Human Communication Research, 22,* 39-64.

Kramer, M. W., Callister, R. R., & Turban, D. B. (1995). Information-receiving and information-giving during job transitions. *Western Journal of Communication, 59,* 151-170.

Krinsky, L. W. (Ed.). (1984). *Stress and productivity.* New York: Human Sciences.

Krugman, R. D., Lenherr, M., Betz, L., & Fryer, G. E. (1986). The relationship between unemployment and the physical abuse of children. *Child Abuse and Neglect, 10,* 415-418.

Kunda, G. (1992). *Engineering culture.* Philadelphia: Temple University Press.

Kutscher, R. E. (1995). Summary of BLS projections to 2005. *Monthly Labor Review: Bureau of Labor Statistics, 118*(11), 3-9.

Laabs, J. (1995). Balancing spirituality and work. *Personnel Journal, 74*(9), 60-76.

Laabs, J. (1996). Eyeing future HR concerns. *Personnel Journal, 75,* 28-37.

LaClau, E., & Mouffe, C. (1985). *Hegemony and socialist strategy.* London: Verso.

Lakoff, R. (1975). *Language and women's place.* New York: Harper & Row.

Langer, S. (1951). *Philosophy in a new key.* Cambridge, MA: Harvard University Press.

Lawler, E. (1986). *High involvement management.* San Francisco: Jossey-Bass.

Lax, D. A., & Sebenius, J. K. (1986). *The manager as negotiator: Bargaining for cooperation and competitive gain.* New York: Free Press.

Leana, C. R., & Feldman, D. C. (1990). Individual responses to job loss: Empirical findings from two field studies. *Human Relations, 43,* 1155-1181.

Leana, C. R., & Feldman, D. C. (1995). Finding new jobs after a plant closing: Antecedents and outcomes of the occurrence and quality of reemployment. *Human Relations, 48,* 1381-1401.

LeBaron, M., & Carstarphen, N. (1997). Negotiating intractable conflict: The common ground dialogue process and abortion. *Negotiation Journal, 13,* 341-361.

Lee, R. T. (1993). A further examination of managerial burnout: Toward an integrated model. *Journal of Organizational Behavior, 14,* 3-20.

Lehrer, J. (1996, March 18). *The newshour with Jim Lehrer* (Show #5486). Overland Park, KS: Strictly Business Transcription Service.

Levine, D. I., & Parkin, R. J. (1994). Work organization, employment security, and macroeconomic stability. *Journal of Economic Behavior and Organization, 24,* 251-271.

Lewicki, R. J., & Litterer, J. A. (1985). *Negotiation.* Homewood, IL: Irwin.

Lewicki, R. J., Weiss, S. E., & Lewin, D. (1992). Models of conflict, negotiation, and third party intervention: A review and synthesis. *Journal of Organizational Behavior, 13,* 209-252.

Lim, S. G., & Murninghan, J. K. (1994). Phases, deadlines, and the bargaining process. *Organizational Behavior and Human Decision Processes, 58,* 153-171.

Lin, N., Woelfel, M., & Light, S. C. (1986). Buffering the impact of the most important life event. In N. Lin, A. Dean, & W. M. Ensel (Eds.), *Social support, life events, and depression* (pp. 215-230). Orlando, FL: Academic Press.

Littlejohn, S. W. (1995). Moral conflict in organizations. In A. M. Nicotera (Ed.), *Conflict and organizations: Communicative processes* (pp. 101-125). Albany: SUNY.

Locke, M. F. (1997). Striking the delicate balances: The future of African American women in the academy. In L. Benjamin (Ed.), *Black women in the academy: Promises and perils* (pp. 340-346). Gainesville: University Press of Florida.

London, M. (1998). *Career barriers: How people experience, overcome, and avoid failure.* Mahwah, NJ: Lawrence Erlbaum.

Longino, H. E. (1993). Feminist standpoint theory and the problems of knowledge. *Signs: Journal of Women in Culture and Society, 19,* 201-212.

Lopate, C. (1974). Women and pay for housework. *Liberation, 18,* 8-11.

Lorber, J. (1994). *Paradoxes of gender.* New Haven, CT: Yale University Press.

Lorde, A. (1983). The master's tools will never dismantle the master's house. In C. Moraga & G. Anzaldua (Eds.), *This bridge called my back: Writings by radical women of color* (pp. 98-101). New York: Kitchen Table Press.

Lorde, A. (1984). *Sister outsider.* Freedom, CA: Crossing Press.

Louis, M. R. (1980). Surprise and sense making: What newcomers experience in entering unfamiliar organizational settings. *Administrative Science Quarterly, 25,* 226-251.

Louis, M. R. (1990). Acculturation in the workplace: Newcomers as lay ethnographers. In B. Schneider (Ed.), *Organizational climate and culture* (pp. 85-115). San Francisco: Jossey-Bass.

Louis, M. R. (1996). Creating safe havens at work. In D. T. Hall & Associates (Eds.), *The career is dead, long live the career: A relational approach to careers* (pp. 223-245). San Francisco: Jossey-Bass.

Lovelace, K., & Rosen, B. (1996). Differences in achieving person-organization fit among diverse groups of managers. *Journal of Management, 22,* 703-722.

Luce, R. D., & Raiffa, H. (1957). *Games and decisions.* New York: John Wiley.

Lukes, S. (1974). *Power: A radical view.* London: Macmillan.

MacKinnon, C. (1989). *Toward a feminist theory of the state.* Cambridge, MA: Harvard University Press.

Maguire, M., & Mohtar, L. F. (1994). Performance and the celebration of a subaltern counterpublic. *Text and Performance Quarterly, 14,* 238-252.

Mander, J., & Goldsmith, E. (Eds.). (1996). *The case against the global economy.* San Francisco: Sierra Club.

Manning, R. (1992). *Speaking from the heart: A feminist perspective on ethics.* Lanham, MD: Rowman & Littlefield.

Manusov, V., & Billingsley J. (1997). Nonverbal communication in organizations. In P. Y. Byers (Ed.), *Organizational communication: Theory and behavior* (pp. 58-89). Boston: Allyn & Bacon.

Manz, C. C., & Sims, H. P., Jr. (1987). Leading workers to lead themselves: The external leadership of self-managing work teams. *Administrative Science Quarterly, 32,* 106-128.

Manz, C. C., & Sims, H. P., Jr. (1989). *Super-leadership: Leading others to lead themselves.* New York: Berkley.

Mar, D., & Ong, P. M. (1994). Race and rehiring in the high-tech industry. *Review of Black Political Economy, 22*(3), 43-54.

Markels, A. (1996, February 26). Top down: A boss can do a lot to raise an employee's sagging spirits. Finding a long-term cure means that everybody wins. *Wall Street Journal,* p. R7.

Markels, A., & Murray, M. (1996, May 14). Slashed and burned—call it dumbsizing: Why some companies regret cost-cutting. *Wall Street Journal,* pp. A1, A6.

Marshall, J. (1989). Re-visioning career concepts: A feminist invitation. In M. B. Arthur, D. T. Hall, & B. S. Lawrence (Eds.), *Handbook of career theory* (pp. 275-291). Cambridge, UK: Cambridge University Press.

Marshall, J. (1993). Viewing organizational communication from a feminist perspective: A critique and some offerings. In S. Deetz (Ed.), *Communication yearbook 16* (pp. 122-143). Newbury Park, CA: Sage.

Marshall, J. (1995). *Women managers moving on: Exploring career and life choices.* London: Routledge.

Martin, B. (1988). Feminism, criticism, and Foucault. In I. Diamond & L. Quinby (Eds.), *Feminism and Foucault: Reflections on resistance* (pp. 3-19). Boston: Northeastern University Press.

Martin, P. Y. (1990). Rethinking feminist organizations. *Gender & Society, 4,* 182-206.

Maslach, C. (1982). Understanding burnout: Definitional issues in analyzing a complex phenomenon. In W. S. Paine (Ed.), *Job stress and burnout: Research, theory, and intervention perspectives* (pp. 29-40). Beverly Hills, CA: Sage.

Maslach, C., & Jackson, S. E. (1982). Burnout in health professions: A social psychological analysis. In G. S. Sanders & J. Suls (Eds.), *Social psychology of health and illness* (pp. 227-251). Hillsdale, NJ: Lawrence Erlbaum.

Mason, E., & Mudrack, P. (1996). Gender and ethical orientation: A test of gender and occupational socialization theories. *Journal of Business Ethics, 15,* 599-604.

Mather, L., & Yngvesson, B. (1980-1981). Language, audience, and the transformation of disputes. *Law & Society Review, 15,* 775-821.

Matteson, M. T., & Ivancevich, J. N. (1982). *Managing job stress and worker health.* New York: Free Press.

Mattson, M., & Buzzanell, P. M. (1999). Traditional and feminist organizational communication ethical analyses of messages and issues involved in an actual job loss case. *Journal of Applied Communication Research, 27,* 49-72.

McKay, N. (1983). Black woman professor—white university. *Women's Studies International Forum, 4,* 143-147.

McKay, N. (1997). A troubled peace: Black women in the halls of the white academy. In L. Benjamin (Ed.), *Black women in the academy: Promises and perils* (pp. 11-22). Gainesville: University Press of Florida.

McKendall, M. A., & Margulis, S. T. (1995). People and their organizations: Rethinking the assumptions. *Business Horizons, 38*(6), 21-28.

McNay, L. (1992). *Foucault and feminism: Power, gender, and the self.* Cambridge, MA: Polity Press.

McPhee, R. D. (1986, May). *Political and critical perspectives on socialization.* Paper presented at the annual conference of the International Communication Association, Chicago.

McPhee, R. D., & Poole, M. S. (in press). Organizational structure, configuration, and communication. In F. M. Jablin & L. L. Putnam (Eds.), *The new handbook of organizational communication.* Thousand Oaks, CA: Sage.

Mead, G. (1934). *Mind, self, and society: From the standpoint of a social behaviorist.* Chicago: University of Chicago Press.

Melia, J. (1995). An honest human body: Sexuality and the continuum of resistance. *Women's Studies International Forum, 18,* 547-557.

Menkel-Meadow, C. (1994). Portia Redux: Another look at gender, feminism, and legal ethics. *Virginia Journal of Social Policy & the Law, 2,* 75-115.

Michelini, R. L. (1971). Effects of prior interaction, contact strategy, and expectation of meeting on game behavior and sentiment. *Journal of Conflict Resolution, 15,* 97-103.

Miller, J. B. (1976). *Toward a new psychology of women.* Boston: Beacon.

Miller, K. I. (1998). Nurses at the edge of chaos: Application of "New Science" concepts to organizational systems. *Management Communication Quarterly, 12,* 112-127.

Miller, K. I., Birkholt, M., Scott, C., & Stage, C. (1995). Empathy and burnout in human service work: An extension of a communication model. *Communication Research, 22,* 123-147.

Miller, K. I., Ellis, B. H., Zook, E. G., & Lyles, J. S. (1990). An integrated model of communication, stress, and burnout in the workplace. *Communication Research, 17,* 300-326.

Miller, K. I., & Monge, P. (1985). Participation, satisfaction, and productivity: A meta-analytic review. *Academy of Management Journal, 29,* 727-753.

Miller, K. I., Stiff, J. B., & Ellis, B. H. (1988). Communication and empathy as precursors to burnout among human service workers. *Communication Monographs, 55,* 250-265.

Miller, K. I., Zook, E. G., & Ellis, B. H. (1989). Occupational differences in the influence of communication on stress and burnout in the workplace. *Management Communication Quarterly, 3,* 166-190.

Miller, V. D. (1996). An experimental study of newcomers' information seeking behaviors during organizational entry. *Communication Studies, 47,* 1-24.

Miller, V. D., & Jablin, F. M. (1991). Information seeking during organizational entry: Influences, tactics, and a model of the process. *Academy of Management Review, 16,* 92-120.

Mills, A. J., & Tancred, P. (Eds.). (1992). *Gendering organizational analysis*. Newbury Park, CA: Sage.

Milwid, B. (1992). *Working with men: Women in the workplace talk about sexuality, success, and their male coworkers*. East Rutherford, NJ: Berkley.

Minkler, M., & Biller, R. P. (1979). Role shock: A tool for conceptualizing stresses accompanying role transitions. *Human Relations, 32*, 125-140.

Mintzberg, H. (1983). *Power in and around organizations*. Englewood Cliffs, NJ: Prentice Hall.

Mirvis, P. H. (1997). "Soul work" in organizations. *Organization Science, 8*, 193-206.

Mirvis, P. H., & Hall, D. T. (1994). Psychological success and the boundaryless career. *Journal of Organizational Behavior, 15*, 365-380.

Mirvis, P. H., & Hall, D. T. (1996). New organizational forms and the new career. In D. T. Hall & Associates (Eds.), *The career is dead, long live the career: A relational approach to careers* (pp. 72-101). San Francisco: Jossey-Bass.

Morris, K. (1998, May). The rise of Jill Barad. *Business Week*, pp. 112-119.

Morrison, A. M., & Von Glinow, M. A. (1990). Women and minorities in management. *American Psychologist, 45*, 200-208.

Morrison, A. M., White, R. P., Van Velsor, E., & the Center for Creative Leadership. (1987). *Breaking the glass ceiling*. Reading, MA: Addison-Wesley.

Morrison, E. W. (1993). Newcomer information seeking: Exploring types, modes, sources, and outcomes. *Academy of Management Journal, 36*, 557-589.

Moses, Y. T. (1989). *Black women in academe: Issues and strategies*. Washington, DC: Project on the Status and Education of Women, Association of American Colleges.

Moses, Y. T. (1997). Black women in academe: Issues and strategies. In L. Benjamin (Ed.), *Black women in the academy: Promises and perils* (pp. 23-38). Gainesville: University Press of Florida.

Mowday, R. T., Porter, L. W., & Steers, R. M. (1982). *Employee-organization linkages: The psychology of commitment, absenteeism, and turnover*. New York: Academic Press.

Moynihan, D. P. (1965). *The Negro family: The case for national action*. Washington, DC: U.S. Department of Labor, Office of Policy Planning and Research.

Mullings, L. (1994). Images, ideology, and women of color. In M. B. Zinn & B. T. Dill (Eds.), *Women of color in US society* (pp. 265-289). Philadelphia: Temple University Press.

Mumby, D. K. (1988). *Communication and power in organizations: Discourse, ideology, and domination*. Norwood, NJ: Ablex.

Mumby, D. K. (1993a). Critical organizational communication studies: The next ten years. *Communication Monographs, 60*, 18-25.

Mumby, D. K. (1993b). Feminism and the critique of organizational communication studies. In S. Deetz (Ed.), *Communication yearbook 16* (pp. 155-166). Newbury Park, CA: Sage.

Mumby, D. K. (1996). Feminism, postmodernism, and organizational communication: A critical reading. *Management Communication Quarterly, 9*, 259-295.

Mumby, D. K. (1997). The problem of hegemony: Rereading Gramsci for organizational communication studies. *Western Journal of Communication, 61*, 343-375.

Mumby, D. K. (1998). Organizing men: Power, discourse, and the social construction of masculinity(s) in the workplace. *Communication Theory, 8,* 164-183.

Mumby, D. K., & Putnam, L. L. (1992). The politics of emotion: A feminist reading of bounded rationality. *Academy of Management Review, 17,* 465-486.

Mumby, D. K., & Stohl, C. (1996). Disciplining organizational communication studies. *Management Communication Quarterly, 10,* 50-72.

Murphy, A. G. (1998). Hidden transcripts of flight attendant resistance. *Management Communication Quarterly, 11,* 499-535.

Murphy, J., & Gilligan, C. (1980). Moral development in late adolescence and adulthood: A critique and reconstruction of Kohlberg's theory. *Human Development, 23,* 77-104.

Nadesan, M. H., & Trethewey, A. (1998). *The entrepreneurial subject: Gendered strategies of success?* Manuscript submitted for publication.

Nakayama, T. K., & Krizek, R. L. (1995). Whiteness: A strategic rhetoric. *Quarterly Journal of Speech, 81,* 291-309.

Nanus, B. (1992). *Visionary leadership: Creating a compelling sense of direction for your organization.* San Francisco: Jossey-Bass.

Neal, J. A. (1997). Spirituality in management education: A guide to resources. *Journal of Management Education, 21,* 121-139.

Neale, M. A., & Bazerman, M. H. (1991). *Cognition and rationality in negotiation.* New York: Free Press.

Newman, K. S. (1988). *Falling from grace: The experience of downward mobility in the American middle class.* New York: Free Press.

Newman, K. S. (1993). *Declining fortunes: The withering of the American dream.* New York: Basic Books.

Nicholson, L. (Ed.). (1990). *Feminism/postmodernism.* New York: Routledge.

Nielsen, J. (1990). *Feminist research methods.* Boulder, CO: Westview.

Nierenberg, G. (1973). *Fundamentals of negotiating.* New York: Hawthorn Books.

Nkomo, S. M. (1992). The emperor has no clothes: Rewriting race in organizations. *Academy of Management Review, 17,* 487-513.

Noddings, N. (1984). *Caring: A feminine approach to ethics and moral education.* Berkeley: University of California Press.

Nonaka, I. (1988). Creating organizational order out of chaos: Self-renewal in Japanese firms. *California Management Review, 31*(3), 57-73.

Notter, J. (1995, April). *Trust and conflict transformation.* Washington, DC: Common Ground Network of Life and Choice.

Oakley, A. (1981). Interviewing women: A contradiction in terms. In H. Roberts (Ed.), *Doing feminist research* (pp. 30-61). London: Routledge & Kegan Paul.

O'Connell, D. (1990, December 17). It's still a wonderful life. *Wall Street Journal,* p. A10.

O'Connell, D., & Louis, M. R. (1997). *Changing contexts of organizational socialization: Implications for theory and research.* Unpublished manuscript.

O'Connor, K. M., & Adams, A. A. (1999). What novices think about negotiation: A content analysis of scripts. *Negotiation Journal, 15,* 135-147.

Olsen, T. (1978). *Silences.* New York: Dell. (Original work published 1965)

Omolade, B. (1994). *The rising song of African American women.* New York: Routledge.

Ong, P. M. (1991). Race and post-displacement earnings among high-tech workers. *Industrial Relations, 30,* 456-468.

Orbe, M. P. (1998). *Constructing co-cultural theory: An explication of culture, power, and communication.* Thousand Oaks, CA: Sage.

Orr, C. M. (1997). Charting the currents of the third wave. *Hypatia, 12*(3), 29-45.

Ostroff, C., & Kozlowski, S. W. J. (1992). Organizational socialization as a learning process: The role of information acquisition. *Personnel Psychology, 45,* 849-861.

Ostroff, C., & Kozlowski, S. W. J. (1993). The role of mentoring in the information gathering processes of newcomers during early organizational socialization. *Journal of Vocational Behavior, 42,* 170-183.

Owens, E. L. (1987, March). Project management deadlines: Are they necessary? *Data Management, 25,* 16, 30-31.

Pacanowsky, M. E., & O'Donnell-Trujillo, N. (1982). Communication and organizational cultures. *Western Journal of Speech Communication, 46,* 115-130.

Papa, M. J., Auwal, M. A., & Singhal, A. (1997). Organizing for social change within concertive control systems: Member identification, empowerment, and the masking of discipline. *Communication Monographs, 64,* 219-249.

Parker, P. S., & Ogilvie, D. (1996). Gender, culture, and leadership: Toward a culturally distinct model of African-American women executives' leadership strategies. *Leadership Quarterly, 7,* 189-214.

Parker, V. A. (1996). Growth-enhancing Relationships Outside Work (GROWs). In D. T. Hall & Associates (Eds.), *The career is dead, long live the career: A relational approach to careers* (pp. 180-195). San Francisco: Jossey-Bass.

Pateman, C. (1983). Feminism and democracy. In G. Duncan (Ed.), *Democratic theory and practice* (pp. 204-217). Cambridge, UK: Cambridge University Press.

Pateman, C., & Gross, E. (Eds.). (1987). *Feminist challenges: Social and political theory.* Boston: Northeastern University Press.

Pearce, W. B., & Littlejohn, S. (1997). *Moral conflict: When social worlds collide.* Thousand Oaks, CA: Sage.

Perrow, C. (1996). The bounded career and the demise of the civil society. In M. B. Arthur & D. M. Rousseau (Eds.), *The boundaryless career: A new employment principle for a new organizational era* (pp. 297-313). New York: Oxford University Press.

Peters, T., & Waterman, R., Jr. (1982). *In search of excellence: Lessons from America's best run companies.* New York: Harper & Row.

Peterson, K. S. (1998, March 19). Strain of stress can be drain on brain. *USA Today,* p. 8D.

Pfeffer, J. (1994). *Competitive advantage through people: Unleashing the power of the work force.* Boston: Harvard Business School Press.

Pfeffer, J. (1995). Producing sustainable competitive advantage through the effective management of people. *Academy of Management Executive, 9*(1), 55-72.

Phillips, K. R. (1996). The spaces of public dissension: Reconsidering the public sphere. *Communication Monographs, 63,* 231-248.

Phillips, S., & Bach, B. (1992, February). *"Did you hear about the guy who retired from the physical plant?" Retirement stories as organizational sense-making.* Paper presented at the meeting of the Western Speech Communication Association, Boise, ID.

Pines, A. M. (1982). Helpers' motivation and the burnout syndrome. In T. A. Wills (Ed.), *Basic processes in helping relationships* (pp. 453-475). New York: Academic Press.

Pitelis, C., & Sugden, R. (1986). The separation of ownership and control in the theory of the firm. *International Journal of Industrial Organization, 4,* 71-86.

Pollock, E. J. (1996, July 15). Angry mail: CEO takes on nun in a crusade against "political correctness." *Wall Street Journal,* pp. A1, A7.

Pollock, T. (1991, November). Cultivate time consciousness. *Supervision, 54,* p. 24.

Pollock, T. (1992, June). The pressures of time. *Supervision, 53,* pp. 23-24.

Pope, J., & Joseph, J. (1997). Student harassment of female faculty of African descent in the academy. In L. Benjamin (Ed.), *Black women in the academy: Promises and perils* (pp. 252-260). Gainesville: University Press of Florida.

Porter, L. W., Lawler, E. E., & Hackman, J. R. (1975). *Behavior in organizations.* New York: McGraw-Hill.

Posner, M. E. (1985). Minimizing weighted completion times with deadlines. *Operations Research, 33,* 562-574.

Poulin, J. E., & Walter, C. A. (1993). Social worker burnout: A longitudinal study. *Social Work Research and Abstracts, 29*(4), 5-11.

Powell, G. N. (1998). The abusive organization. *Academy of Management Executive, 12*(2), 95-96.

Power, M. (1992). After calculation? Reflections on critique of economic reason by Andre Gorz. *Accounting, Organizations and Society, 17,* 477-499.

Pribble, P. T. (1990). Making an ethical commitment: A rhetorical case study of organizational socialization. *Communication Quarterly, 38,* 255-267.

Priesmeyer, H. R. (1992). *Organizations and chaos: Defining the methods of nonlinear management.* Westport, CT: Quorum.

Prigogine, I., & Stengers, E. (1984). *Order out of chaos: Man's new dialogue with nature.* Toronto, Canada: Bantam New Age Books.

Pruitt, D. G. (1981). *Negotiation behavior.* New York: Academic Press.

Pruitt, D. G. (1983). Achieving interactive agreements. In M. H. Bazerman & R. J. Lewicki (Eds.), *Negotiating in organizations* (pp. 35-50). Beverly Hills, CA: Sage.

Pruitt, D. G., & Carnevale, P. J. D. (1993). *Negotiation in social conflict.* Buckingham, UK: Open University Press.

Putnam, L. L. (1990a, April). *Feminist theories, dispute processes, and organizational communication.* Paper presented at the Arizona State University Conference on Organizational Communication: Perspectives for the 90s, Tempe, AZ.

Putnam, L. L. (1990b). Reframing integrative and distributive bargaining: A process perspective. In B. H. Sheppard, M. H. Bazerman, & R. J. Lewicki (Eds.), *Research on negotiation in organizations* (Vol. 2, pp. 3-30). Greenwich, CT: JAI.

Putnam, L. L. (1994). Challenging the assumptions of traditional approaches to negotiation. *Negotiation Journal, 10,* 337-357.

Putnam, L. L., & Geist, P. (1985). Argument in bargaining: An analysis of the reasoning process. *Southern Speech Communication Journal, 50,* 225-245.

Putnam, L. L., & Holmer, M. (1992). Framing, reframing, and issue development. In L. L. Putnam & M. E. Roloff (Eds.), *Communication and negotiation* (pp. 128-155). Newbury Park, CA: Sage.

Putnam, L. L., & Jones, T. S. (1982). The role of communication in bargaining. *Human Communication Research, 8,* 262-280.

Putnam, L. L., Phillips, N., & Chapman, P. (1996). Metaphors of communication and organization. In S. R. Clegg, C. Hardy, & W. R. Nord (Eds.), *The handbook of organizational studies* (pp. 375-408). Thousand Oaks, CA: Sage.

Putnam, L. L., & Roloff, M. E. (1992). Communication perspectives on negotiation. In L. L. Putnam & M. E. Roloff (Eds.), *Communication and negotiation* (pp. 1-17). Newbury Park, CA: Sage.

Putnam, L. L., Wilson, S. R., & Turner, D. B. (1990). The evolution of policy arguments in teachers' negotiation. *Argumentation, 4,* 129-152.

Quick, J. C. (1984). *Organizational stress and preventive management.* New York: McGraw-Hill.

Quintillian. (1922). *Institutio oratoria* (Vol. 4; H. E. Butler, Trans.). Cambridge, UK: Cambridge University Press.

Raiffa, H. (1982). *The art and science of negotiation.* Cambridge, MA: Harvard University Press.

Rakow, L. (1992). *Gender on the line: Women, the telephone, and community life.* Urbana: University of Illinois Press.

Ralston, S. M., & Kirkwood, W. G. (1995). Overcoming managerial bias in employment interviewing. *Journal of Applied Communication Research, 23,* 75-92.

Rawlins, W. K. (1987). Gregory Bateson and the composition of human communication. *Research on Language and Social Interaction, 20,* 53-77.

Rawls, J. (1971). *A theory of justice.* Cambridge, MA: Harvard University Press.

Ray, E. B. (1987). Supportive relationships and occupational stress in the workplace. In T. L. Albrecht & M. B. Adelman (Eds.), *Communicating social support* (pp. 172-191). Newbury Park, CA: Sage.

Ray, E. B. (1990). Assessing the ties that bind: Social support versus isolation in communication networks. In B. D. Sypher (Ed.), *Case studies in organizational communication* (pp. 150-160). New York: Guilford.

Ray, E. B. (1991). The relationship among communication network roles, job stress, and burnout in educational organizations. *Communication Quarterly, 39,* 91-102.

Reed, M. (1992). Introduction. In M. Reed & M. Hughes (Eds.), *Rethinking organization: New directions in organization theory and analysis* (pp. 1-16). London: Sage.

Reichers, A. E. (1987). An interactionist perspective on newcomer socialization rates. *Academy of Management Review, 12,* 278-287.

Reynolds, A. (1992). Charting the changes in junior faculty. *Journal of Higher Education, 63,* 637-652.

Rich, A. (1979). *On lies, secrets, and silence: Selected prose 1966-1978.* New York: Norton.

Rich, J. T., & Bailey, G. (1993). Downsizing costs, not people, through needs-matching. *Public Utilities Fortnightly, 1131*(10), 30-34.

Richardson, L. (1995). Narrative and sociology. In J. Van Maanen (Ed.), *Representation in ethnography* (pp. 198-221). Thousand Oaks, CA: Sage.

Rifkin, J. (1995). *The end of work: The decline of the global labor force and the dawn of the post-market era.* New York: Jeremy P. Tarcher/Putnam.

Riger, S. (1994). Challenges of success: Stages of growth in feminist organizations. *Feminist Studies, 20,* 275-300.

Rixecker, S. S. (1994). Expanding the discursive content of policy design: A matter of feminist standpoint epistemology. *Policy Sciences, 27,* 119-142.

Roberts, M., & Harris, T. (1989). Wellness at work. *Psychology Today, 22*(3), 54-58.

Roberts, S. V. (1995, February 13). Affirmative action on the edge. *U.S. News & World Report, 118,* pp. 32-38.

Rolfe, A. (1993, July 5). Reorganization: A time to rethink. *Industry Week, 242,* pp. 11-12.

Rose, H. (1983). Hand, brain, and heart: A feminist epistemology for the natural sciences. *Signs: Journal of Women in Culture and Society, 9,* 73-90.

Rose, N. (1996). Identity, genealogy, history. In S. Hall & P. du Gay (Eds.), *Questions of cultural identity* (pp. 129-150). London: Sage.

Rosener, J. B. (1990). Ways women lead. *Harvard Business Review, 68*(1), 119-125.

Rousseau, D. M. (1995). *Psychological contracts in organizations: Understanding written and unwritten agreements.* Thousand Oaks, CA: Sage.

Rousseau, D. M. (1996). Changing the deal while keeping the people. *Academy of Management Executive, 10*(2), 50-61.

Rousseau, D. M., & McLean Parks, J. M. (1993). The contracts of individuals and organizations. *Research in Organizational Behavior, 15,* 1-43.

Rubin, J. Z., & Brown, B. R. (1975). *The psychology of bargaining and negotiation.* New York: Academic Press.

Rubin, J. Z., Pruitt, D. G., & Kim, S. H. (1994). *Social conflict: Escalation, stalemate, and settlement* (2nd ed.). New York: McGraw-Hill.

Rubinstein, S., Bennett, M., & Kochan, T. (1993). The Saturn partnership: Co-management and the reinvention of the local union. In B. Kaufman & M. Kleiner (Eds.), *Employee representation: Alternatives and future directions* (pp. 339-370). Madison, WI: Industrial Relations Research Association.

Ruddick, S. (1989). *Maternal thinking: Towards a politics of peace.* Boston: Beacon.

Saltzman, A. (1991). *Downshifting: Reinventing success on a slower track.* New York: HarperCollins.

Sandler, B. R. (1986). *The campus climate revisited: Chilly for faculty, administrators, and graduate students.* Washington, DC: Project on the Status and Education of Women, Association of American Colleges.

Sartre, J. (1956). *Being and nothingness* (H. E. Barnes, Trans.). New York: Philosophical Library. (Original work published 1943)

Sass, J. S., & Canary, D. J. (1991). Organizational commitment and identification: An examination of conceptual and operational convergence. *Western Journal of Speech Communication, 55,* 275-293.

Sawicki, J. (1991). *Disciplining Foucault: Feminism, power, and the body.* New York: Routledge.

Schein, E. H. (1970). *Organizational psychology* (2nd ed.). Englewood Cliffs, NJ: Prentice Hall.

Schein, E. H. (1971). The individual, the organization, and the career: A conceptual scheme. *Journal of Applied Behavioral Science 7,* 401-426.

Schein, E. H. (1978). *Career dynamics: Matching individual and organizational needs.* Reading, MA: Addison-Wesley.

Schellenbarger, S. (1995, February 1). When workers' lives are contingent on employers' whims. *Wall Street Journal*, p. B1.

Schiappa, E. (1989). "Spheres of argument" as topoi for the critical study of power/ knowledge. In B. E. Gronbeck (Ed.), *Proceedings of the Sixth SCA Conference on Argumentation*. Annandale, VA: Speech Communication Association.

Schmenner, R., & Lackey, C. (1994). "Slash and burn" doesn't kill weeds: Other ways to downsize the manufacturing organization. *Business Horizons, 37*(4), 80-86.

Schmookler, A. (1993). *The illusion of choice: How the market economy shapes our destiny.* Albany: SUNY.

Schor, J. B. (1991). *The overworked American.* New York: Basic Books.

Schwartz, J. (1990, November 5). How safe is your job? *Newsweek, 116,* pp. 44-47.

Scott, J. C. (1990). *Domination and the arts of resistance: Hidden transcripts.* New Haven, CT: Yale University Press.

Scott, J. W. (1988). Deconstructing equality-versus-difference: Or, the uses of post-structuralist theory for feminism. *Feminist Studies, 14,* 33-50.

Scott, W. G. (1985). Organizational revolution: An end to managerial orthodoxy. *Administration and Society, 17,* 149-170.

Scott, W. G., & Hart, D. K. (1989). *Organizational values in America.* New Brunswick, NJ: Transaction Publishers.

Sebenius, J. K. (1992). Negotiation analysis: A characterization and review. *Management Science, 38,* 18-39.

Segura, D. (1994). Inside the work worlds of Chicana and Mexican immigrant women. In M. B. Zinn & B. T. Dill (Eds.), *Women of color in the U.S. society* (pp. 95-111). Philadelphia: Temple University Press.

Sells, L. (1997, November). *Thinking in the third wave: Standpoint theory and the reinvention of identity politics.* Paper presented at the meeting of the National Communication Association, Chicago, IL.

Sharpe, R. (1993, September 14). Losing ground: In the latest recession, only blacks suffered net employment loss. *Wall Street Journal*, p. A1.

Sheldon, A. (1992). Preschool girls' discourse competence: Managing conflict and negotiation power. In K. Hall, M. Bucholtz, & B. Moonwomon (Eds.), *Locating power* (Vol. 2, pp. 528-539). Berkeley, CA: Berkeley Linguistic Society.

Sheldon, A., & Johnson, D. (1994). Preschool negotiators: Linguistic differences in how girls and boys regulate the expression of dissent in same-sex groups. In R. J. Lewicki, B. H. Sheppard, & R. Bies (Eds.), *Research on negotiation in organizations* (Vol. 4, pp. 37-67). Greenwich, CT: JAI.

Shelton, L. C. (1993). Leadership as dialogue. *Third Annual Chaos and Network Conference,* pp. 111-115.

Sheppard, D. (1989). Organizations, power, and sexuality: The image and self-image of women managers. In J. Hearn, D. L. Sheppard, P. Tancred-Sheriff, & G. Burrell (Eds.), *The sexuality of organization* (pp. 139-157). London: Sage.

Shiva, V. (1989). *Staying alive: Women, ecology, and development.* London: Zed Books.

Shiva, V. (1991). *Ecology and the politics of survival.* London: Sage.

Shuter, R., & Turner, L. H. (1997). African American and European American women in the workplace: Perceptions of conflict communication. *Management Communication Quarterly, 11,* 74-96.

Siefert, K., Jayaratne, S., & Chess, W. A. (1991). Job satisfaction, burnout, and turnover in health care social workers. *Health and Social Work, 16*(3), 193-202.

Siegel, D. L. (1997). The legacy of the personal: Generating theory in feminism's third wave. *Hypatia, 12*(3), 46-75.

Silvestri, G. T. (1995). Occupational employment to 2005. *Monthly Labor Review: Bureau of Labor Statistics, 118*(11), 6-84.

Simon, H. (1945). *Administrative behavior.* New York: Free Press.

Sims, H. P., Jr., & Manz, C. C. (1996). *Company of heroes: Unleashing the power of self-leadership.* New York: John Wiley.

Singh, R. (1998). Redefining psychological contracts with the U.S. work force: A critical task for strategic human resource management planners in the 1990s. *Human Resource Management, 37*(1), 61-69.

Sloan, A. (1996, February 26). The hit men. *Newsweek, 127*(9), 44-48.

Smith, A., & Stewart, A. J. (1983). Approaches to studying racism and sexism in black women's lives. *Journal of Social Issues, 39*(3), 1-15.

Smith, D. E. (1987a). *The everyday world as problematic: A feminist sociology.* Boston: Northeastern University Press.

Smith, D. E. (1987b). Women's perspective as a radical critique of sociology. In S. Harding (Ed.), *Feminism and methodology* (pp. 84-96). Bloomington: Indiana University Press.

Smith, D. E. (1993). High noon in textland: A critique of Clough. *Sociological Quarterly, 34,* 183-192.

Smith, D. E. (1997). Comment on Hekman's "Truth and method: Feminist standpoint theory revisited." *Signs: Journal of Women in Culture and Society, 22,* 91-97.

Smith, R. C., & Turner, P. K. (1995). A social constructionist reconfiguration of metaphor analysis: An application of "SCMA" to organizational socialization theorizing. *Communication Monographs, 62,* 152-181.

Sobkowski, A. (1994, November/December). How on earth can I manage any faster? *Executive Female, 17,* pp. 73-74.

Soderfeldt, M., Soderfeldt, B., & Warg, L. E. (1995). Burnout in social work. *Social Work, 40,* 638-646.

Sotirin, P., & Gottfried, H. (1996). Resistance in the workplace. In P. J. Dubeck & K. Borman (Eds.), *Women and work* (pp. 367-371). New York: Garland.

Spender, D. (1980). *Man made language.* London: Routledge & Kegan Paul.

Spitzack, C. (1998). Theorizing masculinity across the field: An intradisciplinary conversation. *Communication Theory, 8,* 141-143.

Spitzack, C., & Carter, K. (1987). Women in communication studies: A typology for revision. *Quarterly Journal of Speech, 73,* 401-423.

Spradlin, A. (1998). The price of "passing": Lesbian perspectives on authenticity in organizations. *Management Communication Quarterly, 11,* 598-605.

St. John, Y., & Feagin, J. R. (1997). Racial masques: Black women and subtle gendered racism. In N. V. Benokraitis (Ed.), *Subtle sexism: Current practice and prospects for change* (pp. 179-200). Thousand Oaks, CA: Sage.

Stacey, R. D. (1992). *Managing the unknowable: Strategic boundaries between order and chaos in organizations.* San Francisco: Jossey-Bass.

Stacey, R. D. (1996). *Complexity and creativity in organizations.* San Francisco: Berrett-Koehler.

Stahl, S. D. (1989). *Literary folklores and the personal narrative.* Bloomington: Indiana University Press.

Starnaman, S. M., & Miller, K. I. (1992). A test of a causal model of communication and burnout in the teaching profession. *Communication Education, 41,* 40-53.

Staton-Spicer, A. Q., & Darling, A. L. (1986). Communication in the socialization of preservice teachers. *Communication Education, 35,* 215-230.

Stearns, A. K. (1995). *Living through job loss: Coping with the emotional effects of job loss and rebuilding your future.* New York: Simon & Schuster.

Steers, R. M., & Black, J. S. (1994). *Organizational behavior* (5th ed.). New York: HarperCollins College.

Stohl, C. (1986). The role of memorable messages in the process of organizational socialization. *Communication Quarterly, 34,* 231-249.

Stout, K. R. (1995). *Communication dialectics in a music community: The anti-socialization of newcomers.* Unpublished master's thesis, University of Montana.

Stout, K. R. (1997, May). Exclusionary socialization: The socialization of organizational members to being "outsiders within." In J. Hollowitz (Chair), *Workplace socialization: Perspectives on organizational entry, training, and exit.* Symposium conducted at the fifth meeting of the A. F. Jacobson Symposium, Omaha, NE.

Stout, K. R., & Bullis, C. (1997). Socialization turning points among medical students. In J. Hollowitz (Chair), *Workplace socialization: Perspectives on organizational entry, training, and exit.* Symposium conducted at the fifth meeting of the A. F. Jacobson Symposium, Omaha, NE.

Strober, M. H. (1994). Can feminist thought improve economics? *American Economic Association Papers and Proceedings, 84*(2), 143-147.

Stroh, L. K., Brett, J. M., & Reilly, A. H. (1994). A decade of change: Managers' attachment to their organizations and their jobs. *Human Resource Management, 33,* 531-548.

Sugalski, T. D., Manzo, L. S., & Meadows, J. L. (1995). Resource link: Re-establishing the employment relationship in an era of downsizing. *Human Resource Management, 34,* 389-403.

Sullivan, P. A., & Goldzwig, S. R. (1995). A relational approach to moral decision-making: The majority opinion in *Planned Parenthood v. Casey. Quarterly Journal of Speech, 81,* 167-190.

Sullivan, P. A., & Turner, L. H. (1996). *From the margins to the center: Contemporary women and political communication.* Westport, CT: Praeger.

Sutton, R. I. (1991). Maintaining norms about expressed emotions: The case of bill collectors. *Administrative Science Quarterly, 36,* 245-268.

Swinth, R. L. (1967). The establishment of the trust relationship. *Journal of Conflict Resolution, 11,* 335-344.

Takahashi, K. (1997, May). A tough day, one that lasts: Myths and facts of organizational entry in Japan. In J. Hollowitz (Chair), *Workplace socialization: Perspectives on organizational entry, training, and exit.* Symposium conducted at the fifth meeting of the A. F. Jacobson Symposium, Omaha, NE.

Tancred-Sheriff, P. (1989). Gender, sexuality, and the labour process. In J. Hearn, D. L. Sheppard, P. Tancred-Sheriff, & G. Burrell (Eds.), *The sexuality of organization* (pp. 45-55). London: Sage.

Tannen, D. (1990). *You just don't understand: Women and men in conversation.* New York: William Morrow.

Tannen, D. (1994). *Talking from 9 to 5: How women's and men's conversational styles affect who gets heard, who gets credit, and what gets done at work.* New York: William Morrow.

Tautenhahn, T. (1994). Scheduling unit-time open shops with deadlines. *Operations Research, 42,* 189-192.

Tavris, C. (1987, March 3). Is thin still in? *Woman's Day,* p. 114.

Tavris, C. (1992). *The mismeasure of woman: Why women are not the better sex, the inferior sex, or the opposite sex.* New York: Simon & Schuster.

Taylor, F. (1903). *Shop management.* New York: Harper & Row.

Taylor, M. S., & Giannantonio, C. M. (1993). Forming, adapting, and terminating the employment relationship: A review of the literature from individual, organizational, and interactionist perspectives. *Journal of Management, 19,* 461-515.

Teboul, JC. B. (1995). Determinants of new hire information-seeking during organizational encounter. *Western Journal of Communication, 59,* 305-325.

Teboul, JC. B. (1997). Scripting the organization: New hire learning during organizational encounter. *Communication Research Reports, 14,* 33-47.

Tetrick, L. E., & LaRocco, J. M. (1987). Understanding, prediction, and control as moderators of the relationships between perceived stress, satisfaction, and psychological well-being. *Journal of Applied Psychology, 72,* 538-543.

Thoits, P. A. (1995). Stress, coping, and social support processes: Where are we? What next? *Journal of Health and Social Behavior* [Extra issue], 53-79.

Thomas, D. A. (1989). Mentoring and irrationality: The role of racial taboos. *Human Resource Management, 28,* 279-290.

Thomas, D. A. (1990). The impact of race on managers' experiences of developmental relationships (mentoring and sponsorship): An intra-organizational study. *Journal of Organizational Behavior, 11,* 479-492.

Thompson, J. (1995). *The media and modernity: A social theory of the media.* Stanford, CA: Stanford University Press.

Thompson, L. (1998). *The mind and heart of the negotiator.* Upper Saddle River, NJ: Prentice Hall.

Thorne, B., Kramarae, C., & Henley, N. (Eds.). (1983). *Language, gender, and society.* Rowley, MA: Newbury House.

Tompkins, P. K., & Cheney, G. (1985). Communication and unobtrusive control in contemporary organization. In R. D. McPhee & P. K. Tompkins (Eds.), *Organizational communication: Traditional themes and new directions* (pp. 179-210). Beverly Hills, CA: Sage.

Tong, R. (1989). *Feminist thought: A comprehensive introduction.* Boulder, CO: Westview.

Towler, J. (1991). How to stop spinning your wheels. *Canadian Banker, 98*(1), 56-59.

Trethewey, A. (1997a, November). *Professional bodies: The construction of professional women's identities in and through organizational discourses.* Paper presented at the meeting of the National Communication Association, Chicago, IL.

Trethewey, A. (1997b). Resistance, identity, and empowerment: A postmodern feminist analysis of clients in a human service organization. *Communication Monographs, 64,* 281-301.

Trethewey, A. (1999). Disciplined bodies: Women's embodied identities at work. *Organization Studies, 20,* 423-450.

Tucker, S. H. (1994). Black women in corporate America: The inside story. *Black Enterprise,* 60-66.

Turner, B. S. (1984). *The body and society.* Oxford, UK: Basil Blackwell.

Turnley, W. H., & Feldman, D. C. (1998). Psychological contract violations during corporate restructuring. *Human Resource Management, 37*(1), 71-83.

Tutzauer, F. (1997). Chaos and organization. In G. Barnett & L. Thayer (Eds.), *Organization communication: Emerging perspectives: Vol. 5. The renaissance in systems thinking* (pp. 213-227). Greenwich, CT: Ablex.

U.S. Department of Labor. (1998). *Occupational outlook handbook.* Washington, DC: Bureau of Labor Statistics.

U.S. General Accounting Office. (1994, September). *Equal employment opportunity: Displacement rates, unemployment spells, and reemployment wages by race* (GAO-HEHS Publication No. 94-229FS). Washington, DC: Health, Education, and Human Services Division.

Van Maanen, J. (1975). Police socialization: A longitudinal examination of job attitudes in an urban police department. *Administrative Science Quarterly, 20,* 207-228.

Van Maanen, J. (1976). Breaking-in: Socialization to work. In R. Dubin (Ed.), *Handbook of work, organization, and society* (pp. 67-120). Chicago: Rand McNally.

Van Maanen, J. (1978). People processing: Strategies of organizational socialization. *Organizational Dynamics, 7,* 19-36.

Van Maanen, J., & Schein, E. H. (1979). Toward a theory of organizational socialization. In B. M. Staw & L. L. Cummings (Eds.), *Research in organizational behavior* (pp. 209-264). Greenwich, CT: JAI.

Vicere, A. A., & Graham, K. R. (1990). Crafting competitiveness: Toward a new paradigm for executive development. *Human Resource Planning, 13,* 281-295.

Wall, J. A., Jr. (1985). *Negotiation: Theory and practice.* Glenview, IL: Scott, Foresman.

Walton, R. E., & McKersie, R. B. (1965). *A behavioral theory of labor negotiations: An analysis of a social interaction system.* New York: McGraw-Hill.

Wanous, J. P. (1980). *Organizational entry.* Reading, MA: Addison-Wesley.

Waring, M. (1988). *If women counted: A new feminist economics.* New York: Harper & Row.

Warner, C. (1992). *The last word: A treasury of women's quotes.* Englewood Cliffs, NJ: Prentice Hall.

Watzlawick, P., Beavin, J. H., & Jackson, D. D. (1967). *Pragmatics of human communication: A study of interactional patterns, pathologies, and paradoxes.* New York: Norton.

Watzlawick, P., Weakland, J. H., & Fisch, R. (1974). *Change: Principle to problem formation and problem resolution.* New York: Norton.

Weber, M. (1947). *The theory of social and economic organization.* Chicago: Free Press.

Weedon, C. (1987). *Feminist practice and poststructuralist theory.* New York: Basil Blackwell.

Weick, K. (1995). *Sensemaking in organizations.* Thousand Oaks, CA: Sage.

Weitz, R., & Gordon, L. (1993). Images of black women among Anglo college students. *Sex Roles, 28,* 19-34.

Wendt, R. F. (1995). Women in positions of service: The politicized body. *Communication Studies, 46,* 276-296.

Wertheimer, M. M. (Ed.). (1997). *Listening to their voices: The rhetorical activities of historical women.* Columbia: University of South Carolina Press.

Wessel, D. (1997, June 24). Low unemployment brings lasting gains to town in Michigan. *Wall Street Journal,* pp. A1, A13.

West, C., & Zimmerman, D. (1987). Doing gender. *Gender & Society, 1,* 125-151.

Wheatley, M. J. (1992). *Leadership and the new science: Learning about organization from an orderly universe.* San Francisco: Berrett- Koehler.

Wheatley, M. J. (1993). Let's stop taking ourselves, and the science, so seriously. *Third Annual Chaos Network Conference,* 107-110.

Wheeler, C. (1994, November/December). Confessions of a time management freak. *Executive Female, 17,* pp. 48-52.

White, J. B., & Lublin, J. S. (1996, September 27). Some companies try to rebuild loyalty. *Wall Street Journal,* pp. B1, B7.

Wicks, A. C., Gilbert, D. R., Jr., & Freeman, R. E. (1994). A feminist reinterpretation of the stakeholder concept. *Business Ethics Quarterly, 4,* 475-497.

Wilcox, B. L. (1981). Social support, life stress, and psychological adjustment: A test of the buffering hypothesis. *American Journal of Community Psychology, 9,* 371-386.

Williams, G. R. (1996). Negotiation as a healing process. *Journal of Dispute Resolution, 1,* 1-66.

Williams, P. J. (1991). *The alchemy of race and rights: Diary of a law professor.* Cambridge, MA: Harvard University Press.

Williamson, A. D. (1993). Is this the right time to come out? *Harvard Business Review, 71*(4), 18-27.

Willis, P. (1977). *Learning to labor: How working class kids get working class jobs.* New York: Columbia University Press.

Winner, L. (1993, November/December). Losing the cooperative edge. *Technology Review, 96,* p. 68.

Wolf, N. (1991). *The beauty myth: How images of beauty are used against women.* New York: William Morrow.

Wood, J. T. (1992a). Gender and moral voice: Moving from woman's nature to standpoint epistemology. *Women's Studies in Communication, 15,* 1-24.

Wood, J. T. (1992b). Narratives as a basis for theorizing sexual harassment. *Journal of Applied Communication Research, 20,* 349-363.

Wood, J. T. (1994). *Who cares? Women, care, and culture.* Carbondale: Southern Illinois University Press.

Wood, J. T. (1999). *Gendered lives: Communication, gender, and culture* (3rd ed.). Belmont, CA: Mayfield.

Wood, J. T., & Conrad, C. (1983). Paradox in the experiences of professional women. *Western Journal of Speech Communication, 47,* 305-322.

Woods, J. D. (1994). *The corporate closet: The professional lives of gay men in America.* New York: Free Press.

Wright, S. H. (1985, June). A matter of time. *Data Management, 23,* p. 62.

Wysocki, B., Jr. (1997, September 8). The outlook: Retaining employees turns into a hot topic. *Wall Street Journal,* p. A1.

Yeatman, A. (1987). Women, domestic life, and sociology. In C. Pateman & E. Gross (Eds.), *Feminist challenges: Social and political theory* (pp. 157-172). Boston: Northeastern University Press.

Young, I. (1990a). The ideal of community and the politics of difference. In L. Nicholson (Ed.), *Feminism/postmodernism* (pp. 300-323). New York: Routledge.

Young, I. (1990b). *Throwing like a girl and other essays in feminist philosophy and social theory.* Bloomington: Indiana University Press.

Yovovich, B. G. (1995, October). Downsizing anxiety can stifle innovation. *Business Marketing, 80,* p. 53.

Yukl, G. (1989). Managerial leadership: A review of theory and research. *Journal of Management, 15,* 251-289.

Zaleznik, A. (1977). Managers and leaders: Are they different? *Harvard Business Review, 55*(3), 67-78.

Zappert, L. T., & Stansbury, K. (1987). *In the pipeline: A comparative analysis of men and women in graduate programs in science, engineering, and medicine at Stanford University.* Stanford, CA: Stanford University School of Medicine.

Zimmermann, S., & Applegate, J. L. (1994). Communicating social support in organizations: A message-centered approach. In B. R. Burleson, T. L. Albrecht, & I. G. Sarason (Eds.), *Communication of social support: Messages, interactions, relationships, and community* (pp. 50-70). Thousand Oaks, CA: Sage.

Index

About the Contributors

Brenda J. Allen (Ph.D., Howard University) is an Associate Professor in the Department of Communication at the University of Colorado at Boulder. Her primary area of study is organizational communication, with an emphasis on workplace diversity and computer-mediated communication. Her work has been published in *Management Communication Quarterly,* the *Journal of Applied Communication Research, Communication Studies,* the *Southern Journal of Communication,* and *Sex Roles.* She also wrote a chapter in *Our Voices: Essays in Culture, Ethnicity, and Communication* (1996). *Brenda.J. Allen@Colorado.edu*

Connie Bullis (Ph.D., Purdue University) is an Associate Professor of Communication at the University of Utah. She has authored numerous convention papers and published articles on organizational socialization. Her work has appeared in such journals as *Communication Monographs,* the *Western Journal of Communication, Communication Quarterly, Communication Studies,* and the *Journal of Organizational Change Management.* Her more recent work has focused on standpoint feminism as an approach to organizational socialization. *Bullis@admin.comm.utah.edu*

Patrice M. Buzzanell (Ph.D., Purdue University) is an Associate Professor in the Department of Communication at Purdue University. Her research interests focus primarily on gendered organizational communication and on career issues in the workplace, particularly the ways in which individuals and societies construct careers to manage identities and work processes on multiple levels. For her work on career uncertainty, she received the W. Charles Redding Dissertation Award from the International Communication Association. She has contributed chapters to several books and has published in journals, including *Communication Monographs, Human Communication Research,* the *Journal of Applied Communication Research, Health Communication,* and the *Western Journal of Communication.* She is currently serving as editor of *Management Communication Quarterly,* incoming chairperson of the organizational communication division of the International Communication Association, and president of the Organization for the Study of Communication, Language, and Gender (OSCLG). *Pbuzzanell@sla.purdue.edu*

Robin Patric Clair (Ph.D., Kent State University) is an Associate Professor at Purdue University. Her primary research and teaching interests are in organizational communication. She draws from critical, feminist, postmodern, and aesthetic theories to develop her work on power, politics, and identity. Her areas of study include sequestered stories of sexual harassment, silence as oppression and resistance, pay inequity, organizational socialization, the gendered construction of reality, and the artful practices of resistance. She has published in such journals as *Communication Monographs, Western Journal of Communication, Management Communication Quarterly,* and *Journal of Applied Communication Research.* Her most recent book is *Organizing Science* (1998). *Rpclair@omni.cc.purdue.edu*

Stanley Deetz (Ph.D., Ohio University) is a Professor of Communication at the University of Colorado at Boulder, where he teaches courses in organizational theory, organizational communication, and communication theory. He is the author of *Transforming Communication, Transforming Business: Building Responsive and Responsible Workplaces* (1995) and *Democracy in an Age of Corporate Colonization: Developments in Communication and the Politics of Everyday Life* (1992); coauthor of *Doing Critical Management Research* (Sage, in press) and *Communication and Cultural Change* (Sage, 2000); and editor or author of eight other books. He has published numerous essays regarding stakeholder representation, decision making, culture, and communication in corporate organizations in scholarly journals and books, and he has lectured widely in the United States and Europe. In 1994, he was a Senior Fulbright Scholar in the Företagsekonomiska Institutionen, Göteborgs Universitet, Sweden, lecturing and conducting research on managing knowledge-intensive work. He has also served as a consultant on culture, diversity, and participatory decision making for several major corporations. He offers an on-line course on communication and cultural change for the executive masters at Seton Hall University. He also served as president of the International Communication Association from 1996 to 1997. *stanley.deetz@colorado.edu*

Gail T. Fairhurst (Ph.D., University of Oregon) is a Professor of Communication at the University of Cincinnati. Her research interests focus primarily on leadership communication and language analysis: leadership communication during organizational change and workforce restructuring, the communication of corporate philosophy statements, and leader-member relationships. In addition to several book chapters, she has published in *Human Communication Research, Communication Monographs, Communication Yearbook, Management Communication Quarterly,* the *Academy of Management Journal,* the *Academy of Management Review, Organization Science,* and *Organizational Behavior and Human Decision Processes,* among others. She is also the coauthor (with Bob Sarr) of *The Art of Framing: Managing the Language of Leadership,* honored in 1997 with the National Communication Association's Best Book Award for Organizational Communication. She has consulted with Procter & Gamble, Boeing, the U.S. Air Force, Fluor Daniel, Kroger, and General Electric, among others. *Fairhug@email.uc.edu*

Marlene G. Fine (MBA and Ph.D., University of Massachusetts) is a Professor of Communications and Management at Simmons College, where she also directs the Graduate Program in Communications Management. Her research interests include cultural diversity in the workplace; gender, race, and communication; and feminist theory and research. She is the author of *Building Successful Multicultural Organizations: Challenges and Opportunities* (1995), in addition to numerous journal articles and book chapters. She previously was on the faculty of the College of Management of the University of Massachusetts, Boston, and served as graduate dean at Emerson College. Her research interests in management have been informed by her work as an organizational consultant and her numerous university and college administrative positions, including department chair, associate dean, MBA director, and graduate dean. *fine@simmons.edu*

Tanni Haas (Ph.D., Rutgers University) is an Assistant Professor at Brooklyn College. In addition to the present chapter, he has written two other essays on organizational communication ethics to be published in *The Handbook of Public Relations* (Sage, in press) and *The Foundations of Management Knowledge* (in press). *thaas@brooklyn.cuny.edu*

Deborah M. Kolb (MBA, University of Colorado; Ph.D., M.I.T., Sloan School of Management) is a Professor of Management at the Simmons College Graduate School of Management and the Director of the Center for Gender in Organizations there. From 1991 to 1994, she was executive director of the Program on Negotiation at Harvard Law School. She is currently a senior fellow at the program, where she codirects the Negotiations in the Workplace Program. Her current research looks at how women (and men) can become more effective problem solvers by mastering the dual requirements of the shadow negotiation—empowering themselves and connecting with others. Her latest research projects include *When Women Negotiate: Empowering Ourselves, Connecting With Others* (with Judith Williams, in press) and

Negotiation Eclectics: Essays in Memory of Jeffrey Z. Rubin (1999). She is the author of *The Mediators* (1983), an in-depth study of labor mediation, and coeditor of *Hidden Conflict in Organizations: Uncovering Behind-the-Scenes Disputes,* a collection of field studies about how conflicts are handled in a variety of business and not-for-profit organizations. She has also published a study of the practice of successful mediators, *Making Talk Work: Profiles of Mediators* (1994). Her dissertation won the Zannetos Prize for outstanding doctoral scholarship. She is also involved in a number of action research and consulting projects that link strategic business concerns with gender, diversity, and work-life issues. *Dkolb@vmsvax. simmons.edu*

Adrianne Dennis Kunkel is an Assistant Professor at the University of Kansas in the Department of Communication Studies. Her research interests include the study of personal relationships, emotion and emotional support, socialization processes, sex/gender, and quantitative/qualitative research methodologies. Recently, she has investigated associations between different modes of emotional disclosure and cognitive, affective, and health benefits. She has published several chapters and articles in journals, including *Communication Monographs, Human Communication Research,* and the *Journal of Applied Communication Research.* She has also received the Outstanding Thesis/Dissertation Award given by the Interpersonal Communication Division of the International Communication Association. *adkunkel@falcon.cc. ukans.edu*

Marifran Mattson (Ph.D., Arizona State University) is an Assistant Professor at Purdue University. Her research and teaching interests explore the intersection of health communication, organizational communication, and ethics. Her current research foci include uncomfortable support, HIV/AIDS prevention, aviation safety, and job loss. Her research has expanded accepted understandings of social support by addressing the communicative use of uncomfortable support in a community program for troubled youth. She has worked with HIV test practitioners to develop a patient-centered, harm-reduction model of counseling. She is involved in an interdisciplinary research team that considers the implications of human factors (e.g., stress, burnout) in maintaining safety and productivity (e.g., on-time flights) in the aviation industry. She has also challenged and reframed traditional ethics models used to study job loss and interaction in the global workplace. She has published in *Communication Monographs, Management Communication Quarterly, Human Communication Research,* the *Journal of Applied Communication Research,* and *Health Communication. mmattson@purdue.edu*

Dennis K. Mumby (Ph.D., Southern Illinois University) is a Professor of Communication at Purdue University. His research focuses on power, discourse, and control issues in organizational contexts. He has published in journals such as *Communication Monographs,* the *Academy of Management Review, Discourse & Society,* and *Management Communication Quarterly.* His books include *Communication and Power in Organizations* (1988) and *Narrative and Social Control* (ed., Sage, 1993). He is currently working on a book for Sage titled *Organizing Gender: Feminism, Postmodernism, and Organization Studies.* *dmumby@purdue.edu*

Linda L. Putnam (Ph.D., University of Minnesota) is a Professor of Organizational Communication and the Director of the Program on Conflict and Dispute Resolution in the Center for Leadership Studies of the George Bush School of Government and Public Service at Texas A&M University. Her current research interests include communication strategies in negotiation, conflict, language analysis in organizations, and groups in organizations. She has published more than 70 articles and book chapters in management and communication journals. She is the coeditor of the *New Handbook of Organizational Communication* (2000), *Communication and Negotiation* (1992), *Handbook of Organizational Communication* (1987), and *Communication and Organization: An Interpretive Approach* (1983). She is the 1993 recipient of the SCA Charles H. Woolbert Research Award for a seminal article in the field and was elected a fellow in 1995 and president of the International Communication Association in 1999. *LPUTNAM@tamu.edu*

Cindy Reuther is a partner in NRG, an organizational training and development group. She uses her MA in communication from the University of Cincinnati along with experience-based learning techniques to help individuals and teams explore current organizational issues, including leadership, change, creativity, and risk taking. Her work with client groups includes Procter & Gamble, Children's Hospital, United Stationers, Association of Women Students-Miami University, and the Minneapolis YWCA. *Ckreuther@yahoo.com*

Pamela A. Chapman Sanger is a doctoral candidate at Purdue University. Her main research and teaching interests are in organizational communication. Her work emphasizes critical, postmodern, and feminist approaches to the study of a variety of organizational phenomena. She is currently studying workplace violence. She has published in the *Handbook of Organization Studies.* *sangerpt@sprintmail.com*

Karen Rohrbauck Stout is a doctoral candidate at the University of Utah. Her doctoral studies focus on organizational socialization. She is working to develop exclusionary socialization, a phenomenon that emerged from her thesis research. She has been the recipient of a Cannon research scholarship from the University of Utah the last 2 years and has won two International Communication Association teaching awards. She has presented 12 convention papers and written an instructor's manual for an organizational communication text. *K.Stout@m.cc.utah.edu*

Angela Trethewey (Ph.D., Purdue University) is an Assistant Professor in the Department of Communication at Arizona State University. Her research centers on the relationships among organizational discourse, power, resistance, and identity formation. Her work has been published in *Communication Monographs,* the *Western Journal of Communication,* and *Organization Studies,* as well as in a variety of edited volumes. She directs research and teaches both undergraduate and graduate students in courses such as organizational communication, qualitative research methods, and gender and communication. *Atreth@asu.edu*

A000018294132